WHERE NO FLAG FLIES

MARK ROYDEN WINCHELL

WHERE NO

WHERE NO

FLAG FLIES

FLAG FLIES

Donald Davidson and the
Southern Resistance

UNIVERSITY OF MISSOURI PRESS
COLUMBIA AND LONDON

Library of Congress Cataloging-in-Publication Data

Winchell, Mark Royden, 1948–
    Where no flag flies : Donald Davidson and the Southern resistance / Mark Royden Winchell.
        p.   cm.
    Includes bibliographical references (p.   ) and index.
    ISBN 0-8262-1274-3 (alk. paper)
    1. Davidson, Donald, 1893–1968.   2. Davidson, Donald, 1893–1968—Political and social
views.   3. Politics and literature—Southern States—History—20th century.   4. Criticism—
Southern States—History—20th century.   5. Poets, American—20th century—Biography.
6. English teachers—United States—Biography.   7. Critcs—United States—Biography.
8. Nashville (Tenn.)—Biography.   9. Agraians (Group of writers) 10. Fugitives (Group).
I. Title.
PS3507.A666 Z87   2000
818'.5209—dc21
    [B]   00-036387

Text design: Stephanie Foley
Jacket design: Susan Ferber
Typesetter: Bookcomp, Inc.
Printer and binder: Edwards Brothers, Inc.
Typeface: Garamond

Publication of this book has been supported by contributions from Ward Allen, the
Earhart Foundation, the Mary Noel Kershaw Foundation, and the Wilbur Foundation.

Acknowledgments appear on page 386.

In memory of M. E. Bradford

CONTENTS

On March 3, 1993, I received a phone call from Charles Hamel, publisher of the *Southern Partisan* magazine. "I have some sad news to report," he said. "Mel died this morning." I did not have to ask "Mel who?" To the many friends and admirers of M. E. Bradford, there was only one "Mel." He was a true believer in the causes to which he was devoted, but also, in the hackneyed phrase that in his case really did apply, a scholar and a gentleman. He left an impressive legacy of critical writing on literature, rhetoric, history, and politics. But, as is often the case when a productive man dies before his time (Mel was only fifty-eight when he left us), there was also work left undone. The major project that engaged him at the time of his death was a biography of his old teacher and mentor Donald Davidson. Mel had accumulated several boxes of photocopied letters and other documents, but the only text he had written was a long chapter on Davidson's later poetry. This was not a project that was far enough along to be "completed" by someone else. If a life of Davidson were to be written, another biographer would have to do the job.

At the request of Mel's widow, Marie, I undertook this task in 1995. When writing my biography of Cleanth Brooks (a project Mel himself had recommended to me), I had the opportunity to visit my subject on several occasions during the last three years of his life. Not having known Davidson, I was approaching a stranger. Nevertheless, I have come to appreciate the affection and loyalty that Davidson inspired in so many of his former students. Donald Davidson was a complex and imperfect man but one whose achievements demand more attention than they have received from the community of scholars.

Davidson may well be the most unjustifiably neglected figure in twentieth-century southern literature. He is universally regarded as one of the four most important poets of the Fugitive movement, which is itself one of the two most important groups of poets to write in English during the twentieth century (the Imagists being the other). Moreover, his achievement is probably closer to that of the three "major" Fugitives (John Crowe Ransom, Allen Tate, and Robert Penn Warren) than it is to that of the dozen or so "minor" Fugitives. As a social and political writer, he was also one of the most significant influences on conservative thought in the twentieth century. In addition to these accomplishments, he produced a substantial body of literary criticism, the libretto for an American folk opera, a widely used composition textbook, and a remarkable novel, which was published nearly three decades after his death.

Despite the range and importance of Davidson's achievement, he has been the subject of only a handful of scholarly and critical essays and a single book—a study published by Thomas Daniel Young and M. Thomas Inge in Twayne's United States Authors Series in 1971. Even if the scholarly world (with a few notable exceptions) has been slow in taking the full measure of Davidson's importance, interest in his work remains high. Between 1985 and 1996, five of Davidson's books were either published or reissued. The Foundation for American Education published *Singin' Billy* in 1985; in 1991, Transaction Books reissued *The Attack on Leviathan;* J. S. Sanders brought out new editions of *The Tennessee* volumes one and two in 1992; and the University Press of Mississippi published Davidson's novel, *The Big Ballad Jamboree,* in 1996. A critical and intellectual biography of Donald Davidson would seem to be long overdue.

Davidson is not a figure of mere antiquarian interest. In some ways, his political thinking is more timely as we move into the twenty-first century than it was during his own lifetime. When Davidson and his fellow Agrarians were arguing for regional autonomy, the New Deal was centralizing greater political and economic power in the federal government. The national emergencies of depression and world war were used to justify this effort. Then, in the fifties and sixties, defenders of local culture and state's rights (particularly if they spoke with a southern accent) were dismissed as racists. In the years since Davidson's death in 1968, the tide seems to have turned against the coercive big government that Davidson termed the Leviathan. In his own writings, and through his influence on Richard Weaver, Russell Kirk, and Mel Bradford himself, Davidson helped define a traditionalist political vision that is taken more seriously today than it was when he made his lonely stand as its chief intellectual defender.

This book would not have been possible without the assistance of many generous people. In addition to Mel Bradford, I thank the staff of the special collections section of the Jean and Alexander Heard Library at Vanderbilt University and the interlibrary loan staff of the Robert Muldrow Cooper Library at Clemson University. I am particularly grateful to Ward Allen, the Earhart Foundation, the Mary Noel Kershaw Foundation, and the Wilbur Foundation for crucial financial assistance and to Kevin Murphy for help in preparing the index for this book.

As always, the moral support of my wife, Donna, and my sons, Jonathan and Matthew, has helped sustain me in ways beyond measure. Donna's proofreading and editorial advice have also proved invaluable.

The following individuals consented to interviews, provided information in conversation or letters, or otherwise assisted me in my research: Thomas Daniel Young, M. Thomas Inge, Walter and Jane Sullivan, Harriet Owsley, Rosanna Warren, Vince Davis, George Core, Sarah Little, Ward Allen, William Pratt, Tom Landess, Clyde Wilson, Eugene Genovese, David Moltke-Hansen, Lloyd Davis, Ruel Foster, Jack Kershaw, and Peter Stanlis.

I am also grateful to director Beverly Jarrett, managing editor Jane Lago, copy editor Sara Davis, and various members of the staff of the University of Missouri Press. At a time when scholarly publishing is suffering from a plague of political correctness and fashionable opinion, it is comforting to know that at least one university press is still upholding the principle of reasoned inquiry in a free society.

My largest single debt, however, is to the Davidson family, particularly to Donald Davidson's granddaughters Molly Kirkpatrick and Theresa Sullivan. In addition to sharing their memories of their grandfather and a treasure trove of rare photographs, they have allowed me to quote extensively from his unpublished letters and personal diary. These materials brought the intensely private "Mr. Davidson" alive to me. I hope that something of that life has been conveyed to the readers of this book.

WHERE NO FLAG FLIES

An outlaw fumbling for the latch, a voice
Commanding in a dream where no flag flies.

"Lee in the Mountains"

PART ONE

THE ATHENS OF THE SOUTH (1893-1924)

MIDDLE TENNESSEE

From the very beginning, the South was two nations. One was a land of planters and aristocrats—a group that included the original leaders of this country and the first noteworthy southern writer, William Byrd of Westover. At least two generations older than most of America's founding fathers, Byrd was born in England more than a century before the Declaration of Independence was drafted and died in Virginia the year after Thomas Jefferson was born. He helped foster the myth of the Virginia cavalier in a lifelong effort to gain recognition and status in London. But in his classic memoir *A History of the Dividing Line,* Byrd also wrote of another South. This land was populated by rough frontiersmen such as the workers who surveyed the Virginia–North Carolina border. These men were uncouth, violent, and frequently illiterate. They would have been viewed with condescension and scorn in polite British society. Although they are almost always identified with a later period of American history, they were as much a part of the birth of this nation as any philosophe in a powdered wig. One such individual, an emigrant from Ireland named John Goolman Davidson, settled in southwest Virginia in the middle of the eighteenth century.

Although the date of John Davidson's birth is unknown, it was probably sometime before 1729. We know approximately when he immigrated with his family to America: his son William was born in County Down, Ireland, in 1759, and a second son, Joseph, was born in Pennsylvania in 1762. By 1767, John Davidson had left Pennsylvania for what is now Rockingham County, Virginia.[1] Then, in 1780, he and a friend named Richard Bailey settled their families at Beaver Pond Spring near Bluefield, Virginia. There, they built what came to

---

1. Interview with Molly Kirkpatrick, January 3, 1996.

be known as the Davidson-Bailey Fort. According to the historian David E. Johnston, "These men, as well as their sons and daughters, were a brave and courageous people, and maintained their position on the border at the settlement they had made from the day they came in 1780, until the close of the Indian wars in 1795. Often in battles with the Indians, [they were] frequently compelled to flee for their lives, and shut themselves up in their strong quarters."[2]

In 1783, a neighbor named Rice made the mistake of stealing one of John Davidson's hogs. When Rice was convicted of this crime, he was sentenced to "forty lashes minus one." After the sheriff had administered thirty-eight of the required lashes, he handed the whip to Davidson, who inflicted the final one himself. Rice was so incensed that he vowed revenge, even if he had to wait for years and get the Indians to help him. Ten years later, when John Davidson was returning home to Bluefield through Rocky Gap, Virginia, he was attacked and killed by Rice and a band of hostile Indians. His descendants later erected a granite monument, which bears the inscription: "John Goolman Davidson, Scotch-Irish Pioneer, Killed Here By Indians, March 8, 1793."[3]

This was not the first time the Davidson family had fallen victim to Indian brutality. In early April 1791, John Davidson's son Andrew left his home in what is now Tazewell County, Virginia, to conduct some important business in Smithfield. Remaining at home were Andrew's pregnant wife, Rebecca Burke Davidson, his three small children (two girls and a boy), and two orphans by the name of Bromfield, who were bound servants of the family. Two or three days after Andrew's departure, his brother-in-law, John Bailey, along with Bailey's own sister, left the Davidson-Bailey Fort to look after the isolated family. When they reached a gap in the ridge above the Davidson cabin, the pair saw heavy smoke. Bailey left his sister and her horse in the gap while he descended into the valley. He found the house on fire and the family gone, apparently abducted by Indians. According to David E. Johnston, "Mr. Bailey and his sister rode rapidly to the fort, gave the alarm to the neighborhood, and a party gathered as quickly as possible and pursued the Indians, but the leaves being dry the savages had left but few, if any marks, and the party was unable to overtake them."[4]

Earlier that day, Mrs. Davidson had been gathering sap from sugar maple trees close by her house, when hostile Indians (probably of the Shawnee tribe) appeared and ordered her to go with them to their homes beyond the Ohio River. "Taking such plunder as they could carry," writes Johnston, "they set fire to the house and with their prisoners departed; the Indians helping along with the children.

---

2. David E. Johnston, *A History of Middle New River Settlements and Contiguous Territories*, 73.

3. Kirkpatrick interview.

4. Johnston, *New River Settlements*, 101.

On the way, near where Logan Courthouse, West Virginia, now stands, Mrs. Davidson by reason of the exertion and anxiety of mind gave birth to her child. Only two hours of relaxation from the march was allowed her and they again pushed on. The little stranger after a day's time, they drowned."[5] When they arrived at their settlements, the Indians tied Mrs. Davidson's two daughters to a tree and shot them before her eyes. Her son was given to an old squaw, who accidentally drowned him when she upset her canoe while crossing a river. The fate of the Bromfield children remains unknown.

There is no record of the anguish and terror that Andrew Davidson must have experienced when he returned home to discover his family gone. We know only that he searched for them for several years, traveling as far northwest as the present location of Detroit. His wife had been sold into servitude and remained in captivity from April 1791 until some time after Mad Anthony Wayne's victory over the United Indian Tribes at Fallen Timbers in August of 1794. Prior to his second trip in search of his wife, Andrew Davidson received information from an old Indian that led him across the Canadian border. Stopping for food and lodging at a French Canadian farmhouse, Andrew noticed something eerily familiar about the haggard old servant woman who worked for the farmer. When he nodded to her on his way to bid his host good night, the woman followed him into the parlor, looked him in the eye, and said: "Andrew, don't you know me? I'm your wife." It was indeed Rebecca Burke Davidson, her once black hair turned snow white by her ordeal. Unfortunately, the happy reunion proved short-lived, as Rebecca Davidson died soon after her return to Virginia.[6]

By this time, Andrew Davidson was in his early thirties. Although no official record has survived, he appears to have been born shortly after his family immigrated to Virginia in the 1760s. A decade later, he and his two older brothers fought in the American Revolution (a struggle that patriotic southerners would later call the "first war for independence.") Having lost his first family, Andrew Davidson started over by marrying a Virginia woman named Sarah Muse on November 2, 1801. They soon pulled up stakes and moved to Pulaski County, Kentucky, where Andrew and his brother-in-law Issac Muse served briefly as law officers. At the dawn of the nineteenth century, Andrew Davidson moved again, eventually settling in the Tennessee Territory in Blue Stocking Hollow, near the town of Shelbyville. His descendants have lived in Middle Tennessee ever since.

Virtually nothing is known about the last fifty years of Andrew Davidson's life. One son, Isaac S. Davidson, attained sufficient distinction as a physician and property owner to be mentioned in *Goodspeed's History of Tennessee*. Another son, Bluford Davidson, was born in 1813, when his father was fifty-three, and

5. Ibid., 100.
6. Kirkpatrick interview.

died thirty-five years later. Andrew himself died a few years after Bluford, at the age of ninety, just after the census of 1850. Born a subject of King George III, he lived to see the nation he had helped to build be torn apart by sectional animosities. The persistence that took him deep into the continent in search of a lost wife must have had its unattractive features as well—especially as he grew older. After his death, his granddaughter Sarah Elliot sent a rather ambivalent note of condolence to Andrew's widow and son. "I was sorry to hear of my old grandfather's death," she wrote. "The poor old man must have been a heap of trouble before he left this world."[7]

I

As Wilma Dykeman has observed, "All Tennessee, like Caesar's Gaul, is divided into three parts."[8] East Tennessee is bordered on the north by Virginia, on the south by west Georgia, on the east by North Carolina, and on the west by the Cumberland Mountains. The region is defined geographically by its mountains and is connected historically to an older America. Middle Tennessee is bordered on the north by Kentucky, on the south by east Alabama, on the east by the Cumberlands, and on the west by the Tennessee River. Although it was a frontier region when Andrew Davidson settled there, the boundaries of the frontier were pushed even farther west when the area between the Tennessee and Mississippi Rivers was won for the state by the Chickasaw Treaty of 1818, thus creating the area known as West Tennessee.

By the mid-nineteenth century, Middle Tennessee had become a land of small farmers. It is rich limestone country and the home of the Tennessee walking horse. In the early 1860s, a distiller named Jack Daniel began brewing his legendary whiskey in Lynchburg. James K. Polk, a politician from up the road in Columbia, had become the nation's eleventh president (and the eighth from the South) in 1845. (It would be over 130 years before another southerner would be elected to that office.) "Like the Bluegrass of Kentucky," one observer writes, Middle Tennessee "represented a westward expansion of the Virginia tradition, in which the planter set the tone of society and was willing to live up to his responsibilities. Yet he did not make any too absurd pretensions to aristocracy. The rough-and-tumble tradition of Old Hickory and the negligible distance between planter and farmer forbade that."[9]

7. Ibid.
8. Wilma Dykeman, *Tennessee: A Bicentennial History,* 3.
9. Donald Davidson, *The Tennessee,* vol. 2, *The Old River: Frontier to Secession,* 298–99. Subsequent references will be cited parenthetically in the text.

It was into such a world that Andrew Davidson's great-grandson William Bluford Davidson was born on July 1, 1862. He was the eldest son of Thomas Andrew Davidson, who was himself the eldest son of Bluford Davidson. During the hard times of Reconstruction, young Will Davidson acquired an unusually thorough education. Having matriculated at Holbrook Normal School in Lebanon, Ohio, he was "among the first generation of Southern boys who went north to study to become a *teacher*."[10] In 1891, Will became principal of the school at Mooresville, Tennessee. There, he met Elma Wells, a music and elocution teacher, who had graduated from the Haynes-McClean School in Lewisburg, Tennessee. A year after their marriage in 1892, the Davidsons moved to nearby Campbellsville, where Will was to be principal of the local school. Elma was expecting their first child.

Elma's mother, Rebecca Mar Patton Wells, came from Chapel Hill, Tennessee, where her family owned land adjacent to that of the Forrest family, kin to one of the South's most colorful and controversial heroes, Gen. Nathan Bedford Forrest. (Although he grew up in Mississippi, Forrest had been born in Bedford County, Tennessee, and his uncle still owned a tailor shop in Chapel Hill.) A man of the frontier, Forrest lacked the patrician polish of many of his fellow Confederate officers. Not a professional soldier like Lee and Stuart nor a scholar like James Johnston Pettigrew, he was a scarcely literate farmer and slave trader.

A hero to the common man, Forrest led by flamboyant example. If his fellow generals resembled aristocrats such as William Byrd, Nathan Bedford Forrest reminded one of the vulgar laborers who actually laid the dividing line. He was accused of wanton brutality in the conquest of Fort Pillow, and he served as the first Grand Wizard of the Ku Klux Klan. If Jefferson Davis and Robert E. Lee have won a kind of grudging respect from northern historians, Forrest remains an unreconstructed pariah. Nevertheless, Shelby Foote regards him as one of the two most remarkable figures to emerge from the War Between the States (Abraham Lincoln being the other).

Rebecca Patton Wells's father, Elisha Patton, served all four years with Forrest, having enlisted in the Confederate army at age fifty-three. Two of his sons, Addie and John, also served under the backwoods general, although John, who weighed over three hundred pounds, was deemed fit only to drive the wagons.[11] Another member of the company, Capt. Alfred Dysart, gave his last full measure of devotion for the Confederacy. On March 4, 1863, lead elements of Confederate cavalry encountered a substantial Union force at Thompson's Station, just north of Columbia, Tennessee. It was nine-thirty or ten o'clock the following morning

---

10. Donald Davidson, "Donald Davidson's Notes for an Autobiography: The Early Years," 202. Subsequent references will be cited parenthetically in the text.

11. Kirkpatrick interview.

before the Union commander, Col. John Coburn, moved against the center and left of the Confederate forces. "From his place at the extreme right end of the Southern line, Forrest watched as the Federals advanced, briefly held their ground, and finally fell back."[12] Upon orders of their commanding general, Earl Van Dorn, "the bulk of the Confederate forces, including two of Forrest's regiments, repeatedly assaulted the Union flank and front, while Bedford, with the remainder of his command, worked his way around to the enemy's rear."[13]

Despite strong Federal resistance, Forrest eventually broke through the Union line and forced the enemy to surrender. A portion of his command rode off to chase down the few Yankee soldiers who had gotten away. It was in this final charge that Captain Dysart lost his life. In his report on the battle of Thompson's Station, Forrest wrote: "No one can regret more than I do the loss of Lieutenant Colonel Trezevant, commanding Cox's regiment of cavalry, Capt. M. Little, of my escort, and Captain [A. A.] Dysart, of the Third Tennessee Cavalry. They were gallant men and fell with their faces to the foe."[14] Alfred Dysart was Rebecca Patton's fiancé.

A lecture her grandson gave nearly a century later suggests that Alfred Dysart may not have been the only suitor that Rebecca Mar Patton lost to the cause of southern independence. As Donald Davidson recalled,

> The old folks of my childhood had precious few evenings to sit in the moonlight and listen to banjos. But now and then they did find time to pass on some information to us young folks. A good deal of it was rather grim. . . . [I]n the Sixties, [my grandmother] had seen her boyfriends captured by marauding Federal soldiers and shot in cold blood on the main street of her home town. Her view of reconciliation of the Gray and Blue was about that of some French Villagers that I talked to, near the Western Front, soon after the Armistice of November 11, 1918. Those French people wagged their heads skeptically and said: *"Les Boches, ils reviendront!"*[15]

The war-hardened Rebecca Patton did not marry until she reached the comparatively advanced age of twenty-eight. And her husband, John Henry Wells, was a far cry from the heroic Alfred Dysart. A tailor like Elisha Patton, he had been excused from military service because of an unspecified illness. Remaining in Chapel Hill, he made Confederate uniforms, which had to be hidden whenever Union soldiers were in town. (Apparently, John Henry Wells had once been in

12. Brian Steel Wills, *A Battle from the Start: The Life of Nathan Bedford Forrest,* 104.
13. Ibid.
14. *The War of the Rebellion,* 121.
15. See Virginia Rock, "The Making and Meaning of *I'll Take My Stand:* A Study in Utopian Conservatism," 25.

business with an uncle of Nathan Bedford Forrest, because records of the 1856 Marshall County Fair indicate that the five-dollar prize for best suit of clothes went to Forrest and Wells.) Pictures of John Henry Wells show a frail man, who shared the dark good looks of Edgar Allan Poe and John Wilkes Booth. After the birth of their two daughters, John and Rebecca Wells were divorced for a time, probably because of his fondness for drink. (Divorce records indicate that she was awarded the couple's house.) They later reconciled and produced three sons. An old family Bible contains a joint temperance pledge. By all accounts, it was a pledge that John didn't keep and that Rebecca didn't need.[16]

In 1893, the year that John and Rebecca's daughter Elma and her husband, Will Davidson, moved to Campbellsville, Tennessee, Grover Cleveland was inaugurated as the nation's twenty-fourth president. (He was the only Democrat to serve in that office in the fifty-two years between 1860 and 1912.) In Ireland, a young poet named William Butler Yeats wrote "The Lake Isle of Innisfree." Walt Whitman and Alfred Lord Tennyson had both died the previous year. Closer to home, the *Sewanee Review,* which had been founded by William P. Trent in 1892, celebrated its first anniversary. The Chicago World's Fair commemorated the four hundredth anniversary of Columbus's voyage a year late. It was at this exposition that Henry Adams saw the dynamo and proclaimed it a moral force equal to the Cross. Also at the World's Fair, on July 12, a young professor named Frederick Jackson Turner pondered the significance of the frontier in American history. A little over a month later, on August 18, Elma Davidson gave birth to a child who would be among the first generation of Americans to know that frontier only through the alchemy of myth.

II

Reflecting on the origin of his names, Donald Grady Davidson observed over sixty years after his birth: "It was my mother, under my grandmother's influence, I am sure, who gave me a Scottish first name—out of Jane Porter's *Scottish Chiefs,* no doubt. It was my father, a hopeful young school teacher, who chose for his son's middle name the name of the admirable Peacemaker—Grady."[17] Although he had been in his grave for four years by 1893, Henry W. Grady was still regarded as a prophet of everything the South could become if only it would abandon its benighted heritage and rejoin the Union. When he addressed the New England Society of New York in 1886, the legendary editor of the *Atlanta Constitution*

16. Kirkpatrick interview.

17. Donald Davidson, *Southern Writers in the Modern World,* 33. Subsequent references will be cited parenthetically in the text.

envisioned the New South as "the home of fifty millions of people, who rise up every day to call from blessed cities, vast hives of industry and of thrift; her country-sides the treasures from which their resources are drawn; her streams vocal with whirring spindles; her valleys tranquil in the white and gold of the harvest; . . . her wealth diffused and poorhouses empty, her churches earnest and all creeds lost in the gospel."[18]

As the son of a schoolteacher, Donald Davidson developed an early reverence for education. He remembers his father quoting from Shakespeare's *Richard III* and reading to the family from Bryant's translation of the *Iliad*. ("I was disturbed—and to this day remain disturbed—by the treachery of the Goddess Athena, in taking the form of Hector's brother, Deiphobus, and deceiving Hector into thinking he would have help if he made a stand" ["Notes," 205].) The boy's first memories were of the "handsome old Southern mansion, with white pillars and porches" that served as the schoolhouse in Pulaski, Tennessee, where his father was principal in the mid-1890s (see "Notes," 203).

Years later, Davidson recorded in his private journal one of his earliest recollections:

> One day in early childhood I ran away to school. How I escaped my mother's eye, I do not remember. But I do remember a long hill leading up to a building with white columns. I somehow wandered through a hall way and into a room where my father was teaching. Surprise and amusement when I made my entrance seemed to me quite out of place. My father took me up in his arms and, I think, went on with his teaching until presently, knowing or sensing what company I liked, he turned me over to my best friend at that time, a very good-humored man with large moustaches and a considerable expanse of vest. I sat on his lap and played with his elaborate watchchain with its seals that some time or other, before this, had engaged my infantile attention. And soon afterward, when the bell rang and classes changed, I was duly returned to my anxious mother. This was my first hour in a schoolroom.[19]

By the time Donald was four, his father was teaching in Prospect, Tennessee, "just a little piece up the railroad from Pulaski." One frosty morning in 1897, Will Davidson and his brother-in-law Wallace Wells (who was living in the Davidson household) got up to take the early train to the centennial celebration in Nashville. Donald "remembers this with painful exactness because he stepped on the kindling wood near the stove where the fire was being started, and stuck nails in his bare feet." He also recalls his baby brother Thomas crawling across

18. See Dewey W. Grantham, "Henry W. Grady and the New South," 243.
19. This journal is in the possession of the Davidson family.

the floor and clapping his right hand on a hot stove lid. From that moment on, Thomas was lefthanded ("Notes," 203).

The presence of an extended family was an important influence on Donald Davidson's childhood. Will's youngest brother, Gordon, would often stay with the Davidsons. "There were all sorts of uncles around at Christmas and some other holidays," Donald later recalled, "and you can imagine the tale-telling and joking, for they were all naturally very merry and talkative persons" ("Notes," 201). Donald's Grandmother Wells also lived for a time with her daughter and son-in-law. She brought with her complete furnishings for her room, including pictures in oval frames, an old rocking chair, and a small cherry table that her husband had had in his tailor shop during the War Between the States. Not only did he listen to her stories of the past, young Donald also slept for a time in his grandmother's room. After he got to college and began to write verse in the manner of Longfellow, he published a poem called "Grandmother's Room" in the student literary magazine. The opening lines read:

> Grandmother's room, my Grandmother's room,
> There was never a thought of sorrow or gloom
> When I sat at your side in my own little chair
> And watched the dark shadows go flickering there. ("Notes," 202)

Donald's mother helped instill in him a passion for music that would nearly equal his love of literature. He recalls her teaching him the keyboard, the notes, the scales, and finally simple pieces to play from a book called *Landon's Pianoforte Method*. Unfortunately, his mother was too busy with her other piano pupils to take Donald beyond the beginning stages. After he had passed from finger exercises to simplified versions of Beethoven's "Bagatelles," he developed a modicum of proficiency performing popular compositions by Ethelbert Nevin and the less difficult short pieces of Schubert and Chopin. But he soon realized that he lacked the dedication to practice long enough and hard enough to develop superior technique. Instead, he and his playmates dreamed of becoming railroad men when they grew up and spent their idle time engaging in fistfights or playing baseball with homemade balls and bats.

If music never became Davidson's vocation in life, it remained a consuming avocation. He tried to teach himself the rudiments of composition by working at his mother's one book on harmony and buying books on counterpoint and other elements of musical structure. Years later, he recalled that

> music was a part of everybody's life in those days. People sang a lot—sang at work, sang or hummed while walking. It was the great day of light opera and "musical comedy"—of brass bands, minstrel shows (blackface), strolling Italian organ players with a monkey or a dancing bear. The

Edison phonograph was just beginning to come in—the first of the noise-makers, the beginning, alas, of the age of more passive reception of canned music of all sorts, including now the canned "commercial" on radio and TV. ("Notes," 206)

Throughout Donald's boyhood, his father moved from one teaching position to another within a small area in Middle Tennessee. These jobs were all quite similar—low-paying and generally short lived. His longest tenure was at Lynnville Academy, where he became coprincipal in 1898. (The only thing Donald remembers about the other coprincipal was that his name was Walker and that his daughter Lorraine was a beauty with dark eyes and long chestnut curls.) The job at Lynnville lasted until 1908, when a rich man put up money for a rival school on the other side of town, and patronage for the academy dropped off markedly. For a short time thereafter, Will Davidson taught at McCain's, a school located in a prosperous agricultural area on the Columbia Pike. He would ride horseback from Lynnville to McCain's, stay five days, and return home on weekends.

Even as his social and economic status remained precarious, Will Davidson guided his son's education. Although Dumas and Dickens were considered acceptable authors, Will sternly forbade Donald to read popular "trash" such as George Alfred Henty's adventure books for boys, while merely disapproving of the sensational psychic novels of Marie Corelli. By the time he left for college, Donald had read extensively in the works of Cooper, Scott, Poe, and other canonical writers. He recalls that his father "was always quoting his long favorite passages from 'The Vision of Sir Launfal' or the famous first sentence of Johnson's *Rasselas*" (*Southern Writers*, 10). Another favorite was the Middle Tennessee poet John Trotwood Moore. Donald also remembers reading Byron's poetry and hearing his father recite large portions of Scott's *The Lady of the Lake* and *Marmion*. Donald himself committed to memory passages from Longfellow's *Hiawatha*.

Given the erratic quality of the public schools during this period, much of a child's education came from what he learned at home. Because Will Davidson didn't believe in sending children to school until they were eight or nine, Donald was ready for the fifth grade by the time he entered Lynnville Academy in 1901. (His excellence in spelling was such that his teacher, Miss Jenny Worley, gave him a leatherbound copy of Longfellow's *Evangeline* as a prize.) After they left Lynnville, the family's frequent moves disrupted Donald's formal schooling to the point that some greater degree of permanence was needed. Fortunately, during the early decades of the twentieth century, Tennessee boasted some of the nation's finest preparatory schools for boys. Unlike their counterparts in New England, these schools were not reserved for the elite members of society. They were places where farmboys of the upper South could study Latin and Greek, play sports, develop character, and learn to live away from home. In 1905, the Branham and Hughes School in Spring Hill, Tennessee, became such a place for young Donald Davidson.

III

The school had been founded by William Hughes and W. C. Branham in 1892. Originally called the Campus School, it was located near Vanderbilt University and was intended to provide a preparatory curriculum for young men planning to enter Vanderbilt. After graduates of the Campus School enrolled in the Vanderbilt freshman class in 1897, the school's entire operation was moved to Spring Hill, Tennessee, where Branham and Hughes took possession of the property and buildings of the Spring Hill Male College. In 1898, the institution changed its name from the Spring Hill School to the Branham and Hughes School. Under that name, it continued to function until June 1932, when it became a casualty of the Great Depression and the changing fashion in education.

The school's founders were remembered for their contrasting but complementary personalities. If the levelheaded and practical Branham was often skeptical of his partner's grand visions, he more often used his common sense and industry to make those visions a reality. One of Hughes's pet projects was a proposed lake, which he planned to create in an area behind the Spring Hill campus. Although this scheme nearly sent the school under financially, both the lake and the school were flourishing at the time of Hughes's death on May 14, 1916. An absentminded eccentric, Hughes would allow unopened letters to accumulate in his pockets until his coat began to sag noticeably on both sides. One former student recalls that "he had so many plans and schemes on his mind that he often had a preoccupied manner which caused him to be hardly conscious of the boys whom he met on the campus or in the village."[20]

Because the Branham and Hughes School was thirty miles distant from the Davidson home in Lynnville, Donald was forced to live away from his parents at the age of twelve. For his first year, he stayed with his mother's youngest brother, Wallace. Only ten years older than Donald, Wallace Wells was a senior at the school and manager of the Branham and Hughes Book Store. Having lived for a time with his sister's family, Wallace seemed more like an older brother than an uncle to his young nephew. (The awe in which Donald held Wallace is suggested by some worshipful doggerel he wrote about the family while still a boy: "Wallace the preacher / The football player, / He may be a bishop, / He may be a mayor."[21])

---

20. W. O. Batts, ed., *Private Preparatory Schools for Boys in Tennessee,* 30.
21. This poem is found in one of several notebooks containing Davidson's youthful writings and drawings. These are in the possession of the Davidson family.

On September 9, 1905, Wallace wrote to Elma to apprise her of the expenses Donald would incur over the coming school year: "Beginning at the biggest thing first, the tuition, as I told you while I was there, that I am responsible for that. . . . As to his board, that is $9.00 for the first month and $7.00 [a month] for the remainder of the time. This is a month of four weeks, or by the year $72.00."[22] Wallace assures his sister that he can help pay for half of Donald's board and include his nephew's washing with his own at no extra cost. With money matters out of the way, he offers Elma some personal observations about her son's progress and adjustment.

> I am sure now that there was no mistake made in letting him come to school[,] for he has been getting along very nicely. . . . The door was open from the book store into chapel where Mr. Branham was hearing his Ancient History lesson a day or so ago and I heard [Donald] catch a question and his long explanation of the point in question attracted my attention. When he had finished Mr. Branham said "Good[,]" which is a very welcome sound from that dignitary because it rarely comes. [Donald] does nicely in Arithmetic from what he says, and seems to have no trouble with any of his class[es]. He said today that he did not expect to be home sick, as he had not been so far, but am sure that he has suffered but covered it all up.

Six days later, Donald wrote to his mother with news of his life away from home. "I have been enjoying myself all this week," he begins. "This evening I took a long tramp away out in the sticks. I had a good time for I filled up on apples and such, but got permission." He announces that he has been doing well in his classes and working out in the gym every night. "We will have to have a holiday this week to get the field ready for Saturday's football game. They have already measured off the field and put up the goal posts." He concludes his letter by asking about Grandma and the children (he was the oldest of five siblings) and promising to write every Sunday.

It is not known whether he kept his promise of a weekly letter, but one surviving note, from April 1, 1906, gives us a glimpse into Donald's spiritual life at prep school. He begins by informing his mother that he has just come back from a meeting of the Epworth League (a club in the Methodist Church) and that the leader had made a good talk, which he enjoyed. "We are going to have a regular treat tomorrow night. I guess you have heard of Miss Ellen Stone, the missionary who was held in captivity in Turkey so long. She is going to lecture here tomorrow night and will show some of her situations and so on with a magic lantern, a steriopticon. . . . I belong to the Cheerful Workers, a little missionary society,

---

22. This and other letters cited in this chapter are in the possession of the Davidson family.

and am very much interested. I hope the children will continue Sunday School. I have not missed a single Sunday since school began."

On that same day, Wallace wrote to his sister to indicate that during the past year Donald had more than fulfilled the promise he had shown back in September. He had not made less than a ninety on any of his examinations. "I read his history paper the other night," Wallace notes, "and you might think it was written by a mature person by the fitness of words and good English he used. The only thing that showed his age was the handwriting and hope we can get that improved in the course of time." An acquaintance among the first-year students had told Wallace that he liked to see Donald play basketball. "He said Donald went in with all his might to get his side to win, and that he liked to see that spirit in a boy in school." On a more philosophical plane, Wallace observes: "I saw somewhere a comment on the great value of the virtue 'Innocence.' I hope and pray the boy will continue to have this through his manhood. He seems to be well thought of by all his associates and class fellows and am sure will have a great influence in school when he is older."

By Donald's second year at prep school, Will Davidson had left Lynnville to become coprincipal of the county high school in Columbia, Tennessee. This was near enough to Spring Hill that Donald was able to live at home and commute to school by train. (He had to leave early enough in the morning to make it to class by eight o'clock after a train ride of thirty to forty minutes and a mile walk.) That year, Wallace Wells enrolled at Vanderbilt and even made starting center on the varsity football team before being forced to drop out of school for lack of money. When he returned to Spring Hill, he went into the poultry business with William Hughes.

During his time at Branham and Hughes, Donald was required to take Latin, English, and mathematics all four years and Greek for three. The curriculum for a typical school day might include readings from Caesar, Homer, Euclid, world history, and English grammar. "By the senior year, the Branham and Hughes scholar was required to read the Greek hexameters of Homer's *Odyssey* aloud in proper meter, scanning them at sight."[23] Looking back on his prep school experience forty years later, Davidson was convinced that he got "more solid learning than most college graduates" of a later generation.[24]

His exposure to literature at Branham and Hughes caused Donald to abandon his boyhood ambition to become a railroad engineer. He began writing verse for the school paper, *The Purple and White,* and helped to represent one of the school's two literary societies in a debate held during commencement. (Debate between "literary societies" was one of the major extracurricular activities in Tennessee

23. See Thomas Daniel Young and M. Thomas Inge, *Donald Davidson,* 22.
24. Louise Davis, "He Clings to Enduring Values," 7.

prep schools and at Vanderbilt itself.) He and a classmate named Horace T. Polk successfully argued the negative side of the question, "Should the U.S. Navy be increased for defense purposes?" Years later, he recalled that during his senior year in prep school he had earned part of his tuition as Head Spelling Corrector. "The whole school took a spelling lesson—written on uniform blank books—every day, immediately after noon recess. The errors were marked by student correctors and recorded by me as Head Spelling Corrector. If a student missed more than 3 words out of the 10 'given out' by Mr. Branham out of the day's lesson, he had to 'stay in' a half hour after school was dismissed" ("Notes," 208).

Davidson remembers with particular vividness the evening that former governor Robert Love Taylor visited the Branham and Hughes School. When the legendary Bob Taylor ran for governor as a Democrat in 1886, his Republican opponent was his brother, Alf Taylor. (Running against both of them on the Prohibitionist ticket was their father, Nathaniel Green Taylor.) The two brothers stumped the state together—fiddling, swapping tales, and pulling tricks on each other—in Tennessee's "War of the Roses." The night two decades later when Bob Taylor came to Branham and Hughes, Donald Davidson was "a little boy in knee pants, long black stockings, and high stiff collar . . . , wearing a pair of Walkover shoes that did not cost over two or three dollars."[25] Recalling that evening more than fifty years later, Davidson describes Bob Taylor as being not very tall and plump around the middle. He had "a shiny bald head and rather prominent dark eyes with a friendly twinkle . . . [and] a good sturdy handlebar moustache" (17). Bob Taylor's speech was strewn with flowers of rhetoric and some good belly laughs thrown in for good measure. But it was when he picked up his fiddle that the young boys and assorted townspeople were transfixed, convinced for that moment that they lived in the grandest country in the world, stretching "From Maine's dark pines and crags of snow / To where magnolia breezes blow."

> Then suddenly we were sad, and we sang Kathleen Mavourneen because the last rose of summer had lost all her lovely companions. We dreamed that we dwelt in marble halls, but far, far better than the glory that was Greece and the grandeur that was Rome was our dear old cottage home in Tennessee. We were swinging in the grapevine swing, a barefoot boy with cheeks of tan, down by the old millstream, where we could listen to the mockingbird and dream of Hallie. But there was a gal in that grapevine swing—and we saw those downward drooping eyes, that mantling blush, that heaving breast, and we heard that whispered "Yes," wherein a heaven lies. So we picked a sweet

25. Donald Davidson, "The New South and the Conservative Tradition," 16. Although a shorter version of this essay later appeared in *National Review,* the material quoted in this chapter comes from the typescript of the lecture Davidson delivered at Bowdoin College in Brunswick, Maine, on April 16, 1958.

bunch of daisies, brought from the dell, and said "Kiss me once, darling, daisies won't tell." But quickly the scene changed and we saw the victim of love's young dream, at midnight's holy hour, clad in a long mother-hubbard nightshirt, walking the floor, in his bosom an aching heart—in his arms the squalling baby. (18)

Because of the poverty to which he was accustomed as the son of a school-teacher, Donald took it for granted that he would have to help earn his way in life. He recalls that "the first money I ever made was one dollar—a silver dollar—from the peanuts that I raised in a part of my father's large vegetable garden at Lynnville" ("Notes," 207). Also, as a boy in Lynnville, he failed miserably in his efforts to sell the *Saturday Evening Post.* (One is reminded of Eugene Gant's similar experience in *Look Homeward, Angel.*) Looking back on that fiasco from the perspective of early adulthood, he observed that after some halfhearted attempts to sell the magazine, he simply gave up and refused to sell it at all. "Thus, no doubt, I was saved from a business career."[26]

By the time Donald graduated from Branham and Hughes in 1909, he was committed to furthering his education. Will Davidson was now principal of the high school in Bell Buckle, Tennessee, and had become friends with William R. ("Sawney") Webb, headmaster of one of the most respected prep schools in the South. During his summer vacation, Donald did chores on Webb's farm. Impressed with the boy's industry and ambition, Webb recommended him for a loan from the Boddie Fund, a program that had been established at Vanderbilt for the benefit of Webb School graduates. Because no Webb graduate had claimed the money for that fall, "Old Sawney" used his influence to secure the loan for Donald. In addition, he provided his young friend with a letter of introduction to the Vanderbilt chancellor. As a journalist profiling Davidson noted years later: "It never occurred to the innocent freshman, completely unaware of the usual procedure of registering, that there was anything unusual about his refusing to see anyone except the head of the university."[27]

---

26. See Young and Inge, *Donald Davidson,* 22.
27. Louise Davis, "Clings," 7.

TWENTIETH AVENUE

When Donald Davidson entered Vanderbilt in the fall of 1909, William Howard Taft was president of the United States. With the exception of a brief imperialistic romp in Cuba and the subjugation of the Indians in the Wild West, America had been at peace for over forty years. Despite intermittent financial panic, there seemed to be no limit to the growth and prosperity the country might enjoy in the new century. In England, H. G. Wells predicted a utopian future through technology in his novel *Tono-Bungay*. In Stockholm, the Nobel Prize for literature was awarded to Selma Lagerlof. Closer to home, Henry James published the last volumes of the New York edition of his works. In Jackson, Mississippi, Eudora Welty was born. (Mark Twain and Leo Tolstoy would both die the following year.) And at Vanderbilt, the school's poetic tradition was epitomized by the sportswriter Grantland Rice.

The city of Nashville was 130 years old in 1909. It had been founded on Christmas Day 1779, when James Robertson established a settlement on the west bank of the Cumberland River and called it Fort Nashborough in honor of the Revolutionary War general Francis Nash. In 1862, it was the first major Confederate city to fall under the control of Federal troops. Three years later, it became the site of the last battle of the War Between the States, when Rebel forces tried unsuccessfully to regain the city shortly before the surrender at Appomattox. By the time Nashville observed its centennial in 1880, it had risen from the ashes of Reconstruction to become a model for the progressive New South. The railroads were expanding, and new industry was flocking to the city. Seventeen years later, when Tennessee celebrated the centennial of its admission to the union, Nashville was already calling itself the "Athens of the South." As if to emphasize that claim, organizers of the celebration constructed a full-size reproduction of the Greek Parthenon at the center of the exposition grounds. "The Parthenon, in the eyes of one approving observer, proved that Nashville's and the South's traditions of art and poetry had not been swept away in the New South's tide of industrial spirit."[1] After the centennial, the Parthenon remained, dominating the landscape of a city park in the west end of Nashville.

In many respects, Nashville had moved west between 1880 and 1897. As the downtown fell victim to urban blight, wealthy residents began relocating in the suburbs. Perhaps more important was the presence of Vanderbilt University, which had opened its doors in West Nashville in 1875. In 1873, Holland McTyeire, a bishop of the Methodist Episcopal Church South, had persuaded Commodore Cornelius Vanderbilt to endow the school that would bear his name. (Vanderbilt's second wife was a southerner, a Methodist, and a distant relative of McTyeire.) Although the Commodore's avowed purpose was to reconcile North and South, Vanderbilt University drew its first students primarily from central and western Tennessee and Kentucky, from northern Georgia, Alabama, and Mississippi, and from parts of Arkansas and Texas.[2] As a Methodist who had been educated at a Tennessee prep school, Donald Davidson fit perfectly the profile of the typical Vanderbilt student in the early years of the twentieth century.

During the first six years of the university's existence, the English program had been combined with modern languages and classics. In 1881, however, William Malone Baskervill was made chairman of an independent school of English. Although his academic training (at Randolph-Macon College and the University of Leipzig) had been in Anglo-Saxon and Middle English literature, Baskervill was intensely interested in modern letters. He was also the first historian of southern literature. In his book *Southern Writers* (published in 1897 as the first volume of a projected two-volume work), Baskervill tried to place the writings of George Washington Cable, Joel Chandler Harris, Sidney Lanier, Maurice Thompson, Irwin Russell, and Mary Noailles Murfree within a national, rather than a regional, perspective. He was also instrumental in encouraging Cable, Thompson, James Lane Allen, Thomas Nelson Page, and other contemporary southern writers to lecture at Vanderbilt.

In addition to his scholarly eminence, Baskervill exerted considerable influence at Vanderbilt simply because he was Bishop McTyeire's son-in-law. In fact, he was considered a strong candidate to become chancellor of the university when that position became vacant in 1893, the year of Donald Davidson's birth. After the appointment went instead to James H. Kirkland, a professor of Latin, Baskervill grew increasingly disengaged from campus affairs. He died suddenly in 1899, the second volume of *Southern Writers* still incomplete. When Baskervill was

1. Don H. Doyle, *Nashville in the New South: 1880–1930,* 153.
2. See Paul K. Conkin, *The Southern Agrarians,* 4.

replaced as chairman of English by Richard Jones, a less distinguished scholar, the program suffered accordingly.

During the early years of the twentieth century, student life at Vanderbilt took on a distinctive character. According to the university's official historian, Paul K. Conkin:

> Campus life now had its annual rhythms. In the fall new students first gathered at a college night sponsored by the YMCA and then heard an opening address by Chancellor Kirkland. Immediately, those so inclined were swept up in what was then called "spiking" (rushing). They also quickly began attending football games and then in lesser number other sports. During the year each fraternity had at least one dance, often two, and several campuswide social events clustered around Christmas. The YMCA had ongoing activities—Bible classes, charitable efforts, and various social gatherings. . . . The pace of events increased as commencement neared. The literary societies still vied for speaking honors. Factions formed around the highly contested election of a Bachelor of Ugliness, which occurred in a convention-like meeting in the chapel. . . . Commencement week was full of events—speeches, sermons, moot courts, and from 1902 on a senior prom.[3]

Although Donald Davidson had been to Vanderbilt once before (to attend a high school track meet in 1906), his first day as a student in the fall of 1909 remained more vivid in his memory. That day he took his first train trip alone and his first streetcar ride ever. Following Sawney Webb's instructions to the letter, he presented himself to Chancellor Kirkland in the administration building in College Hall. After waiting for what seemed like hours, Donald was finally admitted to see the chancellor. Everything went well until he discovered that he had not brought his entrance credits from prep school. As luck would have it, his former headmaster, Mr. Billy Branham, was in the building that day. Branham immediately got the proper forms and asked Donald what he had taken at Branham and Hughes. With his paperwork complete, Donald Davidson officially entered Vanderbilt University.[4] It was a relationship that would last for nearly sixty years.

With the one hundred dollars he had gotten from the Boddie Fund and what little additional money he could scrape together, Donald had to pay his tuition and establish living quarters in Kissam Hall. His room (86 Kissam) was located on the fourth floor of the north central wing of the dormitory. When he arrived there, he discovered that the place was completely unfurnished. The basement was filled with secondhand furniture that older students were eager to sell. A

---

3. Paul K. Conkin, *Gone with the Ivy: A Biography of Vanderbilt University,* 211.
4. See Rollin Lasseter, interview with Donald Davidson, 4.

deposit was required to obtain even a simple table lamp. Because the university had not yet begun providing washbowls and pitchers, students had to bathe in the basement of the south wing of the building. (For Donald, this meant a trip outside.) He remembers that the young faculty members who lived in the building took their baths with the students. One professor, John Luck of the math department, was grossly obese, while George "Birdy" Mayfield of languages was all "skin and bones." To watch the two "taking a showerbath at the same time . . . was quite a spectacle."[5]

Every day at noon classes would stop for required chapel. Everyone had an assigned seat, and student monitors took attendance. Although the service was supposed to last no more than half an hour, "the school of religion was always on the platform in full force, and they were likely to pray very long prayers." Even the benediction could drag on as the student body began chafing to get to lunch. Years later, Davidson recalled that "Dean Tillett would start to give the final prayer after we had sung a hymn, . . . and he would go on and on in his nasal voice, . . . and then there would be a stampede over to Kissam Hall to get something to eat."[6]

Academic life at Vanderbilt held little challenge for young Donald Davidson. After the rigid curriculum at Branham and Hughes, the work at Vanderbilt did not seem particularly demanding. His education took place mostly outside class through a habit of constant reading. His mentor in this endeavor was his freshman English teacher, Lawrence G. Painter. Although Painter was the only member of the three-man English staff without a Ph.D., he was well liked by his students. He was the first adviser of the Vanderbilt Dramatic Club, and he regularly invited students to his suite (two little rooms and a central room on one of the upper floors in the north central wing of Kissam) to read and discuss literature. Painter unplugged his chimney and maintained a fireplace. (Davidson recalls him opening a box of cigars and reminiscing about George Lyman Kittredge.[7]) It was at Painter's urging that Donald read through all of Kipling and some of Dostoyevsky and Tolstoy.

Among Donald's acquaintances during his first year at Vanderbilt were two juniors from Ashland, Kentucky, Ben and Varnell Tate. Although not wealthy, the Tate brothers lived far more comfortably than a schoolteacher's son from Middle Tennessee. (Ben would later become a coal executive in Ohio, a political adviser to Sen. Robert A. Taft, and a member of the Vanderbilt Board of Trust.) The Tates gave Donald "free run of the personal library that they had installed in sectional bookcases in their room in Kissam Hall." He recalls

5. Lasseter, Davidson interview, 6.
6. Ibid., 8.
7. Ibid., 6.

"with special vividness . . . their deluxe edition of the complete works of Guy de Maupassant—in translation," which he read through, volume by volume (*Southern Writers,* 11).

With his money exhausted and no prospect of acquiring any more, Donald Davidson, like his Uncle Wallace before him, dropped out of Vanderbilt after his freshman year. At that point, he could have gone into business or sought the sort of manual work he had done while growing up. His fledgling efforts at verse while in prep school had not caused him to dedicate himself to the writing of poetry, and criticism seemed to be the province of scholars with advanced degrees or smart-aleck journalists writing for the big city newspapers. Nevertheless, the love of learning had taken far too deep a root to be dislodged. Even though Will Davidson's life had been one of poverty and frustration, his son rejected other lines of work in favor of teaching school.

I

From 1910 to 1912, Davidson taught at the Cedar Hill Institute in Cedar Hill, Tennessee, approximately thirty miles north of Nashville. Nearly forty years later, he remembered that "in those days, a teacher was expected to handle classes in English, Arithmetic, Plane and Solid geometry, Greek, Latin, and perhaps History, all in a normal day's teaching schedule. . . . I leaped from bloody tragedies like Shakespeare's *Macbeth* to sentimental idylls like Storm's *Immensee* without undue discombobulation. It is a wonderful thing to be a young teacher and to have confidence in your powers."[8] In addition to his academic responsibilities, Davidson also coached the baseball and football teams and composed a children's operetta based on the Pandora myth. This latter experience caused him to fantasize about applying to Harvard to study music.

For at least part of the time that he taught at the Cedar Hill Institute, Davidson roomed and boarded with a local couple, Frances and Will Melvin. (The nearest hotel was in Springfield, Tennessee, a ride of eight to ten miles by horse and buggy.) Virtually every small southern town of that era had such room-and-board facilities, some of which were clearly commercial operations to support needy widows in their own homes. The Melvins, however, ran their establishment out of a fondness for young people. They had no children of their own and enjoyed providing accommodations for some young teacher or preacher who might be in the area for awhile.

---

8. Donald Davidson, "On Teaching Democracy through Literature," 1. Subsequent references will be cited parenthetically in the text.

Frances Melvin's nephew Vince Davis, who would later take classes from Davidson at Vanderbilt, recalls that when he was a boy, his aunt would tell funny stories about the transients who stayed in her spare bedroom.

> She described DD as the "oddest duck." She said "he loved the girls but never knew what to do about it." On one occasion, it seems, he fell desperately in love with some young woman in the community, but was never able to convey this to her. When he finally tried to alert her to his sentiments, she failed to notice and he took this as a rebuff. Humiliated, he retreated to his room and stayed there for weeks in hermit-like isolation, abandoning his teaching duties. Aunt Fannie and Uncle Will faithfully put his meals on a tray and left them outside his room on the family's regular eating schedule. Later, they would pick up the empty tray. He refused to communicate with anybody. When he moved out at the end of the semester, they found in his room scraps of what seemed to be love poems addressed to this young woman.[9]

The years 1912 to 1914 found Davidson teaching in the rural community of Mooresville, the same town where his parents had met. He recollected over half a century later that "while the village had only a store or two, a blacksmith shop, and a church, [Mooresville] was in no sense 'remote'—not 'in the sticks.' The country in those times was quite populous. . . . It is still lovely country around Mooresville but Goldsmith's 'Deserted Village' would describe its present loneliness. . . . When I taught at Mooresville there were only two automobiles (of the more primitive type) in that area—owned by two very prosperous farmers."[10] During the summers, when school was not in session, Davidson made money at various jobs. When his family was still living in Bell Buckle, he pitched hay on Sawney Webb's farm for a dollar a day. Later, when they had moved to Mulberry, Tennessee, he performed the same job for Bob Motlow, who was the brother of Lem Motlow, owner of the Jack Daniels distillery in nearby Lynchburg.

Although he was making his own living during these years away from Vanderbilt, Davidson remained in close touch with his family. By the time the First World War broke out in 1914, his parents and siblings had established themselves at Mulberry, in Lincoln County. Years later, Davidson observed: "I would have to write you a Hardy novel to describe how beautiful country life was there, in that then very fine farming country" ("Notes," 204). It was at the home in Mulberry that Elma Davidson died, after a long illness. Her son passed his twenty-first birthday before acquiring the finances to return to Vanderbilt as a sophomore in

9. Quoted in a letter to me from William Pratt, dated June 8, 1996.
10. Undated letter from Donald Davidson to M. Thomas Inge, in the possession of M. Thomas Inge.

the fall of 1914. By that time the university was significantly different from the one he had left four years earlier.

In 1912, a former Vanderbilt undergraduate named Edwin Mims had replaced "Dickey" Jones as chairman of the English department. Mims was forty and a man of settled convictions, very much committed to the critical temper that was trying to shape a New South. Probably the most influential mentor in forging that commitment had been Mims's undergraduate Latin teacher, James H. Kirkland. The similarities between Mims and Kirkland were striking. Both had been reared in middle-class southern Methodist families (Mims in Arkansas, Kirkland in South Carolina). Both had used a university education as a means of gaining social stature in a culturally backward region of the country. And both saw education as a kind of secular salvation for the entire South. To their supporters, Mims and Kirkland were visionary leaders. To their detractors, they were narrow-minded autocrats. Mims's devotion to Kirkland was such that in the 1940s he would write both a history of Vanderbilt and a biography of its chancellor. For his part, Kirkland tried for several years to lure his former student to the Vanderbilt faculty and gave him virtually free rein once he arrived. Years later Davidson wrote: "For me there was excitement in Dr. Mims' courses, partly from the stunning revelation that English and American literature offered subjects to study, not just books to read" (*Southern Writers,* 10).

In 1914, the Vanderbilt English department still had only three faculty members. The lone holdover from Davidson's freshman year was S. N. Hagen, a philologist educated at Johns Hopkins University, who taught half-time in the German department. In addition to Mims, the other new face was that of a twenty-six-year-old Rhodes scholar and former Vanderbilt student named John Crowe Ransom. During his first year back at Vanderbilt, Davidson was enrolled in courses with both Mims and Ransom. "Ransom's teaching methods were in obvious contrast to those of Mims," Thomas Daniel Young notes. "If Mims made [Davidson] aware that 'English and American literature *had a history,*' Ransom made him conscious of poetic techniques and devices besides music and sound."[11]

Ransom's seemingly diffident classroom manner contrasted markedly with Mims's histrionics.

> Ransom read poetry in a voice flat, quiet, and almost inflectionless. Although Davidson changed his mind before the term was over, at first he considered Ransom a dull teacher because he almost never summarized, synthesized, or uttered pronouncements about the greatness of the selection under consideration. Instead, quietly, patiently, and almost pedantically, he analyzed the

11. Thomas Daniel Young, *Gentleman in a Dustcoat: A Biography of John Crowe Ransom,* 85.

plays [of Shakespeare], sometimes devoting the whole hour to one scene or, more frequently as the year advanced, to a few lines. Although Ransom never assigned specific passages to be committed to memory, as Mims and many other teachers of the time did, Davidson was surprised to learn years later that he could not only quote many of the passages that Ransom had discussed but that he remembered Ransom's specific comments about them.[12]

In 1915, a fourth English professor joined Mims, Hagen, and Ransom. Walter Clyde Curry was a medievalist who had been born in Gray Court, South Carolina, in 1887. After completing his undergraduate degree at Wofford College in nearby Spartanburg, he went west to do his graduate work at Stanford University. Besides teaching Old and Middle English, he developed a popular undergraduate course in Shakespeare. The range of his literary interests is reflected by the fact that his two best-known books are *Chaucer and the Medieval Sciences* (1926) and *Shakespeare's Philosophical Patterns* (1937). In addition to taking a class in Chaucer from Curry, Davidson remembers getting from him "on the side, out of his own library, an informal reading course in modern European drama— Ibsen, Strindberg, Rostand, Hauptmann, Sudermann, and the like" (*Southern Writers*, 11).

Still painfully lacking in finances, Davidson made ends meet by teaching classes in English and German at Wallace University School, a highly respected private institution in Nashville. Along with his expected chores, he was put in charge of "a class of unruly small boys—all from the best Nashville families—to whom I was supposed to teach Biblical History" ("On Teaching Democracy," 1). In some autobiographical notes he made half a century later, Davidson recalls:

> My five-day-a-week schedule at Wallace University School called for me to teach from 8:00 A.M. to about 9:45 A.M. I would just have time to walk to my 10 o'clock Vanderbilt classes. Immediately after my 11–12 V. U. class— or, rather, after the required 12–12:30 chapel was over—I would get back to Wallace School, take a bowl of soup and a meagre sandwich at the very spartan Wallace lunch-room, then teach until 3 P.M. I managed somehow (I don't remember how) to get in Chemistry Lab. I would take Dr. Mims's and Curry's late afternoon classes. ("Notes," 208)

Because this hectic regimen did not allow him time to schedule the required physics course, Davidson failed to graduate with the class of 1916.

In the midst of all his hard work and diligent study, Davidson also found time for fun and entertainment. In the fall of 1909, he had pledged the Alpha Tau Omega fraternity and had been initiated in a large horse pond facing the entrance

---

12. Ibid., 86.

to the university on Twenty-first Avenue. (It was in the fraternity house that he learned to play bid whist and to dance the waltz and the two-step.) "There were informal musical evenings," Davidson recalls, "when one found in some friendly house a little orchestra of flute, violins, and piano. . . . Or there were nights at the Vendome Theatre—to see *The Merry Widow,* or something from Victor Herbert, or Kennedy's *The Servant of the House,* or Forbes Robertson in *Hamlet,* or even Geraldine Farrar in *Madame Butterfly*—and afterwards the long walk back to the Vanderbilt campus where Halley's Comet was blazing across the sky above Kissam Hall. It was not exactly Bohemian; nor was it anything like a Parisian salon; but it was not academic, either" (*Southern Writers,* 13, 14). Davidson's most memorable evenings as an undergraduate had nothing to do with music, however. Less than a year after he returned to Nashville, he and several friends began meeting for informal philosophical discussions with an eccentric autodidact named Sidney Mttron Hirsch at the Hirsch family home on Twentieth Avenue, not far from the Vanderbilt campus.

II

In the years between the War Between the States and the First World World, southern poetry was in a lull. Edgar Allan Poe had died in 1849 and Henry Timrod in 1867. Although Paul Hamilton Hayne survived until 1886, the most important southern poet to write in the last third of the nineteenth century was Sidney Lanier. Not only did he merit the longest chapter (162 pages) in Baskervill's study of southern writers, but he was also the only southern poet of his time known to a national audience. (This may have been owing less to his verse than to his children's book *The Boy's King Arthur.*) Lanier, however, was less a forerunner of southern modernism than a lingering vestige of nineteenth-century ideality. (He would be the subject of a highly regarded biography by Edwin Mims.) Louis D. Rubin, Jr., speculates that had Lanier "been a New Englander rather than a Georgian and grown up in the orbit of transcendentalism, he would have led them all in the intensity of his response to life."[13]

In the thirty-four years after Lanier's death in 1881, no poet of comparable stature had appeared in the South. The only southern poet who seemed fully aware of the modernist revolution in literature was an expatriate—John Gould Fletcher of Little Rock, Arkansas, who had moved to England in 1908. In the spring of 1913, when Fletcher met Ezra Pound in the Closerie des Lilas café on the Left Bank in Paris, he began an association that would make him one of the six poets most prominently associated with the Imagist movement. Although

13. Louis D. Rubin, Jr., "The Passion of Sidney Lanier," 107.

Pound soon abandoned Imagism for the even more revolutionary Vorticism, Fletcher remained with the group for the balance of the decade. It was during this period, after Amy Lowell had transformed the new poetry into what Pound derisively called "Amygism," that Fletcher wrote the verse for which he would be best remembered.

In the summer of 1915, Donald Davidson was not aware of these literary developments in Europe and entertained only vague ambitions of becoming a poet himself. He had remained in Nashville simply to work and to take courses at the George Peabody College for Teachers. As was the custom in those days, he and some of his friends would call on local girls in their parents' homes. Years later, he told an interviewer that he was expected to report to the ATO house in his best clothes on Sunday afternoon. From there, he and several of his fraternity brothers "would go out in small groups, two or three or four together maybe, to call on the various girls." Typically, they "would sit around and play the piano and sing a song that was popular then. Then there would be a knock at the door and somebody would look out the window and see the Dekes coming. When the Dekes would come, we would get out politely and say 'How do you do' to them, not too warmly. And then we would go and call on another girl. . . . [T]he choice ATO girl . . . was Dimples Neely. She was a very beautiful girl, a small girl, a very fragile girl, very beautiful. We would go through this process nearly every Sunday afternoon. We were dressed up in our well-pressed pants, high collars, and hats."[14]

On one such occasion, Davidson's friend Stanley Johnson introduced him to a popular young Jewish woman named Goldie Hirsch. Also at the Hirsch home that afternoon was Goldie's older half brother, Sidney. A native of Nashville, Sidney Hirsch was eight years older than Davidson. Although his father was a successful merchant, Hirsch succumbed to wanderlust early in life and ran away to join the navy. A large and athletic man, he quickly became heavyweight boxing champion of the Pacific Fleet. During a two-year tour of duty in China, he began an idiosyncratic study of oriental languages and religion. After returning briefly to Nashville, he left for Paris, where he became a model for Rodin and an acquaintance of the poets A. E. and Gertrude Stein. Before returning permanently to Nashville, he lived for a time in New York, modeling for the sculptress Gertrude Vanderbilt Whitney and attempting to establish himself as a writer. Although his literary efforts failed, Hirsch did form a close friendship with Edwin Arlington Robinson, which lasted for the balance of Robinson's life.

In the spring of 1913, Sidney Hirsch had recently returned to the city of his birth with a verse play about the goddess Athena. At that time, the Nashville Art Association and Board of Trade were planning a spectacular May festival at the

14. Lasseter, Davidson interview, 13–14.

Parthenon in Centennial Park. Hirsch's play, *The Fire Regained*, was the pageant chosen to launch this ambitious venture.

> A cast of 600 spent three months in rehearsal. . . . Professional drivers were engaged to race chariots drawn by four white and four black horses. Huge papier-mache wings were prepared for the stallion representing Pegasus. Three hundred sheep and 1,000 pigeons were made ready. The railroads reduced their fares for out-of-town visitors drawn to Nashville by full-page advertisments inviting them to see "The Flight of a Thousand Doves, the Revel of the Wood Nymphs, the Thrilling Chariot Race, the Raising of the Shepherd from the Dead, the Orgy of the Flaming Torches."[15]

This production created such a stir that the U.S. State Department seriously considered staging it on the Acropolis in Greece as an international gesture of goodwill. Unfortunately, that plan was scrapped when war broke out in Europe. After the May festival (complete with a new Hirsch pageant) proved less of a success in 1914, the Nashville business community decided not to continue it in 1915. Thus, by the time Davidson met him, Sidney Hirsch had slipped back into obscurity, a twenty-eight-year-old aesthete living with his father and stepmother. But before long, a group of young men from Vanderbilt would begin gathering at his feet on occasional Saturday evenings.

Because of his wide travels and exotic manner, Hirsch appeared to be the very essence of worldly sophistication to Davidson and his circle of friends, all boys with intellectual curiosity but minimal experience in the world beyond Middle Tennessee. Over forty years later, Davidson remembered those gatherings, which would begin in the Hirsch home and then drift out to the large second-floor balcony that overlooked Twentieth Avenue. All "fell silent and became listeners when . . . Sidney Hirsch picked out some word—most likely a proper name like Odysseus or Hamlet or Parsifal, or some common word like *fool* or *fugitive*—and then turning from dictionary to dictionary in various languages, proceeded to unroll a chain of veiled meanings that could be understood only through the system of etymologies to which he had the key."

> This, he assured us, was the wisdom of the ages—a palimpsest underlying all great poetry, all great art, all religion in all eras, in all lands. All true poets possessed this wisdom intuitively, he told us, solemnly, repeatedly. Furthermore, he proved it later on . . . by pointing out that some image that had crept into our verses, no matter what we intended it to mean, revealed exactly the kind of mystic symbolism he had traced from the Ramayana to Homer to Sophocles to Dante to Shakespeare to William Blake. Probably

---

15. John L. Stewart, *The Burden of Time*, 7.

no group of poets ever before received just this kind of assurance. (*Southern Writers,* 12)

Within the Hirsch circle, Stanley Johnson was Davidson's oldest and closest friend. Throughout the summer of 1915, Davidson and Goldie Hirsch made up a foursome with Johnson and his girlfriend, Will Etta Tatum. The philosophical discussions presided over by brother Sidney, which now loom so large in the history of modern southern literature, seemed at the time to be only part of a more general social and cultural ambience. In November 1957, Davidson observed that it was through Stanley Johnson and Goldie Hirsch that he "came into the company of other Nashvillians, especially a group of Southernized Jews and art-minded Gentiles that Stanley frequented" (*Southern Writers,* 13). It was Johnson who first urged his friend to take an interest in modern poetry. "One day he took Davidson up to his room in Wesley Hall and solemnly showed him a new book—*Spoon River Anthology.* 'We should have done this,' he said grimly. 'He's beaten us to it.' "[16]

For all the literary interest and energy that existed among the young men who gathered around Sidney Hirsch, it is doubtful that the group would have turned its focus so fully to poetry had Donald Davidson not invited his Shakespeare professor John Crowe Ransom to join the Saturday evening gatherings. At first, Ransom was seen as the sort of disciplined thinker who was needed to serve as a counterbalance to the mystical Hirsch. After Ransom began showing up on Twentieth Avenue, he slowly guided the discussions away from philosophical abstractions and toward the analysis of specific poems. Initially, these were poems Ransom had assigned in his class. Then, as Davidson recalls, "One day of days I remember well. My teacher, John Ransom, beckoned me aside and led me to a shady spot on the campus near the streetcar stop called 'Vanderbilt Stile'— though the stile had long since yielded to an open entrance. Ransom drew a sheet of paper from his pocket. Almost blushingly, he announced that he had written a poem. It was his very first, he said. He wanted to read it to me. He read it, and I listened—admiringly, you may be sure. The title of the poem was 'Sunset' " (*Southern Writers,* 14).

Ransom's experience in the tutorial setting of Oxford made him an ideal mentor for Davidson and other young men just beginning to discover literature. If the Olympian Mims was a more stirring classroom orator, he was a distant figure for that very fact. To use the jargon of our own times, Ransom taught in a classroom without walls. As a bachelor, he lived on campus in Kissam Hall, and students were constantly dropping by his rooms to borrow books or continue a conversation cut short by the end of class. Although Ransom could have made

16. Louise Cowan, *The Fugitive Group: A Literary History,* 20.

more money had he remained in the New England prep school where he taught for a year upon his return from Oxford, it is doubtful that he would have found life as congenial anyplace other than at Vanderbilt.

Ransom's influence on Davidson at this time was not as a poetic model. Davidson would never emulate Ransom's ironic and whimsical tone. (He later conceded that he did not care as much as he pretended to for Ransom's earliest verse.) He was impressed rather with Ransom's seriousness about his art. Davidson himself had written verse intermittently since his days at Branham and Hughes, but he had not yet developed his mature voice. As Louise Cowan points out, Davidson still regarded poetry as "principally song, with no great burden of thought." When he did turn his attention and passion to poetry, it was to acquire thought, not to lose music. For all their intellectual substance, "his mature poems . . . were still to have a structuralizing aural quality."[17]

In addition to Davidson, Ransom, Hirsch, and Stanley Johnson, the group that Ransom's poem "Ego" would later call "a seven of friends" included two Vanderbilt undergraduates—William Yandell Elliott and Alec Brock Stevenson. As a graduate of the Webb School, Elliott had come to Vanderbilt with four years of Latin and two and a half of Greek. He would later become a Rhodes scholar, a highly respected professor of government at Harvard, and an adviser to Richard Nixon. Stevenson was a native of Toronto, who had moved with his parents to the Vanderbilt campus shortly after his birth on December 29, 1895. His father, J. H. Stevenson, had been a circuit rider for the Methodist church in Ontario before being called to fill a temporary position at Vanderbilt. That position soon became permanent, and the elder Stevenson proceeded to distinguish himself as a professor of Semitic languages. Young Alec grew up in the company of Vanderbilt professors and proved so precocious that he could read *Uncle Remus* in dialect by the age of five. Possessing an impressive command of verse forms, Stevenson became editor of the student literary magazine. From that bully pulpit, he lamented the quality of poetry being produced at Vanderbilt and the lack of an advanced course in writing.[18]

In 1915, the "seven" became complete when Walter Clyde Curry joined the group. Because Sidney Hirsch had suffered a spinal injury while in the military, he would hold court while reclining in a chaise longue. ("Hirsch, half guru and half clown, always ready to find great truths in any youthful comment, provided the needed stimulus toward originality," writes Paul Conkin; "Ransom, with his dry detachment, set the standard for rigor and for intellectual self-discipline."[19]) Although his young friends sometimes found his views suspect, they always

17. Ibid., 22.
18. Ibid., 12–13, 30.
19. Conkin, *Southern Agrarians*, 9.

treated Hirsch with deference, as they discovered the life of the mind on the Saturday nights they spent at his house. Once, when Alec Stevenson was away in Canada, Bill Elliott wrote to him about a particularly memorable evening: "Out on the Hirschs' porch, with the cigar ends glowing occasionally, a debate always insured from the nature of the company, it is the *Happiness*."[20]

These magical nights on Twentieth Avenue came to an end when world war called several of the participants away from Nashville. As American involvement in the European struggle became imminent, the Vanderbilt community closed ranks behind the Allies. Although several Vanderbilt professors (including Chancellor Kirkland) had attended German universities, only Herbert Sanborn in the philosophy department defended the Central Powers, and he was officially silenced once America entered the war. Throughout the spring of 1917, students began preparing for military service. Kirkland approved substituting classes in military science for the undergraduate gym requirement, and anti-German sentiment reached a fever pitch.

Davidson, who was away teaching at the Massey School in Pulaski, Tennessee, volunteered for the army and was reunited with his friend Ransom at Camp Oglethorpe, Georgia, in May 1917. As Davidson recollects that experience, "in campaign hats and khaki, we sat in a grove of pines on the battlefield of Chickamauga, at the foot of Snodgrass Hill. Again Ransom drew a manuscript from his pocket. This time it was a large sheaf of poems. Under the pines he read me parts of what was published in 1919 as *Poems about God*, by Lieutenant John Crowe Ransom" (*Southern Writers*, 14). Although the great war had a profound effect on the literature of the twenties, we tend not to think of Ransom and Davidson as World War I poets. Unlike the young British writers of the era, their sensibility was not shaped by the war. Unlike Hemingway, they suffered no unreasonable wounds and failed utterly to experience the postwar disillusionment of the lost generation.

In more subtle ways, however, the years 1917 to 1919 were crucial ones for both men. Ransom continued writing while in the army and returned from war more committed than ever to his vocation as poet. Davidson carried Ransom's verse with him overseas, wondering if he would ever be able to write like that himself. "When I read those poems in France, by candlelight in some peasant's home in the Cote d'Or or Yonne, or some ruined village near the Western front," he recalls, "they still blurred my exploring, eager eyes, even though at that distance I could more gratefully recognize in them the Tennessee country I had left. I was not only a long way off from writing poetry. I did not even know how to read poetry—if this was poetry, and surely it must be" (*Southern Writers*, 15).

---

20. See Young, *Gentleman*, 91.

3

OVER THERE

When Donald Davidson received his commission as a second lieutenant in August 1917, he was assigned to Camp Jackson in Columbia, South Carolina, where he helped organize Company E, 324th Infantry of the 81st Division. This predominantly southern contingent, which was popularly known as the Wildcats, was transferred across the state to Camp Sevier in Greenville, in May 1918, to replace the Thirtieth Division, already heading overseas. Davidson's communications with his family throughout this period reflect a mild homesickness. In an undated letter to his sister Rebecca, sent from Camp Jackson in the summer of 1917, he writes: "I would like to be with you now, where there is green grass, and growing crops, and real dark earth—not this dull sand and monotonous pinetrees."[1] However, in another letter to Rebecca, which appears to have been written somewhat later, he observes: "It does not do to think of the things one is missing. We are all proud to do what we are doing[,] sure that it is the best thing to do in a time like this which calls for service from everybody."

In addition to his immediate family, Davidson had left his future wife behind. While teaching in Pulaski, Tennessee, in 1917, he had met Theresa Sherrer, who was teaching Greek, Latin, and mathematics at nearby Martin College. No longer the lovesick boy who had boarded with Will and Frances Melvin four years earlier, Davidson had acquired a measure of sophistication and social grace from life in Nashville, especially his association with the Hirsch circle. For her own part, Theresa Sherrer was hardly a provincial country girl. She came from Oberlin, Ohio, a major stop on the Underground Railroad and a hotbed of midwestern liberalism. (In a letter he wrote from Pulaski on February 8, 1917, Davidson tells

1. The letters cited in this chapter from Donald Davidson to his sister and father are in the possession of the Davidson family.

Rebecca that he is learning to ice-skate because "I could not stand off and see my Northern and Western friends get the best of me.")

If her Yankee origins were not sufficient to set her apart, Theresa Sherrer was also a woman of considerable intellect, with career aspirations of her own. (This was enough to scandalize some members of the rigidly traditional Davidson family.[2]) At the time that Donald met her, she already had bachelor's and master's degrees in the arts from Oberlin College. In 1922, she earned a law degree from Vanderbilt and served as librarian in the law school. Later, her interest in Roman law led to her earning a Ph.D. in classics. She worked with Professor Clyde Pharr in translating the Theodosian Code and even taught for a time in the classics department at Vanderbilt.

Because Donald could not secure leave to travel to Ohio, Theresa and her father came to Greenville, where the couple was married on June 8, 1918—by the same Methodist minister who had married Will and Elma Davidson. In late July, the 324th Infantry was ordered to Camp Mills, Long Island. As one might expect, Davidson's diary entries at this time are filled with longing for his new wife. On July 27, he writes, as if speaking directly to Theresa: "I have just gotten my first letter from you since we were separated. The tears *will* come. You are so dear. How I wish you could see into my heart. It is with me just as it is for you. When feelings are deepest, words are hardest. And I have never truly told you how much I love you. How I do regret that now—how I wish I could have said more. If you ever read this you will know." Then, on July 30, he writes: "Theresa comes tomorrow[,] I hope. A day or two more of best happiness[,] then—the long parting. It is better to think of the happiness of meeting again."[3]

On August 5, the Wildcats began their departure for England. Although the morning was dark and gloomy with the threat of rain, the weather had cleared by the afternoon. Davidson had spent his last night on American soil sleeping comfortably with a mattress, a blanket, and a cot. (Some officers had already sent their bedding ahead to the ship.) In the morning, they boarded a train. "I could hardly bear to look at the scenes around Garden City," Davidson writes, "—[a] place once so unknown to us, now so sacred. The trip across by ferry was a panorama of never ceasing wonder to me—City unrolled before us—living tapestry against the sky, proud buildings, thronging people and clanging traffic. The Statue of Liberty seemed to make us a gesture of farewell."

By 5:15, they were in midchannel. The people aboard passing ships cheered them as they steamed out, the sun already bright on the water. Off the coast, they picked up a convoy of two destroyers, which stayed with them for about a day. The first two days went smoothly. Then, on the third day, when Davidson prepared to

2. Molly Kirkpatrick in conversation.
3. Donald Davidson's World War I diary is in the possession of the Davidson family.

go on guard duty, "the heavens descended, the earth came up." Seasick, Davidson was reduced to eating hardtack and apples for the next twenty-four hours. At last, on a bright Sunday morning, five U.S. destroyers rushed out to meet the ship in convoy formation. The next day, the crew of Davidson's ship sighted land. "We steamed up the Irish Sea, saw the Welsh Coast and . . . anchored in the River Mersey at about 12 o'clock to wait for the tide. Finally after much agony we docked. A British band played ragtime American airs for us. We crossed the gangplank and set foot on English soil in the good city of Liverpool. It was August 12, 1918."

On the march from Liverpool to the army rest camp, Davidson and his fellow soldiers were besieged by hordes of children, all crying, "Any cents, Joe?" and the like. Along with the throngs of dirty children, Davidson noticed English and American soldiers, nearly all of whom seemed to have girls. Never had he seen such open displays of affection. "It was altogether the most loose, careless place I ever saw," he observed, "vice everywhere apparently open and above board." After spending two nights at the camp, which they called "Knobby Ash," the men boarded a train that took them across England to Southampton. When they were all seated, they were handed a letter from the king, which was given out to all American troops passing through. Later, Major Humphreys, whom Davidson had known at Camp Jackson, came by to bid them goodbye. "His monocle glittered bright as ever. The whistle blew. We were on our first trip by rail in Europe."

Upon arriving in Southampton, after an eight-hour train trip through England, the soldiers were marched to another rest camp. The next afternoon, they set sail for France, rounding the rocky banks of the Isle of Wight at twilight. They docked in France at dawn and marched through the narrow cobblestone streets of Le Havre just as the little town was waking up. Butchers and bakers were opening their shops, as people passed carrying great loaves of French bread. It was there that Davidson heard for the first time the patter of a foreign tongue. They spent the day in another "rest camp," in some cases crowding eight to ten men into a single small tent. That evening, they learned that they were to leave that very night for the training area in Tonnerre. "A moon shone down on us," Davidson notes in his diary, "—there was much singing and laughter. In the moonlit distance we could see the harbor, with its points of land projecting far into the water, and the ships riding at anchor."

The Eighty-first Division was assembled in Tonnerre on August 16, 1918, and then moved to the town of Dye. Despite the constant drilling, Davidson found the life at Dye to be half-idyllic. The soldiers soon became acquainted with the principal inhabitants of the village—including the merry host of the cafe and an "old man who sang, but only in his cellar, away from all gossiping ears." At night, the soldiers sat until late outside their billets, watching the moon and talking of the people and places they had left behind. Often, they would sing in the streets—the Stephen Foster favorites "My Old Kentucky Home" and "Old Folks at Home," along with other laments for homes far away.

On September 1, Davidson wrote to his father to describe "what you might call a rise in the world." He had been assigned to the battalion staff as the officer in charge of billeting. Whenever the troops entered a town, he would visit the town authorities and, "after a great deal of 'parley-vooing' through an interpreter," manage to secure lodging for all his men. As he would tell the story later, French housewives recoiled in horror when they heard the interpreter, a Cajun private from Louisiana, "mutilate their language."[4]

In his letter to his father, Davidson describes the texture of everyday life for an American infantryman in France:

> It is hard to realize, sometimes, that we are so very far away from home. It seems that one would only have to look up a train, get on it, and in a little be back in Sunny Tennessee. But there is no morning paper, no mail, no automobiles (practically)—in fact all we see from day to day is an occasional car bearing a staff officer or some such dignitary, a truck maybe, and always the French horses trundling their queer carts, and the enormous French cows, and old women carrying burdens, and the jolly village baker, and the moustache of the Major, and the town crier as he goes about beating his drum and reading notices that we can't understand.

One unambiguously happy note was the fact that Vanderbilt had written to inform Davidson that his diploma was being sent to Theresa in Oberlin. The university had allowed military training to substitute for the required physics course he had been unable to fit into his schedule.

On September 9, Davidson received his first two letters from Theresa. Both had been mailed to Camp Mills, Long Island, over a month earlier. The following day, three more letters arrived. "My dear girl has been writing a letter every day," he records in his diary. "More joy—a regular celestial aura about me everywhere I go, despite toothache, rain & cold wind, and a thousand worries. This fine love of yours, Theresa, what a blessing it is." One fact that he does not mention (and may not even have known at the time) was that Theresa was nearly three months pregnant with their first (and only) child.

I

For seven of the ten months that Davidson was overseas, the war was over, and he was waiting with increasingly frayed patience to be sent home. However, in

4. Walter Sullivan, *Allen Tate: A Recollection*, 25.

the two months before the armistice on November 11, 1918, the 324th Infantry saw plenty of action. According to Thomas Daniel Young and M. Thomas Inge:

> First casualties came when German airplanes bombed the troop trains before they reached the Bruyeres area. The lengthy sector that the division took over extended some fifteen miles from Lusse to Allencombe. Preparatory to entering the great Meuse-Argonne offensive, the division was moved to another sector and occupied a line equal in length to the first from Fort Douamont (northeast of Verdun) to Fresnes, with Davidson's 324th Infantry at the south end.[5]

On October 7, Davidson found himself in a seemingly tranquil valley about a mile away from the little village of Allarmont, which was held by the Germans. Because both sides were there to rest and recuperate, there was little fighting. Once, before Davidson and his division came down, the Germans had held a grand party, singing in the valley and walking openly in the fields with the region's French inhabitants. But things had begun to grow more tense in recent days. The "Boche" (as Davidson calls the enemy) no longer dared to put their horses out to pasture. Still, they retained some of their gentle, fun-loving ways. "Yesterday[,] being Tuesday," Davidson writes, "he [the Boche] decided that a little sweet music would fit the occasion. So from the mountainside[,] about ten in the morning[,] the notes of a bugle come to our ears and for half an hour the musician plays for us martial calls, marches, & gentle airs. He was no amateur that Boche. There was . . . an appealing tenderness about his notes that bespoke an artist, at least in his class."

On October 12, after he had gotten his men settled, Davidson and his companion Stevens found their own billet. The first person they encountered was an old, crazy woman, who wept profusely and kept showing her American visitors pictures of the Virgin and various saints. The man of the house looked knowingly at Davidson and Stevens and said "Malade!" After Davidson struck a bargain with the man for eggs, a basket of apples also appeared on the table. They tasted good to soldiers who had been subsisting on salmon and bully beef. Davidson and Stevens slept soundly that night in narrow French beds.

The following night, Davidson ventured closer to an encounter with the enemy. The idea was to push "a patrol up to the Boche lines to see where he was & what he was doing." Davidson asked permission to go along as a spectator because he did not want to send his men to places where he would not go himself. They started out on time and arrived at their jumping-off place without any trouble. There, the lieutenant in charge of the strong point informed Davidson that the

5. Young and Inge, *Donald Davidson*, 28.

Germans had been bombarding him with shrapnel for most of the evening. "The words had hardly left his mouth before the Boche guns behind the mountain began to roar, and the shells began to pop and whistle in our close neighborhood." The men ducked in the trench until the spasm of firing seemed to be finished, then climbed out and continued on their way.

They soon discovered that their own barbed wire had not been cut to aid their passage, although they had been promised that this would be done. After making a slow and noisy progress through the various belts of wire, Davidson learned that his corporal had a pair of wire cutters. Fifteen minutes after they began cutting the wire, they sighted a German flare up ahead. At first, Davidson thought it was from one of their own positions, but the other men convinced him that was not the case. They all crouched low and remained still until the flare had gone out and then proceeded on their path. "All went pleasantly enough for a while, though progress in cutting the path was very slow. But more trouble was ahead. The German gun behind the mountain got into action again. Shrapnel began to burst overhead and fell all around us. Again we clung close to mother-Earth while the fragments whistled in our ears. One piece struck the ground by my side." Because they had taken so long with the barbed wire, the men had been out longer than expected. Having accomplished little, they decided to retreat and returned to the barracks safely. Again, Davidson laments, Battalion Headquarters "had failed in making reconaissance & providing us with proper information."

In a letter to his father, dated October 15, Davidson admits: "I haven't captured any machine-guns, or even shot a Boche or captured one. But I do know now how it feels to be out in No Man's Land at night and what it means to be under fire. Not enough for you to worry about[,] however. It is exciting while it lasts, but doesn't seem particularly grand when one gets back to barracks to talk it over." Writing again to his father, on October 21, he brags: "When we get a real good crack at the Hun, Mr. Boche will know we have arrived." He then goes on to describe an incident that had taken place on the evening of October 17.

Davidson had been looking for some drunken American soldiers in a mostly deserted village up in the lines. ("As usual, wherever the French are," he writes, "is wine also—hence the drunks.") With his sergeant and a sentinel, Davidson immediately found and arrested one of the drunks. A French boy who accompanied Davidson and acted as an interpreter told him that two American soldiers had locked themselves up in a certain house and would not let the proprietor in. Suspicious of this story, Davidson found the proprietor and went (with lighted candle) to force the door. Upon entering the house, the men saw three ragged persons revealed in the light. They were not wearing American or French uniforms, but neither did they seem to be civilians. When the interpreter spoke French to them, they responded with only blank stares. The three men were Germans, who claimed to have lost their way while on patrol. Upon further examination, they were proved to be "arrant liars." Their coats and shirts bore the letters "PG," which stood for "prisoners of war" in French. Quite by accident, Davidson had captured his first two enemy soldiers.

There were lighter moments, as well. On October 27, Davidson describes in his diary an encounter between a colonel and a sentry:

> Sentinel (whispering): Halt! Who's there?
> Colonel (whispering): Friends!
> Sentinel (whispering): Advance one with the countersign.
> Colonel is somewhat alarmed by now. Dismounts & goes forward on tiptoe, pistol in hand.
> Sentinel (whispering): Halt. Give the countersign.
> Colonel (whispering): Jackson.
> Sentinel (whispering): Advance.
> Colonel (more and more alarmed at his proximity to danger) (whispering): Say, sentinel, how far is it to the front line?
> Sentinel (whispering): Seven miles.
> Colonel (out loud—thoroughly angry): Seven Miles!!! Well, what the *** are you whispering for?
> Sentinel (whispering): Sir, I've had this *cold* for three days.

On October 31, only a week before his final and most intense experience of warfare, Davidson reflects on his situation and appraises the soldiers with whom he has served. "Finer men there never were than these we are so fortunate to lead," he writes in his diary. "It is an honor to take them into action. May victory rest on our banners. We know that these lads will do honor to themselves and their country, whatever may happen. 'Dulcie et decorum est pro patria mori'—the old poet's words come back to remembrance."

II

On November 14, 1918, Davidson finally had sufficient leisure to reflect on his experiences of the previous week. Like the men in Stephen Crane's *Red Badge of Courage*, Davidson and his fellow soldiers could see only what was going on around them, with but a fragmentary appreciation of the larger context in which they acted. The 322nd and the 324th Infantry were sent in at the head of the final offensive movement of the war. Marshall Foch had designed this strategy in an attempt to intimidate the Germans during the armistice negotiations. By the end of the day on November 10, each unit had lost over two hundred men. Reading his vivid and previously unpublished account of the events of

November 7 to 10, one realizes how easily Donald Davidson could have been one of those casualties.[6]

Three days passed at Manheuelles before the day of all days arrived. It was hard work. The enemy opposite us was exceedingly nervous, patrols on both sides were active. Rain continued to fall unceasingly. We slopped around in the mud, keeping up our spirits as best we could. All meals had to be carried to us at night, as movement between front and support lines was dangerous in the day time. We generally ate in the evening about 8:30 and in the morning between 7:00 and 8:00. There was no sleep for anyone at night, and very little at daytime. On Nov. 7 Maj. Todd & Lt. Boulloche came by my C. G. [campground] about 3 pm and called for a squad of riflemen & automatics to back up a patrol which Lt. Brown was taking out in broad daylight. . . . While Brown with his patrol was maneuvering in the valley in front of the supposed enemy lines, a machine gun opened fire on him. Nobody was hurt, although Brown's trousers were badly torn by bullets. We located the position of this machine gun[,] and I was ordered to take out a patrol of 12 men the following night to capture it.

We were to have a little barrage to precede us, beginning at 5:30 & lasting till 5:40. We were then to follow it up rapidly, encircle the machine-gun enplacement, capture it & make a quick get-away. The barrage began, but a little late. It was rather too close for comfort, so all of us moved back a bit. The Major was right with us, watching. After 15 or 20 minutes of absolutely useless bombardment, the artillery ceased. But instead of lifting and playing on the . . . emplacement, as it was supposed to, it quit altogether, and fired no more. Nevertheless, at a word from the Major[,] we moved out into No Man's Land.

We bore considerably to the right of our destination in order to be able to come in on the flanks. It was this, I suppose, which threw us off our course. For after a while we became hopelessly lost. We cut through two belts of wire, crouched low when flares went up or bullets whizzed by. We walked, we crawled, we bumped along, seemingly for miles. But the trees which marked the position of the gun so plainly in daytime could not be seen. The farther we went, the clearer it was that we were lost. We tried the compass; but there was too much metal near. It would not work. No stars were out. Presently some stray shells began to drop near. I decided it was best to go back. No machine guns were firing or flares going up now, although we were making a devil of a noise. We about-faced and started in what seemed the direction of our own trenches. My intention was, as per directions, to patrol in front of Brown's C. G. & return by way of his trenches.

6. Other than the alterations indicated by brackets and ellipses, I have made no changes in the following extract from Davidson's diary except to consolidate several extremely short paragraphs by removing some paragraph breaks from the text.

We pushed on. We reached no familiar landmarks. The horizon was a vast dim bowl around us, all sides just alike. Intermittent artillery fire was in progress, but we could not tell from what side the shells came. Still we went on, stopping every now and then to listen and to try vainly again our compass. Presently we came to barbed wire. This seemed better. Surely it must be our own. We cut through this belt and then another, and struggled painfully through. Then after a few minutes progress, a vacant trench. What was it? No one remembered it. I decided to cross. We went on further and stopped again to cast about in different directions for a guide. Presently to our great joy, we discovered on our left the old blown-up dugout, from near which we had taken our departure. The rest was easy. We moved up the crest of the hill, found the road, and dragged our weary, but cheerful way into our C. G. Here Brown was waiting anxiously, ready to push out with a patrol of 25 men to locate & help us if we did not come in by midnight. It was then 11:30 p.m.

[At 3:30 A.M., Davidson was awakened with orders to be ready to move out at dawn. Just after breakfast, the departure time was moved back to 8 A.M.]

In great haste we made ready. The men threw together packs. Many did not even have time to change from rubber boots to shoes. I took my pack, consisting of one blanket and a few toilet articles, tied my overcoat on it, stuffed a few things in my bag, donned my raincoat, and got the platoon down where the main road enters Manheuelles. Then and only then we received definite orders. They were short and sweet. "The Battalion will attack in the direction N 55 E [and] H Co will be in the front line on the left. F will support H. G will support E. Approach formation."

The morning was dark and cloudy. The wind blew obliquely toward us from the enemy line. We were in position behind a long low crest and somewhat concealed from the enemy's view. We could not see the German lines from our position. . . . It is hard to tell what my own feelings were. Before we left Manheuelles, they were rather dubious. I was not anxious, and I am sure nobody was, to attack. We felt somehow that somebody had made a mistake or that orders were gone wrong. But when we once got on the field, all those feelings vanished. There was too much to do. One must look after the men, watch toward the enemy, watch toward the flanks. Men were smoking cigarettes. I myself longed ardently for a smoke, but could not locate a match.

Just before we moved forward, before even our last platoon had cleared the village, enemy artillery began to bombard Manheuelles. I thanked my stars we were already out of it. We were moving slowly forward, crossing first two belts of barbed wire, and then a road, where we paused a minute to steady our lines. At this juncture four aeroplanes suddenly appeared from the east and flew low over our heads. I was ready to fire on them if they came near me, but they did not come directly over. . . . They buzzed hither and thither a minute or two, then darted swiftly back to their lines. In less than five minutes the enemy barrage began to fall ahead of us. No shells fell very near me, but they were coming close on the right and left and in front. The men were very steady and cool. It was, however, hard to guide correctly. I could now see a line of houses among some trees, apparently about a kilometer ahead. Here no doubt was the chateau which Major Todd had given me as a guide. Part of my platoon was supposed to go to the right of it, part to the left. Our pace was slow and steady.

The barrage had ceased now. We moved on. I wondered if there could be any gas mixed in the bombardment. We were approaching a road fringed with trees. Brown's platoon on the left was astraddle of it. The scouts were far ahead. Suddenly, to the left, the crack-crack-crack of a machine-gun. The men were down instantly. With great difficulty we deployed them in two waves. The fire ceased. Apparently it was too far to the left to bother us. I decided to assemble in groups and move on. H Co was getting far ahead by now. We had gone perhaps four or five hundred yards when machine-guns opened in on us in dead earnest. Bullets whistled around our ears. We were all in it now.

In a flash everybody was under cover and out of sight. They had caught us when it was almost impossible to deploy. I could see only a part of my platoon—the two squads nearest me. I cast about for the others, but they were too widely separated. It seemed best to push forward with the men I had, hoping that the rest would see and follow suit. Just at this time enemy artillery began to lay down a terrific barrage. Support groups were entirely lost to view. The fire was falling heavily on my own rear wave. We were just ahead of it with our little handful of men. I could see that Brown was moving forward on the left, and could hear him shouting encouragement to his men. I had with me by now most of the 1st half-platoon. It was probably about this time that Sgt. Woodell was wounded. The 2nd half-platoon[,] behind without a leader, lost touch with us, and fell behind. There was an intermittent fire on us from machine guns straight ahead. I made up my mind to advance as far as possible, locate the enemy position, and try to bring up groups from the rear to out flank them.

The ground had been cultivated in former years in parallel strips from 15 to 20 yards wide. They ran about parallel to the enemy lines. Each one was high in the middle, so as to leave a considerable depression between them—which was defiladed from fire & afforded good cover. We tumbled from one to another of these depressions, advancing steadily. After we had gone about 200 yds. Corp Martin was wounded in the arm. About the same time Pvt. Wm. Smith was wounded in the mouth by the explosion of his own discharge when he attempted to fire a rifle grenade.

At last we came to within 200 yard[s] of the line of houses and trees from which the fire came. It was much hotter by now. We could not move without drawing a stream of bullets. Brown on the left had evidently stopped progress. I had with me about 10 men. The rest of the company I could neither see nor hear. I sent back a message to Stevens reporting the situation. It was impossible also to determine the exact positions of the enemy machine guns. They were many and all too cleverly camouflaged. After getting well set in the place & looking the ground over thoroughly, I determined to try to go back and get together nine men, then make an attempt on the right flank. A little wooded ravine there seemed to offer good ground for a flank move.

I tumbled rapidly from shellhole to shellhole, from hollow to hollow, some three or four hundred yards back. Here I discovered Sgt. Melia with half of the second platoon. He had orders from Stevens to move to my support, but being out of touch with . . . his own platoon commander[,] he was somewhat hesitant about moving. Here also was one squad of my own automatics. I told Sgt. Melia to move up close behind me with these men, figuring then that I would just about have the equal of a platoon formed in two waves & ready to maneuver. Also I still had some ideas of trying the flanking movement. But at this juncture here came a runner with a message from the major looking for Stevens. As I firmly believed by this time that Stevens had been knocked out, I sent an answer myself, and also relayed it on to Stevens.

Rejoining my platoon I found that my other squad of automatics had come up on the right and taken up a good position. Our casualties were light, but no forward move could be made. The Major's order was to hold the present line until ordered to advance. This we proceeded to carry out cheerfully by digging in with whatever tools we had, bayonets, trench knives etc. Most of the men had thrown away their packs & so lost their trenching tools. All this time the enemy was putting down a terrific barrage just in [the] rear and to our right and left. Our own artillery was silent. The situation was fit to terrify the strongest, but not a man quailed. All were cheerful, cool and calm, at all times. I got in connection with Stevens at last, and with Brown.

[From Brown, Davidson receives the major's latest order—to retire at dusk and take up a defensive position on the road they had crossed that morning. On the way back, he is fortunate enough to recover the pack and bag he had earlier discarded.]

The men sank down in utter weariness. I found some hard-tack in my bag, munched some with great gusto, changed my socks, and awaited orders. The battle was over, but the sequence was just as bad. Darkness settled on us, half-frozen, tired, but not dispirited. We had given our best and done all that mortal men could do. In the darkness I sat down and changed my socks. That was the greatest relief of all. How I thanked the providential forethought which made me put an extra pair into my pack. This done I felt better. All I wanted now was a smoke. But this was impossible outside. It was necessary to locate some sort of hut or dugout. . . .

Brown & I shifted around in the cold for some time before we had courage to signify our presence to the Major. Finally we sent word through Stevens that we would like to get in a little while swiftly to take a smoke. The Major, god bless him forever, invited us in right away. We smoked, we rested, and tried to warm ourselves. It was not so bad as the outside. One by one the other officers of the battalion drifted in[,] and some of them stayed in for the rest of the night. We huddled around the stove.

It was a wretched night. Cold racked our bones. The Boche shelled us almost without ceasing, first to the right, then to the left, then all along the road. We did not know what moment might bring one down on us. It would have sealed the fate of the Major and many officers. But it never came. Only we always heard the faraway ominous mutter of heavy guns, then after minutes the whistle of the shell & the explosion. It was all very trying on the nerves. To add to our hard situation, we believed that we would have to renew the attack at dawn. This, in our present, fatigued, disorganized situation was not an evil to be desired. We waited the night long with tense nerves. The candle flickered, runners came and went, officers reported. I could not get one wink of sleep, tired as I was. We smoked, talked in low tones, and waited.

Sgt. Wan of E Co was so far the only one reported killed. Three of my N. C. O.'s had been wounded, one man was down with shell-shock and two others were slightly wounded, but not out. [While I was in the Major's dugout during the night a shell fell close by killing one H Co man & wounding two. A soldier came in to tell Lt. Falkin immediately after it happened.7] No officer in our Battalion was wounded or killed—by a miracle. We heard that the 1st & 3rd Bns had been badly cut up. The sad news also came that Major Ward had been mortally wounded. [He was hit almost point-blank by a machine gun concealed in the woods.] All this was very depressing, especially considering the haste, lack of orders & supplies, & absence of artillery or other kind of support with which that day's operations had been carried out. Yet there was not a man in the Battalion who, if the word had come, would not have gone to the attack again with high and courageous heart. I heard never a word of complaint about the hardships of the fight. Many[,] however[,] did comment on the lack of artillery support. We all felt alike about that.

At about 5:00 a.m., receiving no answer from a message which he had sent the Colonel, the Major gave orders for a further withdrawal. . . . I went immediately out to the trench, waked my men and set out in single file toward Bonzee. We struck out across country, aiming to strike the Manheuelles-Bonzee road. It was just before dawn. I followed my nose and my memory, stumbled through barbed-wire, over trenches, through winding paths, & finally hit the road. Just about this time it was geting light. The Boche, evidently in expectation of a new attack, began a terrific bombardment. I

7. This passage appears elsewhere in the diary but is labeled as an insert. I have placed it where it seems logically to belong.

feared much for those who were moving near Manheuelles, for the barrage seemed to be falling directly on them. We hastened our steps & arrived at Bonzee without mishap. Here I found good dugouts for the men. Brown came up with his platoon, and together we sat down by the road, in the cold morning, hungry, exhausted, frozen, but almost happy at getting a chance to rest. Here we had the first good look at ourselves since the battle of the day before. We were muddy from head to foot, clothes were torn, cockleburrs stuck here and there, faces unwashed & unshaven—altogether we were as thoroughly disreputable as we could possibly be.

One of my old 239 Co men, Roberts, now in the MG Co, came by and offered me warm breakfast from the MG Co kitchen. I complied gratefully & received a plate of warm beans, which I will never forget. This with some hard-tack I had & some chocolate which Brown produced, made a wonderful meal. We found a dry room with an open fireplace. . . . Here we rested all day in grand comfort, dried out clothes, cleaned up, and enjoyed ourselves immensely. We prayed that we might be able to spend a quiet night there and get some sleep at last. We had had none since being in the sector. But alas, our hopes were doomed. We were informed by Bn Hq that we would probably move that night to Handimont. . . . We were to hold ourselves in readiness. A solemn evening it was there by the open fireside. Brown joined—so did Stevens & I. But all knew what was in our hearts. Thoughts of home, and peace (so far away, we thought) and the attack we thought would come the next day.

About 9 p.m. we moved out. It was a long hard march, terribly fatiguing to our already wornout troops. We started out with an open formation, but when we came to Reg. Hq. we abandoned it & did not take it up again. We marched through Handimont in column[s] of twos[,] in plain column[s] of companies. Boche shells at this juncture would have worked terrible havoc with us. It is a wonder he did not turn loose. We stopped finally at a quarry beyond Handimont, and all were turned loose to find bunks wherever they could. There was only the ground. The officers got into a salvage dump. We bundled up together all four, on a pile of overcoats with god knows whose blankets over us. And we slept the sleep of the blest—the tired soldiers' sleep.

On Nov. 11 we awoke early, threw together hasty packs and set out again. As we passed over the mountain American batteries were firing (though we did not know it) their last shells. One time we heard some cheering, but paid no attention to it. When we came to the little shot-up village of Ronvaux, the Major halted us and summoned the officers. It was then 10 a.m. He announced that an armistice would go into effect at 11 o'clock. We could hardly believe our ears. But at 11 o'clock we retraced our steps to the top of the mountain. The guns were quiet. An immense quiet rested over all. We stacked arms in an open field on the road to Verdun, and made preparations for a hot meal. Many slept from utter weariness. At night the long hidden campfires flared up everywhere. We rested till about 9 p.m. then marched our weary but happy way to Camp Les Reums.

III

After the armistice there was considerable criticism of the costly actions taken in the final two days before peace. In some undated notes in his diary, Davidson contends that it was not the division headquarters but somebody farther back who was responsible for the attack—"playing with us like pawns on the chess-board." American prisoners who returned later said that the Germans were astounded by the attack. Unlike the Americans, the Boche had been told that an armistice had been negotiated and were waiting to lay down their arms, but they felt they had to return fire when their enemies kept coming. To make matters worse, General McFarland's repeated pleas for artillery support were ignored.

Throughout the attack, Davidson's immediate superior, Colonel Moses, was nowhere to be seen. (He was an extremely unpopular commander who had earlier angered the men by laying hold of a box of cigars and some chocolate belonging to Stevens and Brown.) While the entire regiment went into the attack, the colonel remained three or four kilometers behind. On the night of November 9, when the village of Manheuelles was being shelled, he complained of being gassed, even though those who were within eight to ten feet of him did not. He was also heard to say: "All you Captains & Lieutenants can walk around with some safety, but if I stick my head out a sniper opens up on me." (When the major from one of the other battalions of the 323rd came to relieve Davidson's First Battalion, he asked the colonel for directions. Instead of giving him the information, Colonel Moses barked: "It is *your* job to find out where they are.") It was later discovered that the First Battalion had entered the woods on the night of November 10 at the written command of Colonel Moses. The colonel explained this by saying the order should have been "to penetrate the woods with strong patrols," and that the stenographer to whom it was dictated had mistakenly omitted the qualifying phrase. The following February, Davidson learned that Colonel Moses was to receive the Croix de Guerre for bravery.

During the relative calm and frequent boredom that characterized the remaining months before his return to the United States, Davidson made some general notes in his diary. In one such note, he tells of men lying in their places all day, separated into two groups, rushing the machine guns that had held them at bay. "Five German prisoners were taken and lined up. The Lieutenant said: 'Well, you have killed too many of us, for you to be let live.' Then he took his pistol and shot them one after the other."

Davidson personally recalls a sergeant singing "Homeward Bound" at Somme-dieu on the night of November 8. On November 11, he led a combat group over the top. A shell struck the group, and nothing remained. On another occasion, during maneuvers, a trench mortar battery was firing. When a soldier thoughtlessly stepped in front of a piece as it was being fired, the shell entered his body under the armpit, about four inches protruding. A nearby captain "seized the shell, pulled it out of the body, and threw it into a trench or somewhere out of harm's way. It did not explode after all. But if it had, and the captain had not acted as he did, many people would have been killed. The Captain received the D[istinguished] S[ervice] C[ross] for this. The man was instantly killed."

Writing to his sister Rebecca on December 22, 1918, Davidson makes it clear that he has no intention of becoming a career soldier once his present duty was over. Although some of the injured men have swaggered back to camp proud of their wounds, he is delighted to have no bullet-torn clothes to flaunt. Instead, he compares himself to a boy from Montaud "who said that he got down behind a log to take cover, and later[,] when he put his hand on it and started to get up[,] he found it was a cigarette paper." You can't get much flatter than that.

Davidson spent Christmas 1918 in Belau. On Christmas Eve, he and several other officers shared a dinner of turkey, nuts, apples, and oranges. (Although the major growled at the cook because there was not more turkey, the other men were thankful for what they had.) Davidson later noted in his diary that he and his companions joked and sang and went home afterward, down a rainy, muddy street, "with much Christmas spirit in our bones." The next day, General MacFarland passed by and complimented the men on the festive appearance of their kitchen. (He asked if he could bring the local count and countess down from their chateau.) The meal the officers ate on Christmas day was a gala affair. Donald even played the piano for awhile after dinner.

About three weeks into the new year, Davidson's wisdom tooth began to bother him. When a dentist examined him, he discovered the infection commonly known as trench mouth. By the afternoon of January 16, Davidson was in the hospital. The enforced idleness grated on him, as he felt healthy enough despite a sore gum. The only consolation in his condition was that he would be able to miss attending classes at a wretched military school in Clemecy. (He later turned down a chance to attend a French university, fearing that it might delay his return to the United States.) After being kept in the hospital for eleven days with virtually no medical treatment, Davidson was released on January 27. He then spent a few more days at Clemecy before being allowed to return to his unit in Belau.

Fortunately, his travel enabled Davidson to take a side trip to Paris, where he visited the Cathedral of Notre Dame. He remembers a dim light and rows of pillars rising to a lofty roof. There were "candles burning, a few stray worshippers.

Then the music of an organ. The harmonious chant of beautiful voices, the solemn intonation of a soloist." He "stood enchanted for many minutes, almost breathless with sheer delight." On his way out, he bought a little pamphlet at the candle shop near the door. An old nun held out a basket and accosted all passersby with the words "pour les pauvres—pour les pauvres." Davidson dropped in a few sous and went on his way.

Back at Belau, he was relieved to be among friends and free of the mindless regimentation of Clemecy. He proceeded to catch up on mail (which had not been forwarded during his absence), and to contemplate his future. "My plans are necessarily very indefinite," Davidson writes to his father in a letter dated February 8. "It seems now that Theresa's people wish her to be at or near her home for awhile, so I may try to locate temporarily in Ohio. But I do not know. I do not think that anything can keep me long away from the South. It is my country."

In early April, Davidson was able to spend some time on leave in Nice, enjoying total rest and relaxation. However, the thought was never far from his mind that his baby might be born at any minute. When he returned to Belau on April 6, he found the long-expected cable waiting for him. On March 26, his daughter, Mary Theresa, had been born. On April 20, he wrote to Rebecca with recent news of the child: "Your little *niece,* from all I can hear, is quite a credit to the family, for she is a most *wonderful* child, very good, very attractive, in fact she already prefers smiling to crying." The new father concludes: "Myself—I'm in the best of spirits and health—longing more than ever for the day when I'll get back to God's country." It would be nearly two more months before that would happen.

At 4:20 P.M., June 4, 1919, Lt. Donald Davidson and the rest of the 324th Infantry caught a troop train to St. Nazaire. Arriving early the next morning, they were taken to Camp number 2, where the men ate breakfast and underwent physical examinations. Davidson soon discovered that he and his cohorts were scheduled to sail the following morning on the USS *Martha Washington.* Unfortunately, coaling the ship postponed their departure by another day. Finally, on June 7, at 9:25 A.M., they marched to the dock. They boarded the *Martha Washington* around 11 A.M. and, after an additional delay, departed at 12:30. A French band played a farewell concert from the wharf. Davidson remembers casting his last look on the shores of France at about 1 P.M. "France has grown so familiar," he writes in his diary, "it is almost like leaving a friend. But to return to America is like returning to a sweetheart."

4

ROBIN GALLIVANT

Service in the war had done nothing to improve Davidson's dire financial straits. When he returned to America in 1919, he had no job and a wife and child to support. He landed at Charleston, South Carolina, in mid-June and was detained for several days of processing at Fort Jackson before he was allowed to return to civilian life. On his way to meet Theresa and Mary in Oberlin, Ohio, he passed through Nashville in the hope of seeing old friends and securing employment in the Vanderbilt English department. Edwin Mims, with whom he had exchanged letters while he was in France, received Davidson warmly on the swing in front of his house but could not offer him a job. Finding virtually none of the Hirsch circle in town, Davidson proceeded to Oberlin disconsolate and uncertain about his future. He spent the next several months pursuing a fruitless job search around Cleveland.

Davidson's dislike of bureaucracy in general, and the urban Northeast in particular, may well date from this time. His first stop was a government agency formed to help relocate returning veterans. The office clerks, who seemed to be on a "1919 version of the coffee break," simply ignored him.[1] Although he applied for positions with an advertising agency and with the Cleveland public schools, he never heard from either one. After several other disappointments, he finally got in to see the managing editor of the *Cleveland Plain Dealer,* who suggested that he come back after he had gained some experience on a smaller paper. Almost at the end of his tether, Davidson was offered a position as chairman of the English department at Kentucky Wesleyan College in Winchester, Kentucky. In addition to his administrative duties, he taught five classes—freshman composition,

1. Young and Inge, *Donald Davidson,* 33.

survey of English literature, and advanced courses in Chaucer, Shakespeare, and American literature.

Although there is little surviving record of Davidson's year at Kentucky Wesleyan, one can glean some sense of what the job entailed from a handwritten letter sent to him on August 27, 1919, by Dean J. L. Whiteside. "If you teach with us," Dean Whiteside writes, "would you be willing to conduct our devotional exercises say once a week, and take an active part in the Y. M. C. A. work occasionally?"[2] A couple of lines later, he inquires: "How are you on discipline in the school room? In our college work, there is not much discipline necessary, but you know a member of the faculty who proves very weak as a disciplinarian would necessarily throw more work and responsibility upon the dean." Years later, Davidson recalled that his students made up for their lack of academic preparation with industry and an eagerness to learn. He was disappointed, however, by the college library. Although adequate for class assignments, it held little that interested him personally.

Apparently, the closest thing to professional writing Davidson did during his time at Kentucky Wesleyan was a six-page handwritten letter to the editors of the *Home Sector,* a weekly magazine for the "new civilian" published by the former editors of *Stars and Stripes.* On January 16, 1920, he called the *Home Sector* to task for falsely asserting that the Eighty-first Division had had no part in the Meuse-Argonne offensive. Throughout his life, Davidson remained proud of his service in the war and committed to seeing his division given full credit for its accomplishments. After setting the record straight, he writes: "If we did not take part in the Meuse-Argonne, what did we do? Where did all those 250 men killed and 801 wounded come in? Do you think we could have lost them in the Vosges? Or do you imagine that we got those 101 prisoners there, too?" Not having developed the appetite for public controversy that he would show in later life, Davidson concludes: "If you care to print all or parts of my letter, you may do so provided you keep my name out of it."

Perhaps the greatest benefit of the job at Kentucky Wesleyan was the opportunity it provided Davidson to establish a home and experience the pleasures of family life. In a letter he wrote to his sister Rebecca on February 22, 1920, he promised to send some pictures of his daughter, Mary, who was now almost eleven months old. "Mary can stand up and walk now by holding on to things," he writes. "We think it will not be long before she is standing alone. . . . Her vocabulary is still quite limited, of course. She has a few sounds she can make and apparently knows their meanings." One gathers that Mary began to walk alone while she and her mother were on a trip to Oberlin later that spring. In a letter to Rebecca dated May 2, Donald writes that Theresa had urged him to

2. The letters cited in this chapter are in the possession of the Davidson family.

"hurry up and send the 'baby fence,' so I know the little rascal is already making herself at home by getting into things." "I am lonesome, of course," he continues, "—but am kept so busy, except on Sunday, that I don't have a lot of time to think about it. We only have a month more of work. Then I shall shake the dust of Winchester off my feet with a great deal of pleasure."

When he finally did leave Kentucky, it was to become an instructor at Vanderbilt for the next academic year. Mims offered the position to Davidson in a letter sent on May 19. Although the salary of $1,400 was $100 less than what he was making at Kentucky Wesleyan, the teaching load was lighter and the academic atmosphere much more stimulating. The appointment also permitted Davidson to pursue a master of arts degree, which he would need if he wished to continue teaching in college. With Theresa and Mary still in Oberlin, Davidson returned to Nashville in June to search for a suitable apartment and to begin his summer job as a reporter for the *Evening Tennessean*. By fall, the Davidson family was settled in the first of several west Nashville apartments they would occupy before setting up long-term residence in Wesley Hall on the Vanderbilt campus. Meanwhile, Donald was teaching four sections of freshman composition and becoming reacquainted with his literary companions from before the war.

If the country at large was returning to normalcy in the 1920s, Vanderbilt was a substantially different institution from the one Donald Davidson had known before his departure for France. Since its recent separation from the Methodist Church, the university had survived wartime austerity, reorganized several of its programs, and launched ambitious plans for the future. At the end of the war, Latin and Greek were dropped as requirements for the B.A. degree. By 1921, student enrollment had increased significantly. And by the middle of the decade, graduate education, which had languished for many years, was once again on a sound footing. Also, by the middle of the decade, Chancellor Kirkland had realized his dream of a new medical school. The official mood at Vanderbilt was one of comfortable self-congratulation as the university prepared to celebrate its semicentennial in the fall of 1925.

As Paul Conkin notes, Vanderbilt tried to steer a safe middle course in all matters social and spiritual. More than anything else, James Kirkland craved a kind of bland respectability.

> He sought professors who would "fit" at Vanderbilt, who would be coopera-
> tive, and not rock the boat. . . . [This] meant that one either fit somewhere
> within the Christian spectrum or kept quiet on religious issues. Avowed
> atheists did not fit within the narrow repressive world of Nashville or the
> South. It meant that one could not openly espouse political or economic
> views outside the mainstream, not even to the extent of advocating milder
> forms of socialism. It meant that Vanderbilt professors should not openly

attack their prime benefactors, the large corporate managers, those who led in collectivizing production, in subverting the old proprietary society. They fit best of all if they joined Mims in celebrating a new South.[3]

What Mims and Kirkland were loath to admit was that, as the 1920s wore on, any celebration of the New South became increasingly forced and problematic. If southern liberalism had risen to its apogee with Woodrow Wilson's election as president, it was dealt a severe setback by Wilson's failure to win approval of the League of Nations. By the mid-1920s, quite a few leading southern liberals, including Wilson and Walter Hines Page, were dead. The Ku Klux Klan was enjoying a resurgence. Stereotypes of the backward South were known to millions who would never read a word of Ellen Glasgow or James Branch Cabell. Almost as an act of desperation, Edwin Mims published *The Advancing South* in 1926. Meant as an encouragement to disheartened southern liberals and as propaganda for the rest of the nation, the book reminded its readers of the tremendous strides that had been made in the South during the preceding three decades. Although *The Advancing South* enjoyed popular success and came close to winning a Pulitzer Prize, it failed to convince the region's detractors. H. L. Mencken "dismissed Mims and his ilk as 'amiable obfuscators' and 'mere windjammers.' "[4]

I

Although the future of the American South was an issue that would absorb him later in life, this and other social controversies were of little interest to Davidson in the early 1920s. At that time, his professional energies were devoted to teaching his classes, writing his poetry, and completing work on his master's degree. Under Ransom's direction, he wrote a thesis on Joseph Conrad's narrative technique. Although much of Davidson's argument would later become received critical wisdom, his attempt to read Conrad as a modernist rather than as a Polish-born Robert Louis Stevenson seemed fairly original in 1922. In an article derived from his thesis, which he published in the spring 1925 issue of the *Sewanee Review,* Davidson contends that Conrad's distinctive contribution to the art of the novel was in his manipulation of time, particularly his distortion of chronology, to emphasize character and mood at the expense of plot and action. Prior to Conrad's death in 1924, far too many critics had ignored or minimized these structural innovations in order to comment on his language, "as if criticism were distracted

3. Conkin, *Gone with the Ivy,* 229–30.
4. Michael O'Brien, "The Middle Years: Edwin Mims," 147.

from close analysis by the interesting spectacle of a native-born Pole in masterful employment of the English tongue."⁵

Much of Davidson's essay is devoted to a discussion of individual works, particularly *Karain, Lord Jim, Nostromo, Chance, Victory, The Arrow of Gold,* and *The Rescue.* Of Conrad's eighteen books of fiction—twelve novels and six volumes of short stories—fourteen make prominent use of inversive narration. To be sure, Conrad was not the first writer to use this technique. Davidson identifies five common types of stories that employ distorted chronology: the story-within-a-story; the pluperfect summary (or flashback); parallel narratives; the mystery story ("which trace[s] a crime backward from its fatal end"); and the newspaper report (sometimes called an inverted pyramid). "Conrad does not, then, employ a downright revolutionary technique in the device of inversion *per se.* It is his exploitation of the possibilities of the method that makes it a unique feature" (167).

In revealing important elements of his plot up front, Conrad makes a calculated trade-off. "The reader, possessed in advance of knowledge which the participating characters do not have, looks down on the scene with Olympian foresight and with pity for brave mortal strife. Like the audiences in the golden age of the Attic theatre, he witnesses a drama the outcome of which he knows in advance. His emotions are thereby released and tempered for the suspense of an evolving character rather than for mere incidental outcome" (165). Davidson argues that in *Lord Jim,* we lose the suspense of melodrama in order to gain "a different sort of suspense, akin to the curiosity of a scientist examining under his microscope a portion of diseased tissue. It is a suspense as to character" (171). Along with Marlow, we know from the outset that there is something fatally wrong with this man, and we read on to discover what it is.

In terms of his approach to art, Conrad was closer to modernists such as James Joyce and Virginia Woolf than to his Victorian predecessors. In fact, Davidson asserts that Conrad's work "is in line with a predominant tendency in every field of modern art—the tendency to overthrow the old fallacy that art should represent life in a photographically methodical way. In the new scheme of art, distortion becomes an inevitable feature. The artist conceives life, not in terms of the flat realities of nature, but in terms of his own spirit, through which his expression must find its own unique form" (177).

An essay by Davidson that had an even more profound effect on literary history remains unpublished. Cleanth Brooks, who would help reshape criticism during the second third of the twentieth century, recalls that as an undergraduate, he first became aware of the possibilities of literary interpretation when he heard

---

5. Donald Davidson, "Joseph Conrad's Directed Indirections," 163. Subsequent references will be cited parenthetically in the text.

a graduate teaching assistant read a paper Davidson had written on a book by Kipling. By the time he was enrolled at Vanderbilt in the mid-1920s, the Fugitives had already discovered the value of reading poetry closely; however, Brooks found it something of a revelation that fiction could also be discussed in aesthetic terms. Two decades later, Brooks and Robert Penn Warren would dedicate their textbook *Understanding Fiction* to Donald Davidson.

Davidson's discussion of Kipling was originally delivered as a lecture to an undergraduate literary organization called the Calumet Club. Although he is concerned primarily with *A Diversity of Creatures,* which was published in 1917, the lecture itself could not have been delivered before Davidson's return to Vanderbilt in 1920. No date is given on the only surviving typescript of the paper, but we know that Davidson was in the army in 1917. Moreover, the essay is written with a worldy sophistication that would be more characteristic of a veteran returning from France than of an undergraduate, even one who had discovered poetry in the company of Sidney Hirsch and John Crowe Ransom. Unfortunately, it is a sophistication that seems a bit pretentious in places. The heavily subordinated Jamesean prose style lacks the clarity and directness that one finds in Davidson's later critical writing. Also, Brooks's admiration notwithstanding, there is little in this essay that clearly anticipates the New Criticism. Nevertheless, Davidson renders aesthetic judgments with a wit and conviction that indicate a developed critical intelligence.

The first ten and a half pages of Davidson's "The Recrudescence of Kipling" pronounce a withering indictment on the poet laureate of British imperialism. Kipling's technical ineptitude and general vulgarity are roundly condemned. Making a particularly astute observation, Davidson writes:

> There is more than a generation between Poe and Kipling—there is a whole world of lost and mutilated art, for Kipling's ghost stories are no more like those of Poe than a cadaver is like a spirit; the imitator has merely caught the trick of evoking the emotion of terror and horror which was only one of the ends for which the master worked, and, most unfortunately, has quite overlooked the more delicate, precise, and subtle working out of the activities of abnormal psychology—the despair of all imitators of Poe's genius.[6]

Then, just as one becomes convinced that there are no redeeming qualities in Kipling's art, Davidson pulls a rabbit out of the hat. For the final three and a half pages of his essay, the critic more than gives the devil his due by heaping praise upon the story "Regulus" and the sketch "Swept and Garnished." He speaks of

6. Donald Davidson, "The Recrudescence of Kipling," 7. Subsequent references will be cited parenthetically in the text.

the "superlative artistry . . . of Mr. Kipling at his best." That artistry includes a sense of the dramatic, sympathetic tenderness for the suffering of children in war, and "a wealth of pathos." Because of these virtues, "we are disposed to forgive Kipling for all his perpetrations of an earlier—and if need be of a later—date, and to take him to our hearts" (14).

From a biographical standpoint, the most interesting aspect of Davidson's paper is its view of Kipling's politics. Given his later career as a defender of the racial caste system in the American South, one might have expected Davidson to regard the British rule in India with a sympathetic eye. As it turns out, nothing can be further from the truth. Early in "The Recrudescence of Kipling," Davidson writes:

> In most of Mr. Kipling's Indian stories one hears the continual roaring of the British lion, rampant, raging, bloody-mouthed—I use the term in the approved English sense—to the complete exclusion of even the yelp of a poor jackall [sic]—all of which cannot but prove at least mildly distasteful to the whole tribe of jackalls. Your Englishman, as Mr. Kipling is so fond of painting him, is nothing if he is not the natural conqueror and ruler of the universe which, in the accepted order of things, should be properly grateful that it is cuffed and kicked by such a demi-god in the uniform of a lancer or a lascar. Now I had imagined, in what I considered to be a rather inoffensive sort of manner, that perhaps all men are born free and equal or at least that the people of India—with a short six thousand years of civilization behind them, to be sure, but nevertheless a civilization of a sort—might know something of the true meaning and significance of freedom. (14)

II

Even as Davidson was in exile at Kentucky Wesleyan, the other members of the Hirsch circle were beginning to regroup in Nashville. Although Ransom had no advanced degree, Edwin Mims was eager to bring him back to Vanderbilt on a parity with Walter Clyde Curry, who possessed the union card of a Ph.D. and conventional scholarly interests. However, Ransom's experience in France had made him restless with the parochialism of Tennessee. It was only when he realized that his parents were in declining health that he abandoned his search for a teaching or newspaper job in the Northeast and accepted an assistant professorship at Vanderbilt. By now, Sidney Hirsch had moved in with his sister and her husband, Nashville businessman James Frank, who lived a few miles west of the Vanderbilt campus at 3802 Whitland Avenue. Before long, the returning veterans began gathering there on alternate Saturday nights.

At a time when creative writing workshops had yet to become fixtures in the curricula of university English departments, the young men who gathered around Sidney Hirsch informally exchanged poems and criticism with each other. "When the talk began to subside around eleven o'clock," John L. Stewart writes, "Mrs. Frank would put aside the curtains which separated the talkers from the adjoining dining room, and everyone would help himself to cold cuts, sausages, potato salad, cheeses, several kinds of bread, and, if he wished, beer or wine, which were not hard to come by in Nashville despite the new Prohibition Laws."[7]

Donald Davidson, who rejoined the group upon his return to Nashville in 1920, describes a typical meeting:

> Every poem was read aloud by the poet himself, while the members of the group had before them typed copies of the poem. The reading aloud might be followed by a murmur of compliments, but often enough there was a ruminative silence before anyone said a word. Then discussion began. It was likely to be ruthless in its exposure of any technical weakness as to rhyme, meter, imagery, metaphor and was often minute in its analysis of details. . . . It was understood that our examination would be skeptical. A poem had to prove its strength, if possible its perfection, in all its parts. (*Southern Writers,* 21)

Walter Clyde Curry, who had stayed in Nashville during the war, continued to write sonnets and to be involved with the group on an irregular basis. (His Stanford degree and his training in philology added academic authority to the etymological discussions initiated by Hirsch.) William Elliott was back in graduate school, and Alec Stevenson, brought home by the death of his father, went first into journalism and then into banking and securities. William Frierson, an undergraduate who had joined the group briefly before the war, had returned to finish his senior year. (He and Elliott both left for Oxford on Rhodes Scholarships in 1920 and remained members *in absentia*.) Stanley Johnson, who had taught at the University of Manila for two years after the war, returned to Nashville to marry his old girlfriend Will Etta Tatum and to enter graduate school in 1921. The newer members of the group included Alfred Starr, a student who would later become a local motion picture entrepreneur, and a junior from Kentucky named John Orley Allen Tate.

Born on November 19, 1899, Allen Tate was the younger brother of Ben and Varnell Tate, Davidson's old friends from his freshman year at Vanderbilt. Their father, John Orley Tate, was a Free Thinker of vague Episcopalian provenance, while their mother, Eleanor Parke Custis Varnell Tate, was a Presbyterian with

7. Stewart, *The Burden of Time,* 22–23.

family ties to the Virginia aristocracy. (It was not until he reached the age of thirty that Allen discovered he had been born in Kentucky, not Virginia.) Because John Tate was generally unsuccessful in business, the family had moved frequently during Allen's childhood. As a result, he had received a sporadic education at a succession of private and public schools in Ohio, Kentucky, Indiana, and Tennessee. In 1917, his mother enrolled him in the Georgetown University Preparatory School in Washington, D.C. The following year, Allen entered Vanderbilt, where he experienced a stability he would know only infrequently in an otherwise chaotic life.

As Louis D. Rubin, Jr., observes, "At Vanderbilt, Tate found himself. His brilliant intellect and his bookishness were no longer social liabilities, but distinct assets. The sophistication and the formal polish that a rather withdrawn and insecure young man had erected as a defense to keep the world at a distance became, in the social environment of a university campus and among young men and women who were striving to seem and be worldly-wise adults, qualities that elicited admiration and attention."[8]

Disdaining mathematics and dropping chemistry, Tate concentrated his energies on literature and philosophy. He took a philosophy course from Herbert Sanborn his sophomore year and all of Sanborn's classes from then on. Also that year, he took English courses from Edwin Mims and Walter Clyde Curry. Although his experience in Mims's class inspired what would be a lifelong antipathy for the pompous old autocrat, Tate formed a warm friendship with Curry, who lent him books and entertained him in his bachelor quarters in Kissam Hall. The following year, Tate joined the Calumet Club, where he met Ransom, Stevenson, and Davidson. (Tate's first published poem, "A Ballade of the Lugubrious Wench," was published in the club's humor magazine.) Then, in the fall of 1921, Davidson invited Tate to a meeting of the Hirsch circle. Over twenty years later, Tate wrote of that evening: "I cannot remember whether I felt any excitement except in my own vanity, for Don and John were professors; and when I got there, . . . being the only undergraduate present, I was flattered. Who read poems I do not know; yet I seem to remember that Don read a long romantic piece called "The Valley of the Dragon," in which the monster shielded lovers from the world. I imitated it soon afterwards; but neither the original nor its echo was allowed to survive."[9]

As the Hirsch circle expanded, strain began to develop between those members who were committed to a career in literature and the talented amateurs who enjoyed writing poetry without seeing it as the single most important activity in

8. Louis D. Rubin, Jr., *The Wary Fugitives: Four Poets and the South,* 71.
9. Allen Tate, "The Fugitive, 1922–1925: A Personal Recollection Twenty Years After," 24.

life. The most abrasive member of the first faction was Tate, with Ransom and Davidson sharing his values if not his manner. (After the publication of T. S. Eliot's *The Waste Land* in 1922, Tate became a faction of one by being the first member of the group to appreciate the greatness of that historic poem.) The amateurs in the circle included the older and less talented traditionalists Hirsch and Frank, who seemed like throwbacks to another age; younger veterans such as Alec Stevenson, Bill Elliott, and Alfred Starr; and three new members—Merrill Moore (son of the Middle Tennessee poet John Trotwood Moore) and the cousins Ridley and Jesse Wills. When Stevenson, Elliott, Moore, and Jesse Wills all attended a reunion of the group in 1956, none was making his living in literature. Moore (a prominent Boston psychiatrist who included the young Robert Lowell among his patients) had nevertheless written approximately 100,000 sonnets in his spare time.

In March 1921, Sidney Hirsch decided that the group had produced enough good poetry to warrant publishing a magazine. The first issue of *The Fugitive: A Journal of Poetry* appeared in April 1922. With sporadic backing from the Nashville business community and modest subscription revenue, this venture continued several times a year until 1925. Although Sidney Hirsch coined the name *Fugitive,* no one was ever quite certain what it meant. (Paul Conkin suggests that Hirsch may have been making a veiled allusion to "the diaspora of the Jews."[10]) The penultimate stanza of Ransom's "Ego," the opening poem of the first issue, closes with the lines: "I have run further, matching your heat and speed, / And tracked the Wary Fugitive with you." The editorial foreword to that same issue declares, "Official exception having been taken by the sovereign people to the mint julep, a literary phase known rather euphemistically as Southern Literature has expired, like any other stream whose source is stopped up. The demise was not untimely: among other advantages, THE FUGITIVE is enabled to come to birth in Nashville, Tennessee, under a star not entirely unsympathetic. THE FUGITIVE flees from nothing faster than from the high-caste Brahmins of the Old South."[11]

Prior to the War Between the States, literary magazines had flourished throughout the South. One thinks of the original incarnation of the *Southern Review* (1828–1832), the *Southern Literary Messenger* (1834–1864), the *Southern Literary Journal* (1835–1838), *Orion* (1842–1844), the *Southern Quarterly Review* (1842–1857), and *Russell's Magazine* (1857–1860). (The pantheon of southern critics and editors included Edgar Allan Poe, William Gilmore Sims, Henry Timrod, Paul Hamilton Hayne, Daniel Whittaker, and Hugh Swinton Legaré.) Perhaps just as important, a semblance of literary culture was essential to the persona of the antebellum southern aristocrat—even if its scope did not extend

10. Conkin, *Southern Agrarians,* 16.
11. *The Fugitive: A Journal of Poetry,* April 1922, 2.

beyond the reading matter Huck Finn discovered in the Grangerfords' parlor. For over half a century after Appomattox, however, the South produced no literary magazine of note and scant readership for those being published elsewhere.[12] That situation would begin to change in the aftermath of the First World War.

Among the by-products of literary modernism was the appearance of what Monroe K. Spears calls "the exciting, rebellious, and unpredictable little magazines of the twenties." It was "a period of vigorous experimentation and revolt in the arts" and of low printing costs. "*Broom, Blast, Transition, Little Review,* and other little magazines were founded to publish experimental poetry and fiction. . . . They were intense and impudent, carefree about deadlines and business arrangements, living very much for the moment."[13] In 1921, three such magazines were founded in the South: the *Double Dealer* in New Orleans, the *Reviewer* in Richmond, and the *Lyric* in Norfolk. When the *Fugitive* of Nashville joined this company in April of 1922, it was with a smaller budget and more modest circulation. Nevertheless, Donald Davidson recalls that "when all agreed that we would, we *must* publish a magazine, it was for me one of my moments of highest, undiluted joy—one of the few such moments of peculiar elation and, I could almost say, triumph."[14]

Unfortunately, the officials at Vanderbilt were considerably more restrained in their reaction to the *Fugitive*—none more so than Edwin Mims. This was not because Mims was a stuffy academic with an instinctive aversion to creative writing. After all, he had hired Ransom and Davidson when neither had a Ph.D. (Ransom had no "advanced" degrees beyond his B.A. from Oxford) and treated their published poems the same as he would traditional scholarship in determining academic advancement. What disturbed him were the bohemian overtones of the Fugitive phenomenon. The mingling of students and faculty on terms of social equality must surely have offended his sense of academic hierarchy. (It was inconceivable for his younger colleagues, much less students, to be on a first-name basis with the imperious Mims.) It was bad enough that these young men met in the house of a Jew, but it was bruited about campus that women had been seen creeping from the poets' bedroom windows. (Michael O'Brien points out that Mims, a notorious lecher, seemed more intent in maintaining appearances than in punishing vice.[15]) The kind of verse the Fugitives wrote lacked the high moral seriousness of Victorian poetry and would certainly have fallen flat if declaimed from the lecture platform. And yet, all of this might have been tolerated had the Fugitives not decided to publish a magazine over which the university could exercise no control.

12. See Richard J. Calhoun, "Literary Magazines in the Old South."
13. Monroe K. Spears, "The Function of Literary Quarterlies," 111.
14. See Young and Inge, *Donald Davidson,* 111.
15. See O'Brien, "The Middle Years," 148.

When Mims got wind of the fact that the Whitland Avenue poets were planning to go public, he invited them to lunch and tried to talk them out of it. When that didn't work, he simply hoped for the best. After the *Fugitive* proved to be a noncontroversial success, Mims not only breathed a sigh of relief, he praised the venture so fulsomely one would have thought that he had backed it from the start. In *The Advancing South,* he lauded Davidson's lyricism and said that "Ransom may never be popular; but for a combination of intellectual subtlety, refined sentiment, originality, boldness of poetic diction, and withal a certain whimsical imagination, his poetry is destined to increasing recognition."[16] When these same two men had received praise in a leading literary magazine three years earlier, Mims had written to Davidson: "I rejoice in this recognition. It confirms my judgment with regard to your promise (you have the makings of the poet) and Ransom's critical achievement."[17]

III

In the year the *Fugitive* first saw the light of day, it was party time in America. Warren G. Harding was entertaining his girlfriends in the White House, while his cronies were swilling at the public trough. An overvalued stock market created a false sense of prosperity, and the nation was awash in bathtub gin. F. Scott Fitzgerald gave the era its name with his book *Tales of the Jazz Age,* but the real literary sensation of the year was created by Sinclair Lewis's *Babbitt.* Edwin Arlington Robinson's *Collected Poems* won the Pulitzer Prize for poetry. Eck Robertson and Henry Gilliland produced the first commercial recording in the history of country music. Mussolini became dictator of Italy. James Joyce published *Ulysses* in Paris, while T. S. Eliot's *The Waste Land* appeared in London. Back in Nashville, a precocious sophomore from Guthrie, Kentucky, enrolled in Donald Davidson's survey course in English literature.

Over thirty-five years later, Davidson recalled that the seventeen-year-old Robert Penn Warren was "a freckled, angular, gawky boy, yet a prodigy whom at birth the Muse had apparently vested with a complete literary equipment" (*Southern Writers,* 16). Although the course covered the traditional canon of English literature from Beowulf to Hardy, Davidson was anything but a conventional teacher. Warren found him to be "a darkly handsome man with an intense gaze, passions and convictions, though kindly and generous in human relations."[18] He allowed exceptional students such as Warren to write imitations of the authors being studied rather than typical term papers. These were the first poems that

16. Edwin Mims, *The Advancing South: Stories of Progress and Reaction,* 201.
17. See Michael O'Brien, "Edwin Mims and Donald Davidson: A Correspondence," 908.
18. Joseph Blotner, *Robert Penn Warren: A Biography,* 35.

Warren would ever write. Also, during that term, Davidson showed his student a copy of *The Dial,* which contained *The Waste Land.*

Because Warren had taken freshman English and an advanced composition class under Ransom the previous year, he had already developed an interest in writing and literature by the time he met Davidson. "Warren was the brightest student they had ever seen around there," Davidson recalls. "His daily or weekly themes were the ones that always got read with admiration by the instructor [and] his mind seemed to work with extraordinary speed."[19] This newfound calling as a writer was a far cry from the direction Red Warren had plotted for his life while growing up in southern Kentucky just across the Tennessee border. (He actually graduated from high school in Clarksville, Tennessee.) Although he had been unusually close to his bookish grandfather, an eccentric veteran of the Confederate army who hated all aspects of modern life except for fly screens and painless dentistry, Warren's primary ambition in life was to become a naval officer. He had even received an appointment to the U.S. Naval Academy when a freak accident severely damaged his left eye and prevented him from passing the physical examination. During his first year at Vanderbilt, he was majoring in science when he found his English classes under Ransom to be far more interesting than freshman chemistry. The courses he took the following year under Davidson and Curry completed his conversion to the literary life. Then, in February 1923, he met Allen Tate.

During the spring term of that year, Tate, Warren, and Ridley Wills roomed together on the top floor of Wesley Hall, the theological building on the Vanderbilt campus. Nearly two decades later, Tate described their living arrangements:

> It was one large room with two double-decker beds, and Ridley and I being older than Red made him sleep above. In order to get into bed at night we had to shovel the books, trousers, shoes, hats, and fruit jars onto the floor, and in the morning, to make walking space, we heaped it all back upon the beds. We stuck pins into Red while he slept to make him wake up and tell us his dreams. Red had made some good black-and-white drawings in the Beardsley style. One day he applied art-gum to the dingy plaster and when we came back we saw four murals, all scenes from *The Waste Land.* I remember particularly the rat creeping softly through the vegetation, and the typist putting a record on the gramophone.[20]

It was during this time that Warren began attending meetings of the Fugitives. Later that year, he won a poetry contest sponsored by the group. Then, in

19. Ibid., 35.
20. Tate, "The Fugitive," 32.

February 1924, Robert Penn Warren was officially listed as one of the editors of the *Fugitive*, then completing its second year of publication.

Throughout most of the two previous years, the group had debated the organization of its magazine with a passion that exposed fundamental differences in philosophy and personality. When they had simply been meeting fortnightly to share and discuss their work, the enterprise was truly communal. The only material labor involved was making carbon copies of one's poems. (It was taken for granted that James Frank would provide the meeting place and refreshments.) The members could gather without rank or primacy and allow their verse to be the focus of attention. However, publishing a magazine that would appear four to six times a year involved soliciting subscriptions, handling correspondence (which increased substantially once the pages of the *Fugitive* were opened to poets not in the group), negotiating with printers, and managing circulation. Because the journal was not self-supporting, financial contributions from local businesses were also required.

For over a year and a half, the lion's share of these duties were assumed by Davidson and, to a lesser extent, Tate. In a letter to his father, dated November 25, 1923, Davidson hints at the burden he is bearing: "My work goes on just the same, with plenty to do at the university and plenty to do in other respects, for wherever I turn I seem to find new tasks. My main interest now is the editorial work on 'The Fugitive,' which takes a great deal more time than you might think. Always there are letters to answer, manuscripts to consider, and details of administration to attend to, all very interesting, but also all very greedy of my time." What Davidson does not reveal in this letter is his anger over the fact that other members of the group were doing less work and receiving more recognition than he was.

Although all the brethren were listed equally on the masthead, most readers of the *Fugitive* assumed that Ransom was its real editor. (In the *Literary Review of the New York Evening Post* for July 7, 1923, Christopher Morley praised "John Crowe Ransom's *Fugitive*.") Thus, when Ransom initially resisted any change in the masthead, the actual workhorses (primarily Tate and Davidson) were quietly resentful. That summer, when Davidson and Ransom were both away from Nashville, Tate and Stanley Johnson proposed a plan for the group to elect an "editor" and "associate editor" each year. After Johnson convinced him that Ransom concurred with such an arrangement, Davidson eagerly accepted appointment as editor for the following year and credit for the job he was already performing anonymously.

During its three and a half years of existence, the *Fugitive* itself became a progressively less anonymous publication. In the first two issues of the magazine, the contributors wrote under humorous pen names. (Ransom was "Roger Prim"; Tate, "Henry Feathertop"; Hirsch, "L. Oafer," and Davidson, "Robin Gallivant.")

In addition to the sheer fun of this ruse, the Fugitives may have been trying to focus attention away from the identity of the poets and onto the poetic text itself. (In his famous essay on Milton's "Lycidas," written over a decade later, Ransom would laud the quality of anonymity in poetry.[21]) One unfortunate consequence was that many readers thought that all of the poems had been written by Ransom under various pseudonyms. By the third issue, the personae had been abandoned, and the contributors were beginning to take pride in the favorable notices their work was receiving. At first, recognition came from the local Nashville papers— the *Tennessean* and the *Banner*—and later from such nationally prominent critics as Witter Bynner, Louis Untermeyer, and William Stanley Braithwaite.

Perhaps the most enthusiastic and gratifying notice the magazine received was from Braithwaite, a leading African American poet and anthologist. Writing in the *Boston Evening Transcript* of October 6, 1923, Braithwaite declared that the *Fugitive* "displayed more character and originality during the last year than any magazine in the country."[22] Davidson was particularly elated by this praise and by the fact that Braithwaite selected three of his poems for inclusion in the *Anthology of Magazine Verse* for 1923. In a note of thanks sent to Braithwaite on October 13, Davidson remarks that "it is no mean encouragement to a group of writers, isolated from the main stream of current letters in an environment none too friendly to the arts, to be able to feel that we are understood by a critic for whose work we have no inconsiderable respect."

21. John Crowe Ransom, "A Poem Nearly Anonymous," in *The World's Body*, 1–28.
22. See Cowan, *Fugitive Group*, 135.

5

DEMON BROTHER

In the summer of 1922, when Allen Tate had retreated to the mountains of Valle Crucis, North Carolina, for his health and Donald Davidson was working as a counselor at Camp Kawasawa in Lebanon, Tennessee, the two friends began a correspondence that would last for the balance of Davidson's life. Perhaps the greatest significance of these letters was the consequence of a casual suggestion that Davidson made when writing to Tate on July 2, 1922. After mentioning that he has enclosed a poem for Tate's consideration, Davidson writes: "I would like to propose to you that we hereby agree to exchange *new* poems constantly,—that is, if one sends the other a poem, the obligation will be on the receiver to transmit a newly composed poem in turn."[1] In a sense, this project was a continuation of the Fugitive enterprise. Lacking any record of the Fugitive meetings, we can only imagine the critical exchange that transpired on those long-ago nights in Nashville. The Tate-Davidson letters provide a transcript of such an exchange conducted through the mail.

These letters are also valuable for the personal information they give us about the correspondents. For example, in a letter dated January 23, 1923, Davidson describes a day in his life:

> Having put *The Fugitive* to bed by the process of carrying it to the printer this evening, having answered sundry communications, returned sundry manuscripts, filed sundry letters, recorded sundry subscriptions, also having attended a luncheon meeting of the Vanderbilt Lecture Bureau, having run most of the way home in order that my wife might get over to Ward-Belmont

1. *The Literary Correspondence of Donald Davidson and Allen Tate,* 10. Subsequent references will be cited parenthetically in the text.

[College] for her tutoring work there, having graded sundry themes, having cut out sundry paper dolls for my little Mary, having inserted an ad in the paper for a new servant, having fired the furnace sundry times (yea, even having burned the infernal thing out), having telephoned to sundry people about sundry things, having studied my lesson for tomorrow with the freshman, and having smoked sundry cigarettes while being engaged with these other sundries,—having done all these things, O Poet, O Allen Tate, O Hot Youth, I salute you, and close my twenty-six hours a day with this letter. (67)

We also learn that, during the summer of 1922, Davidson entertained ambitions of breaking into the cinema as a screenwriter. In the same letter in which he proposes the exchange of poems, Davidson describes the photoplay he is working on during his idle moments at Camp Kawasawa: "I've got the most bang-up plot you ever heard of, with an impractical young hero falling in love with the daughter of his father's enemy (quite an old theme, that), and a revolutionary plot in South America (not à la Conrad, however), and a noble villain who is three parts good and only one part bad" (10). An earlier letter indicated that the atmosphere for this story was suggested by the work of W. H. Hudson, a romantic novelist of the twenties who was a particular favorite of Ernest Hemingway's Robert Cohn.

It is clear from their comments on contemporary writers that Davidson was far less sympathetic than Tate to the revolution in modern letters. When Tate sent him a copy of the experimental magazine *Secession,* Davidson responded: "It rather strikes me as hokum,—very smart, very sophisticated, but nevertheless hokum. If the fellows who are guilty of that magazine went to Europe in search of art, it seems pretty obvious to me that they didn't find any" (18). Ten days later, on July 25, Davidson stated his aesthetic case against the sort of "abstract" art produced by the Cubists, Futurists, and Imagists. Music was the only art in which he believed that pure abstraction was possible, and even there he was doubtful. Music had the advantage of a mathematical precision that no verbal art could ever attain. Davidson then makes a specific comparison.

I believe that most of the poems of the Dadaists, for example, have no meaning whatever, nor impression, except to their authors, who probably had something in mind to convey, but other people do not get that thing, whatever it is. However, a piece by Debussy, besides the conception it had for the author, produces a definite impression on every hearer, which to be sure will vary as far as interpretation is concerned with the individual culture and experience of the person listening. So I could not admit an analogy between poetry and music, except in the minor matters of rhythm and tone-color. There is where the Free Verse set went wrong, with that vague talk of "cadence." Their idea of a musical cadence transferred into a form of language-art pleased me very much until I found out how very unsatisfactory it was—it simply could not be done with words as a medium. (24)

Having returned to Nashville and set up temporary residence in an apartment in Kissam Hall once occupied by Walter Clyde Curry, Davidson expresses his distaste for T. S. Eliot in a letter he sent to Tate on August 23, 1922. What he found most lacking in Eliot's verse was "memorableness"—that is "happiness and ultimateness of expression." He chides Tate and Eliot both for an excessively narrow conception of poetry. "The longer poems of Eliot strike me as weak because of the presence of the qualities you applaud. Maybe it's a cheap ideal, but I still can't help but think that it doesn't hurt anything for lines to be worth quoting (PARDON AN INTERRUPTION. A LARGE KISSAM COCK-ROACH IS ABOUT TO DRAG OFF MY EVENING PAPER TO HIS DEN, A THING WHICH I WON'T PERMIT EVEN IF HE IS BIGGER THAN ME)" (40). On December 14, Davidson wrote to Tate, now in Ashland, Kentucky, to lament violations of syntax in Eliot's poetry. "No matter how adequate a form of expression may seem to you as a poet, you must consider that artistic expression in a void is a pretty poor proposition; that is where Eliot is going, in my opinion. He is as far as I am concerned talking in a vacuum, in [The] Waste Land, which I have read three times, with no gleam whatever of comprehension. I would like, by the way, to hear your interpretation of that poem" (59–60).

Davidson's aversion to experimental modernism also extended to fiction. On August 29, he wrote to Tate about some issues of the *Little Review* his friend had sent him: "the chapters from Ulysses are unique and interesting, but I am not inclined to accept them as art—My God, think of reading 782 pages of that blooming stuff" (43). (The closing of that letter reads: "Yours for the Moderns [excluding the Dada's, the Vers Librists, the Secessionists, and other ultra-ultra's."]) Nearly ten months later, in a letter dated June 26, 1923, Davidson scolds Tate for starting to write too much like Eliot and Joyce: "I could never grant to you or T. S. Eliot or James Joyce or anybody the right (the literary right) to decompose thought into these unwelded and amorphous combinations" (73).

In the letters of late December 1922 and early January 1923, it appears that fondness for one's fellow Fugitives increased with distance from them. Writing from Ashland, Kentucky, on December 7, 1922, Tate waxes elegiac about the literary fellowship back in Nashville:

> Your account of the meeting is actually thrilling (and people say poets are *so* dull), and all I can do now is mourn my own absence. It must have been a great night—Stanley delivering his usual damnations on the evils of sophistication or the pose of it, alias Me, as He would probably say; Mttron expounding his etymologies with a sweet contempt for accuracy; John sitting there with a cigar out of all proportions to the man, amused often, bored occasionally, disgusted with such thickness all the time; and then you, my dear Don, mule-like in your standards of beauty and rhythm, which I am always trying to understand with a blast of entrails and livers! I can't afford

to miss many more meetings; if I do my nostalgia will become a disease and I shall be a dear little idiot boy. (56)

In a letter dated January 13, 1923, Davidson, who was still in Nashville, appears considerably less sentimental about his own blue-collar role on the *Fugitive:* "I have finally gotten a pretty clear idea of my function with regard to the magazine. . . . I am to do all of the damn detailed work, . . . without having any sort of voice as to the general tone of things, which would be reward enough. . . . It seems to be taken for granted that I will meekly take all the burdens of Atlas on my shoulders, while the rest of the members here in Nashville are busily writing poems, writing novels, reading contemporary literature, and otherwise enjoying themselves." (65)

Nearly three years later, the *Fugitive* ceased publication when no one else was willing to assume the editorial labors that Davidson had performed for so long. By that time, he was on the verge of depression and beginning to question his own future in Nashville. Although he had won promotion from instructor to assistant professor with the appearance of his first book the previous year, he was feeling increasingly isolated at Vanderbilt. Most of his fellow Fugitives had departed, and he was convinced that Ransom would soon be gone as well. On November 29, Davidson wrote to Tate about his desire to leave the South. He was hoping that Allen might intercede on his behalf with Mark Van Doren, a prominent New York critic who taught at Columbia University. His major concern was a fear that Theresa might not be able to get as good a job elsewhere as she had working at the Vanderbilt law library. (Her salary was then higher than Davidson's had been when he first came to Vanderbilt.) He was also realistic about his academic marketability. "[Y]ou know I can't show any array of Ph.D.'s and contributions to PMLA," he writes. "My appeal to the scholarly bugs is flabby; to literary bugs, however, it might be less motheaten. . . . I do fear New York somewhat, and am not anxious to be swallowed; but I don't think the Battle of New York would be more dreadful than the Battle of Nashville, 1925" (151–52).

As it turned out, Donald Davidson was not destined to leave Nashville in 1925. Whatever dissatisfaction he may have felt at Vanderbilt, he would remain there for another four decades, the only one of the major Fugitives to spend his entire career where the movement began. Surprisingly, one of the reasons he stayed was Edwin Mims. If several of the other brethren would have gladly left the South simply to get away from Mims, that was not the case with Davidson. (In fact, one of his reasons for wishing to leave Vanderbilt was the fear that Mims would soon be lured away by a more attractive job offer.) If young turks such as Tate and Warren saw Mims as the devil incarnate, Davidson was more inclined to defend the old man, however tepidly and ineffectually.

Even if Davidson was not an unblinking apologist for his employer, he was always eager to give him the benefit of the doubt and to take others to task for their ungenerous attitudes toward Mims. When Allen Tate complained that the chairman was demanding an apology for past irreverences as the price for writing him a letter of recommendation, Davidson saw some justice in Mims's position. On September 10, 1923, he wrote to Tate:

> As I told you before (and so I believe has Curry) you and Ridley weren't quite fair in your attitude toward Dr. Mims last spring. I am sure that he felt very much hurt and bothered by a belief that you and Ridley were in the ranks of the enemy, and that you were on occasion not losing opportunities to make sport of him. . . . Probably he felt that in addressing the committee, however much he might praise your scholarship, he would in all conscience and justice be required to say that he had some doubts as to your seriousness with regard to academic matters. But, with a statement from you which cleared up that feeling of his, he would be able to give you an unqualified recommendation which would benefit, not injure, your case. (91)

If anything, Davidson's dependence on Mims increased when it became apparent that he would not follow Tate into the literary world of New York. (Mark Van Doren was unable to find him a suitable position at Columbia, and Davidson, unlike Tate, was unwilling to make his family's financial security hostage to the vagaries of a free-lance writer's career.) As long as Mims did not hold his lack of an advanced degree against him and valued his poems and literary journalism as much as he did conventional scholarship, Davidson had a more secure home at Vanderbilt than he could expect at any other university.

I

By 1925, Donald Davidson had already developed a distinctive poetic style and formed his first critical principles. In the four volumes of the *Fugitive,* he had published three book reviews, two editorials, and forty-eight poems. (Because thirty-three of those poems were later republished in various books and anthologies, they cannot be dismissed as mere juvenilia, even if they are radically different from his later, more mature work.) Even though he and his friends edited the magazine, it would be wrong to assume they were uncritically promoting their own work. No poem appeared in the *Fugitive* without close critical scrutiny and a vote of the editors. If nothing else, a desire to win acclaim for the magazine prevented the Fugitives from publishing second-rate verse— by themselves or others. Only two poems appearing in the first volume of the magazine received more votes than Davidson's "The Dragon Book" and "The Demon Brother."[2] Because versions of "The Demon Brother" would be published in different contexts over the next four decades, it is obvious that Davidson wished to preserve it. "The Dragon Book," which has never been republished, is more typical of the youthful vision that he eventually discarded.

The speaker in "The Dragon Book" lives in a world of quotidian realism, from which he is tempted to journey to an exotic land beyond the mountains. (The voice that beckons him describes his present domain as "plainlands, flat and thin / Roofs that are dusty, gray with sin.") Not only is this faraway retreat a lush realm of "cherry-tree blossoms," it is also where his young love now dwells. When he visualizes her, she is reading an old book: "Across the pages a dragon crawls, / Glittering under the ancient scrawls." The young woman never sees the dragon, but is enchanted by the words of the book, which indirectly indicate his presence. As her reading becomes an ever more sensuous experience, perfume and music both rise from the page. This insidious spell reaches its apogee in the penultimate stanza.

> The music dies to a thin, low theme,
> Painful and sweet as the pain of a dream.
> And still the snow of blossoms falls,
> And she turns the page,—and the dragon crawls.

In the final stanza, the speaker realizes that a journey to this mythological country is likely to reveal one of two results: " . . . my young love dead, / Or, smiling, to the dragon wed."

The diction of this poem is romantic to the point of decadence, and the form (rhyming couplets) is timidly conventional. If the poem possesses any complexity at all, it is in the speaker's awareness that romanticism is dangerous as well as alluring. (As we shall see, this theme is repeatedly sounded in *An Outland Piper.*) Although he does not develop the notion with any sophistication, Davidson has nevertheless written a kind of metapoem, one that is about the power of literature itself. The irony of the poem lies in the fact that that power appears to be primarily destructive. Although Davidson had by now committed himself to the literary life, he depicts a protagonist who will almost certainly resist its blandishments. The tension inherent in this attitude was not resolved until Davidson discovered a social use for poetry that transcended the limits of mere aestheticism.

Although he did not yet have a fully articulated critical theory during his Fugitive days, Davidson was beginning to develop definite notions about the nature of poetry. For example, his editorial "Certain Fallacies in Modern Poetry,"

---

2. These poems were John Crowe Ransom's "L'Egoist" and Stanley Johnson's "Sermons," with eight votes each.

published in the June 1924 issue of the *Fugitive,* tells us much about what Davidson believes by what he rejects. The first "fallacy" he identifies is the notion "THAT A GOOD POET MUST BE POSSESSED OF AN AESTHETIC."[3] What he means is that the creative act is primary and the critical act secondary. Poets who try to write according to a particular theory or set of rules are frequently revealing a lack of imagination. "Deliberateness justly comes only after the poem has been written," he notes, "and then, even in revision, it is often a highly treacherous business, about as likely to spoil as to make perfect. . . . The Imagist Movement has labored, and brought forth in the main only a few tinted and splashy jellyfish that now grow sick and wan in the light cast by time" (66).

For fallacy two, Davidson specifies a particular aesthetic, one that is far removed from the sophistication of the Imagists. This is the notion "THAT A GOOD POET MUST PERFORCE HAVE 'LOCAL COLOR.' " For a critic who would later become identified with a regional approach to art, such a rejection might seem the product of youthful impulse. But the slightly redundant expression "must perforce" and the quotation marks around "local color" indicate that Davidson is spurning a superficial parochialism, not true regionalism. As he points out: "Frost has written of New England, Sandburg of Chicago, but whatever is good in their poetry is not good merely because they wrote of specific places. . . . The poem, not the 'scene,' . . . must be uppermost in his consciousness" (67).

The third fallacy holds "THAT VOCABULARY IS IN ITSELF IMPORTANT." By "vocabulary," Davidson means an inherently poetic language. In his famous essay on the metaphysical poets, T. S. Eliot would decry the "dissociation of sensibility" that entered English poetry at the end of the seventeenth century. This development had the effect of defining a certain kind of language and subject matter that was appropriate to poetry. Modernist critics such as Eliot and I. A. Richards would argue for a more inclusive aesthetic, one that was closer to the practice of the metaphysical poets. Although Davidson does not use grand terminology or historical schematics, he too is rejecting a prescriptive view of poetic language. As his students Cleanth Brooks and Robert Penn Warren would do over a decade later in *Understanding Poetry,* Davidson is arguing that poetic language should be judged according to its contextual appropriateness. "The word must be judged where it stands," he writes. "How it is used,—that is what counts; how it blends with the ring and color of line and stanza; how economically and happily it presents the idea. Therefore, even the *cliche,* now so utterly abhorred of Moderns, is not absolutely to be purged away" (67).[4]

3. Donald Davidson, "Certain Fallacies in Modern Poetry," 66. Subsequent references will be cited parenthetically in the text.
4. Robert Penn Warren would later echo this sentiment in "Pure and Impure Poetry," in *New and Selected Essays* (New York: Random House, 1989), 1–28.

If Davidson seemed to be a thoroughgoing modernist in his rejection of a specifically poetic vocabulary, he was careful not to substitute one exclusivist dogma for another. Consequently, he disagrees with those minimalists who argue "THAT THE GRAND STYLE IS IMPOSSIBLE TO MODERN POETRY." This fallacy is, in its own way, as limiting as the neoclassical insistence that poetry can be written only in the grand style. "If there are no epic poems today," Davidson writes, "it is because we have no epic poets. . . . For all our hatred of the Victorians, we are more Victorian than they in our refusal to be daring—and this is likewise true even of our experimentalists, whose apparent daring comes from writing according to a set of very inelastic principles. They are more unyielding in their dogmas than the traditionalists whom they denounce" (67–68). It is interesting that even as he was writing lyric poems about imaginary worlds, Davidson believed that epic poetry was still possible, perhaps even desirable. This belief may help to explain what might otherwise seem to be an inexplicable shift in poetic strategy between Davidson's first and second books of verse.

The final fallacy that Davidson decries is the notion "THAT ANY VERY SPECIFIC LIMITATIONS CAN BE SET FOR POETRY." This principle would seem to be implied in the position he had taken on the preceding four fallacies. Were it not for the qualifiers "very specific," he would be arguing that criticism was quite literally impossible. Some limitations are necessary if we are to define poetry, much less judge whether a particular poem is any good. Rather than suggesting even flexible standards for that task, Davidson argues for a pluralism that is virtually indistinguishable from aesthetic relativism. "Let the poem, of whatever sort, be judged for and of itself alone," he urges. "Poetry comes from the individual, and will have as many variations as there are individuals writing it" (68). As sensible as that position might seem as a corrective against excessive dogmatism, it was one that Davidson even more sensibly abandoned in his own critical practice. It would not be long before he realized that poetry comes from a community of individuals and that it is properly judged by the standards of that community. That is certainly what the Fugitive experience was all about.

II

In 1924, two southern poets published their first books of verse. Despite obvious differences, there were also striking similarities between William Faulkner's *The Marble Faun* and Donald Davidson's *An Outland Piper*. Both books were clearly influenced by the decadent romanticism of the late Victorian and fin de siècle periods. Rather than drawing nourishment from his own little postage stamp of soil, Faulkner preferred to trespass on a stylized British countryside. As Cleanth

Brooks has demonstrated, A. E. Housman was his true Penelope.[5] If anything, Davidson's muse was even more exotic. The imaginative landscape of *An Outland Piper* was populated not only by nymphs and dryads, but by dragons and tigers, as well. If one would be hard put to find the seeds of *The Sound and the Fury* or *Absalom, Absalom!* in *The Marble Faun, An Outland Piper* offers little evidence of the writer that Donald Davidson would eventually become.

The title poem of *An Outland Piper* (which is written in octosyllabic couplets, like Faulkner's *The Marble Faun* and Yeats's "Song of the Happy Shepherd") is a considerably revised version of one that Davidson had published in the first issue of the *Fugitive* in April 1922. Four years later, it became one of five selections by Davidson included in Addison Hibbard's influential anthology *The Lyric South*. Finally, over four decades after its original publication, it was among only a handful of poems from *An Outland Piper* that Davidson chose to preserve in the definitive edition of his verse—*Poems, 1922–1961*. The theme of this lyric is one repeated throughout the rest of the volume—the vast gulf separating the world of mundane experience from the realm of the imagination. What keeps that theme from sounding like a plaintive whine is the suggestion (already broached in "The Dragon Book") that the world of art is an alien and dangerous place, which human beings enter at their own peril. (The notion that beauty cannot exist without an element of strangeness suggests a particular affinity with the British decadents and the French symbolists.)

The fact that the piper hails from the outland makes him a foreigner. (The title of the poem when it appeared in the *Fugitive* was "A Demon Brother"; the version published in *Poems, 1922–1961* is "The Demon Brother.") The piper himself warns the speaker of the poem to "Follow me no more. . . ."

> And cherish not my outland grace
> Nor pride in likeness to my face,
> For children of an earthly mother
> Cry out upon their demon brother.[6]

For all these ominous overtones, the speaker is "agape to see / How like that piper was to me" (3). (He is a brother as well as a demon.) The eerie combination of strangeness and familiarity is again suggested when, at the end of the second stanza, the figure is referred to as "That alien piper, so like me" (3). Immediately after warning the speaker not to follow him, the piper says "Though I be of thy

---

5. See Cleanth Brooks, *William Faulkner: Toward Yoknapatawpha and Beyond* (New Haven: Yale University Press, 1978).

6. Donald Davidson, *An Outland Piper*, 4. Subsequent references will be cited parenthetically in the text.

father bred, / And though I speak of thine own blood, / Yet I am not of mortal brood" (4).

In a sense the piper tries to have it both ways. While uttering these ritualistic disclaimers, he plays a song so seductive that it literally transforms the town through which he passes: "Streets tipped, I thought, in ravishment; / Roofs clapped, and windows blazed. . . ." (3). The speaker himself is even more profoundly transformed. Even though he does not follow the piper, he cannot remain the same person he was before encountering him. He is constantly hearing the piper's melody and peering at "all men's charactery / To find that image so like me" (5). Rather than leaving him ennobled, the piper has simply made the speaker dissatisfied with the world of common day. It has "left me to know a world's deceit, / Left me to seek an unknown kin / Through all the streets I travel in" (5).

If there is any hint of the later Davidson in the precious aesthete who speaks to us in "An Outland Piper," it is in the suggestion that the piper is calling modern man back to a lost heritage. The contrast of a vital past with an enervated present is even more pronounced in "Old Harp," the second poem in the volume. Originally published in the *Fugitive* in October 1923, this poem is addressed to an ancient harp placarded in a museum. The speaker imagines the "shame and hurt surprise" that would have been felt by the owner of the harp if he could see this instrument, which had once played a useful role in a human community, reduced to the status of a decorative artifact. At one time, the harp might have entertained a Viking society and served its storytelling tradition. Today, art has been removed from the common people and put on a shelf for an elite few to observe from a distance. Poetry, which once was song, has become nothing more than words on a page. Davidson lamented this development, even as he spent most of his career resisting it.

A more ironic, and modern, tone characterizes "A Dead Romanticist," the third poem from *An Outland Piper* to be preserved in Davidson's final volume of verse. At the outset of the poem, we are told that the romanticist has no quarrel with analytic men. This is not because he agrees with them but because he is concerned with a completely different realm of experience. Rather than engaging them in witty repartee, "He copied old Diogenes in his barrel / And cried 'The sun!' O reverend little sirs" (31). The reference is apparently to the Greek cynic Diogenes, who lived in a barrel and used a lantern to search for an honest man. When Alexander the Great asked if he could do anything for him, Diogenes replied, "Yes, move out of my sunshine." This modern Diogenes has learned everything that mathematics can teach him, "But by such matters he could not set much store / As pointing ways to scotch a life's abuses" (31). The tone of understatement is crucial here. The world of science is not so much a fraud as it is an irrelevancy. Not only does it fail to create an earthly paradise, it cannot even provide a temporary antidote to the manifold woes that flesh is heir to.

What equations and theorems cannot do images can:

> For he has seen a road by healing waters,
> Hushed into wintry slate against the sand,
> And spoken there with the wind's elfin daughters,
> And mingled in their dusty saraband. (31)

We also learn that "he has known winds that blow from blossomy closes, / Rich with the fruity smell of summertide, / And kissed warm faery lips. . . ."

Davidson employs a subtle shift in verb tense. When the romanticist encounters the empirical world, it is in the past perfect: "With analytic men he had no quarrel. . . . He had remarked that two and two make four." However, his dealings with the realm of art, being less definite, are rendered in the present perfect: "He has seen a road of healing waters. . . . He has known winds that blow from blossomy closes." The open-endedness of his imaginative life is emphasized by the four ellipses points after "warm faery lips," followed by a piece of uncertain information: "Now he reposes, / While we are not quite certain he has died" (31). If the romanticist, and—by implication—romanticism itself, has died, it is not with a bang but a whimper. Are we to assume that in making a truce with science, art has lost its claim to a position of importance in life, that it has been reduced to a collage of solipsistic images in the mind of one who is neither living nor dead? Even if these inferences are far from certain, Davidson's oblique style makes them at least plausible.

For reasons that are not altogether clear, Davidson chose to reprint "Redivivus" in *Poems, 1922–1961*. Although Harriet Monroe quoted this poem in her review of *An Outland Piper*, Thomas Daniel Young and M. Thomas Inge believe that it is one of Davidson's weaker efforts.[7] While the poem may add little to his stature as a craftsman, it does give us some insight into Davidson's sensibility in the early 1920s. The speaker in "Redivivus" sees the world as a place where one may occasionally encounter unexpected good fortune: "Thin lips can make a music. . . . Cold cheeks can feel kisses. . . . The surly heart of clowns / Can crack with ecstasy." In such a world, the speaker pleads for a spiritual resurrection:

> Then let my skeleton soul
> Writhe upward from the loam,
> Drink red morning again,
> And look gently home. (46)

In hoping for an extraordinary blessing, the speaker expresses optimism. However, the fact that he feels compelled to do so is a measure of how desperate he perceives

---

7. See Young and Inge, *Donald Davidson*, 52.

his condition to be. A skeleton soul that must "writhe upward from the loam" hardly reflects the image of God. Significantly, his fondest hope is to be able to "look gently home." Although Davidson had yet to identify home with the myth of the Old South, he obviously believed that some unidentified lost heritage would prove to be the source of artistic and spiritual renewal.

One of the most successful poems in *An Outland Piper,* and the fifth to be reprinted in Davidson's definitive selection of verse, reveals the influence of both Allen Tate and literary modernism in general. The basic technique of "The Wolf" is that of the implied controlling metaphor. Just as Emily Dickinson wrote of a train as if it were a horse in "I like to see it lap the Miles," Davidson writes of a predatory southern storekeeper as if he were a wolf. Although the poem makes no explicit social commentary, the choice of analogy implies a severe criticism of the storekeeper. (Young and Inge believe that Davidson was thinking of the unscrupulous country storekeepers who operated in the South during Reconstruction.[8]) The second stanza of the poem should be sufficient to suggest its tone and method:

> Drooling, like one who should be crunching bones,
> He mouths the figured column of his kill.
> A sneaking blast rattles the locked door;
> The cat looks on, oracular and still. (51)

As Louis D. Rubin, Jr., notes, "the image in the second line has a radical quality that does violence to customary poetic expectations. Only Tate, of all the Fugitives, would have used images that on the literal level clash so drastically. There is also more than a little hint of Eliot here in the savage, dissecting objectivity of the description."[9]

III

Among the most successful verse that Davidson wrote during his early career was the Pan series, a group of four poems composed in the summer of 1922 and later published in the *Double Dealer.* All four appeared in *An Outland Piper* but were dropped from *Poems, 1922–1961.* Although these poems inhabit the realm of mythology (not quite that of myth), they are more closely connected to the quotidian realities of the modern world than were the poems about dragons and tigers that Davidson wrote during his early Fugitive days. Moreover, as Martha E.

8. Ibid., 54.
9. Rubin, *The Wary Fugitives,* 148.

Cook observes, "in these poems in which Davidson skillfully utilizes the materials of his contemporary society, he also first develops in full the theme of the value of the past. Here specifically the past becomes a way to save oneself from the insanity of the modern world, of the Jazz Age."[10]

The protagonist of "Dryad" is a young woman who, like the speaker in "An Outland Piper," is lured away from the everyday world. (We are told that her hopes are "mured at the gingham counter.") In this case, the seducer is a faun disguised as a man, his ears barely visible "beneath a Leghorn (latest cut), / And goat-legs, underneath his suit, / Crooked with a strangely familar strut." This faun plays an oaten pipe and shouts with an "old delirious satyr's laughter" (35). Unlike the outland piper, this figure bears no familial resemblance to the human being he seduces. (Cook nevertheless argues that the faun's "strangely familiar strut" identifies the woman as the dryad referred to in the title of the poem.[11]) She is simply captivated by the contrast between the boredom of her life in the modern city and the arcadian delights promised by the faun. In following him, she finds "what cities could not give, / Bare beauty by a careless pool." There is not even a suggestion of danger or ambiguity in her decision to follow the faun. When the poet asks what she has lost by following the faun, he responds: "That is for reasoners / And titillators of the School" (36). In other words, only the sort of people who would delight in arguing over how many angels can dance on the head of a pin would criticize the choice this woman has made.

In "Twilight Excursion," a man mired in the world of commerce is lured away into a dream landscape by the image of a woman. He is touched by "twilight warm as a woman's flesh" as he sits at a "littered desk." Seeing the firmament outside his window, he realizes that his office is actually a "chamber of the dead." Ordinary men looking on him with "fragmentary sight" cannot "guess the forest in his brain, / Nor hear a fevered drum's long beating." The vague hint of another world begins to take definite shape when he sees "a satyr, stamping a cloven hoof, / White forms, stainless against the green, / Bare throats, under the leaves' mad roof" (37). The poem then turns surrealistic as we are invited to wonder what the protagonist is "groping for there in the dusk." The answer is "not a bell— but a bush for the hand to cleave! / Not a door—but a slough of the garment's husk!" (38).

The protagonist leaves the world of commercial obligation behind him ("the lordly buildings drooped to grotesque") to find that "the summoning drum in the wood kept beating / As she came, with lips of flesh and blood." In an ironic reversal, his waking life now seems less concrete than the dreamworld he enters. But what he actually experiences in that other realm is far from clear.

10. Martha E. Cook, "Dryads and Flappers: Donald Davidson's Early Poetry," 18–19.
11. Ibid., 21.

There is a cryptic reference to "a table's white and silver," which somehow arrests "the passion of a renegade." Also, what had first been a "fevered" and then a "summoning" drum is now reduced to a "muted drum." Instead of kissing the lips of flesh and blood, the protagonist becomes a kind of Prufrockian onlooker "considering, . . . / The tainted posturings of a maid" (38). Rather than describing an escape from "the pits of livelihood," Davidson may be lamenting the difficulty of such an escape. In some ways his protagonist is closer to Walter Mitty than to Paul Gauguin.

In contrast, "Naiad" is an unabashedly sensual poem in which a female protagonist pays the ultimate price for turning her back on the straitened conformity of contemporary life. In a letter to Tate dated July 25, 1922, Davidson summarizes the poem: "A young girl, very beautiful of body, is bathing in a river with a group of companions,—men and women in the tawdry attire which custom imposes. She slips away to a place beyond a bend of the river, strips off her bathing suit, and goes into the water alone. There something happens to her,—perhaps the river god drags her down, but perhaps she merely drowns. Anyway, a certain insight comes to her in those moments,—something very mystical and beautiful" (*Literary Correspondence,* 25).

"Naiad" is certainly a more ambitious poem than "Dryad" or "Twilight Excursion." The erotic imagery gives it a richer texture, and the death of the girl poses as starkly as possible the risk of leaving the familiar human world behind. The fifth stanza depicts her surrender to death in terms of sexual climax:

> The skittering dragon-flies beheld her lust,
> And her plunging whiteness deep in the green deflected.
> The penumbral depths received her slim trunk's thrust,
> Like lover gesturing, "Come, O Long-expected!"[12]

The poem does not conclude with an experience of resurrection. Instead, the focus shifts back to the other swimmers the woman has left. When a search party finally finds her body, "A rustic, stumbling in a sandy bight, / Gloated upon the dead with obscene woe" (40). To return to such a world and such a community, Davidson implies, would be a fate worse than death.

Perhaps the most effective poem in the Pan series, and the first of Davidson's poems to win Tate's wholehearted approval, was "Corymba." Once again, Davidson contrasts a vital mythic past with the cultural sterility of modern life. (As much as Davidson instinctively disliked the mannerisms of Eliot's life and art, he could not completely avoid the wasteland theme in his own verse.) However,

---

12. The sexual pun on "come" is fairly obvious here. One wonders if Davidson might also be echoing the title of Charles Wesley's hymn "Come, Thou Long-Expected Jesus."

Corymba does not effect a passage from the Jazz Age to the Age of Faith. Instead, images from ancient religions surface in her consciousness as she is dancing in a nightclub in the 1920s. Surprisingly, these images do not cause her to reject or even question her current way of life. Whatever social criticism Davidson may be implying is left for the reader to infer.

Davidson suggests his attitude toward the recreation of his own age when he tells us that Corymba "has gone with a jaded youth / To a sudatorium." The dance, which had religious significance in ancient times, has been reduced to its physical essence: "The sweating there is of movement / To a cacophonic drum" (32). In the midst of this delirium, "She has heard a silvery jangle / From the slight harps of the moon." This reminds Corymba of "Isis's warm commune" and "the dark aisle where Shiva / Nods to the trembling ballet" (33). For all that we know, Corymba may be aware of no incongruity. She may even regard the twentieth-century flapper as a kind of secular priestess. Immediately after the reverie in which she imagines the dances of Isis and Shiva, we see the protagonist back in her natural element:

> Corymba has not rejected
> Familiarities.
> It is past noon. She dozes,
> With half drawn-up knees,
> Thinking of new stockings
> And other such verities. (33–34)

With the gestures of love reduced to a litotes (unrejected familiarities), Corymba resembles the clerk typist in *The Waste Land*, just as her partner, the "jaded youth," seems a spiritual second cousin to the "young man carbuncular." By sleeping past noon in a fetal position (apparently after a late night on the town), she is withdrawing from any vital connection with life. Significantly, her dreamworld is populated not by fauns and nymphs and demonic pipers but by "new stockings / And other such verities." Like Pope's Belinda, who makes no distinction between Bibles and billets-doux, Corymba equates truth with materialism and sensuality. To paraphrase Hemingway's Brett Ashley, new stockings are what she has instead of God.

Rebecca Patton Wells, Davidson's maternal grandmother. (Unless otherwise noted, all photographs courtesy Davidson family collection.)

John Henry Wells, Davidson's maternal grandfather

Thomas Andrew and Louisa Snell Davidson, Davidson's paternal grandparents

William Bluford Davidson,
Davidson's father

Elma Wells Davidson,
Davidson's mother

Elma Wells as a girl

Donald Davidson as an infant

Davidson, 1910

Davidson's birthplace in Campbellsville, Tennessee

Mrs. Adams's Sunday school class in Lynnville, Tennessee. Davidson is in the bottom row, second from left.

Branham and Hughes Glee Club, 1909. Davidson is in the top row, fourth from left.

Vanderbilt sophomore football team, 1914–1915. Davidson is in the middle row, far left.

Davidson and his daughter, Mary, at his ancestor's marker in Bluefield, West Virginia, about 1937

(l to r) William Bluford Davidson and his sons, Donald, Tom, Bill, and John

PART
TWO

PARADISE RECLAIMED
(1924-1936)

6

TWO CHEERS FOR MODERNISM

Donald Davidson's career as a literary journalist did not end when the last issue of the *Fugitive* appeared in December 1925. By that time, he had devoted nearly two years to editing the weekly book page of the *Nashville Tennessean.* In January 1924, the managing editor of the *Tennessean,* John H. Nye, had approached him with the idea of doing a book page, and the project was launched a month later. Nye offered pay of ten dollars a week and review copies of the books. With a wife and child to support, Davidson welcomed the opportunity to supplement his salary at Vanderbilt. (His pay at the *Tennessean* was eventually increased to two hundred dollars a month, which was equal to what he was then making at Vanderbilt.) During the first year, he wrote a column of book news and one or two reviews of his own for each Sunday paper. This column was called "The Spyglass" until 1928, when it was renamed "The Critic's Almanac." A selection of these reviews was edited by John Tyree Fain and published in 1962 under the title *The Spyglass.*

Because so much of Davidson's writing about literature was published on this book page, even his most fervent admirers tend not to think of him as a critic. Unlike John Crowe Ransom, he was no theoretician. Unlike Cleanth Brooks, he did not change the way we look at individual texts and the canon as a whole. Unlike Allen Tate, he was not on the cutting edge of literary modernism. For that matter, it is hard to imagine one gaining any kind of reputation as a literary critic by writing book reviews for a local newspaper in a provincial city such as Nashville. As Joseph Epstein notes, "Something of the odor of Grub Street still clings to the activity of book reviewing; something of the foul reputation of hackwork, however undeserved it may be."[1]

1. Joseph Epstein, *Plausible Prejudices: Essays on American Writing,* 52.

Even if this were not the case, relatively few individuals in the larger republic of letters ever saw Davidson's book page. Although it was syndicated from 1928 to 1930 in the *Memphis Commercial-Appeal* and the *Knoxville Journal,* its circulation was minuscule compared to the book review of the *New York Times.* Nor could the *Tennessean* boast the highbrow readership of the literary quarterlies. Nevertheless, the book page brought genuine literary culture to tens of thousands of ordinary people who read neither the *Times* nor the quarterlies. By sharing his opinions with citizens of his own community, Davidson also developed a greater sense of himself as a southerner. Although he wrote about the literature of various regions, one can discern the beginnings of his Agrarian sensibility emerging in the comments about southern culture he published in his hometown paper.

In 1931, a year after he stopped editing the book page, Davidson wrote an extended essay for the *Bookman* on the unique situation of being a book editor in the provinces. While suffering all the practical difficulties of trying to work far removed from the nation's center of culture, he notes, the provincial critic enjoys some advantages. For one thing, his remoteness affords him a superior degree of independence. Because he is unlikely to know the authors he is reviewing, he need not curry their favor or fear their disapproval. Nor can he "be seduced, even unconsciously, by publishers' advertising, because publishers do not advertise in his page."[2]

Over the six years that he edited the book page for the *Tennessean,* Davidson employed as many as three or four hundred different reviewers. Although established critics such as Allen Tate and John Crowe Ransom were among them, Davidson generally had to rely on the services of amateurs. (This included such Vanderbilt undergraduates as Andrew Lytle, Cleanth Brooks, and Robert Penn Warren.) They worked simply for free copies of the books they were reviewing and to see their opinions in print. At their worst, such reviewers could produce perfunctory and shallow criticism. What amazed Davidson, however, was the frequency with which the amateur reviewer did a better job than his professional counterpart. "[T]hey are more impressed with the obligation of doing a good review (not necessarily a favorable one) and have not yet learned the sad lesson that criticism is one of the most impermanent and least respected forms of writing" (247).

If those who read and wrote a provincial book page might have seemed unsophisticated in the eyes of New York, the cosmopolitan publishers themselves were often laughably ignorant about the interests and habits of the reading public west of the Hudson River. Although some of the more established publishing houses paid attention to the peculiarities of the local book page, others sent

---

2. Donald Davidson, *The Spyglass: Views and Reviews, 1924–1930,* 242. Subsequent references will be cited parenthetically in the text.

and withheld review copies for no discernible reason. Davidson recalls "getting numerous review copies of obscure Scandinavian or Polish novels from a certain publisher and missing entirely a novel by a Tennessean, published by the same firm; . . . [of] being refused a review copy of the diary of President Polk, whose tomb is a few steps away from the newspaper I worked for; but . . . always getting diaries or biographies of other worthies in whom I could take no possible interest" (249–50). Even as these commercial houses were hawking a new list of masterpieces every spring and fall, as if they were disposable commodities, the typical provincial reader preferred to hunker down with the classics. And why not? "Wells was after all no adequate substitute for Thackeray, and . . . Isadora Duncan and Bertrand Russell were featherweights in comparison with Plutarch and Shakespeare" (252–53).

One who knew Davidson only from his criticism would not guess that his own muse was far more committed to poetry than to fiction. While his critical writing about novelists from Joseph Conrad on is extensive and usually perceptive, he had much less to say in print about the art of verse. On the book page, he tried to present himself as a defender of modern poetry; however, it is clear from his comments on individual poets that his sympathy for experimentation and eccentricity was limited. In praising Thomas Hardy's continuing productivity at age eighty-five, Davidson can't resist comparing the "old man's exuberant store [with] the publication recently of T. S. Eliot's 'collected' poems, in which the young expatriate American puts together all of his work that 'he cares to preserve' (a slim volume indeed!) and thus signifies the drying-up of the springs of poetry in his soul" (103).

Davidson can express only guarded admiration for a poet as experimental as Hart Crane. In his review of Crane's *White Buildings,* published on April 3, 1927, he begins by deferring to the criticism of Allen Tate and Waldo Frank. As for his own response, Davidson admires the musicality of Crane's verse and the originality of his imagery but wonders "how far can the process of telescoping metaphors be carried? Or, how far can Mr. Crane favor his entirely personal verbal associations and still achieve a poetical effect?" (108). In partial answer to this question, Davidson observes "that the 'contemporary' parts of [Crane's] poetry are often unabsorbed and jangle; that his meticulous striving for precision, together with his crowding of metaphors, makes his poetry stiff in texture; that his tone is too often sticky and sepulchral" (108). "Nevertheless," Davidson concludes, "his phrases stay with me whether I understand them or not. Crane's poetry is masculine and bold and serious, and, with all its defects (as I see them) I prefer his poetry to that of the trivial soupy sycophants and pink-tea artists who monopolize the space given in most magazines to poetry" (109).

Davidson is on far more comfortable ground when he praises Josephine Pinckney's first book of verse, *Sea-Drinking Cities,* in a review published on

January 15, 1928. In this piece, one finds none of the reservations about local color that Davidson had expressed a few years earlier in the *Fugitive*. If anything, he thinks that Pinckney may have been a little too influenced by the techniques of modernism. "[P]erhaps she has been guided a little too much by imagism, or whatever influence it is that makes her see things nearly always in pictorial terms, so that her poetry is at times not only in repose, but static. And there is the slight diffidence that one finds often in the moderns, the shrinking from direct utterance, the finical carefulness" (111). Nevertheless, Pinckney has not succumbed to what Davidson considers some of the more baneful aspects of the modernist sensibility: "her conviction is not, like Mr. Wheelock's or Mr. T. S. Eliot's, a product of defeat rendering itself in melancholy beauty" (112). On the basis of this single volume, Davidson ranks Josephine Pinckney as the best of the South Carolina poets and finds her verse comparable to any then being written in America.

If Davidson's unabashed provincialism is obvious in his enthusiasm for a poet such as Josephine Pinckney, it is equally evident in his antipathies. In a scathing review of Harriet Monroe's *Poets and Their Art,* published on August 1, 1926, Davidson charges the founder of *Poetry* magazine with responsibility for all that is fashionably meretricious on the national literary scene. Unknown to most of Davidson's readers, Monroe had first raised the hackles of the Fugitives in May 1923 with her review of Dubose Heyward and Hervey Allen's *Carolina Chansons*. She had gushed a bit too patronizingly that the "soft silken reminiscent life of the Old South is becoming articulate" and had urged southern poets to be interpreters "of a region so specialized in beauty, so rich in racial tang and prejudice, so jewel-weighted with a heroic past."[3]

Davidson responded to this bit of regional condescension a month later in an unsigned editorial in the *Fugitive*. "Undoubtedly the Old South is literary material to those who care to write about it," he asserts. "But many may not. It is not the province of any critic to dictate the material these many shall choose. They will guffaw at the fiction that the Southern writer of today must embalm and serve up an ancient dish. They will create from what is nearest and dearest in experience—whether it be old or new, North, South, East, or West, and what business is that of Aunt Harriet's."[4]

Now, over three years later, Davidson begrudgingly credits Monroe with having championed the new poetry when she started her magazine in 1912; however, he argues that that enterprise has become insular and self-regarding. One of the problems is that Monroe herself possesses the mind of a clubwoman, not a critic. Her essays "play earnestly over the surface of poetry. They introduce us

3. Harriet Monroe, "The Old South," 92, 91.
4. [Donald Davidson], "Merely Prose," 66.

with a pleasant feminine urbanity to a series of notables, breathing recollections, recording tilts and encounters, volleying opinions and dogmatic preferences which have little systematic dogma to uphold them. They represent crusades rather than analyses" (123). While Aunt Harriet is adept at dropping names, she is deficient in literary judgment. The poets she discusses in her book are, on the whole, less distinguished than the ones she excludes. "Miss Monroe has fought for poetry nobly but blindly," Davidson concludes. "She has wanted to be a general, but her strategical capacities are thin. She claims to be the friend of poetry and of poets, but has little of real importance to say to them" (124).

Compared to his contempt for Harriet Monroe, Davidson's view of the infinitely more articulate H. L. Mencken seems positively benign. Although Mencken would eventually become a kind of Antichrist for defenders of southern culture, he had been a largely irrelevant figure for the Fugitives. As one of the critics who thought that all of the verse in the first issue of the *Fugitive* was written by the same person, he proved himself to be an obtuse reader. "Although he could detect the movement of a national or regional literature," Fred Hobson notes, Mencken "could often not recognize distinction in the *individual poem*—and he could not distinguish one poet from another when the two poets happened to belong to the same broad 'school.' " To the Fugitives, Mencken was primarily a critic and editor who had power in the world of literature, not a polemicist who said provocative things about the South. (To the extent that they took notice of what he said about the artistic climate in the South, they tended to agree with him.) What they found most limiting about him was his insensitivity to poetry. "They did not respond at all when Mencken attacked the South," Hobson writes; "they responded only when he attacked poetry."[5]

Throughout the 1920s, and intermittently thereafter, Davidson expressed a guarded respect and admiration for Mencken. (As we shall see, it was only after Mencken persisted in attacking the Agrarian movement that relations between the two men were permanently ruptured.) While accusing him of comical exaggeration, Davidson shared Mencken's low esteem for mass society. Writing in the *Tennessean* on December 12, 1926, he argues that the most accurate way of reading Mencken is not as a serious social critic, whose opinions are supported by data and arguments, but as an entertainer who encourages us to laugh at the world much as Mark Twain did. Davidson allows that "Mr. Mencken is sorry he was born, and that life offers him no pleasure except an occasional tickling, a sensual excitement, or sardonic laughter at the ridiculousness of the world." Even so, he believes that Mencken was fortunate to have been "born in the United States, which, with England, is the only country democratic enough to permit a

5. Fred Hobson, *Serpent in Eden: H. L. Mencken and the South,* 73, 77.

confirmed and lowly misanthrope to rise to his present position of honor, wealth, and power, or to tolerate his persistent rowdyism after he has arrived" (130).

If Davidson felt drawn to the warmth and vigor of Mencken's style even as he disagreed with the substance of his thought, much the opposite was true of his reaction to T. S. Eliot. After reading *For Lancelot Andrewes,* Davidson expressed the same populist impatience with Eliot's prose that he had felt upon finishing *The Waste Land.* "The Sacred Wood of literary tradition that Mr. Eliot explores critically," Davidson writes, "is a carefully picketed area, rarely extending beyond the seventeenth century. . . . A chilly hauteur is part of his manner; one suspects it to be the psychological defense of a lonely heart. At any rate one feels icily repelled, put in one's proper uncouth place" (140, 141). Despite these reservations about Eliot's style, Davidson can't help agreeing with much of what the critic has to say. (He especially likes Eliot's essays on Arthur Symons, Thomas Middleton, and Irving Babbitt.) Davidson believes that the dilemma of contemporary criticism is reflected equally in the superficial timeliness of a literary journalist such as Henry Seidel Canby and the esoteric pontifications of a dogmatic elitist such as Eliot. "We may wish that Mr. Canby would be more deliberate," he concludes; "even more heartily we could wish that Mr. Eliot could be more expansive" (142).

I

For all the involvement the Fugitives had with poetry and criticism, the majority of people who read Davidson's book page were more interested in what he had to say about fiction. What they found in his reviews of novels was an unusual comprehensiveness of judgment. Because he generally knew the other works of a given novelist, Davidson was able to place the book he was discussing in context. Consider, for example, his review of Dubose Heyward's *Mamba's Daughters.* Davidson believes that in *Porgy,* Heyward had proven himself a good storyteller who could depict the primitive virtues of the Negro with sympathy and understanding. However, his later book "shows him to be wavering between the demands of his own artistic integrity and the demands made by outside influences, including no doubt the public, the metropolitan critics, and the publishers—all three as likely to operate for ill as for good" (29–30). Davidson goes on to say that

> If I did not know Mr. Heyward is the author, I could easily have imagined
> the book to have been written by some fly-by-night millionaire novelist from
> the Riviera or Gopher Prairie, who put his yacht into Charleston harbor for
> the winter season and picked up enough local color to fill out his contract
> for a fifteenth best-selling novel. . . . The book, in brief, though seeming

to be an "inside" interpretation, is without the passionate absorption in the subject that we must demand of a regional novelist. It is written as if to order. (31–32)

What we hear in this passage is clearly the voice of the writer-critic, not the scholar-pedant. No amount of theorizing about literary regionalism would have been nearly as effective as Davidson's image of the millionaire novelist from Gopher Prairie docking his yacht in Charleston harbor.

Although he did not believe that Dubose Heyward always wrote convincingly about the Negro, Davidson voiced wholehearted praise for Julia Peterkin's and Roark Bradford's efforts to imagine life on the other side of the racial divide. In discussing Peterkin's *Black April,* he identifies three types of literature about the Negro: the folk literature of the African Americans themselves, the sophisticated texts of educated Negroes such as Walter White and Countee Cullen, and the depictions of black life by such white writers as Joel Chandler Harris, Thomas Nelson Page, "and that prurient modern, Carl Van Vechten" (21). Davidson, who was most impressed with what he had read in the first and third of these categories, believed that no one had written more effectively about the Negro than Julia Peterkin. For him, *Black April* was "the first genuine novel in English of the Negro as a human being" (23).

In contrast to Peterkin, Roark Bradford clearly dealt with the Negro as stereotype. However, given the genre in which he was working, that was to be expected and excused. By translating various stories from the Old Testament into the form of Negro folktales, Bradford had "slipped up on the American public and taken a left-handed advantage that no minister of the Gospel could assume. Without seeming to intend it, he ha[d] got a hardheaded people interested in religion" (54). Because cosmopolitan white audiences did not demand the same logic from black people that they demanded from themselves, they could safely suspend their disbelief in the Negro fables presented in Bradford's stories (not to mention *Green Pastures,* the play Marc Connelly based on those stories). Although one can't help discerning Davidson's racial condescension here, he does stress the superior wisdom of myth and even asserts the integrity of what would later be called Black English. "The most powerful appeal is never through logic and reason," he writes; "but when ideas attach themselves to a certain manner of speaking which by common consent is privileged against hard and fast criticism, and which has rules of its own that suit our inmost sense of rightness—then a myth is created to which we ally ourselves only too gladly" (55).

Displaying a remarkable evenhandedness, Davidson often gave writers for whom he must have felt little affinity their just share of approbation. For example, in a review published on January 31, 1926, he appears genuinely impressed by Theodore Dreiser's depiction of American life. While admitting the stylistic awkwardness of Dreiser's *An American Tragedy,* he confesses that the power of the narrative made that fact seem almost irrelevant. "The very multiplicity of detail arises from an honest and sympathetic desire to allow nothing pertinent in [the protagonist's] life to remain undiscovered. . . . And even the gawky, sprawling sentences may be the product of the same unflinching honesty. . . . The result is an overwhelming book; a book convincing, terrible, and true; a book that tears you away from whatever you are doing and incorporates you into itself; a massive and pitiful document of human verity; a book from which may be gained, as from George Eliot's *Romola,* an overpowering sense of the reality of evil" (68–69).

Unfortunately, Davidson's criticism was not always so sympathetic and judicious. By the mid-1920s, he had become increasingly committed to interpreting life and art from a partisan southern perspective. Although this disposition would have an overwhelmingly positive effect on his writing, it could also cause him to form aesthetic opinions for largely ideological reasons. A case in point is his response to Ernest Hemingway. Discussing *Men without Women* in a review published on January 22, 1928, Davidson writes:

> The sentences must be as flat and brief as possible. [Hemingway] never attempts a complicated sentence, except when at intervals he gives a long succession of clauses tied together with "and," like a child's story of an adventure. . . . The result is that he has developed a style of his own, which I am obliged to respect because it is so perfectly done after its design; but I cannot read it with any great pleasure, unless you would say it is a pleasure to see a butcher carving a hind quarter or slicing lamb chops. There is exactly the same sort of execution—cut, slice, whack. (78)

Even more obtuse is the review of *A Farewell to Arms* that Davidson published on November 3, 1929. Not only does he manage to misspell the names of both of Hemingway's principal characters, he also gives the book an embarrassingly simplistic reading, dismissing it as a failed attempt to achieve scientific objectivity in the form of a novel. According to Davidson, *A Farewell to Arms* "is a splendid imitation, but only an imitation, of science. It is a hybrid beast, ill-begotten and sterile. It is a stunt, a tour de force, and no matter how blindingly brilliant, no matter how subtle in artifice, it is in effect a complete deception (possibly a self-deception) and can exist only as a kind of marvelous monstrosity" (92).

In the two years prior to the first of his Hemingway reviews, Davidson's poetry was shifting from the decadence of his early Fugitive verse and the modest experimentation of *An Outland Piper* to the visionary regionalism of his second book, *The Tall Men.* This was also a period when the Fugitive group had ceased to function, even as reactions to the Scopes trial focused national attention on the cultural peculiarities of the South. As a result of all these developments, Davidson found himself growing increasingly hostile toward literature that did not seem congenial to the southern ethos. Two months after his review of *A Farewell to Arms,* he admitted as much. In a letter to Allen Tate, who knew Hemingway and admired his work, Davidson writes, "I am afraid that I sacrificed Hemingway (to some extent) in order to make a point against science. . . . I certainly respect him, and I'm glad to have your opinion of him to take to heart. And with what you say about literary judgments in general, as not to be made from a sectional basis, but on a higher level, I'm in perfect agreement. I've felt for quite a while that I was in danger of losing balance and becoming merely a cantankerous localist, and your admonishment warms my conscience to its task" (*Literary Correspondence,* 249).

II

Even as Davidson was becoming more deeply rooted in his native region, he began a voluminous correspondence with John Gould Fletcher, an expatriated southerner who wished that he had never left home. When Fletcher lectured on American poetry at Oxford in 1922, his audience had included the Rhodes scholar and Fugitive poet William Yandell Elliott. After the lecture, Elliott expressed his surprise that Fletcher had not mentioned the Fugitives. Fletcher quickly made his acquaintance with the work of the Nashville group and contributed two poems to the *Fugitive* the following year. During a trip to America in 1927, he lectured at the Centennial Club in Nashville, where he met Ransom and Davidson. By this time, Fletcher was growing tired of the European literary scene and was increasingly eager to escape a bad marriage.

On March 21, 1927, Davidson wrote to Fletcher to thank him for commenting on two poems he had sent him.[6] "Your criticism is generous and fair," Davidson notes, "and I am very grateful for it, all the more because you are the most disinterested literary person who has come this way in a long time." He then proceeds to speak of his work in progress, a major poem that would be published later that year as *The Tall Men:*

> In the revision of my manuscript, now in process, I am trying to get more of the color and intensity that you suggest. It will not always be possible in this book, I realize, for I am in many ways committed to the "gray against gray" procedure. This came about because I felt that I would run the danger of being too splashingly heroic if I plunged too boldly into my potentially epic material; and I wanted the poems to be partially a mixture, with an affirmative warmth gradually emerging toward the end of my series of subjective but partly dramatic inquiries. I know I carried the process too far—I toned down

6. This and other letters between Davidson and Fletcher are housed in the University of Arkansas Library at Fayetteville.

too much, and maybe cannot fully remedy the fault in this book. But you see, I believe, what few of my friends have seen who have read the whole manuscript, that the work is in many ways prefatory; it is a self-orientation, after which I may go on with a feeling that I know where I am headed. Meanwhile, the book can be published for what it is worth. I do not delude myself into believing that it is anything immense.

On March 25, Fletcher responded to Davidson with a brief note, in which he writes: "[T]hough I had to live for forty years before I arrived at any contact with another Southern poet that I could in any way respect, I am glad to see that there are now three. You and Tate and Ransom are now envisaging the same problem from different angles, . . . and I feel sure you personally will somehow make as important a dent in it as the other two I mention." It would be hard to overestimate the impact these words had on Davidson at a transitional point in his poetic career. Not only did Davidson revere Fletcher's international reputation, he also admired his verse.

Writing on June 13, 1927, Davidson tells Fletcher: "Your *Branches of Adam* impressed me most tremendously. I do not believe that any American poet of this century has done anything finer; I doubt whether anyone has indeed equalled your performance. . . . You have dared to treat an epic theme in a style which is epic in a modern way." Perhaps thinking of Tate, he continues: "I have never agreed with those poets and critics who seemed to think that a 'grand style' was impossible in modern times; if we had no 'grand style,' it was only because of the insufficiency of our poets, not of our times." Davidson goes on to say: "The problem of *being* grows enormously acute for us; we cannot endure many more *Waste Lands*. Myths must undergo reexamination, or we must have new ones; and I believe the purport of your work lies in this direction."

Davidson and Fletcher discovered each other at a time that proved useful to both men. An older and far more celebrated poet, Fletcher provided Davidson with a soul mate at a time when the Fugitives were no longer functioning as a group. For his part, Davidson gave Fletcher both an appreciative audience and the hope that his native region might not be a cultural desert. The son of a Confederate officer and gentleman, Fletcher had been traumatized as an adolescent when his father lost a race for governor of Arkansas to a populist demagogue named (of all things) Jeff Davis. Fletcher had not lived in the South since leaving for Harvard in 1903 but was very eager to reestablish his sectional roots. In his autobiography, published over a decade later, he reveals that in Davidson he had found a kindred spirit: "Davidson was, like myself, far more discontented and unhappy at bottom than Ransom. He was, indeed, more or less lost amid the confused sophistications of modernity, and had set himself directly against the popular current, feeling that in so far as he cared for the South at all, it was only for the premechanical, agrarian, plantation South which had gone to defeat at Appomattox that he cared. I could understand and even share this point of view, for all its pessimism; for it was indeed largely my own."[7]

On June 26, Fletcher wrote to Davidson to say that "you and the few others who in the South are trying to keep some spark of the human spirit alive in this mechanical age, are, in the only real sense, my nearest kinsmen." He then adds: "I have always believed that the South would some day awaken, and always hoped to take some part (however small) in that consummation. My own isolation (which I feel every day and hour with a keenness which is almost unbearable) would be a small price to pay if I could feel that the South was preparing to take steps toward the recovery of its own intellectual and cultural heritage."[8]

Two months later, Fletcher publicly abandoned the Imagists and embraced the Fugitives in a major essay in the *Saturday Review of Literature*. There he writes of the Nashville group: "It takes the innovations of form of the free-verse school more or less for granted; what it quarrels with is fundamentally their attitude toward art. It begins by challenging the importance of emotion in poetry; it asserts that intellect and not emotion is the true basis of poetic art; and it proposes a return to classicism as the only possible remedy for the common looseness and facility of much present-day poetic art."[9]

In their correspondence from this time, Fletcher and Davidson offer revealing observations about other contemporary writers. While praising *Branches of Adam* in his letter of June 13, Davidson notes: "I have grown a little weary of the timidities of Robinson and Frost." In his response of June 26, Fletcher voices partial agreement: "Frost has always been a puzzle to me—he so definitely limits himself spiritually that I have never been able to appreciate him perhaps as much as he deserves. I am much more drawn to Robinson. . . . I sometimes feel a very perceptible irritation at his *New England correctness*. But when all is said, he has written two major poems: 'The Man Against the Sky' and 'Ben Jonson.' " Fletcher then observes: "I am even more interested in the Lindsay-Masters question. If these two could have been fused: if you could combine the lyric fire of the one with the often uncompromising realism of the other, the result would have been a very great poet. Unfortunately, there was no fusion, and the crass vulgarity of the Middle West arrested the development of both."[10]

In a letter dated October 24, 1927, Fletcher comments on a poet much closer to Davidson:

7. John Gould Fletcher, *The Autobiography of John Gould Fletcher*, 349.
8. John Gould Fletcher, *Selected Letters of John Gould Fletcher*, 96.
9. John Gould Fletcher, "Two Elements in Poetry," 65–66.
10. Fletcher, *Selected Letters*, 97.

I agree with you that there is a romantic irony at the bottom of Ransom—a sort of dandified disillusionment which I do not altogether like. I prefer your work with its harsher and raggeder outlines to his. Ransom has done his job very perfectly and very finely—he is an artist—whereas Miss Millay . . . is neither a poet nor an artist, but a *fake* from first to last. But Ransom's work has a sort of self-imposed limitation of slightly bored superiority which I mistrust (this in confidence). I prefer work that is not always so polished, so brittle. I believe it is possible to be intellectual without being a sort of Laforgue super-ironist about life. Life is too serious a business and commands too large issues to be met with a faint mockery. The best poet has to be dissatisfied with himself as well as with the world, and has to fuse his own dissatisfaction with that of the world. That is why I pointed out Dante as the supreme type of intellectualist. But no doubt you realize this better than I.[11]

Less than four months later, on February 13, 1928, Davidson informed Fletcher that Tate would soon send him a copy of a recent volume that included work by several of the Fugitives.[12] With a becoming modesty, he observes that the book shows its contributors "in our various virtues (if any) and vices." He finds Ransom's offerings to be the most consistent ("mine breaks in the middle") and also praises the work of Wills, Warren, and Moore. Perhaps most significant, he indicates his growing divergence from what he regards as the astringent quality of Tate's recent verse. "Tate is the most overwhelming" contributor, he writes; "—often I like his poetry thoroughly, often I admire it but do not like it, always I respect it, even when I quarrel with him for taking the most devious route to every goal."

---

11. Ibid., 100.
12. *Fugitives: An Anthology of Verse* (New York: Harcourt, Brace, 1928). Davidson's contributions to this volume will be discussed in the next chapter.

7

UBI SUNT

Although the last issue of the *Fugitive* appeared in 1925 and several key members of the group had left Nashville, the brethren still hoped for one final collective effort to give closure to their association. When the prospect of a Fugitive press proved impractical, the group briefly flirted with the idea of a yearbook featuring their most recent work. In July 1926, however, Allen Tate suggested that an anthology of their best earlier verse would be a simpler and more impressive project. Not surprisingly, the task of contacting the various members and soliciting their contributions fell to Donald Davidson, while he and Tate began looking for a northern publisher. At first, Ferris Greenslet of Houghton Mifflin (the firm that had published *An Outland Piper*) expressed interest in the book, but on November 26, 1926, he informed Davidson that the volume contained too much previously published material to make it a sound commercial risk. After Horace Liveright and Harper and Brothers both rejected the manuscript, Harcourt, Brace accepted it in July of 1927.

Fugitives: An Anthology of Verse appeared in 1928 with an unsigned foreword by Davidson and poems by eleven contributors.[1] Among Davidson's own selections were four poems that he would preserve in his late collection *The Long Street* (1960). Each of these, in different ways, reflects a darkly realistic (almost naturalistic) view of life. The most notable of the four poems is "Apple and Mole," a lyric that had originally appeared as "Not Long Green" in the June 1925 issue of the *Fugitive*. At the literal level, this poem describes a thoroughly natural process

---

1. John Crowe Ransom, Donald Davidson, Allen Tate, Robert Penn Warren, Alec Stevenson, Jesse Wills, Merrill Moore, Laura Riding, William Elliott, Walter Clyde Curry, and Sidney Hirsch.

of decay. At the end of the summer, a mole burrows its way to the base of an apple tree:

> Till the root will be sapless and the twig will be dry
> And the long green bough it will be shaken.
> The apple is too old, it has worms at the core,
> And the long green summer will be green no more.
> The apple will fall and not awaken.[2]

Although this may not exactly be a nature red in tooth and claw, it is certainly not a romantic or pastoral environment. By 1925, Davidson was moving beyond the youthful mannerisms of *An Outland Piper* without having developed the regionalist sensibility that would inform his most characteristic verse from 1927 (*The Tall Men*) to 1938 (*Lee in the Mountains and Other Poems*). Nevertheless, two distinguished critics have seen an inchoate Agrarian vision here. Louise Cowan argues suggestively that the original title, "Not Long Green," along with the frequent repetition of the term "long green," serves as a pun for material avarice.[3] Without necessarily endorsing this view, Louis Rubin declares that the poem is about "the intrusion of the commercial spirit into the rural garden." "The apple that will 'fall and not awaken,'" Rubin maintains, "is the fruit of the garden, and one would assume, of the region. The blind mole, powerful, efficient, timeless, manages to bring down the tree which 'is tall . . . green'—and tallness is Davidson's favorite word for the old heroes."[4]

As plausible as such a reading may seem, it should be noted that the apple was already infested with worms before the mole's arrival. Even if industrialism accelerates the process of decay, moles have been attacking apple trees ever since Adam was expelled from the Garden of Eden. Rather than prefiguring Davidson's later Agrarian sentiments, this poem may actually suggest the course that his career would have taken had he not become such an impassioned defender of the Old South.

The poems "Martha and Shadow" and "Cross Section of a Landscape" also belong to that brief period between *An Outland Piper* and *The Tall Men*. The first of these was originally published in the August 18, 1926, issue of *Nation* and reprinted in William Stanley Braithwaite's *Anthology of Magazine Verse for 1927*. Like Ransom's "Bells for John Whiteside's Daughter" and Tate's "The Death of Little Boys," this poem deals with the stark fact of mortality. However,

---

2. Donald Davidson, *The Long Street*, 73. Subsequent references will be cited parenthetically in the text.
3. Cowan, *Fugitive Group*, 202.
4. Rubin, *Wary Fugitives*, 150.

the difference in voice and sensibility is crucial. Although there is nothing maudlin about this poem, it shuns ironic detachment. (If anything, it is vaguely reminiscent of Gerard Manley Hopkins's "Spring and Fall.") It begins by showing us a little girl playing with her shadow (here personified with a capital "S"). In the gold of the morning sun, walking in the dew of the clover, Martha feels infinitely stronger than Shadow. The Shadow is even smaller at noon, "but would not die." That fact alone strikes an ominous note. The second stanza ends: "Shadow not Martha had a long time for growing."

In the third and final stanza, Shadow itself is given a voice. And when Martha speaks again, it is not in innocent baby talk but with a fully mature sense of fatality:

> Shadow said, Martha is little, Martha is not
> Able as I in evening, and evening is last.
> Martha said, Shadow is all, I know thee, O Shadow!
> I will come into Shadow and rest. (*Long Street*, 74)

"Cross Section of a Landscape" looks at the planet in purely geological terms. It is ice girdling a "joyless ocean," water "folding a sphere of quiet slime," and rock covering fire, which is itself lying "over the slag and ash of old decay." When the "bold geometrist" looks at this, all he is able to do is to pinch "space to a point in his vain Euclidean way." The irony and originality of this poem lie in the fact that these observations about the essential nothingness of the earth do not reflect a peculiarly adult cynicism and disillusionment. The speaker had reached much the same conclusion while still a child:

> But when I was a boy I searched from pole to pole
> Of a gaudy globe, a rainbow-colored ball,
> Peeled the cover, unraveled the shiny whole,
> And was vexed to find at center nothing at all. (*Long Street*, 76)

Although Davidson retrieved the poem "Litany" for *The Long Street*, he dropped it from *Poems, 1922–1961*. Having been published in the December 1923 issue of the *Fugitive*, it predates the publication of *An Outland Piper* by a few months. Nevertheless, there is nothing in this poem to suggest either the fairy-tale world of nymphs and druids or the Jazz Age wasteland of "Corymba." The setting of the poem is a bleak rural landscape. Although the region is unspecified, one imagines a northern location, as the wind roars and the ravages of the weather seem particularly severe. The speaker admonishes his listener not to waken "the child," because its lot would be one of nonidyllic agrarian toil: "For field is to plow and furrow's to run / And sheaves are to bind for our bread."

One need not read too much into this poem to infer that not awakening the child to such a world is equivalent to not letting it be born at all. The final stanza reads:

> Do not waken the child
> When wind's at the door
> And weather beats wild.
> Let it slumber, not know
> How lightnings terribly flash and go,
> Leaving worse dark than before. (*Long Street,* 74)

At the time the Fugitives had come on the scene, half a dozen years before the publication of their anthology, the state of southern poetry had not been much different from what it was before the First World War. John Gould Fletcher continued to be an important figure among the Imagists in London; however, his work was virtually unknown in the region of his birth. Although Conrad Aiken of Georgia and John Peale Bishop of West Virginia were each writing modernist verse, both had long since left the South (Aiken for New England and Bishop for Europe). The club women who filled the newspaper poetry columns with what Louis Rubin calls "perishable sentiment" represented the most visible embodiment of southern verse. H. L. Mencken was not far wrong when he said of the South, "Down there a poet is now almost as rare as an oboe-player, a dry-point etcher, or a metaphysician."[5]

The character of contemporary southern verse was evident when Harriet Monroe devoted the April 1922 issue of *Poetry* to the South. The guest editors of that volume were Dubose Heyward and Hervey Allen, two prominent members of the Poetry Society of South Carolina. In addition to publishing copious selections from their own work, Heyward and Allen featured poems by their cronies Henry Bellaman, Josephine Pinckney, and Beatrice Ravenel, as well as verse by several lesser lights. Although individual Fugitives had been devoting themselves to poetry for several years at this time, and John Crowe Ransom had published his first book of verse three years earlier, no work by the Nashville poets was deemed worthy of inclusion.

It would be unfair at this late date to criticize Heyward and Allen for their cliquishness or lack of prescience; however, their editorial selections do suggest how greatly the most revered southern poetry of their time differed from what the Fugitives were trying to do. Even in such a distinguished avant-garde publication as *Poetry,* the concept of southern modernism was a virtual oxymoron. The commentary with which Heyward and Allen concluded their special issue of

5. H. L. Mencken, "The Sahara of the Bozart," 136.

Poetry stressed the distinctively regional aspects of the verse produced in their part of the country. It was a poetry that regarded the Negro and the poor white as rich sources of local color. It also saw the predominantly rural topography of the South as ideally suited to a landscape poetry unlike the verse being produced in the great American cities. By definition, such poetry would keep its distance from the main currents of modernism. According to Heyward and Allen, the South "will accept with modern spirit the new forms in verse, but accept them as being valuable for their loosening effect upon the old rather than as being all satisfactory in themselves."[6]

Despite the revolutionary innovations of the Fugitives, local color *still* dominated the most widely admired southern verse at the end of the 1920s. At the time the Nashville poets were producing their anthology, Addison Hibbard, who was professor of English and dean of liberal arts at Chapel Hill, was editing a collection of poetry titled *The Lyric South*. Although Davidson and Ransom would both be represented in this volume, they became increasingly leery about Hibbard's critical standards as his project neared completion. On June 16, 1927, Ransom wrote to Davidson about the untenable situation they found themselves in. He felt that they could not honorably back out of a promise already made but hoped that the objections they had voiced to Hibbard would cause him to let them out on his own initiative. Ransom indicates how they had gotten into the predicament when he writes, "We made our mistake largely on Dr. Mims's recommendation."[7]

Apparently, Hibbard had disagreed with the Fugitives over which "Southern poets" qualified for inclusion in the volume. Although Hibbard (who was himself born in the Midwest) included several poets from the North then living in the South, he excluded native southerners who were living elsewhere. He also refused to include any poet who had not yet published a volume of verse. Ransom and Davidson objected to these policies because collectively they had the effect of excluding such poets as John Gould Fletcher, Conrad Aiken, and Allen Tate in favor of some fairly marginal figures. Holding firmly to his position, Hibbard wrote to Ransom and Davidson on May 27, 1927: "Aiken, Fletcher and one or two of the others you mention have done their writing in Massachusetts and perhaps in England. They are no more 'southern' than Lady Astor."

Hibbard probably came much closer to identifying the source of his differences with the Fugitives in a letter he wrote to Ransom and Davidson on June 26. "Quite obviously, your contention for 'quality only' is largely influenced by your desire to see the anthology include nothing that is not 'modern,'" he maintains. "Equally

6. Dubose Heyward and Hervey Allen, "Poetry South," 47.
7. This letter and others cited in this chapter are housed in the Fugitive Collection of the Jean and Alexander Heard Library, Vanderbilt University.

obviously, my own purpose is to show what the South is doing conventionally and unconventionally, irrespective of manner. In other words I want to give a cross section of the Lyric South (doesn't that name grate, too) while you want to represent it by the 'new' note almost exclusively."

Not only was Hibbard insufficiently modern to suit the Fugitives, he was also insufficiently southern. The poets who had begun their careers by seeming to reject the very concept of southern literature were becoming increasingly uneasy with the loss of regional identity on their home soil. In his review of *The Lyric South*, published in the September 16, 1928, issue of the *New York Herald Tribune*, Allen Tate all but accuses Hibbard of being a carpetbagger because he disdains sectionalism and extols progress. From his self-imposed exile in New York, Tate was writing a biography of Stonewall Jackson. A year earlier, he had published "Ode to the Confederate Dead." At the same time, Davidson, Ransom, and Warren were also trying to determine what it meant to be *both* a poet and a southerner in the modern world. It was a question that only a few years earlier they would not have thought to ask.

I

Virtually everyone who has studied Donald Davidson's career has been struck by the profound transformation in his views of life and art during the mid-1920s. Among the Fugitives, he and Ransom and Tate had seemed to be the most intent on accommodating southern literature to the innovations of modernism. As we have seen, he was eager to leave Nashville for New York as late as 1925. (Had Mark Van Doren found a suitable place for him at Columbia, he might very well have left at that time.) Fred Hobson has noted that Davidson's early book columns in the *Tennessean* generally extolled the cause of southern liberalism. He praised "such iconoclastic Southern magazines as the *Reviewer* of Richmond and the *Double Dealer* of New Orleans, outspoken Southern rebels such as [Howard] Odum, Gerald Johnson, and novelist Frances Newman, and on occasion even Mencken."[8] He was on friendly terms with the Chapel Hill liberal Paul Green and had submitted poems to Mencken at the *American Mercury.* But perhaps the strongest evidence of Davidson's early progressivism was his enthusiastic response to Edwin Mims's *The Advancing South.*

A combination of personal regard and professional self-interest would have prompted Davidson to deal respectfully with anything that Edwin Mims might have written. However, his review of *The Advancing South,* published in the May 23, 1926, issue of the *Tennessean,* far exceeds the dictates of courtesy. The

---

8. Fred Hobson, *Tell about the South: The Southern Rage to Explain,* 207.

sentiments underlying that review are far different from any that Davidson would have expressed during the last forty years of his life. "It simplifies matters too much," he writes, " . . . to reduce Dr. Mims' book to a question of who does and who does not possess intellectual curiosity, valuable and necessary as that quality is, and *certain as I am that the liberals possess it and the reactionaries do not*" (emphasis added). Throughout his review, Davidson lauds the cause of progressivism and those who champion it, as if the politically correct opinions needed only to be uttered, not defended. For example, in describing Mims's narrative, he writes: "Over and against the belligerancy of fundamentalist leaders and the folly of the Dayton episode is set the clear-cut preaching of men like Bishop Mouzon, the frank liberalism of editors here and there, the determination of religious and educational leaders not to yield ground."

Not only does Davidson agree with Mims, he also believes that *The Advancing South* itself is a significant chapter in the history of southern progress. All that is necessary to make the book complete is a chapter on "The College Professor as a Social Individual." The paradigm of such a figure would be Mims himself:

> What he has taught in his classes has constantly been the relation of literature to life. In writing this book he has gone just one logical step farther, carrying his natural gift for interpretation beyond the bounds of his profession, making Southern life more significant for humanity in this part of the world, and thus contributing in a very remarkable and brilliant way to the forward movement of the South itself.[9]

Although Davidson continued to revere Mims personally, he would soon come to very different conclusions about the proper course for southern culture to take.

The explanations that have been offered for Davidson's increasingly strident rejection of the New South seem plausible but insufficient. After the breakup of the Fugitive group, and particularly after the departure of Allen Tate for New York, Davidson became ever more embattled in his position in Nashville. At the same time, his relations with various liberals and modernists began to sour. Paul Green and Mencken both rejected poems he had sent to their respective magazines. When he entered the *Nation*'s annual poetry contest for 1927, his submission lost out to a more modernist poem by Thomas Horsby Ferril. (Allen Tate won an honorable mention.) In letters to Tate, Davidson bitterly surmised that he was moving in a direction different from the prevailing literary fashion.

The difference between *An Outland Piper* and Davidson's second book of poetry, *The Tall Men,* published just three years later in 1927, is as marked as the difference between Faulkner's *The Marble Faun* and his early Yoknapatawpha

---

9. Donald Davidson, review of *The Advancing South,* by Edwin Mims.

fiction. Possibly, Davidson's changing positions on regional issues account for this difference. But it is even more likely that things happened the other way around. I suspect that it was Davidson's intense imaginative engagement with *The Tall Men* that altered his view of contemporary southern culture. Chafing under the technical inhibitions of modernism and without the presence of the Fugitives to help reinforce those inhibitions, Davidson began in the mid-1920s to search for a more expansive and vernacular poetic style.

According to Daniel Joseph Singal, Davidson believed that "the Modernist aesthetic required an intensely introspective style of poetry, informed as much by the intellect as the emotions, heavily symbolic in its language, and addressed principally to a tiny coterie of fellow literati. Most important, because of its strict ban on sentimentality, Modernism severed the poet from his native subject matter, particularly if he happened to be a southerner."[10] In moving away from this constricted approach to art, Davidson naturally gravitated toward more indigenous poetic themes.

Not only did he choose to write about his frontier ancestors in *The Tall Men*, but he dedicated the poem to his parents. Not only did he purge dryads and flappers from his verse, he also got rid of the "packed lines and precise word choices" we find in *An Outland Piper*. "Instead, Davidson drew on his expertise in southern folk music to devise a lyrical style, based on blank verse and colloquial speech, which at once emancipated him from formal restraints and tied his epic to the ancient oral tradition in poetry. Such art, he hoped, would appeal to common people, especially in the South, and not just to the intellectual elite."[11] Ironically, in his rejection of the forms of modernism, Davidson may well have reflected a key aspect of the modernist dilemma.

In his superb study of literary modernism, *Dionysus and the City*, Monroe K. Spears identifies several types of discontinuity that plagued artists and intellectuals in the years surrounding the First World War. Metaphysical discontinuity recognized an unbridgeable gulf separating the realms of the natural, the human, and the supernatural, while aesthetic discontinuity posited a chasm between life and art. Another type—rhetorical discontinuity—held that conventional language was inadequate to convey the fragmented and chaotic state of modern life.

According to such analysis, Donald Davidson would hardly qualify as a modernist. He appears never to have experienced the metaphysical angst that bedeviled so many of his contemporaries in the twenties, and he soon came to see the poet not as an alienated rebel but as the keeper of society's memories. Even his technical experimentation was quite modest in comparison to that of Ransom,

---

10. Daniel Joseph Singal, *The War Within: From Victorian to Modernist Thought in the South*, 222.
11. Singal, *War*, 223.

Tate, and Warren. However, Davidson does seem to have been a quintessential modernist in one important respect. He experienced a fourth affliction that Spears identifies—temporal discontinuity: the sense that we have lost the bonds of tradition that once united the living, the dead, and the yet unborn.[12] In the two years after the *Fugitive* ceased publication, Davidson began increasingly to identify this sense of temporal discontinuity with life in the modern South. To varying degrees, this identification would become the major theme of his subsequent poetry and social criticism.

The fragments that Davidson chose to shore against his ruin are clearly different from the ones we find in *The Waste Land.* If Eliot and Davidson both saw the modern world as a pretty dismal place, they posited different solutions to the problem. In fact, Davidson wrote *The Tall Men* in part to counter the cosmopolitan world-weariness that he found in Eliot's poem. Writing to his publisher on April 9, 1927, Davidson said that he was trying to place "considerable emphasis on the heroic and romantic, in contrast to the disillusionment which afflicts us in the chaotic modern world. The idea is to arrive at some basis for an attitude of acceptance, which, while resting on the past, would not wholly reject the present—a mood of positiveness rather than the gesture of defeat to be found, say, in *The Waste Land.*"[13]

The speaker in *The Tall Men* is a modern urban southerner, whose life is divorced not only from history but also from nature. He paces a long street, where industrialism seems to have blurred any distinction among the seasons of the year. "Only the blind stone roots of the dull street / And the steel thews of houses flourish here."[14] The speaker yearns for release from this indigenously southern wasteland. But the vehicle of that release is neither oriental religion nor figures from ancient mythology. As we move from the prologue (titled "The Long Street") into the body of the poem, we find the speaker trying to recover an heroic regional heritage. As Louis Rubin points out, the situation in this poem bears some superficial similarity to that of Tate's "Ode to the Confederate Dead." The differences, however, are even more important.

> Davidson's modern speaker [unlike Tate's] is not really cut off from the past; rather he is out of place in the present, and infinitely prefers the values of the past, and he seems to blame his present unsatisfactory circumstance not on the fact that *he* is a modern, but on the historical and social circumstances

12. See Monroe K. Spears, *Dionysus and the City: Modernism in Twentieth-Century Poetry,* 3–34.

13. Quoted in Michael M. Jordan, " *The Tall Men:* Davidson's Answer to Eliot," 50.

14. Donald Davidson, *Poems, 1922–1961,* 115. Subsequent references will be cited parenthetically in the text.

that force him to play so false a *role*. His heart is with the men of old time; he views the present from their vantage point, and with their values.[15]

After the prologue, the title poem of the collection juxtaposes the speaker in his comfortable modern life with his violent forebears, who cleared the land and fought the Indians. (Singal believes that "what Davidson valued most in the frontier was precisely its violence, . . . [the fact that] the tall men were brave enough to act before they thought, and [that] their actions took place on the grand scale of life and death."[16]) In contrast to these vital ancestors, the speaker "is flung up from sleep against the breakfast table / Like numb and helpless driftwood." At first, the remnants of history seem remote to this man who has "my teeth to wash / And a cigarette to light before I catch / A car at eight-fifteen. . . ." He remembers always to look before crossing at an historic corner, because a man was killed "the other day / For failing to look while civilization crept / Upon him with rubber wheels and a stench of gas" (*Poems,* 118).

When a northern acquaintance asks the speaker whether it is the milk, the air, the cornbread, or the climbing of hills that causes Tennesseans to grow so tall, he replies: "Tallness is not in what you eat or drink / But in the seed of man" (119). This declaration causes him to reflect on particular figures from the past—a fictitious Indian fighter named McCrory and the historical titans John Sevier, Andrew Jackson, and Davy Crockett. The speaker laments that he did not live in that glorious past:

> . . . I was not there,
> At Talledaga, Horseshoe Bend, King's Mountain,
> Not at Suwannee, Mobile, or Pensacola
> In days when men were tall. . . .

A few lines later, he confesses: " . . . I have not sung / Old songs or danced old tunes. I have read a book" (124). He is forced to confront the dispiriting prospect that "The songs of my own race and the ways of fighters / Are something read in a book only, or graven / Only in stone and not in the hearts of men" (125).

The elegiac tone continues in "The Sod of Battle Fields," as we move into the era of the War Between the States. When the speaker drives his car along Battery Lane, he realizes that, for most modern southerners, the battles fought nearby have no more meaning than the new paint factory being built in the same region. Fortunately, this is not true of the old men who still remember "names that are not names to them / But panoplied moments, exultations made / Visible in the flesh that woke their banners" (126). The speaker, who is not old enough to have

---

15. Rubin, *Wary Fugitives,* 170.
16. Singal, *War,* 223–24.

experienced the war firsthand, nevertheless feels greater affinity with those who have than with the hollow men of his own generation. He says of himself: " . . . I who was born by the battlefields cannot / Escape a sorrow that dwells, a valor that lingers, / A hope that spoke on lips now still" (127).

As might be expected, the sectional bitterness is more acute here than in the title poem, which dealt with a frontier heritage that all Americans can claim to share. In what is surely an autobiographical reference, the speaker recalls his grandmother telling him stories of Yankee atrocities during the war. In one case, the Yankees came at night "Plundering the stables, leading the horses out. / They said, *Why you won't need your old barn now, / And so we'll burn it*" (127). In another instance, southern boys who had slipped home from the Confederate army for a snack and a change of clothes were rounded up and shot as spies.

> One tried to run. He got across a garden
> And over a paling-fence before they stopped him . . .
> Full of bullet holes . . . riddled . . . The bodies
> Lay in three pools of blood until the women
> And old men carried them in by candlelight . . .
> Dressed them decent . . . buried them.
> Riddled . . . the blood lay in pools. (130; ellipses in original)

The speaker obviously laments the fact that time has healed these old wounds. In the present day, "Lee is a granite face on a mountain. / And the grandsons of Confederate soldiers learn / About Abe Lincoln, the sad-eyed rail-splitter" (131).

It is in the third poem, titled "Geography of the Brain," that Davidson first identifies industrialism, and the creature comforts it provides, as part of the problem afflicting modern man. The contemporary American, North or South, finds himself:

> . . . . attended by bellowing
> Of Kansas steers (they go in animals;
> They come out packages); attended by
> The harried eyes of men on subway trains
> And pale children staring from tenement windows.
>> Assisted to a chair (Grand Rapids) by
>> Two slippers (from St. Louis) bites cigar
>> (Perhaps Havana) strikes a match (Bellefonte)
>> Unwrinkled trousers (Massachusetts) leafs
>> The *New York Times* (by U.S. Postal Service). (133–34)

Although the speaker can easily summon up appealing images from the past, actually recovering the old way of life is a far more difficult matter. His father, who tells him about the past, admits that it is all gone because of the war. " . . . I had rather tell you about Julius Caesar or Captain John Smith or read / Out of Plutarch's Lives" (137). But the father's memory keeps returning compulsively to the war and its aftermath. One scene he recalls with evident delight is of "the Ku Klux riders all in white parading / Around the square at Pulaski . . . ," taunting "frightened Negroes" (138).

Davidson confronts the race issue even more directly in section six of "Geography of the Brain." Addressing an unseen black man, he recalls that " . . . when you and I were young together, / We knew each other's hearts." Unfortunately, now that they are no longer children, they recognize that "there is a wall / Between us, anciently erected." Even if it had once been possible for them to cross that wall, the speaker cannot now forget that he was once a master, nor does he suspect that the black man can forget that he was once a slave. In the light of this painful reality, he can only counsel acquiescence. "We did not build / The ancient wall, but there it painfully is. / Let us not bruise our foreheads on the wall" (140). These lines do not sound like any that a Klansman might have uttered and give only the slightest hint of the fiery segregationist Davidson was to become.[17]

II

One of the few opportunities the modern southerner had to experience violent heroism in the early years of the twentieth century was in the First World War. Davidson drew on his own experiences in France to describe that war in the fifth poem of *The Tall Men*. Titled "The Faring," this poem depicts southern boys of Anglo-Saxon origins returning to their European homelands: "Over the Viking road came the Viking blood / Eastward for battle, borne in the Angles' ship, / They who were Angles" (144). In reversing the westward movement of civilization, these boys are returning symbolically to a past even more remote than the one inhabited by their Tennessee ancestors:

> Now they are going
> Somewhere in France on roads where Roman eagles
> Slanted to meet the Nervi or where
> Napoleon, flushed with greetings, galloped from Elba
> A hundred years before. . . . (146)

Once the Tennesseans enter battle, the figure of McCrory reappears. (Whether he is an archetypal soldier or merely a descendant of the Indian fighter in the earlier poem is not made clear.) Just as the McCrory of old had watched for Indians

---

17. As Louis Rubin notes, none of the other Fugitives was nearly as direct in advocating traditional southern attitudes on race. See *Wary Fugitives,* 174.

while thinking of Phoebe who slept in a nearby cabin, his modern incarnation stands sentinel against the Germans "half-wakefully, remembering how a girl's / Deep eyes commanded his in a land far off . . ." (149) (One cannot help visualizing Davidson thinking of Theresa while in the trenches of France with mortars exploding all around him.) Although this war is far more mechanized than the earlier battle against the Indians, there is no indication that the struggle is any less noble.

Commenting on Davidson's universal frame of reference, Michael M. Jordan writes:

> By identifying the doughboys with Tennessee Indian fighters, Anglo-Saxon warriors, Roman legions, and famous Greek soldiers, Davidson's persona has taken us through history, backward along the long street. One might contrast this journey to Eliot's sequence of "unreal Cities" in *The Waste Land*. . . . While Davidson emphasizes a real connection and a fruitful identification with the past in a movement from the present to the past, Eliot's sequence of cities, from the past to the present, underscores modern man's alienation from old traditions identified with the cities.[18]

The tone changes noticeably, however, in the penultimate section of the poem. After the armistice, the time has come for taking stock. The speaker tells us that "heroes are muddy creatures, a little pale / Under two days' beard with gritty mouths that mumble / Oaths like the Ancient Pistol. . . ." Later in the same stanza, the images become considerably more grotesque:

> . . . . Cramped forms in a dugout
> Vomiting smell of gas. Delirious corporals
> Tearing at bloody bandages. Captains in rusty
> Trench-coats mending broken cigars. Dead men
> Wrapped in blankets and earth under wooden crosses.
> Living and dead have different tongues for war. (151)

If the anguish in these lines is not exactly comparable to the bitter disillusionment found in the war poetry of Wilfred Owen, the stark realism reminds us that war is not all honor and glory (an unremarkable point in itself but one that had not been made previously in *The Tall Men*). After a variety of voices reflect on the war, "The Faring" concludes with the Tennesseans returning for discharge to Charleston, South Carolina, where an earlier war had begun.

With the experience of war concluded, the speaker returns home to try to make a life for himself in the postwar world. In "Conversation in a Bedroom," he rejects

18. Jordan, *"The Tall Men,"* 57.

not only the meretriciousness of modern life but most of the fashionable solutions that his contemporaries have found for that condition. The most heavily satirical poem in *The Tall Men*, "Conversation" is filled with savage parodies of Eliot. Davidson begins with an obvious echo of *The Waste Land*: "By the waters of Thames or Meuse in another world / I laid me down and slept" (157). Suffering from insomnia and an inability to adjust to civilian life, he prays for deliverance, only to discover that "God has poor ears. / They are clogged with pontifical wax" (158). He then turns to the Devil, hoping to make a better bargain than Faust did. In a sequence of surrealistic images and sing-song commentary, the Devil appears as a ringmaster to show the speaker two movies—reel one is entitled "Disease of Modern Man"; reel two, which is untitled, purports to bring "the picture to a happy ending." It features the voices of a traveler, a mystic, three expatriates, a satyr in a tuxedo, a bobbed-hair bacchante, and an intellectual—none of whom is a match for the tall men of the Tennessee frontier.

"Conversation in a Bedroom" is the most negative poem in *The Tall Men* because the focus is entirely upon modern culture. Unlike the earlier poems, Davidson does not present a redeeming image of the past, even as a judgment upon the inadequacies of our own time. The only positive image (and it is a powerful one) comes at the very end of the poem in the simple fact of the dawn. In the final stanza, the dawn represents many things to the speaker, but finally, it is simply "a friend crossing the grass with eager feet and calling / Under the window where you sleep, *Oh, come, / Come Down. I have news for you. It is morning!*" (166).

Some readers have felt that in "Conversation in a Bedroom" Davidson protests too much. "None of this is particularly convincing," writes Louis Rubin, "for it is all done with such withering contempt that it is difficult to take the modern scene seriously. Davidson will not concede any virtue to modern culture; he is not tempted by it in the slightest."[19] One might even argue that the lack of ironic resistance makes this poem a rather facile instance of propaganda art. Over seven decades later, one is also struck by Davidson's wrongheadedness in seeing T. S. Eliot as simply a deracinated naysayer, even if that view was widely held in the late 1920s. We must remember, however, that it would be another decade before Cleanth Brooks would reveal the affirmative subtext of *The Waste Land*. Moreover, it was only in his later embrace of Anglo-Catholicism and the religious poetry it inspired that Eliot would do what Davidson himself was trying to do in *The Tall Men*—seize a tradition by the sheer force of his imagination.[20]

In "The Breaking Mould," which is the seventh poem in *The Tall Men*,

---

19. Rubin, *Wary Fugitives,* 176.
20. I am not suggesting that either Anglo-Catholicism or the southern heritage is *simply* a product of the imagination. I do believe, however, that what Edmund Burke calls the moral

Davidson belatedly contemplates the role of religion in shaping his own identity. Two years after the publication of this poem, he would write to Tate that he seemed "to be bothered less by religious matters than anything else" (*Literary Correspondence*, 227). That fact is certainly borne out by the detached tone of "The Breaking Mould." The poem begins with a dramatic re-creation of the scene in which the Anglo-Saxon King Aedwin was converted to Christianity. Rather than celebrating this moment as a triumph for the one true faith, Davidson seems to regret the loss of pagan vigor that it occasioned:

> The hammer of Thor was fallen forever, and Odin
> Looked upon Asgard sadly. Twilight came
> With a mild Christian splendor of bells and incense.
> The Goths unbuckled the sword. The sons of the Goths
> Remembered the saints in stone with arches leaping
> Heavenward like my soul from the desolate earth. (167–68)

Although the speaker still reveres the heroic legacy of paganism, he also admires the courage of such Protestant Reformers as Luther and Tyndale— less for what they believed, one suspects, than for the fearless example they set. (Davidson's own cultural heritage included his upbringing in the southern Methodist Church.) Accordingly, Protestant Christianity forms an additional, and more problematical, aspect of the speaker's religious identity. Davidson was not prepared to celebrate a fundamentalist faith in which he did not believe. To him the rantings of an evangelical preacher were less persuasive than the findings of science and the queries of philosophy. The speaker in "The Breaking Mould" believes that "the prayers of men / Are mightier than the altars where they bow / Their wounded heads in one eternal wish" (170). Nevertheless, he harbors fond memories of learning the Ten Commandments from a gentle mother and reading "the Good Book through at the age of twelve, / Chapter by chapter." He also remembers the hymns of country choirs and the various prohibitions he learned from "the words of stately men / Speaking from ghostly pulpits. . . ." Finally, he is convinced that "the words of God are written in the Book / Which I will keep beloved though earth may speak / A different language unto those who read her" (171).

The conflict among the speaker's three religious traditions (pagan, Methodist, and secular rationalist) might be more easily resolved if only he could return to the days when men saw their gods and religion as more matters of experienced reality than faith in things unseen. He would even settle for a God "who will

---

imagination played an important role in prompting Eliot and Davidson to embrace these respective traditions.

not tame the manliness of men" (170). Unfortunately, he is left not with an affirmation but a question;

> How can three alien men be reconciled
> In one warm mind that like the sparrow flies
> In a great hall lit for feasts and the laughter of men,
> And would be glad before it goes forever
> Out of the opening door? Oh, give me a scroll
> Written anew, for where I pass are lions
> Walking chainless and devils that will not flee. (172)

If *The Tall Men* had ended with "The Breaking Mold," we might be tempted to conclude that the only transcendence that Davidson could find in the modern world (other than brooding about the irrecoverable past) lay in a pagan worship of nature. However, "Epithalamion" (the final poem before the epilogue) suggests another possibility—that even in the contemporary wasteland, one can experience grace through married love. (The title and verse form of this poem indicate an obvious debt to Spenser.) Because of the autobiographical inspiration of his poem, Davidson is forced to suspend his sectional polemics and admit that it is possible for a boy from Tennessee to find happiness with a girl from Ohio. The speaker admits that "in being faithful to you I have been unfaithful / Maybe, this once, to my own" (175).

Such treason is justified not only by the power of love, but also by the fantasy that their union was ordained in a time before the hostility between North and South. The speaker imagines that once an Ohio girl gave a drink of water to a captured Confederate soldier who was led past her farm by Yankee guards. Or perhaps, centuries earlier, when a young herald of the Goths landed on the Frisian coast to make peace with the Franks, the eyes of a young Frankish girl "met his warm through the spears." Not content with just these two scenes, the speaker asserts that throughout history there have been such meetings, "sealed with pledges under a castle window, / Longings unfulfilled when the clear horn sang / Challenge to the battle waged in a foreign land" (177).

"The Fire on Belmont Street," which serves as Davidson's epilogue, was actually written before the other poems in *The Tall Men*. (It was completed in 1926 and won first place in the southern poetry contest sponsored by the Poetry Society of South Carolina.) This epilogue begins with a "worthy citizen" of the town being informed that there is a fire in his neighborhood. (Belmont Street is an actual location in West Nashville.) What the worthy citizen fails to realize is that every house is endangered by the fire, which serves as a symbol for the spiritual conflagration burning away the fabric of society. The city is threatened by neither a natural catastrophe nor an external enemy but by the corrosion of industrialism. The smoke and soot "have turned back to live coals again for shame / On this gray city, blinded, soiled, and kicked / By fat blind fools." Had the speaker lived in a more heroic age, he might have found patriots like the sixty Danish warriors who stood with King Hnaef to hold the palace of the Finns against their foe. Not living in such an age, all that he can do is ask:

> But who will stand tonight,
> Holding this other door against the press
> Of brazen muscles? Who can conquer wheels
> Gigantically rolled with mass of iron
> Against frail human fingers? Who can quench
> The white-hot fury of the tameless atoms
> Bursting the secret jungle of their cells? (180)

After the joyful celebration of "Epithalamion," *The Tall Men* ends on a somber note, which, for all of Davidson's protestations to the contrary, is not appreciably more hopeful than the one struck by Eliot in *The Waste Land*. He seems to lament the fact that the Indians died for nothing (without acknowledging that it was in large part because of the superior industrial firepower of McCrory and his kind), but he is far from confident that his own race will escape the same fate. The best that he can do is issue an impassioned warning in consciously archaic language:

> . . . . White man, remember,
> Brother, remember Hnaef and his sixty warriors
> Greedy for battle-joy. Remember the rifles
> Talking men's talk into the Tennessee darkness
> And the long-haired hunters watching the Tennessee hills
> In the land of big rivers for something. (181)

With the publication of *The Tall Men*, Davidson had completely renounced the sophisticated skepticism that one finds in the poetry of Allen Tate and other literary modernists. Almost as an act of will, he had embraced a southern myth that seemed to be at variance with many of the deplorable tendencies of modern life. Tate, however, believed that such a willed allegiance could not produce convincing poetry. In a letter to Davidson, dated May 14, 1926, he writes: "I am convinced that Milton himself could not write a Paradise Lost now. Minds are less important for literature than cultures; our minds are as good as they ever were, but our culture is dissolving. . . . You can't put your epic of Tennessee in the minds of Tennesseans; the pre-condition of your writing is that it must (in an equivalent of spiritual intensity) be already there" (*Literary Correspondence*, 166, 167). Although he recognized the validity of this criticism, Davidson continued to try to put the southern myth into the minds of southern readers. The fact that it was no longer there made the task all the more compelling.

8

ANGRY AS WASP MUSIC

The history of twentieth-century thought is filled with dramatic political conversions—usually from left to right. The brutality of the Spanish Civil War turned George Orwell and John Dos Passos into staunch anti-Communists. The Moscow show trials and the Hitler-Stalin pact drove even larger numbers of Soviet sympathizers toward a conservative, or at least skeptical, point of view. So many former radicals turned right in the late sixties and early seventies that Michael Harrington coined the term *neoconservative* to describe the phenomenon. American conservative thought would certainly have been much poorer without the contributions of James Burnham, Sidney Hook, Whittaker Chambers, Norman Podhoretz, and numerous other refugees from the political left. In comparison, Donald Davidson's shift from a kind of moderate progressivism to an immoderate sectionalism hardly seems that dramatic.

The one common thread running through Davidson's thought as both a liberal and conservative was a genuine regard for the best interests of the South. Up through the mid-1920s, he had little reason to question the Mims-Kirkland belief that the South was well served by adopting mainstream notions of economic and intellectual progress. To have believed otherwise would have required a period of independent reflection and strongly persuasive evidence. During his early adult life, Davidson was concentrating on other things—trying to earn a living and care for his family while pursuing a literary career. His work at Vanderbilt and the editorial demands of both the *Fugitive* and the book page consumed almost all of his intellectual energies. It was not until he began writing *The Tall Men* that his examination of southern culture went beyond a perfunctory adherence to the conventional wisdom.

When he was finishing *The Tall Men,* Davidson read James Weldon Johnson's recently republished *Autobiography of an Ex-Coloured Man.* This novel tells the story of a light-skinned Negro who moves back and forth between white and black society. At one point, he decides to live as a black man and travels in the South, collecting folk music and writing songs. However, the poverty and discrimination suffered by the black race repels him. After witnessing a lynching, he returns to the North, enters business college, and "passes" as a white man. Although he becomes financially successful and marries a white woman who accepts him, mixed blood and all, he is plagued by the notion that he has forsaken his chance for greatness. At the end of his story, the protagonist observes: "My love for my children makes me glad that I am what I am and keeps me from desiring to be otherwise; and yet, when I sometimes open a little box in which I still keep my fast yellowing manuscripts, the only tangible remnants of a vanished dream, a dead ambition, a sacrificed talent, I cannot repress the thought that, after all, I have chosen the lesser part, that I have sold my birthright for a mess of pottage."[1]

Davidson was very much impressed with this book and reviewed it favorably in the *Tennessean* on September 11, 1927. In identifying the theme of the novel, Davidson writes, "this fictionalized autobiography is . . . , from one point of view, the autobiography of a traitor."[2] One can only speculate what connection, if any, Davidson might have seen between his own situation and that of Johnson's protagonist. Within the larger intellectual community, defenders of the southern tradition were a maligned and ridiculed class. Only those southern writers who were willing to abandon that tradition and embrace the cosmopolitan values of the North would be allowed full citizenship in the dominant culture. Such writers were in a position analogous to that of the mulatto who "passed" for white. Although Davidson would surely have been amused, perhaps even offended, by the metaphor of the southerner as nigger, it is clear that by the time he read *The Autobiography of an Ex-Coloured Man,* he was determined not to sell his own birthright for a mess of pottage.

I

Even though most of the contributors to the *Fugitive* had gone their separate ways by the late 1920s, several of them maintained bonds of friendship. Because Ransom and Davidson remained at Vanderbilt, they were in almost daily contact.

1. James Weldon Johnson, *The Autobiography of an Ex-Coloured Man,* 211.
2. Donald Davidson, review of *The Autobiography of an Ex-Coloured Man,* by James Weldon Johnson.

In addition to writing frequently to Tate and intermittently to Fletcher, Davidson also stayed in touch with Red Warren, who had graduated from Vanderbilt in the spring of 1925. The year before his graduation, Red had suffered a serious emotional breakdown. In the spring of 1924, the sight in his injured eye grew worse, and he feared going blind. At the same time, his lack of discipline had caused him to fall behind in his course work. Finally, he was suffering from an unreciprocated crush on a woman named Catherine Baxter Nichol. One night, he penned a suicide note, in which he despaired of ever becoming a poet, and covered his face with a chloroform-soaked towel.

After Warren survived this ordeal, he returned home to Guthrie, Kentucky, for the summer, where various friends (particularly Allen Tate) visited to show their support and concern. During his recuperation, he sent poems to Davidson for critical comments and contributed reviews to the *Tennessean*. In an undated letter from that summer, he writes to Davidson: "Allen and I wax in faith and strength daily; he is acquiring quite a bit of tan, and his cheeks are rosy even as the red apples that they were before he shaved (I appeal to M. Moore for a metaphor). We take long walks every morning and evening and often swim in the afternoon; at night we read and write. Allen is preparing to endow the mortal maids of Guthrie with an immortal youth by means of a poem; he will also speak of the village Croesus, who is gruff and who rides by our place every day."[3] After completing his B.A. at Vanderbilt, Warren spent the next two years at the University of California at Berkeley, where he earned an M.A. degree in 1927. He entered Yale to pursue a Ph.D. that fall and visited Allen Tate in New York the next summer.

A marginal contributor to the *Fugitive*, who was also living in the Northeast at this time, was Catherine Nichol's cousin Andrew Nelson Lytle. A native of Murfreesboro, a town just outside of Nashville, Lytle received his secondary education at the Sewanee Military Academy. He turned down an appointment to West Point to travel in Europe and lived for a time on the Left Bank of Paris, where he studied fencing. Lytle enrolled in Exeter College, Oxford, in 1921, but withdrew after three weeks upon the death of his grandfather. Returning to Tennessee, he entered Vanderbilt, where he became a student of Davidson's and Ransom's and a classmate of Red Warren's. By the fall of 1926, he was studying drama under George Pierce Baker at Yale. Because of his proximity to New York, Lytle visited Allen Tate and his wife, Caroline Gordon, in 1927. After writing some plays and taking a few temporary acting jobs, Lytle abandoned his theatrical career in 1929 to help his father run Cornsilk, a large plantation near Guntersville, Alabama.

---

3. Except where otherwise indicated, the letters cited in this chapter are housed in the Fugitive Collection of the Heard Library.

Much of Davidson's extensive correspondence with Lytle during the midtwenties concerns reviews Lytle was writing for the *Tennessean;* however, in the spring of 1926, the two men expressed their mutual exasperation with a difficult friend. On May 16, 1926, Davidson wrote to Lytle:

> If you have any influence over Red Warren, you'd better write and advise him to steer clear of Nashville on his return East. There are some very angry people here who are likely to have him arrested the minute he arrives, and I am one of them. He carried off (at Xmas-time) some books that I value—in fact he made a general haul on his Nashville friends, leaving injured feelings and even a bad check behind. Since he left—not a word—not a damn whisper—except a request to write a recommendation. I've written my last one for him. I haven't the slightest interest in being abused any longer. If you're writing Red, you better drop a hint. I don't expect to write him any more or say anything about the affair. Like the fiend Grendel, I am swollen with rage.

Responding to Davidson a week later, on May 24, Lytle offered his own perspective on Warren's recent behavior:

> I am distressed to death over the actions of Red. He has written me only once since Xmas, but I really did not expect many letters. It looks as if he has gone wild out there. He always had a certain weakness—but his present actions appear to have pressed things to the breaking point. He has abused Bill Clark rather badly, until Bill has written him he has charged both the sum of money and his friendship off to bad debts. From every side I hear complaint, and it distresses me very much. I shall endeavor to see what under God's earth has come over him. Red has always felt that he is the offspring of God's second son, and with such lineage he evidently feels that he can treat his friends any way, then soothe their wounds with the balm of his smile. However, he has made a grievous mistake and needs a jacking up.

This crisis, like Warren's attempted suicide, eventually passed—perhaps because the ties uniting the former Fugitives were stronger than the differences in temperament that divided them. If those ties had been forged by a shared devotion to literature, the literary enterprise itself was merged with a greater regional consciousness by the end of the decade. For example, in 1925, Allen Tate wrote "Ode to the Confederate Dead." This poem contrasts the solipsistic modern man with the heroic defenders of the Southern cause. On March 1, 1927, Tate wrote to Davidson: "I've attacked the South for the last time, except in so far as it may be necessary to point out that the chief defect the Old South had was that in it which produced, through whatever cause, the New South" (*Literary Correspondence,* 191). That same year, Tate began touring Civil War battlefields and immersing himself in Confederate history for his biography of Stonewall Jackson (followed in 1929 by a life of Jefferson Davis). These experiences helped convince him that at least potentially the Old South was one of the last bastions of religious humanism in the western world.

At the same time, John Crowe Ransom was also rediscovering the virtues of the Old South. A particularly compelling example of his newfound regionalism is "Antique Harvesters." Published in 1927, this poem is at one level a brutally honest description of rural poverty in the South. Against that realism, Ransom posits the abiding faith of those who remain loyal to the land, which he venerates as a fair lady, suggesting images of medieval chivalry and perhaps even Catholic devotion to the Blessed Virgin. When modern voices try to convince the region's youth that they will prosper more readily in other lands, the speaker of the poem exhorts them:

> Angry as wasp-music be your cry then;
> "Forsake the Proud Lady, of the heart of fire,
> The look of snow, to the praise of a dwindled choir,
> Song of degenerate specters that were men?
> The sons of the fathers shall keep her, worthy of
> What these have done in love."[4]

If John Gould Fletcher was a late convert to the Fugitive cause and a long-term expatriate, his fondness for his native region seems to have flowered even earlier than it did for those who stayed at home. In 1921, he published two experiments in polyphonic prose—"The Old South" and "The Passing of the South." The elegiac quality of these selections is suggested by the sentence that opens and closes "The Passing of the South": "On a catafalque, draped in black, under bronze cannon, forlorn and white, rigid in death, the corpse of the South is borne to its tomb."[5] Even earlier, in 1916, he published "The Ghosts of an Old House," a series of twenty-four poems about his childhood home in Little Rock. In his autobiography, Fletcher writes of these poems: "I may claim for them that they are the only imagistic poems which are also purely southern poems. The later southern school of the Nashville 'Fugitives,' appearing on the literary scene seven years later, would have treated these themes, no doubt, far differently than I. But at the time that I was writing them no one had so much as heard of the Fugitives."[6]

Andrew Lytle and Red Warren were also imaginatively engaged with the Old South as the 1920s came to an end. Lytle was writing a biography of Nathan Bedford Forrest, and Warren a life of John Brown. Like Tate, each man had

---

4. John Crowe Ransom, "Antique Harvesters," 27.
5. John Gould Fletcher, *Selected Poems of John Gould Fletcher*, 167.
6. Fletcher, *Autobiography*, 199.

selected a biographical subject that ideally suited his interests and sensibilities. If Stonewall Jackson and Jefferson Davis appealed to Tate's patrician sympathies, Forrest was Lytle's kind of southerner. As a native of Middle Tennessee and the only one of the Vanderbilt writers to run a farm, Lytle believed that the hope of the South lay in the yeoman farmer. At his best (and even at his worst), Forrest was the paradigm of such a figure. In contrast, John Brown, as both man and myth, revealed the dangers of abstract righteousness. Warren was fascinated by the tragedy and folly of John Brown and continued to write about such characters in his fiction and poetry. He completed *John Brown: The Making of a Martyr* after abandoning doctoral studies at Yale to pursue a Rhodes scholarship. While at Oxford, he also wrote "Prime Leaf," a long story about the tobacco wars he witnessed during his childhood in Kentucky.

II

If Donald Davidson was becoming too provincial to be accepted in New York, his own region did not boast a large enough reading public to make up the difference. In private, Davidson blamed the situation on southern liberals who had abandoned their own patrimony to accept the cultural standards of New York ("a new set of 'scalawags' and carpetbaggers," he called them in a letter to John Gould Fletcher), but in public he continued to maintain a moderate persona.[7] In "The Artist as Southerner," published in the May 15, 1927, issue of the *Saturday Review of Literature,* he considers for the first time an issue that had not much interested the Fugitives—the role of the *southern* writer in twentieth-century America.

Davidson believed that the serious writer in the modern South feels inhibited and self-conscious when he considers the literary tradition of his region. The rich poetic material that is at hand has been so debased by sentimentality that the truly committed literary artist is afraid to touch it. Although northern poets as diverse as Lowell, Whitman, Robinson, Lindsay, and Sandburg have celebrated Abraham Lincoln "with the dignity and seriousness that suited his heroic dimensions," no southern poet has done the same for Robert E. Lee. Even if the contemporary southern poet fully appreciates Lee's potential as a poetic subject, "he is more likely to remember emphatically the rhymes of the more puerile Confederate songsters, and feel an impulsive distaste for a subject of a sort that has already been boggled too many times."[8]

7. This letter is housed in the University of Arkansas Library at Fayetteville.
8. Donald Davidson, "The Artist as Southerner," 782. Subsequent references will be cited parenthetically in the text.

Davidson readily concedes that the truly autochthonous writer ("Frost in New England, Hardy in Wessex, Hamsun and Bojer in Europe") does not experience such inhibitions. Such a writer lives comfortably within an ongoing cultural tradition. The contemporary southern writer, however, senses a radical disparity between the magnolia myths of the Old South and the industrial reality of the new. If he is aesthetically at odds with the former, he is spiritually displaced by the latter. This condition has spawned a literature of protest and a literature of escape, produced by a host of fourth-rate Blakes, Shelleys, Byrons, and Swifts, while those writers who strive primarily for local color rarely reach even that high. "Heyward's church-towers are Charleston towers and Charleston towers only," Davidson writes. "Robert Frost's birches and ax-helves and pasture-lots and rock walls, though they may incidentally be New England, are more definitely the phenomena of the universe, as it is familiar to all men. The true autochthonous writer moves from the particular to the universal, and this process is not very common in contemporary Southern literature" (782).

Davidson's solution to the dilemma of modern southern letters is not nearly so incisive as his diagnosis of the problem. He points with pride to the many fine writers who live and work in the South and hopes for the emergence of some native genius who will encompass all of their best virtues. Because such qualities of the southern character as "exuberance, sensitiveness, liveliness of imagination, warmth and flexibility of temper" are underrepresented in contemporary American literature, there is much room for the truly autochthonous southern writer to make his mark. Unfortunately beyond arguing for the sort of affirmative zest and abandon that southern patriots display when they hear "Dixie" played, Davidson cannot yet offer a particular program for regional literature.

Probably the most significant event for shaping national attitudes toward the South in the 1920s was the Scopes "Monkey" trial. When John T. Scopes, a high school biology teacher, was tried in the summer of 1925 for teaching the theory of evolution, the national press descended on tiny Dayton, Tennessee. Scopes himself turned into a minor player in the drama when two of the country's best-known lawyers (William Jennings Bryan for the prosecution and Clarence Darrow for the defense) faced each other across a sweltering courtroom that has since become an abiding presence in our historical imagination. An equally imposing figure in Dayton that summer was H. L. Mencken. If Bryan and Darrow were putting religious faith and intellectual freedom on trial, Mencken made the South itself the defendant in Dayton. His columns in the *Baltimore Evening Sun,* which were widely syndicated, mercilessly lampooned the backwoods South. (As Fred Hobson notes, "Mencken's greatest prejudice of all—far greater than any against blacks, Jews, 'half-civilized' immigrants from Eastern Europe, or even Methodists—was that against the southern cracker."[9]) As a consequence, southern intellectuals were forced to take a stand on the events in Dayton.

One response, typified by Mims's *The Advancing South,* was to argue that the Scopes trial was an aberration in a region that was making rapid social, economic, and cultural progress. (Mims quotes with approval Chancellor Kirkland at the Vanderbilt semicentennial celebration: "The answer to the episode in Dayton is the building of new laboratories on the Vanderbilt campus for the teaching of science. . . . The remedy for a narrow sectarianism and a belligerant Fundamentalism is the establishment on this campus of a school of religion, illustrating in its methods and in its organization the strength of a common faith and the glory of a universal worship."[10]) On the other extreme, John Crowe Ransom believed that southern intellectuals should embrace fundamentalism for aesthetic reasons. Even as he moved away from the Methodist dogma embraced by his father and grandfather (both of whom were clergymen), he longed to find some system of myth and ritual that would give formal coherence to life. In his idiosyncratic book *God without Thunder* (1930), Ransom argues that the literal Old Testament religion of the South could serve that function. Although he was personally a religious skeptic and near positivist, Ransom was more sympathetic to the culture of fundamentalism than were the liberal Methodists Mims and Kirkland.

To judge purely on the merits of the issue, Davidson was probably closer to Mims than to Ransom. Writing in the *Tennessean* a month before the Scopes trial, he had expressed concern that the proceedings in Dayton might embarrass Tennessee, "and the very week of the trial he had commended Mencken for the number of southerners who appeared in the *American Mercury.*"[11] Davidson had very little interest in religion as such, and he still thought of himself as intellectually progressive. However, the people whom Mencken and other Yankee journalists were ridiculing bore a strong resemblance to Davidson's kin and neighbors. Moreover, he was inclined to see Darrow and his supporters as outsiders trying to use the Constitution to negate local self-government in Tennessee. During his childhood, Davidson had heard enough stories about the War Between the States and Reconstruction to resent any instance of northern meddling. Nevertheless, his first public discussion of the Scopes trial was measured and unpolemical.

Davidson begins "First Fruits of Dayton: The Intellectual Evolution in Dixie," an essay published in the June 1928 issue of *Forum,* by arguing what sounds like the Mims position—that the South is too complex a region to reduce to

9. Fred Hobson, *Mencken: A Life,* 257.
10. Mims, *Advancing South,* 158.
11. Hobson, *Tell about the South,* 158.

caricature. Practically echoing Mims, he writes: "We may recall that Chancellor Kirkland's answer to the Dayton episode was to build new laboratories on the Vanderbilt campus. We may rejoice in the press, the *Journal of Social Sciences* [actually the *Journal of Social Forces*], the notable activities of the University of North Carolina." Even if this praise of the Chapel Hill liberals was perfectly sincere, it served the strategic purpose of making Davidson's limited defense of fundamentalism seem less reactionary. He makes that case initially by arguing that "anti-evolution legislation may even be taken as a kind of progress; for it signifies that Fundamentalism has appealed an issue of battle—already lost elsewhere—to law-making bodies, and that sort of appeal is characteristic of the American idea that law can effect what society in its inner workings cannot." In the next paragraph, Davidson argues that "Fundamentalism, whatever its wild extravagances, is at least morally serious in a day when morals are treated with levity; and that it offers a sincere, though a narrow, solution to a major problem of our age: namely how far science, which is determining our physical ways of life, shall be permitted also to determine our philosophy of life."[12]

If science did not represent an unmixed blessing for the South, Davidson believed that the influence of the business class was even more problematic. Placing the situation in an historical perspective, he writes:

> Colonial Virginia was mercantile before it adopted the genteel tradition of its Cavaliers—a minority who set the tone for the majority of the population. The South has never blushed to acknowledge that the good life has its foundation in economic matters. But the plantation masters of the old days and even the factory builders of the late nineteenth century mixed a considerable amount of civic responsibility and generous paternalism with their business affairs. The Southern business men of to-day seem to be out of touch with this tradition. Their public activities tend to be limited to the familiar process of boosting the home town, or to minor civic enterprises like widening a street or supporting the community chest. . . . [B]ehind their genial front is a determined, though not consciously formulated, policy of aggrandizement. They are ready to egg on their industrial revolution enthusiastically without ever counting the evils they may be dragging in with it, and without considering whether they are hurrying the South into an artificial prosperity. (902–3)

Davidson is quick to point out that it is the ideology of industrialism, not business per se, that he is attacking. He notes several instances of public beneficence

---

12. Donald Davidson, "First Fruits of Dayton: The Intellectual Evolution in Dixie," 898. Subsequent references will be cited parenthetically in the text.

by commercial interests throughout the South. (This included support of the *Fugitive* by the Nashville business community.) Nevertheless, he is wary of what might happen if the South makes industrialization its sole measure of progress. Warming to his argument, he writes, "To make Charleston over into the precise image of Pittsburgh would be a worse crime than the Dayton crime. Those who advocate progress without any positive regard for the genius of the South may presently find themselves in the unenviable company of the carpet-baggers and scalawags of the first reconstruction. They shall be as persons without a country— barren and importunate exiles—dwelling in a land that loves them not, that they have helped to kill" (905). Sounding like a southern Edmund Burke, Davidson concludes that the South can avoid such a fate only by embracing an organic model of progress—"as growth means improvement of what you have, not mere addition or change, the first step toward progress is for the South to turn back upon itself, to rediscover itself, to examine its ideals" (907). As he had made clear earlier in the essay, such a program would involve an enlightened and unabashed provincialism. "The South has been damned for its provincialism," he writes, "but there never was a time when the South needed its provincialism more—if by provincialism is meant its heritage of individual character, the whole bundle of ways that make the South Southern. . . . [P]rovincialism means, not sectionalism, not insularity and bigotry of mind, but differentiation, which is a thoroughly ancient and honorable and American idea" (904, 906).

III

As the 1920s wore on, Davidson's own unabashed provincialism became increasingly evident on his book page in the *Tennessean*. As we saw in his reviews of Hemingway's work, this sometimes could lead to the literary misjudgments of a "cantankerous localist." When he was wearing his regional blinders, Davidson was also capable of reversing earlier assessments in seemingly record time. Two months after heaping enthusiastic praise on Dreiser's *An American Tragedy*, Davidson writes of a character in T. S. Stribling's *Teeftallow* that "he has not even the dignity of ambition and consuming passion that somewhat dignify that other worm of modern American fiction, Dreiser's Clyde Griffiths" (*Spyglass*, 13). As Louis Rubin observes:

> Stribling has written a novel in which life in Tennessee is portrayed unfavorably, and Davidson objects to the negativism of the portrait; since Dreiser also portrayed life in dreary terms, he therefore uses Dreiser to attack the viewpoint. Dreiser's fiction, which had made so powerful an impact upon Davidson, now becomes the victim of a theory about the proper approach

to the portrayal of regional life, and is therefore denounced for what it represents as subject matter, rather than for what it is as art."[13]

In his "Critic's Almanac" column for April 22, 1928, Davidson celebrates the cultural value of provincialism. Although the term had often been used as an epithet, he argues that, properly understood, it "is allied to the self-reliance of Emerson's teaching and to the 'know thyself' of the ancient sages" (*Spyglass,* 3). He believes that provincialism is the enemy of standardization and conformity. Ancient Athens, he contends, was a provincial society because it drew its main strength from its own Greek character. Rome, on the other hand, decayed because it was too cosmopolitan. "It consolidated and selected, but it did not originate" (4). Whatever one might think of this observation as history, it is an early indication of a philosophy that would come to dominate Davidson's writings on literature and society. Although he warned the South against xenophobic hostility to outside influences, he urged southern writers and audiences to know their own region better. The sort of provincialism that Davidson endorsed "believes in unity as a principle of convenience and beauty, but not in uniformity. It knows that harmony comes not from exact correspondence but from a certain amount of diversity" (4–5).

During the time that he edited the book page, Davidson became ever more concerned with reclaiming southern history. He believed that the South had suffered three defeats at the hands of the North. The first was losing the War Between the States. The second was losing the peace during Reconstruction. The third, and more lingering, defeat was losing control of history. "For sixty years and more, at the hands of New England historians," he writes on September 15, 1929, "the South lost something imponderable and precious. . . . It saw monstrous legends persist, not to be refuted by Southern voices, for Southern voices were laughed down under the charge of sectionalism, sentimentalism, and the bloody shirt. . . . It saw the United States of America become the United States of the North and West, with the Solid South as a kind of embarrassing appendage to the 'real' America" (217).

The new southern consciousness of the former Fugitives went public with the appearance of Allen Tate's *Stonewall Jackson: The Good Soldier* in 1928. As one might imagine, Davidson's review of that book is laudatory. Despite a few minor quibbles, he finds the book historically sound and "poetic in implication" (201). What is perhaps most important, however, is Davidson's realization that Tate was trying to substitute a regional mythology for a national one. Tate believed that the Unionists, not the Confederates, had been the true rebels, because it was they who tried to destroy the long-standing constitutional balance between the states

13. Rubin, *Wary Fugitives,* 154.

and the federal government. The "Northern rebels," as Tate calls them, were not trying to preserve the existing union so much as to create a new one. It was Tate's hope to recover the older vision—if only through memory.

Perhaps the most important contributions to a revised history of the South were those made by Ulrich B. Phillips, who was surely the most respected southern historian of his time. In commenting on Phillips's *Life and Labor in the Old South,* Davidson is most impressed with the fact that Phillips offers empirical support for the notion that the South had always been a distinctive region. Although his book ventures few explicit generalizations, the evidence it adduces is generally favorable to the plantation South. Expressing his only major reservation, Davidson argues that Phillips favors the "plantations and gentry too much and does not take into full enough consideration the strong Western character of the part of the South on our side of the Appalachians" (216–17). This conflict between a southern vision centered on the planters and one stressing the yeoman farmer would soon prove to be one of the central issues dividing champions of the Old South. There was little question which side the author of *The Tall Men* would endorse.

What U. B. Phillips did for the image of the old Confederacy, Claude Bowers did for the reputation of the postbellum South. His book *The Tragic Era* tells the shameful story of Reconstruction in all its painful detail. In reviewing that book, Davidson can't help being reminded of Bowers's earlier study of Hamilton and Jefferson. Clearly, Hamilton's centralized industrial vision, which had long dominated life in the North, was threatening to become the wave of the southern future. For that reason, Davidson urges the South to ponder the price such a transformation would exact before surrendering its older Jeffersonian faith. He believes that, in addition to telling us what the past was really like, books such as *The Tragic Era* can help us avoid repeating the mistakes of that past. Consequently, Davidson finds such books cathartic.

The critical response to revisionist southern historians such as Tate, Phillips, and Bowers raised important historiographical questions. The tendency of reviewers had been to praise these writers in terms that denied the importance of their work. An example was the elder Arthur M. Schlesinger, who called Claude Bowers "the greatest living practitioner of personal history." Bowers's primary strength was his vivid presentation of personalities and events. What he ignored, according to Schlesinger, were "the great impersonal tides in human affairs" (see *Spyglass,* 226). This accounts for both his popularity among the masses and his low esteem among professional historians. Schlesinger, of course, is begging an important question. He assumes that history is shaped more by impersonal forces than by the actions of individual men and women. Davidson argues that the perspective of the personal historian is not only more interesting but closer to the truth—at least the truth as southerners see it. According to Davidson, the virtue of the personal historians is that "they brush aside abstract forces, and center our attention on human beings of our own near past who, for good or ill, foolishly or wisely, took responsibility into their hands and by their personal, particular force determined the shame under which we live today" (229).

Davidson's evolving social vision is evident not only in his comments on southern literature and history but in his reviews of books far removed from the confines of the Old Confederacy. In his extremely favorable discussion of Siegfried Sassoon's *Memories of an Infantry Officer*, he reveals an anti-industrial bias that would become far more pronounced in his subsequent social criticism. "The World War," Davidson writes, "was the first war in history to be thoroughly mechanized, on a fully modern, presumably 'efficient' basis. It was also the first war in all history to produce no great generals, no great leaders, and perhaps not a single piece of first-class strategy. In other words, the triumph of the machine!" (193).

As the 1920s wore on, Davidson became convinced that the triumph of the machine would mean the end of much that he loved in the traditional South. Nothing less than the very soul of the South was at stake. If the battle for the Confederacy was long since lost, the war against industrialism was still up for grabs. In a particularly evocative passage from "First Fruits of Dayton," he had warned what losing that war might mean.

> A Southerner visits New York, let us say, as Southerners do. He boards the train at Charleston, leaving behind the marshes with wild birds and deer, the trees heavy with moss, the close, white-fronted houses—a quiet land, gracious and full of ancient peace. He passes the sandy flats, the pines and turpentine camps, the cotton fields, presently the greener country with its different soil, and then the rolling fields and variegated hills of Virginia, where are houses placid, old in generous traditions. Not even yet is it a thickly settled country. There is ugliness around the railroad stations, but not much elsewhere until Washington is passed, and then comes the miles of slums, factories, railroads, a hopeless wreck of the soil, a triumph of ugliness until one plunges into the bowels of the earth and, issuing breathless, feels on his temples the roar of New York. ("First Fruits," 905)

This same animus toward industrialism can be found in Davidson's comments on the work of a whole host of social critics who questioned the blessings of machine technology from a variety of perspectives. For example, James Truslow Adams bemoaned the damage done to society when business determines a nation's culture as well as its economy. Summarizing the argument of Adams's *Our Business Civilization*, Davidson writes: "The leisure essential to a humane civilization is confused with idleness and is depreciated or filled with material things, the sale of which 'helps business.' The professions lose dignity and give up social responsibility for the ideal of wealth. The arts are commercialized or atrophied" (*Spyglass*, 231).

Much the same argument informs Ralph Borsodi's *This Ugly Civilization,* whose main target is the factory and its corrosive influence on community life. Borsodi contends that the factory, not the machine as such, has caused overproduction, manic consumption, "congested cities, stock market crises, wild sprees of inflation, and all such evils" (*Spyglass,* 233). His simplistic remedy is to eliminate all but the most essential factories and to return most economic activity to the home. Expressing agreement with Borsodi, Davidson reminds us that "machines have always existed, but before the days of industrialism they were domesticated, like the spinning wheel, to home use, and they promoted and did not destroy the happiness and well-being of human society" (232–33).

Surely the man most responsible for both the fact and the concept of industrialism was Henry Ford. Ford's ideal society, as envisioned in his aptly titled book *Moving Forward,* would be one in which fewer people worked shorter hours at higher wages to produce more goods. What would happen to the technologically unemployed is not clear. What would happen to the concept of labor for those still on the job is all too clear. In his review of *Moving Forward,* Davidson notes that Ford's machines "are operated under the theory that labor is bad and men ought to do as little of it as possible. . . . One can only conclude that the introduction of more and more labor-saving machines signifies that labor will be held in more and more contempt. Or, still worse, that our lives are to be severely split between work and play, when as a matter of fact the two ought not to be put into opposition. In the ideal life work and play are not at odds, but harmoniously blend and interchange" (237).[14] In order to produce his earthly paradise, Ford would have to convince people "that life is made up of material satisfactions only, and that there are no satisfactions that cannot be purchased. On the one hand, we shall have financial chaos; on the other, a degraded citizenry, who have been taught under the inhumane principles of Fordism always to spend more than they have, and to want more than they get" (*Spyglass,* 238).

In reading Davidson's comments on industrial civilization, one cannot help being struck by their unintended affinities with Marxist thought. Although Davidson does not mention capitalism by name, he laments the condition of the alienated worker who controls neither the source nor the fruits of his labor. This was a theme that had been sounded by southern traditionalists for nearly a century by the time Davidson launched his book page. (One thinks of William J. Grayson's poem "The Hireling and the Slave" and even of the arguments of Augustine St. Clare, the benevolent slaveholder in Harriet Beecher Stowe's *Uncle Tom's Cabin.*) As the Marxist historian Eugene D. Genovese notes: "In the Old South, outstanding political and intellectual figures denounced capitalism ('the

---

14. This is essentially the position taken by John Crowe Ransom in his essay "Forms and Citizens." See *The World's Body,* 29–54.

free-labor system') as a brutal, immoral, irresponsible wage-slavery in which the masters of capital exploited and impoverished their workers without assuming personal responsibility for them."[15]

Making much the same point in the *Communist Manifesto*, Marx and Engels write: "The bourgeoisie, wherever it has got the upper hand, has put an end to all feudal, patriarchal, idyllic relations. It has pitilessly torn asunder the . . . feudal ties that bound man to his 'natural superiors.'"[16] If Davidson and other admirers of the Old South shared Marx's hatred of the new industrial order, their solution to the problem differed from his. As the thirties found many American writers committing themselves to the promise of a socialist future, a group of former Fugitives were busy trying to maintain the values of an arcadian past.

15. Eugene D. Genovese, *The Southern Tradition: The Achievement and Limitations of an American Conservatism*, 31.

16. Karl Marx and Friedrich Engels, *The Communist Manifesto*, 182.

9

SOME VERSIONS OF PASTORAL

On March 17, 1927, Allen Tate wrote to Donald Davidson to inform him that he and John Ransom had been discussing "a Southern symposium of prose" (*Literary Correspondence,* 195). Davidson, who was making final revisions on *The Tall Men,* responded four days later: "I am out-and-out enthusiastic about the project. I'll join in and go the limit. Am willing to write on almost anything" (196). Because Tate was in typically precarious financial straits, he did not pursue the enterprise for more than two years. (He was busy writing the Jackson and Davis biographies and spending a year in Europe on a Guggenheim grant.) During that time, Davidson, Ransom, and several like-minded colleagues began holding meetings on the Vanderbilt campus to advance the idea of a southern symposium on their own. The group included Andrew Lytle (when he was in town) and three Vanderbilt faculty members who had had no involvement in the Fugitive movement—John Donald Wade in English, Lyle Lanier in psychology, and Frank Lawrence Owsley in history.

A native of Marshallville, Georgia, Wade came to Vanderbilt in 1926, when the Fugitives had pretty much gone their separate ways. Largely on the strength of his biography of Augustus Baldwin Longstreet (published the previous year), he had been hired to start a graduate program in American literature. Although he lacked the polemical fire of Ransom and Davidson, he shared their affection for the rural South. Never feeling at home in the urban environs of Nashville, he boarded at a local hotel and returned to his family home in Marshallville at every opportunity.

Lyle Lanier brought the perspective of a social scientist to the discussions. Because social science reigned supreme at Chapel Hill, it was strategically valuable to have someone in the Vanderbilt group who could meet the enemy on his own terms. Born in Madison County, Tennessee, Lanier was the product of an inferior public school system (he began his education in a one-room schoolhouse), who had met the Vanderbilt entrance requirements only after taking a year of study at Valparaiso University in Indiana. Upon completing his graduate degrees at the George Peabody College for Teachers, he did research—on racial differences in intelligence—at the University of Chicago and taught at New York University. He joined the Vanderbilt faculty in 1928. Lanier was a distant cousin of Sidney Lanier and the man who introduced Cleanth Brooks to Robert Penn Warren. (He also married Catherine "Chink" Nichol, the woman who unwittingly helped inspire Red Warren's suicide attempt.) His approach to his academic discipline is suggested in a letter he wrote to Allen Tate on November 20, 1929:

> I want to keep on at scientific work on an intensive basis to provide me with materials for speculation and to deserve the right to evaluate scientific achievements critically. . . . I should like to think that sometime I might get far enough along to be able to demand some consideration and recognition when I try to show that what we have had in "scientific" America is a perversion of science in the disinterested sense. Science for its own sake doesn't get us very far, nor do the applications of it always bring benefits, but science for the sake of stimulating reflection has merits.[1]

If Lanier was just beginning what would prove to be a distinguished academic career, Frank Owsley had already established himself as a brilliant young historian of the American South. Born on a farm in the blackbelt of Montgomery County, Alabama, he completed the bachelor's and master's degrees in history at Alabama Polytechnic Institute (now Auburn University) before pursuing doctoral studies at the University of Chicago. He joined the Vanderbilt faculty in 1920, four years before finishing his Ph.D. dissertation on state rights in the Confederacy. Owsley published his dissertation in 1925 and traveled to England on a Guggenheim grant two years later. This leave enabled him to complete research on his second book, the vastly influential *King Cotton Diplomacy*, which he published in 1931.

David Robertson has suggested that in his early life, Owsley experienced the "savage ideal" that W. J. Cash would later only write about.[2] On the day in 1920 when he announced his departure from Birmingham Southern College to take a position at Vanderbilt, Owsley nearly came to blows with the president of Birmingham Southern, who tried to prevent him from leaving. "[H]e would have made a bad mistake if he had attacked me," Owsley recalls in his unpublished memoirs. "I am six feet, one inch, and I weighed about 185 pounds—all bone

---

1. See Rock, "Making and Meaning," 500.
2. See David Robertson, "Frog-Gigging in a Leaky Skiff," 181.

and muscle; and I am an excellent boxer and a good wrestler, and a most successful bare-knuckles fighter."[3] While a student in Auburn prior to World War I, Owsley had had to defend himself against some rock-throwing thugs. Although he survived that attack with only some cuts and bruises, he was stalked by the same gang while he was studying a few nights later. When he heard the scrape of a ladder against the windowsill of his upper-floor boardinghouse room, he was armed with several kettles of boiling water, which he poured on his attackers. Owsley brought that same combative spirit to his scholarship and his defense of the old South.

When Owsley arrived at Vanderbilt from Birmingham Southern, he brought with him his nineteen-year-old bride, Harriet Chappell Owsley. Eleven years her senior, Owsley had met his future wife when he coached the girls' basketball team on which she was the star center. Holding rather advanced views on the intellectual equality of women, Owsley treated Harriet Chappell with a respect that she did not receive from her other professors. In his memoirs, Owsley recalls: "Harriet was a lovely, shy girl, . . . popular with the boys and girls despite her shyness. She had the most gorgeous brass colored hair I have ever beheld. It is really not possible to describe it—the general effect was a great mass of finely spun, highly polished brass, yet a glint of copper red was there, when the sun shone on it."[4] Shortly after their arrival at Vanderbilt, Mrs. Owsley was waiting one morning to accompany her husband into chapel for the annual convocation. Mistaking her for a student, Edwin Mims pointed to the staircase. "Coeds to the balcony," he barked. "Coeds to the balcony."[5]

By virtue of their regular meetings at Vanderbilt, Ransom, Davidson, Wade, Lanier, and Owsley constituted a local nucleus of contributors for a southern symposium. From their respective locations outside Nashville, Tate and Lytle were also on board. (Red Warren and John Gould Fletcher would both join the project in early 1930.) Still, the symposium might never have gotten beyond the talking stage had Davidson not been spurred into action by the knowledge that Howard Mumford Jones of Chapel Hill was planning a collection of southern essays, which would almost certainly be dominated by North Carolina liberals. Fearing that he and his colleagues would be preempted if they did not move quickly on their plan, Davidson wrote to Tate on July 29, 1929: "I hope very much that you will soon complete your labors and return to the States. . . . [Y]our services are badly needed in a big fight which I foresee in the immediate future" (*Literary Correspondence*, 227).

In an effort to broaden the scope and appeal of the volume, Davidson hoped to

3. See Harriet Owsley, *Frank Lawrence Owsley: Historian of the Old South*, 29.
4. Ibid., 32.
5. Interview with Harriet Owsley, July 8, 1991.

solicit several outside contributors with national reputations. Among those who refused to participate were U. B. Phillips, William Yandell Elliott, and Gerald Johnson. (Not surprisingly, Davidson didn't get very far with the rest of the group when he proposed Edwin Mims as a potential contributor.) For a while it seemed as if Stringfellow Barr, editor of the *Virginia Quarterly Review,* might join the project, but an exchange of letters with Davidson in the spring of 1930 revealed prohibitive differences over the proper attitude to take toward industrialism. Although the correspondence between Davidson and Barr was quite civil, an article Barr published in the October 1930 issue of the *Virginia Quarterly Review* so raised the hackles of the men in Nashville that they wrote an open letter denouncing him. Vigorously defending himself in his own open letter (which was accompanied by a conciliatory personal note to Davidson), Barr proved to be a formidable critic of the Nashville traditionalists.

In his essay, "Shall Slavery Come South?" Barr bemoans the excesses of industrialism and concedes that slavery—for all its injustice—was a more humane system of economic organization. He also ridicules the philistine businessmen who seem to make a religion out of the free market. At the same time, Barr believes that the material goods that industrialism can produce will make it irresistible to the poverty-stricken South. Thus, to oppose industrialism is at best quixotic and at worst morally irresponsible. Rather than waste their time in a futile effort to slay the beast, Barr exhorts men of goodwill to tame it through enlightened social legislation. However, in making this argument, he could not resist taking some cheap shots at the anti-industrialists. At one point in his essay, Barr argues that "the traditionalists, frightened by the lengthening shadows of the smokestacks, take refuge in the good old days and in what I have called the apotheosis of the hoe. They make a charming but impotent religion of the past, make idols of the defunct horse and buggy, and mutter impotently at the radio."[6]

Ransom and Davidson completed the list of contributors to their symposium with Henry Blue Kline, a Vanderbilt graduate student; Herman Clarence Nixon, an economics professor who had recently left Vanderbilt for Tulane; and Stark Young, a New York theater critic who had been born and reared in Mississippi. Of the three, Kline was the least well known and the one most obviously out of his depth. Paul Conkin portrays him as little more than an academic toady who courted Ransom and Davidson in order to secure the professional advantage of having a published essay while still in graduate school. Ironically, Kline soon abandoned academia and spent much of his later career with what Davidson considered the Leviathan itself, the Tennessee Valley Authority. He was information officer for the Atomic Energy Commission when he died of uremic poisoning at the age of forty-six.

6. "Shall Slavery Come South?" 488.

Unlike Kline, Nixon was a well-respected scholar. He had been a classmate of Owsley's at Alabama Polytechnic Institute and was the man Owsley recommended to replace him at Birmingham Southern. Like Owsley, he had taken his doctorate under William E. Dodd at the University of Chicago. However, in his politics, Nixon was radically different from Owsley and the other contributors to the symposium. An admirer of the populist movement, Nixon was an early and ardent supporter of the New Deal. His objections to industrialism were more prudential than romantic. He believed that the glories of technology were being oversold in the South and that the champions of industry were promising more than they could deliver. Nixon was interested in the agrarian way of life because he was concerned with the well-being of the farmer, not because of a poetic or philosophical vision he was trying to advance.

In Stark Young, the Nashvillians landed their most nationally prominent contributor. A generation older than most of the other essayists, he was born in Como, Mississippi, in 1881, the son of one of Bedford Forrest's soldiers. After a sporadic private education in Oxford, Mississippi, Young entered the University of Mississippi at age fifteen. Five years later, he had earned an M.A. degree from Columbia University. For the next fifteen years, he pursued an academic career, teaching at the University of Mississippi, the University of Texas (where he founded the *Southwest Review*), and Amherst College. Then, in 1921, he left academia to assume editorial positions with the *New Republic* and *Theatre Arts Monthly*. By 1930, Young was a poet, a playwright, a translator, and America's foremost drama critic.

Writing to Tate on October 26, 1929, Davidson expressed enthusiasm over the prospect of Stark Young's participation in the symposium, provided "he understands the full import of the affair and does not treat it simply as a literary or sentimental excursion." "These points are in his favor," Davidson concludes: "he knows the tone of Southern life at its best and writes extremely well; he comes from Mississippi originally, but has wandered widely enough not to be accused of narrow parochialism; we need at least one such eminent Southern writer, outside our own circle, to strengthen our array, and he would put us in no danger, I think, of being swallowed up by New York" (*Literary Correspondence*, 235–36).

I

In November 1930, Harper and Brothers published the long-awaited southern symposium, *I'll Take My Stand: The South and the Agrarian Tradition*. As Thomas Daniel Young has noted, "if one were trying to assure the failure of a project, one could hardly improve on the procedure followed in putting together *I'll Take My*

Stand. Everything about arranging for the publication of the symposium, it would seem, was wrong. First of all the contributors [identified on the title page simply as "Twelve Southerners"] were scattered over two continents, from Nashville to New York, London, Oxford, and Paris. Many of them had never met, and some of them never would."[7] Although no editor was assigned, Donald Davidson predictably filled the vacuum. The introductory statement of principles, compiled mostly by John Crowe Ransom, was not even written until more than half the essays had been completed. Then, at the eleventh hour, a dispute over the title of the book nearly derailed the entire enterprise.

The final title was not selected until mid-1930. By then, two thirds of the essays were in, the statement of principles had been drafted, and the contract had been signed. When John Donald Wade suggested the evocative line from "Dixie" and Davidson added a colon and the descriptive subtitle, the rest of the Nashville contingent signaled their approval, or at least their acquiescence. Unfortunately, they did not bother to poll the brethren in exile. In June, Warren wrote to Tate: "I think the title . . . is the Goddamndest thing I ever heard of; for the love of God block it if you can."[8]

Although both Tate and Warren were devoted to the cultural legacy of the Old South, they feared that the sectional title might limit the appeal of the book and even subject it to caricature. On September 3, with publication only two months off, Tate, Warren, and Lytle drafted a letter to E. F. Saxton of Harper and Brothers. The letter, which never got beyond Ransom and Davidson, who talked the authors out of sending it, argues for keeping the subtitle but changing the main title to "Tracts against Communism." In the letter, the authors maintain that the new title has two advantages: "First, it implies the idea at the root of our position: we are opposed to all economic and social organization that imperils individualism, and we are thus opposed to industrialism for the same reasons as we are against Communism; they tend to the same social values. Secondly, this title is just paradoxical enough to attract attention; it will at least startle the ordinary reader who might be inclined to call us 'radical' by charging him with ultimate 'radicalism' if he continues to support the industrial system."[9]

In expressing their fear that the "ordinary reader" might interpret their position as radical, Tate, Warren, and Lytle were admitting that the symposium was at least in part an attack on capitalism. Their proposed title would have emphasized a related, equally important position—that the ills of industrialism could not be cured nor the cause of freedom and individualism be advanced simply

7. Thomas Daniel Young, *Waking Their Neighbors Up: The Nashville Agrarians Rediscovered*, 9.
8. Ibid., 17.
9. See Rock, "Making and Meaning," 68.

by transferring control of the industrial machinery from private capitalists to government bureaucrats. To hold otherwise, as most radical leftists always have, is to succumb to an egalitarian pipe dream. In commenting on the fall of the Soviet Union (some six decades after the publication of *I'll Take My Stand*), Eugene D. Genovese makes just such a point:

> The collapse of the socialist system of state ownership of the means of production has tellingly exposed the futility of the ideal of a radically egalitarian society of free and autonomous individuals. Every step of the way, the socialist experience, as well as the performance of social democracy, whenever it has come to power, has generated bureaucratic forms of stratification that have dashed radical-democratic and egalitarian dogmas. However much Marxists, among others, may ridicule Vilfredo Pareto's theory of the "circulation of elites," those elites, like the poor, we always have with us. The more they are denied in theory—the more we are inundated with anti-elitist rhetoric and compelled to proceed on radical egalitarian premises—the greater the room for irresponsibility and unaccountability in our leaders.[10]

Although the other contributors to the symposium probably agreed that state socialism was simply another form of industrialism, there were several problems with changing the title of the book as Tate, Warren, and Lytle had suggested. As a practical matter, such a change would have produced utter chaos. The book was already being promoted by Harper as *I'll Take My Stand*. That title represented the southern emphasis of the book as it actually existed. The title "Tracts against Communism" would have been seriously misleading. In a letter to Tate, Warren, and Lytle, dated September 5, 1930, Davidson and Ransom write: "The issue of communism is a good one that we might have made central to our exhibit, but did not. Actually, we have only one brief reference to that issue. If you take the title you name, you will have to arrange for a full-length paper to be included in the contents, which will elaborate the issue advertised. The book as it stands at present will have only the slightest relation to such a title" (*Literary Correspondence*, 408).

The issue of Communism might have seemed fairly peripheral to the American South of 1930. A decade earlier, many of the Communists residing in America had been deported and most of those who remained had gone underground. It would still be a few years before much of the American literary community would embrace Marxism as a response to the Great Depression. Nevertheless, milder left-wing alternatives to unbridled industrialism were being proposed by critics of the Nashville Agrarians. Such an argument had been made by Stringfellow Barr in his preemptive attack on the Nashvillians in the *Virginia Quarterly Review*.

10. Genovese, *Southern Tradition*, 35–36.

The issue was raised again when Ransom and Barr met in a debate in Richmond on November 14, 1930.

When Ransom, Davidson, and the Tates arrived at the Richmond City Auditorium a little before 8 P.M. on the evening of the debate, they found that many of the 3,500 seats were already taken. The audience included the governor of Virginia, the president of the University of Richmond, and such literary notables as Ellen Glasgow, James Branch Cabell, Henry Seidel Canby, and H. L. Mencken. "When Sherwood Anderson [who was to serve as moderator] rose to introduce the speakers, every seat in the auditorium was filled, and some of the Boy Scouts who had served as ushers, as well as a few latecomers, lined the back wall."[11]

In his prepared remarks, Ransom made explicit the argument that was implied in the rejected title "Tracts against Communism":

> By the least construction we can put upon Mr. Barr's language, he stands for the strongest unionism. And since he wants state action, he is a laborite—he is prepared to let labor become a political party and run the government as in Great Britain. But let us go further yet. Socialism of the variety practiced in a half-way house like Great Britain is a program of regulation which is merely temporizing. It approaches everyday closer to communism . . . and the grand finale of regulation, the millennium itself, is Russian communism.[12]

I'll Take My Stand was published two days later and has been generating controversy ever since.

II

Donald Davidson begins his contribution to *I'll Take My Stand*—"A Mirror for Artists"—by asking "What is the industrial theory of the arts?" Although such a theory has not been explicitly formulated, "there seems to be the phantom of a theory in the air."[13] If industrialists simply wanted to ban artists from their ideal society, as Plato wished to bar poets from his republic, defenders of art would immediately be on guard. Instead, industrialism poses as a modern equivalent of Maecenas, the Roman statesman who subsidized the work of Horace and Virgil. Industrialism patronizes art indirectly by providing more leisure with which to create and consume art. It can also provide direct patronage through industrial

---

11. Young, *Gentleman,* 220.
12. Ibid., 221.
13. Donald Davidson, "A Mirror for Artists," 28. Subsequent references will be cited parenthetically in the text.

philanthropy (or, as it has turned out, through government endowments). "Through his command over nature," Davidson writes, "the modern man can move his art about at will. Literary masterpieces, chosen by the best critics that can be hired, can be distributed once a month to hundreds of thousands of disciples of culture. Symphony concerts, heavily endowed and directed by world-famous experts, can be broadcast to millions" (32).

The problem with this apparently enlightened scheme of things is that it misconstrues art as simply another industrial commodity. To begin with, the leisure that industrialism produces is too often time stolen from mind-deadening labor. (Like Thoreau, Davidson sees a certain desperation in what we call play.) "We cannot separate our being into contradictory halves," Davidson observes, "without a certain amount of spiritual damage. The leisure thus offered is really no leisure at all; either it is pure sloth, under which the arts take on the character of mere entertainment, purchased in boredom and enjoyed in utter passivity, or it is another kind of labor, taken up out of a sense of duty, pursued as a kind of fashionable enterprise for which one's courage must be continually whipped up by reminders of one's obligation to culture" (34–35). Art as "mere entertainment" can be seen in the mass-produced commodities of our popular culture (movies, romance novels, music from Tin Pan Alley, and, later, prime-time television), while art as cultural obligation is enshrined in museums, libraries, and concert halls.

Davidson's attack on mass culture was not surprising coming from a non-commercial artist and a member of the academy. His criticism of the edifices of high culture was considerably more nuanced. To establish special places for art, even places of honor and reverence, is to separate it from the life of the people. "If paintings and sculptures are made for the purpose of being viewed in the carefully studied surroundings of art galleries, they have certainly lost their intimate connection with life. What is a picture for, if not to put on one's own wall? But the principle of the art gallery requires me to think that a picture has some occult quality in itself and for itself that can only be appreciated on a quiet anonymous wall, utterly removed from the tumult of my private affairs" (39). One could just as easily imagine eating his daily meals from crude dishes, only to be allowed occasionally to dine on fine china at a restaurant museum. Libraries and art galleries encourage their patrons to think "that the state—or some local Maecenas—will take care of their taste for them, just as the police take care of public safety" (40).

If the segregation of art from everyday life has had unfortunate consequences for society, it also has had an unhealthy effect on art. The artist as alienated rebel is a figure far more common in an industrial civilization than in any previous society. For that reason, romantic and lyric poetry have become the dominant modes of artistic expression in the modern world. "The poet sings less and less for the crowd in whose experiences he no longer shares intimately. The lonely artist appears, who sings for a narrower and ever diminishing audience; or having in effect no audience, he sings for himself" (44). Like Ransom, Davidson believes that the neohumanists missed the mark in the way that they lament this tendency in modern art. What they fail to realize is that no other art is really possible in an industrial society.

Davidson agrees with Ransom's assertion that critics who wish to return to a more classical conception of art must first concern themselves with the relationship between the artist and the society in which he lives. No matter how brilliant or well-intentioned, a merely aesthetic criticism will not do. "Harmony between the artist and society must be regained; the dissociation must be broken down. That can only be done, however, by first putting society itself in order. . . . As in the crisis of war, when men drop their private occupations for one supreme task, the artist must step into the ranks and bear the brunt of the battle against the common foe" (50, 51). No dialectical materialist calling for artists in uniform could have made a more explicit argument for socially engaged criticism. It is within this context that Davidson makes his stand for the Old South. In modern America, he argues, the most tangible alternative to industrial civilization and its sundry discontents is the traditional agrarian society that has held on longer in Dixie than in any other region of the country.

Because the society of the Old South was stable and hierarchical, it could be both homogeneous and pluralistic at the same time. When people know who they are and what they believe, they can more easily live in harmony with their neighbors. (Industrialism, in contrast, breeds a kind of dynamic instability.) At least equally important, the life of the agrarian South was lived in harmony with nature. Davidson concedes that, for all these advantages, the Old South did not produce much great art. But then, neither did the rest of America. Perhaps more to the point, the protracted ideological conflict between North and South meant that a disproportionate amount of the intellectual energy of the South was diverted from art to politics. (Ironically, Davidson seems to be proposing a similar diversion of energy in summoning southern artists to mount the barricades on behalf of Agrarianism.) In any event, Davidson rejects the notion that it is the sole, or even primary, function of art to produce "great" works. "If art has any real importance in life," he writes, "it is as a significant and beautiful way of shaping whatever there is to be shaped in life, secular and religious, private and public" (56). He believes that such conditions can obtain only in a provincial society uncorrupted by industrialism.

Curiously enough, Davidson does not turn his attention to the South until two-thirds of the way through his essay. As Daniel Joseph Singal has noted: "For all his talk of championing agrarianism, . . . it is noteworthy that he gives the agrarian existence far less concrete and detailed treatment than one might expect. . . . We find nothing like Lytle's injunction to 'throw out the radio and take down the fiddle from the wall.' " Although Davidson would be far more concrete and detailed about southern life in future essays, such as "Still Rebels, Still Yankees," there is some truth to Singal's observation that "Davidson cared little about rural life, . . . [that] what concerned him most was resolving the cultural conflict inside him, along with the fervent southern patriotism he was scarcely able to suppress."[14] "A Mirror for Artists" concludes with Davidson's lament that not enough of his fellow southern writers share that fervent patriotism.

In contemplating the equivocal southernness of the most heralded writers of the region, Davidson echoes the note of cultural ambivalence he had sounded in "The Artist as Southerner": "Why does Mr. Cabell seem so much nearer to Paris than to Richmond, to Anatole France than to Lee and Jefferson? Why does Miss Glasgow, self-styled the 'social historian' of Virginia, propagate ideas that would be more quickly approved by Oswald Garrison Villard than by the descendants of first families? Why are Dubose Heyward's and Paul Green's studies of negro life so palpably tinged with latter-day abolitionism? Why does T. S. Stribling write like a spiritual companion of Harriet Beecher Stowe and Clarence Darrow?" ("Mirror," 58–59). The answer Davidson gives us is that those writers are alienated from the agrarian tradition of the South. What Davidson could not have realized at the time was that the loss of that tradition would paradoxically make it more accessible to the imagination. The Southern Renascence produced an elegiac literature that might not have been possible without the triumph of industrialism. In literature as in life, death is the mother of beauty.

III

Had *I'll Take My Stand* been published a year and a half earlier, its argument against industrialism would have been regarded as merely quixotic. Coming thirteen months after the stock market crash, it struck many economic "realists" as hopelessly reactionary. Certainly, its celebration of a life of agrarian leisure would have seemed bitterly ironic to the masses of the unemployed, if they had been aware of the book at all. (For their own part, the Agrarians were convinced that the Great Depression simply demonstrated the unreliability of industrialism—what Marxists would call the contradictions of capitalism.) The hostile and sarcastic reviews that the book received from the mainstream press were largely predictable. It seemed that when the reviewers were not ridiculing the Old South itself, they were pointing out the difficulty (even absurdity) of returning to some preindustrial Eden.

14. Singal, *War*, 227.

Reviewing *I'll Take My Stand* along with Broadus and George Mitchell's *The Industrial Revolution in the South* for the *New York Times Book Review* of January 4, 1931, Arthur Krock left no doubt where his sympathies lay. At one point, he quotes the Mitchells with evident approval:

> The Old South expired like a fine gentleman who, after protracted years as a burden to his family, has passed on leaving sons and daughters penniless. What do we owe to the memory of this gallant? He once had a grand manner, but even in his heyday his linen was habitually soiled. Why embalm his remains and keep his few belongings like relics at the shrine of a saint? We paid him too much honor while he lived, and furthermore sad reminders of his handiwork are all about us in the South this long time afterward: poverty, race hatred, sterile fields, the childish and violent crowd gulled by the demagogue.[15]

A similar note was struck by W. B. Hesseltine, writing in the winter 1931 issue of the *Sewanee Review,* a magazine then edited by William S. Knickerbocker, who could never seem to decide whether to scorn or praise the Agrarians. According to Hesseltine: "Cheap novelists, visionless rhymesters, motion picture intellectuals, and writers of advertisements, have seized upon the broad verandas of the mythical manor houses of the old South and burst into rapturous paeans of praise for a civilization which never existed." Later in that same paragraph, Hesseltine contends that "there are even said to be 'professional' Southerners who stand at attention while the band plays 'Dixie,' and interlard their conversation with references to 'befo de wah.' "[16] Although the Agrarians might have pled guilty to being professional southerners, they hardly seem to qualify as cheap novelists, visionless rhymesters, motion picture intellectuals, or writers of advertisements. The fact that Hesseltine felt compelled to deal in such obviously irrelevant caricature reveals more about his own personality than about the book he was ostensibly reviewing.

When Knickerbocker himself discussed *I'll Take My Stand* (in the December 20, 1930, issue of the *Saturday Review of Literature*), he offered a more balanced (some would say schizophrenic) assessment. While praising the book's literary qualities (he compared it to a prose symphony), he found its practical suggestions fatally misguided. Apparently, Andrew Lytle gave the game away when he wrote about his hypothetical farmer visiting the local blacksmith shop. "[I]f we tolerate industrialism in rudimentary forms," Knickerbocker asks, "where shall we stop? Doubtless, the blacksmith didn't mine the iron for his horseshoes." To set up an antithesis between industrialism and the culture of the Old South simply

---

15. Arthur Krock, "Industrialism and the Agrarian Tradition in the South."
16. W. B. Hesseltine, "Look Away, Dixie," 97.

defies history. "Cotton became king only after the invention of the cotton gin, and thereafter maintained his reign through the healthy functioning of the industrial system with its factories, cities, ships, railways, banks."[17] Even if we are speaking only in relative terms and concede that the antebellum South was less industrialized than the North, it is not clear that an independent South would have remained that way. Writing in the spring 1931 issue of *Hound and Horn*, Thomas D. Mabry argues that the Confederacy would have found it easier to secede politically from the Union than to insulate itself from the pressures of the international marketplace.[18]

In a similar vein, Henry Hazlitt employs the tired old argument of the slippery slope. Reviewing *I'll Take My Stand* in the January 14, 1931, issue of the *Nation*, Hazlitt writes: "[I]f Mr. Ransom's fears of Progress had always prevailed we should still be in the savage state—assuming that we had at least accepted such technological advancements as flint and the spearhead. Mr. Ransom may reply that he is merely proposing to dig in and stop progressing *now*, which, we may be confident, was precisely the position of the conservatives among our paleolithic ancestors."[19] The false alternative that Hazlitt poses, and that many other critics of Agrarianism implicitly endorse, is between unlimited industrialization and a return to the Stone Age. Technology does not offer its blessings without demanding something in return. The Agrarians were simply asking whether the South, at this particular point in history, was being asked to give up too much in exchange for too little. Hazlitt's title—"So Did King Canute"—suggests an invidious comparison. The proper Agrarian response might be titled "So Did Dr. Faustus."

An even more thoroughgoing critique of the Agrarians' position was offered by the liberal southern journalist Gerald W. Johnson (who had earlier turned down an offer to contribute to the symposium). Reviewing *I'll Take My Stand* and three other books in the January 1931 issue of the *Virginia Quarterly Review*, Johnson infers that the Nashville Twelve derived their knowledge of the South entirely "from the pages of Joel Chandler Harris and Thomas Nelson Page," while being "completely oblivious to the Vardamans, the Bleases, the Heflins, the Tom Watsons, who are the delight of [contemporary] Southern agrarianism."[20]

The next month, Johnson made a more extended, if qualified, defense of southern industrialism in *Harper's* magazine. While he condemns the brutal suppression of recent strikes in the textile mills of Gastonia and Marion, North Carolina, he argues that industrialism itself was not responsible for these excesses. If anything, industrialism has provided the wealth necessary to maintain such

17. William S. Knickerbocker, "Back to the Hand," 68.
18. Thomas D. Mabry, "Look Away, Look Away," 438–39.
19. Henry Hazlitt, "So Did King Canute," 48.
20. Gerald W. Johnson, "The South Faces Itself," 157.

educational institutions as Duke University and the University of North Carolina. (For that matter, Vanderbilt itself was founded by a northern industrialist.) The real choice facing the South is whether to maintain the current level of economic progress or return to the poverty of 1900. The glories of 1850 (real or imagined) simply cannot be recovered. Referring directly to *I'll Take My Stand,* he writes:

> At first blush it seems incredible that twelve men, all born and raised in the South, all literate, and all of legal age, could preach such doctrine without once thrusting the tongue in the cheek or winking the other eye. . . . Of such a philosophy one can only say that it smells horribly of the lamp, that it was library-born and library-bred, and will perish miserably if it is ever exposed for ten minutes to the direct rays of the sun out in the daylight of reality.[21]

One of the most interesting and oddly sympathetic responses to Agrarianism came from the literary critic Malcolm Cowley. A native of rural Pennsylvania, Cowley became fast friends with Allen Tate in the early thirties. (He recalls singing Stephen Foster plantation songs with Tate while returning from an afternoon visit to a Civil War cemetery: "At last I said weakly, 'You know those songs we've been singing? They were all written by a Pittsburgh boy.'") Although a party-line Stalinist, Cowley found himself emotionally drawn to the vision of the Agrarians. Looking back from the perspective of fifty years, he writes: "I too had been raised in the country and was never happy for long where I couldn't feel the soil under my feet. . . . [Like the Agrarians] I sometimes pictured an ideal society, and it was never situated in a metropolis ruled by workers each of whom had an equal share in the products of antiseptic factories; rather it was an open landscape where the houses were not too thickly scattered in groves of very old trees."[22]

As appealing as he may have found the agrarian dream, Cowley believed that it was wildly impractical. The economic rewards of subsistence farming were far too meager. An aristocratic society might benefit those at the top, but it depended on the exploitation of a peasant class—mostly black and white sharecroppers. Cowley saw the Agrarians as an ironic refutation of their own philosophy. Having themselves been driven off the land, they were prevented from carrying their theories into practice. "Condemned by their superior abilities to live in cities, they might celebrate an earlier way of life, with its good customs, and might gather in sacramental feasts over a country ham, but meanwhile they belonged to the underpaid white-collar staffs of the new educational factories."[23]

21. Gerald W. Johnson, "No More Excuses: A Southerner to Southerners," 333.
22. Malcolm Cowley, *The Dream of the Golden Mountains: Remembering the 1930s,* 199, 201.
23. Ibid., 203.

10

THE LONG CAMPAIGN

The summer after *I'll Take My Stand* was published, Donald Davidson began an association that would last for the rest of his life. He left the sweltering heat and urban congestion of Nashville for the balmy weather and bucolic surroundings of rural Vermont. In 1920, Middlebury College had begun a summer program called the Bread Loaf School of English. The faculty and students for this venture were drawn from all over the United States and from several foreign countries. By the time Davidson joined the Bread Loaf faculty in 1931, the school was known as the most distinguished program of its kind in the world. The summer session of the Bread Loaf School, which generally ran from late June to early August, was followed by a two-week writers' conference that regularly attracted some of the contemporary giants in literature, criticism, and publishing. Davidson often stayed for the conference, where he enjoyed a degree of creative stimulation he had not known since the breakup of the Fugitive group in the midtwenties.

From the mid-nineteenth century until his death on February 23, 1915, the largest landowner in the Bread Loaf region was an eccentric bachelor named Joseph Battell. A sickly youth who suffered from weak lungs, Battell devoted the first two years of the the War between the States to a walking tour of Europe, during which he seems to have spent much of his time ogling milkmaids and serving girls through a spyglass. Upon returning to the United States, Battell became convinced that his health would be improved by recreation and light exercise in the mountain air of Ripton, just southeast of his hometown of Middlebury, Vermont. He so liked the area that he bought three hundred acres of land and never left. By the spring of 1866, Battell had decided to make alterations to his home and open it to the public. Called Bread Loaf Inn because of its location near the famous Bread Loaf Mountain, Battell's establishment grew over the years as wings and outbuildings were added to the original structure. Despite early financial difficulties, the enterprise eventually became a success because of the stunning natural surroundings and Battell's own legendary hospitality.

Because of the short growing season and the rocky soil, the area around Bread Loaf was never particularly good farmland. From the 1830s on, sawmills began springing up. By 1870, much of the Green Mountain slopes had been stripped of their forests. In an effort to halt this scourge, Battell used most of his family legacy to buy up sizable amounts of land surrounding his own. His grounds manager, John Houston, carried blank deeds with him wherever he went so that he could purchase land on the spot from any willing seller. (If there was a dispute concerning the ownership of a piece of land, he would simply buy both claims.) Eventually, Battell increased his holdings a hundredfold and preserved the natural beauty of the region. " 'Some folks go to Europe,' Battell would often say, 'and pay $10,000 for a painting and hang it up in their home where none but their friends can see it. I buy a mountain for that money and it is hung up by nature where everybody can see it. And it is infinitely more handsome than any picture ever painted.' "[1] When the automobile first made its appearance in Vermont, Battell did his best to keep the infernal machine far removed from the sanctity of Bread Loaf.

Upon his death in 1915, Battell left thirty thousand acres of land, including the Bread Loaf Inn and a good deal of the Green Mountain Forest to nearby Middlebury College. Without Battell's magnetic presence and single-minded devotion, the inn lost money for the next five years. By 1920, the Middlebury trustees were ready to get out of the hotel business altogether, when the president of the college and several members of the faculty suggested that the inn could be made the site of a summer graduate school in English language and literature similar to summer programs in foreign languages regularly taught on the Middlebury campus. Thus, in 1920, the Bread Loaf School of English began offering master's level study in English and American literature, teaching methods, public speaking and debate, theory and practice in modern drama, and composition. The writers' conference, which began in 1926, was initially an expedient to keep the inn open and filled nearer to capacity up through Labor Day.

By the time that Davidson arrived in Vermont in 1931, Bread Loaf had been a summer home to such luminaries as Hervey Allen, Joseph Auslander, Stephen Vincent Benet, Willa Cather, Floyd Dell, Max Eastman, Sinclair Lewis, Gorham Munson, Louis Untermeyer, and the spiritual godfather of the place—Robert Frost. Peter J. Stanlis, who was a student at Bread Loaf during the late thirties and early forties, remembers standing outside the Middlebury campus chapel in

---

1. David Howard Bain and Mary Smyth Duffy, eds., *Whose Woods These Are: A History of the Bread Loaf Writers' Conference, 1926–1992,* 9.

1938 and reading the inscription from Psalms 95:4—"The strength of the hills is his also."

> The chapel faced toward the east and was silhouetted on the rim of a long sloping hill overlooking the gray-granite, ivy-covered buildings of "Old Stone Row" on the lower campus. Beyond these buildings, farther downhill, lay the village of Middlebury, shire town of Addison County, largely hidden under green summer foliage, but flecked here and there by the first faint gold of approaching Indian summer. From the northeast the dark gray shadow of Chipman Hill covered the village. . . . Six miles to the southeast lay the tiny village of East Middlebury, nestled against the foot of Ripton Gorge, along which ran state highway 125, the road that wound its way four miles through the first range of the Green Mountains to the village of Ripton.

The Bread Loaf Inn and the campus of the school were located three miles beyond this point. "The cottages of the campus lay on both side of the road, in an open clearing of a large plateau surrounded by evergreen forests and mountain ranges. Almost directly north was the most conspicuous landmark from the campus, Bread Loaf Mountain, rising 3,823 feet high."[2]

Davidson found Bread Loaf in 1931 to be a much more hospitable environment than Vanderbilt. Not only was the area itself more rural, but his colleagues were more congenial. While failing to share his fierce southern loyalties, they did not perceive those sentiments as either a threat or an embarrassment. (The New South types at Vanderbilt saw them as both.) When he delivered a lecture titled "Southern Poets and Current Issues," it was greeted with interest and goodwill by his largely Yankee audience. In their official history of the Bread Loaf Writers' Conference, David Howard Bain and Mary Smyth Duffy speculate that "it was perhaps at the faculty reception later that evening that Bread Loaf saw the genesis of the 'Ten O'Clock Rule': It was forbidden that anyone could discuss the Civil War after ten at night, on pain of expulsion from the faculty club and payment of a fine, the amount of which varied."[3]

On July 29, 1931, with most of his first summer at Bread Loaf behind him, Davidson wrote to Allen Tate:

> Perhaps I am a little of a curiosity among these folks, to whom the South is really *very* remote; and I may be all the more so because I'm unlike James Southall Wilson, who was here the last three years in the Southern niche of the faculty. But I'm having a *good* time. We all are—Theresa & Mary

2. Peter J. Stanlis, "Acceptable in Heaven's Sight: Robert Frost at Bread Loaf, 1939–1941," 181, 182.
3. Bain and Duffy, *Whose Woods These Are,* 24.

have gained in strength & spirits—even in weight, though all of us have been doing strenuous mountain climbing. All in all, I'll be quite content, I think, to accept the invitation to come back here another time—it's an ideal summer school, I should say. (*Literary Correspondence*, 264)

A week later, on August 11, 1931, Davidson wrote to Andrew Lytle: "I have had a glorious summer here. We have all had much outdoor life and good pleasure among good people."[4]

I

Around 4:30 in the afternoon of February 19, 1932, flames were observed in the cupola on the northeast corner of Wesley Hall on the Vanderbilt campus. The fire continued to rage until late that night, destroying much of the interior of the building and leaving only the strongly based brick walls still standing. All that firemen could do was shoot water onto the ruins until noon the following day and fence off the area to prevent anyone wandering near enough to be injured by falling debris. The greatest blow was to the theological library contained in the building. In all, fifteen thousand volumes, many of them old and irreplaceable, were destroyed. Some books that had been thrown from the second floor library were soon covered by falling water and sparks. Several graduate students lost their theses in various stages of completion.

A multitude of images stayed in the minds of those who witnessed the fire. There were "chandeliers hanging in the glow of flame-baked rooms" and "the gaunt face of Wesley Hall as viewed from Hillsboro [Avenue] at 9 p.m., with the windows laced with flames." The towers of the building had seemed to waver for a few minutes before being engulfed in fire and crashing down amid a trail of sparks. A canary sang in its cage on the fourth floor, apparently oblivious to the inferno overhead. An airplane, which had hovered over the building shortly after the fire was discovered, flew back over later after the flames had completely lit up the night sky. Newsreel cameramen proceeded to shoot footage as a group of onlookers formed around a student playing on a rescued piano. A family that lived in the building saved a bale of coat hangers but forgot to bring out a chest of silver. One professor, A. M. Harris, left his scattered belongings because he had to go on stage in *Tweedles* at the Little Theater. John Chu, a Ph.D. candidate from Soochow, China, was heard to say, "I humbly bow to the god of fire. What is, must be."[5]

4. Except where otherwise indicated, the letters cited in this chapter are housed in the Fugitive Collection of the Heard Library.
5. Don Price, "Wesley Hall Burned," 103.

Among the ten faculty members and seventy-five students who became temporarily homeless were Donald Davidson and his family. Although they were not injured, Davidson lost most of his meager possessions, including books, correspondence, and back numbers of the *Fugitive*. The uncertainty and depression that had plagued him ever since the breakup of the Fugitive group now became even more acute. As Michael O'Brien has pointed out, "the time between *The Tall Men* in 1927 and the summer of 1932 was remarkably barren" for Davidson.[6] Although he was deeply involved in the Agrarian enterprise, he had failed to produce a history of southern literature that he had hoped to write in 1929. Despite going away for the summer to the Yaddo writers' colony, he hit a creative block and never completed the book. Now with the loss of his home, less than three years later, it seemed as if Davidson was at the end of his tether personally as well as professionally. He and his family were reduced to accepting charity before they could get back on their feet.

The fire at Wesley Hall was simply the most recent in a series of misfortunes that Davidson had suffered. In late 1930, Sen. Luke Lea, publisher of the *Tennessean*, saw his business empire come apart. Ironically, Lea, who was one of the most ruthless industrialists in the South, had been the patron of Davidson's book page. A hero of the First World World War and the model for Bogan Murdoch in Robert Penn Warren's *At Heaven's Gate*, Lea eventually landed in jail for his role in the $17 million collapse of the Asheville Central Bank and Trust Company. In November 1930, as this disaster was occurring, Lea discontinued the *Tennessean's* book page, thus cutting Davidson's annual income in half. To make matters worse, Will Davidson had fallen critically ill. After his death in February 1931, Donald became engaged in a protracted struggle with the state commissioner of education over the payment of his father's full salary as school superintendent for Lincoln County. On January 18, 1931, he wrote to John Gould Fletcher: "I have simply been in a state of confusion and agitation for two months or more."[7] His frame of mind was not improved by the often hostile reaction to *I'll Take My Stand*.

For the first six months after the symposium appeared, the Agrarians engaged their opponents in several public debates. Although Ransom was the most frequent spokesman for the group, Davidson took the stage against William S. Knickerbocker in Columbia, Tennessee, on May 21, 1931. Because of the proximity to Nashville, a strong contingent of Agrarian sympathizers was on hand to cheer for their side. (The Ransoms, the Tates, and the Laniers left Nashville in the middle of the afternoon in the Ransoms' car and stopped for a picnic near Franklin, just outside of Nashville, before continuing on to Columbia.)

6. Michael O'Brien, "Donald Davidson: The Creed of Memory," 189.
7. Both letters from Davidson to Fletcher cited in this chapter are housed in the University of Arkansas Library at Fayetteville.

As with other debates, the auditorium of Central High School was practically filled when the Nashvillians arrived at 7:30. Twenty-five minutes later, Davidson and Knickerbocker took the stage. Toward the end of his opening statement, Davidson used a metaphor from his Fugitive days, comparing those who would argue for controlled industrialism to "the people who let a dragon into the house and then set about a wild speculation as to whether the dragon should be required to eat in the dining-room or the kitchen, and what his hours of feeding, and his diet should be."[8] This was the last of five debates between defenders of the dragon and his would-be slayers.

On March 30, 1932, Davidson wrote to Edwin Mims to request leave for the next academic year. Explaining the rationale for his timing, he writes: "Since the Wesley Hall fire, my worldly goods are reduced to very small proportions. This is a severe loss, but it may be turned to an advantage of a sort. If I am going to have a leave of absence at all, it is best that I should have it now, while I have no establishment to maintain and before I undertake the expense of starting another one." Although Davidson was not granted a paid leave, he took the year off anyway, moving his family into a small house on John Donald Wade's ancestral farm in Marshallville, Georgia.

Located just southwest of Macon, Marshallville is part of the peach-growing region of central Georgia. His residence there afforded Davidson an opportunity to write and study in what he regarded as a truly agrarian environment. According to Paul Conkin, "he relaxed, felt loved and appreciated, gave plenty of speeches, made lasting friends, and soon dubbed this fertile and friendly land a modern Eden." In addition to pursuing his literary vocation, Davidson used the year in Marshallville to renew his interest in folk music. "He visited, and exalted in, old harp singing at a rural church, and would soon love nothing as much as the ballads and church music preserved from British sources in the backwoods of the South."[9]

On October 2, 1932, Davidson described his new life in a letter to Wade back in Nashville:

> Well, here we are, as you see, and it's a quiet Sunday night in Marshallville, and we are very much at ease with the world and very happy. I should have written you much earlier but for the considerable agony of bustling around to get provisions in the larder and tin pans and knickknacks on the shelves.
>
> We "moved in" on Tuesday last, our freight having arrived Monday. Your dear mother (she is perfect in everything) insisted that we remain with her even for Tuesday morning breakfast. She has been a fountain of

8. Young, *Gentleman*, 277.
9. Conkin, *Southern Agrarians*, 97.

thoughtfulness and kindness—sending Oleen (is it Irish spelling, or what?) over with stuffed peppers, and syrup, and sausage, and Lord knows how many good things. And we have had many good hours of talk and fellowship, in garden, house, and on the porch.

As the letter continues, Davidson paints an increasingly idyllic picture of life on the farm. Although "the condition of the exchequer" has so far forced him and Theresa to do their own domestic work, he cheerfully labels the situation "an experiment in economics." In time, "human weakness" will almost certainly cause them to take on the "beaming Katy Lou" as a full-time cook. At present, she is doing only the laundry and an occasional day or two of cleaning. "[S]he *almost* adopted us *willy-nilly*," Davidson writes. "Is this the way of Georgia negroes?"

After noting that Mary was well started in school and that all the neighbors had proven themselves to be "extremely well-spoken and genial," Davidson assures Wade that his fence is about in place. "We have dug up a few spare yards of earth, back of the garage, and planted a tiny 'winter garden' that may or may not provide food; at any rate it will provide exercise and adventure." The environment has also enhanced Davidson's appreciation of Wade's contribution to *I'll Take My Stand,* "The Life and Death of Cousin Lucius," which he had been rereading "in the surroundings where it ought to be read." "It went to my heart, more than ever," Davidson writes. "I think, as I told your mother the other evening, that it is the one piece in the book that has a chance of living permanently, going beyond the temporal controversy. The others will lose some point with time; yours won't."

Davidson concludes his letter by thinking of his colleagues, whose ill fate it is not to be with him.

> I'm a sort of fortunate Lazarus dwelling in Abraham's bosom right now, and I do wish for sweet charity's sake that they did not have to stay in the smoking cauldron of Nashville (the damned old place, which I nevertheless am quite attached to!) and give them all the best regards and good wishes. Let them picture me sucking a stalk of sugar cane, under a pecan tree, reciting, under these extraordinarily spacious Georgia skies where swallows and night-hawks crowd the evening air, the southern and agrarian equivalent of *Om Mane Padme Om.* I am at any rate blissfully engaged, though slothful, and cannot at the moment conceive how any human being could grade freshman themes and attend committee meetings in order to make a living.

The year in Marshallville provided Davidson a period of intense creativity. Although the end of the book page deprived him of an important outlet for his views (along with much-needed income), it did provide him with an opportunity to write longer essays and to publish more widely. One project to which he contributed was a collection of essays on the South edited by William Terry Couch of Chapel Hill. Running to nearly seven hundred pages, *Culture in the South* (1934) was a more diffuse and less polemical volume than *I'll Take My Stand*. Davidson's own essay, "The Trend in Literature," offers a well-informed survey of the southern literary scene, based largely on his experience as book editor for the *Tennessean*.

Much of "The Trend in Literature" seems dated today, both in its emphases and its judgments. For example, Davidson praises William Faulkner's literary artistry without finding him to be a particularly important or appealing writer. Of *The Sound and the Fury*, he observes: "We know there is tragedy, but it is hardly the tragedy of a single person. Only the Negroes, chirping insensitively as crickets all through, are unmoved by it and furnish an ironic contrast."[10] Faulkner's subsequent work meets with even less approval: "Mr. Faulkner has pushed his horrors so far in his later books—such as *Sanctuary* and *As I Lay Dying*—that he reduces his own theme to something like absurdity. One feels inclined to accuse him of being either a literary sadist or a harlequin who is bound to have his brutal joke, and one wishes that his cool objectivity could be better applied" (206).

The paragraph that sheds greatest light on Davidson's approach to criticism reiterates the theme of social engagement that runs through "A Mirror for Artists." "I am assuming, contrary to much modern doctrine," he asserts, "that a writer's aesthetic acts can not in the last analysis be separated from his other acts as a member of society. Questions of genius must be left out of consideration; they are beyond reach of argument, although it is fair to add that, if society provides no opportunities, the Miltons are likely to remain mute and inglorious in country churchyards" (198).

Taking Milton as his touchstone, Davidson notes that the poet's verse harmonizes with his character; "and back of that, it harmonizes with a literary and social tradition which is English in the national sense and 'classic' and European in the larger sense. Milton was 'integrated.' When he came to do his greatest work, he did not have to repudiate his personal convictions and renounce England, even though he disagreed with the party in power." Davidson argues that Milton was perhaps the last English poet of whom this was true. By the time we get to Dryden later in the seventeenth century, we find a poet "who had trouble in deciding what to believe, and who, under the impact of French culture and the new rationalism, established a critical denial of the English tradition" (198). Apparently, Davidson, like Eliot, believes that English poetry took a wrong turn with Dryden, but he defines the problem in social rather than epistemological

10. Donald Davidson, "The Trend in Literature," 205. Subsequent references will be cited parenthetically in the text.

terms. If there is hope for southern literature, it lies in following the example of Milton, not that of Dryden. If the South is to recover a sense of literary tradition, it must stop listening to the courtly muses of Europe and even to the seductive blandishments of the urban Northeast. It must take its rightful place as a nation within a nation. Although he does not say so in this essay, one of the purposes of the Agrarian movement was to enable the South to do precisely that.

II

Throughout the first half of the 1930s, when the depression was at its lowest ebb, a nucleus of eight brethren located in or near Nashville tried to make Agrarianism into a full-blown literary and social movement. Ransom, Davidson, Owsley, Wade, and Lanier, all of whom were still teaching at Vanderbilt, were joined by Warren, who had accepted a temporary appointment in the English department in the fall of 1931. (After finishing his bachelor's in literature at Oxford in 1930, he had taught for a year at Southwestern College in Memphis.) Andrew Lytle was nearby, at his farm in Guntersville, Alabama, and, in the summer of 1930, Allen Tate moved from New York to a home in Clarksville, Tennessee. (Called Benfolly in honor of Tate's brother Ben, it would become an unofficial way station for Allen and Caroline's many literary friends from both America and Europe.) John Gould Fletcher in Little Rock and H. C. Nixon in New Orleans were too far away to be part of the inner circle in Tennessee, while Stark Young in New York and Henry Blue Kline in Knoxville were pursuing careers divorced from the Agrarian enterprise. (In 1934, Young did publish *So Red the Rose,* a vastly popular novel that celebrated the culture of the Old South.)

"In the dark years of 1931 and 1932," writes Paul Conkin, "the agrarian brethren gathered whenever possible at Benfolly, particularly during the winter months, when they were teaching and the European and New York crowd stayed away. The two 'boys,' Lytle and Warren, were practically family members. On weekends Davidson . . . , the Ransoms, the Laniers, and the Owsleys would also join in parties, picnics, late-night drinking bouts, endless games of charades, interlaced with deep and solemn agrarian conspiracies."[11] For various reasons, none of these conspiracies (buying a county newspaper, starting a new political party, organizing a second symposium) seemed to get off the ground. After five debates in late 1930 and early 1931, public interest in the cause appeared to wane, and the Agrarians themselves were involved with other projects and harried by a variety of personal problems.

11. Conkin, *Southern Agrarians,* 93.

In early 1932, Caroline Gordon won a Guggenheim Fellowship, and the Tates left Tennessee for a year in Europe. In September, Davidson left Vanderbilt for his year in Marshallville. The letters that Davidson and Tate exchanged during this time reflect their mutual frustration at the failure of the Agrarian movement to catch on. Davidson believed that the problem lay in the Agrarians' unwillingness to risk their comfort and security for the cause. In a letter dated October 29, 1932, he writes:

> People who are ill, poor, hard-worked, troubled with family responsibilities, deaths, fires, the woes of relatives, are not in a position to give a great deal of time to civic agitation. . . . [I]sn't it true that not a one of our wives (who are all paragons, the Lord knows,—the top of excellence among womankind) would say to her warrior: Go forth with this spear and shield against industrialism and return with your shield or upon it. That is, take that $500 out of the savings bank and use it to organize a political party among the farmers and small merchants of Alabama. That sort of thing simply doesn't happen among us; it will only happen if times get much worse, and we get much more passionate in our seriousness. (*Literary Correspondence*, 275–76)

The Agrarian movement might have continued to languish indefinitely had it not been for the efforts of the New York editor Seward Collins. The son of a wealthy Syracuse businessman, Collins was educated at the Hill School and Princeton. After working briefly for *Vanity Fair,* he became publisher of a literary magazine called the *Bookman* in 1927. (This was the publication for which Davidson had written his account of the demise of the *Tennessean*'s book page.) By 1933, his interests had turned from literature to politics and economics. On March 8, 1933, he wrote a long letter to Davidson describing his plans for a new magazine, which would soon be called the *American Review.*

Collins tells Davidson that he began his career believing in all of the "delusions and fallacies" of liberalism. When the writings of the neohumanists Irving Babbitt and Paul Elmer More disabused him of these notions, he began pushing neohumanism in the *Bookman.* In the meantime, he began reading some of the European neoscholastics and the British Distributists. But his greatest epiphany came when *I'll Take My Stand* was published: "I was exhilarated and cheered[,] as I have seldom been, to find men right here in my own country sharing and expounding the ideas I had come upon in so painfully roundabout a fashion." Later in that same letter, he writes: "while other points of view are not ruled out, it is the Agrarian view that I want to see emphasized. . . . What I would like would be to have you think of the magazine as being in large measure your own; quite at your disposal for anything you cared to say." This seemed to be precisely what the brethren had been hoping for—a national forum that would not require any of them to withdraw his final $500 in savings. In fact, Collins was promising to pay a penny a word for their thoughts.

Less than a month later, Collins met with eight of the Agrarians at Andrew Lytle's farm in Alabama. Davidson attended the meeting after what he calls "a long and devious bus journey" from Marshallville. What lingered most clearly in his mind, however, was his return trip, when he had to spend several hours waiting to change buses in Rome, Georgia. As he walked around the town, he looked at the statue of General Forrest and "at the bronze she-wolf suckling the infants Romulus and Remus on the lawn of the municipal building." Then he "climbed a high hill, overlooking the meeting of the Coosa and Oostenaula, and found, set apart in a large and beautiful cemetery, a section devoted to the fallen warriors of the Confederacy" (*Southern Writers,* 61). "There," he writes, "I looked upon the tombs of the Confederate dead, but not at all with the eyes and mood of the desolate young man in Mr. Tate's great poem. In the sparkling light of that Sabbath day, after the meeting of the night before, with hopeful prospects ahead, I was not in the least desolate" (61–62).

On the Confederate monument in that cemetery, Davidson found the following inscription:

> This monument is the testimony of the present to the future that these were they who kept the faith as it was given them by the fathers. Be it known by this token that these men were true to the traditions of their lineage. Bold, generous, and free, firm in conviction of the right, ready at their country's call, steadfast in their duty, faithful even in despair, and illustrated in the unflinching heroism of their deaths, the freeborn courage of their lives. How well they served their faith, their people know; a thousand battlefields attest; dungeon and hospital bear witness. To their sons they left but honor and their country. Let this stone forever warn those who keep these valleys that only their sires are dead; the principles for which they fought can never die. (62)

III

Despite the fact that Seward Collins was primarily interested in economics while the Agrarians maintained a broader emphasis on the arts and humanities, the two forces came together out of mutual need. Because the new magazine solicited all its content, it was able to maintain a consistency of viewpoint lacking in such liberal journals as the *New Republic* and the *Nation.* At the same time, it did not promote the strict party line found in Marxist publications. Although Collins initially saw Agrarianism as only one of several related movements to be featured in the *American Review,* it soon gained dominance because of the incredible productivity of the southerners, who had published approximately seventy articles and reviews in its pages by early 1937. With twenty-one appearances, Donald Davidson was one of the magazine's most frequent contributors.

In October 1934, Davidson published "New York and the Hinterland," the first of a two-part article jointly titled "The Lands Were Golden," in the *American Review*. This was one of several essays in which Davidson developed his belief that the real cultural strength of the nation lay in the provinces, or hinterland, rather than in the cosmopolitan Northeast. The dichotomy he defines here is not so much between North and South as between East and West. From the very beginning of our nation, eastern sophisticates had viewed the raw frontiersman with scorn and condescension. By the 1920s, that attitude had become the dominant note in our literature. New York, in particular, had become the worst offender.

> New York transmitted, to the one people on earth who were freest of class-consciousness, the Marxian theory of the war of the classes. To the least neurotic and energetic of races, it offered the Freudian doctrine of repressions and complexes. To a people the greater part of whom were schooled in Protestant religion and morality New York presented, with a knowing leer, under the guise of literary classics, the works of voluptuaries and perverts, the teeming pages of *Psychopathia Sexualis,* and all the choicest remains of the literary bordellos of the ancient and modern world. German Expressionism, French Dadaism, the erotic primitivism of D. H. Lawrence, the gigantic *fin de siecle* pedantries and experimentalisms of James Joyce, the infantilism of Gertrude Stein and various Parisian coteries—these furnished the catchwords of all the clever people.[12]

Although Davidson failed to note that the magazine in which these words were written and the firm that published *I'll Take My Stand* were also located in New York, his larger point would have remained unchanged—the dominant literary culture in America was hostile to the customs and values of the majority of the American people.

At the same time that our imaginative literature lampooned the American provinces (often in novels that became best-sellers in those same provinces), a new generation of historians was discovering cultural vitality in the hinterland. Davidson mentions the achievement of the popular historians Claude Bowers, James Truslow Adams, and Ulrich B. Phillips. Even more impressive are two scholarly works of "revolutionary importance"—Frederick Jackson Turner's *The Significance of the Sections in United States History* and Vernon Parrington's *Main Currents in American Thought.*

---

12. Donald Davidson, *The Attack on Leviathan: Regionalism and Nationalism in the United States,* 163. Subsequent references will be cited parenthetically in the text.

The second part of "The Lands Were Golden," "The Two Old Wests," is considerably less polemical than "New York and the Hinterland." Here, Davidson is describing, indeed celebrating, the trans-Appalachian region that he regards as America's heartland. The region where he felt most at home was not even an area as large as the Old Confederacy but rather the size of the Old Southwest. As Fred Hobson notes, the theory of sectionalism that Davidson was developing in the 1930s regarded the seaboard South as "the home of spiritual Yankees with Southern accents."[13] The tall men who resided across the mountains were Davidson's people. With rich detail and apt generalization, he demonstrates how the Old Northwest and the Old Southwest differed from each other and how both differed from the Old Northeast. Although no brief summary can do justice to the rich texture of this essay, a few key passages capture the essence of Davidson's argument.

In maintaining that certain tendencies inherent in the East are writ large in the Middle West, he notes: "The East thought of factory production; but the Middle West thought of Fordism and mass-production. The Connecticut Yankee got up the wooden nutmeg; but the Middle West devised salesmanship. What is Eli Whitney's lone cotton-gin beside the teeming inventions of Edison of Ohio, who might be said, almost, to have invented the idea of invention?" (*Leviathan,* 186). In contrasting the personalities of the midwesterner and the southerner, Davidson asserts the force of geographic determinism: "Upon the Prairie Plains of the Ohio country, or the Great Plains farther west, the charm of nature, indubitable enough in its enormous features, such as skies, horizons, stretch of earth, nevertheless repels man from tender intimacies. Thoreau in Illinois is as unthinkable as Wordsworth on the Congo" (187).

The one overtly political point Davidson makes is an attack on Lincoln's much-admired contention that "this government cannot endure permanently half slave and half free." Even though the Constitution conceded such a division, and sectional equilibrium demanded it, Lincoln was intent on universalizing "the importance of free labor and free soil to the Northwest" (186). As his student M. E. Bradford would later do, Davidson argues that Lincoln's abstract utopian rhetoric helped to transform the country from a confederation of sovereign states into a "union" held together more by brute force than by common affections. As a northwesterner, Lincoln "furnished political and moral leadership to a panicky East." Moreover, "the North's most successful military leaders were the two Northwesterners, Grant and Sherman, who dropped the polite military orthodoxies of the East and devised obliterating, massive, daring evolutions on a grand scale. Like the march of Henry Ford's machines, these movements were glacial, crushing, and yet somewhat fervent" (187).

13. Hobson, *Tell about the South,* 221.

IV

One of the immediate consequences of Davidson's polemicism in the *American Review* was to bring H. L. Mencken back into the debate over Agrarianism. Mencken had originally reviewed *I'll Take My Stand* in the March 1931 issue of the *American Mercury.* While agreeing with some of the criticisms of southern life raised by the book, Mencken was skeptical about its proposed solutions. "The South," he writes, " . . . can no more revive the simple society of the Jefferson era than England can revive that of Queen Anne." Taking dead aim at the Agrarians, he continues: "The present authors, for all their sincerity, show in their own persons most of the worst weaknesses that now afflict their homeland. There is something dreadfully literary and pedagogical about their whole discussion."[14] Like Gerald Johnson and Stringfellow Barr, Mencken believed that industrialism had to be tamed rather than eliminated.

Mencken's reaction to the Agrarian phenomenon was remarkably temperate considering the extent to which he had been attacked on Davidson's book page. As Fred Hobson points out, from about 1924 to 1928, Mencken and his followers constituted Davidson's single biggest target in the pages of the *Tennessean.*[15] Throughout the early 1930s, after the publication of *I'll Take My Stand* and the suspension of the book page, Davidson continued to attack the spirit of southern liberalism that he traced back to Mencken's polemicism of the previous decade. At the same time, Mencken himself had seemed to mellow in his attitude toward the South. He formed several important friendships in the region and, in the summer of 1930, he married a southern woman, Sara Hardt of Montgomery, Alabama. In his contribution to Couch's *Culture in the South* (1935), Davidson even held out an olive branch to his once and future nemesis. He notes that "Mr. Mencken, once known as the South's bitterest detractor, began in 1932 to look almost like a disguised Confederate raider who had chosen his own methods of devastating a too-Yankeefied civilization." Davidson concludes that "Mr. Mencken stood suspect of being at heart a romantic southerner" ("Trend," 196).

If the surviving correspondence is any indication, Davidson and Mencken maintained a very civil professional relationship, even as they publicly disagreed with each other's opinions. For nearly a decade, Mencken urged Davidson to submit essays to the *American Mercury.* In a letter sent on March 25, 1931, he speaks favorably of the article that would appear two months later in Seward Collins's the *Bookman* under the title "Criticism outside New York." (Perhaps even more significant is Mencken's observation: " 'I'll Take My Stand' interested me very much, though I had to dissent from at least part of its thesis and from

14. H. L. Mencken, "Uprising in the Confederacy," 380.
15. See Hobson, *Serpent,* 158.

more of its manner. Such books always have a good influence—more in the long run than immediately.") Then, in the fall of 1933, Davidson sent the manuscript of his essay "The Dilemma of the Southern Liberals" to Mencken, who was in the process of turning the editorship of the *American Mercury* over to his successor, Henry Hazlitt. On October 13, 1933, Mencken wrote Davidson a cordial note indicating that he had just made up his last number of the *Mercury* (December 1933) but that he would pass the essay on. "It is interesting stuff," Mencken writes, "and I am sure that Mr. Hazlitt will like it." Although it is technically correct to say that Mencken never published Davidson, it is likely that he gave "The Dilemma of the Southern Liberals" the crucial endorsement that resulted in its appearance in the *American Mercury.*

Despite their seeming cordiality, Davidson remained suspicious of Mencken and was launching a new attack on his influence before the more benign assessment he had written for Couch's anthology had even appeared. In "New York and the Hinterland," Davidson decries "Mr. Mencken's volatile dissatisfaction with most things indigenously American" (*Leviathan,* 157). He goes on to say that the works of Mencken and the critics he spawned "were anathemas, not credos." He could not "disentangle from their utterances any positive scheme to which they would give allegiance" (161). Whether from personal pique at Davidson or a mere desire to set the record straight, Mencken would not let this attack go unanswered.

Writing in the *Virginia Quarterly Review* of January 1935, Mencken again challenged what he regarded as the pedantic romanticism of the Agrarians and the particular obscurantism of Davidson. After pointing out some of the social benefits of economic progress, Mencken notes that "even the Agrarian Habakkuks themselves are the clients of industrialism, which supplies them generously with the canned-goods, haberdashery, and library facilities that are so necessary to the free ebullition of the human intellect. Left to the farmers of Tennessee, they would be clad in linsey-woolsey and fed on sidemeat, and the only books they could read would be excessively orthodox."[16] Mencken ignores the more sophisticated agrarian ethos of the antebellum planters (perhaps because it now exists largely in memory). This is clearly what John Crowe Ransom, Stark Young, and John Donald Wade would like to have recovered. Even such champions of the yeoman farmer as Andrew Lytle and Donald Davidson seemed to believe that an aesthetic life was consistent with linsey-woolsey and sidemeat, while questioning whether canned goods and the like were really *necessary* to the "free ebullition of the human intellect."

Throughout his essay, Mencken seeks to distinguish between the sort of cosmopolitan conservatism that he advocates and the ignorant provincialism

16. H. L. Mencken, "The South Astir," 53.

that he attributes to the backwoods South. "Mr. Davidson passes for an advanced thinker," Mencken writes, "—and in many particulars his thought is advanced enough, God knows—, but whenever he observes an eye peeping over the Potomac his reaction is precisely that of the Mayor and City Council of Dayton, Tenn. That is to say, he simply throws up his hands, and yields to moral indignation."[17] The difference between Davidson and the Daytonians, which Mencken does his best to obscure, is that Davidson's reaction was based on an informed understanding of what those on the other side of the Potomac, even the Atlantic, were saying.

Mencken was particularly offended by the fact that Davidson seemed to regard him as a decadent radical when the two men actually shared many of the same antipathies. "Mr. Davidson . . . constantly confuses the quackeries of Greenwich Village with the general body of urban thought," Mencken notes. "In one of his essays ["New York and the Hinterland"] he makes a list of the horrors embraced by the intelligentsia of his imaginary Sodoms and Gomorrahs." These include everything from German expressionism and French dadaism to the more exotic productions of D. H. Lawrence, James Joyce, and Gertrude Stein. As one of Davidson's "chosen Gomorreans," Mencken responds with understandable pique: "I hope I may be permitted to recall that I was denouncing each and every one of these varieties of trash long before any news of them had ever penetrated to Tennessee, just as I was whooping for an unyielding Regionalism in my native Maryland."[18] Except for his attacks on what he considered to be a strain of anti-intellectualism in southern life, there was probably a greater cultural affinity between Mencken and Davidson than there was between Davidson and the high modernist Tate. The fact that tribal loyalty could obscure that affinity suggests how strong Davidson's identity as a southerner had become.

Davidson was less disturbed by Mencken's essay itself than by the fact that it had been published in a southern magazine. Although the *Virginia Quarterly Review* was considered to be in enemy hands when it was edited by Stringfellow Barr, the Agrarians had high hopes that it would prove to be a friendlier journal when Lambert Davis took over the editorship in the early 1930s. This hope seemed to be validated when Davis solicited essays from Ransom, Tate, and Warren for a special anniversary issue of the quarterly. Davidson, however, was miffed that his own invitation to contribute did not come until later and in what he considered a perfunctory manner. (When they were at Bread Loaf together in the summer of 1934, James Southall Wilson, who was one of the editors of the review, taunted Davidson by revealing that his name was not included on a lengthy list of contributors Tate was recommending to Davis for the anniversary issue.) After the

17. Ibid., 55.
18. Ibid., 57.

appearance of Mencken's article, Davidson wrote to Lambert Davis on January 9, 1935, to ask "whether you mean to indicate, by the publication of Mr. Mencken's remarks, that you would prefer to see the discussion of Southern affairs returned to the condition of obfuscation and billingsgate which Mr. Mencken inaugurated a good many years ago." Shortly thereafter, Davidson submitted a history of *I'll Take My Stand* for the anniversary issue of the review.

In a letter dated February 28, 1935, Davis rejected Davidson's submission on the contradictory grounds that it was insufficiently literary for the anniversary issue, while not being suitable for a general issue of the magazine. Incensed by Davis's willingness to publish attacks on Agrarianism without giving him comparable space for defense of the movement, Davidson simply resolved to have nothing more to do with the *Virginia Quarterly Review*. The more combative John Gould Fletcher went much further. In an attempt to present a united Agrarian front against Davis, he circulated a pledge among the brethren demanding that they all boycott the review. When Ransom and Tate refused to sign the pledge or to withdraw their essays from the anniversary issue, Fletcher denounced them as traitors and worse.

Although deeply offended by the whole affair, Davidson tried to mend fences with his old Vanderbilt colleagues while calming the apoplectic Fletcher, whom he feared he had inadvertently set off. (Davidson was convinced that the editors in Charlottesville were trying to breed dissension within the Agrarian ranks.) In a letter to Tate, dated March 17, 1935, he writes: "I think there must be some almost psychopathic cause in F's intense rages, as you suggest." Writing to Fletcher on the same day, Davidson argues that it is impossible for his friend to "resign" from the Agrarian movement "as long as you are the person I know you to be. Being an Agrarian (with whatever name) is a matter of living and believing: it has nothing to do with anything as explicit as organization. Even if you or I should intensely dislike all the other 'Agrarians' (as we don't) we couldn't 'resign' because we couldn't stop being Southerners, ourselves, our fathers' sons. I know you believe that! So I urge you to act accordingly."

PART THREE

THE MEMORY KEEPER
(1936–1950)

11

AGRARIAN POETICS

Although John Crowe Ransom and Allen Tate remained committed to an Agrarian vision of society up through the mid-1930s, the intensity of that commitment varied. Tate published his southern novel *The Fathers* in 1938, and the fate of regional culture was never far from his mind. Nevertheless, from the 1940s on, his writing was more greatly influenced by his religious quest than by social and political issues. As for Ransom, from the time he published *The World's Body* (also in 1938), his artistic and intellectual energies were consumed by literary criticism and theory. In "Ode to the Confederate Dead," Tate wrote his one great Agrarian poem. Ransom did the same with "Antique Harvesters." Beyond these two works, it is difficult to see an Agrarian influence continuing in their verse. That influence is even more attenuated in Robert Penn Warren's muse. Although he remained intensely interested in history, Warren was more concerned with exploring metaphysical conundrums in his fiction and verse than in defending the culture of the Old South.

In contrast, Donald Davidson was upholding the faith polemically in his contributions to the *American Review* and other periodicals. Perhaps more important, his poetry grew more distinctively southern. As the only one of the major Fugitives who continued to live in the South, he saw firsthand the dire prophecies of *I'll Take My Stand* fulfilled with each passing year. If those who had gone north to live could preserve an idyllic image of what the South once was, Davidson found that image assailed by the daily reality of what the region had become. The various selections in *Lee in the Mountains and Other Poems* (including a slightly revised version of *The Tall Men*) contrast the heroic southern past with a spiritually diminished modern world.

If Davidson's conservative vision places his work at odds with much of the poetry being written in the 1930s, his very engagement with social issues puts him in the literary mainstream. It was an era in which American writers of all genres were shunning the aestheticism of the early modernist period and reasserting an interest in the material conditions of their existence. (Of course, Davidson had called for just such an awareness in "A Mirror for Artists.") For a variety of reasons, writers found that this shift in emphasis could be more easily reflected in fiction and drama than in verse. In a review-essay that discusses *Lee in the Mountains* and over forty other books of poetry published between 1937 and 1939, Morton Dauwen Zabel writes:

> In terms of "new poets" it has been as lean a period as any since poetic revivalism became a national industry thirty years ago. If publishers' lists and verse journals are reliable indicators, the young talent has met some abrupt halt, mortification, or check to his energies. It may be that Bacon's law has fallen heavily upon him: that an excess of critical intelligence has lamed his creative confidence. In any case, the past twenty months offer few books of extraordinary consequence by poetic beginners, but an astonishing number by their twentieth-century ancestors. The question at such a moment—a profitable one—becomes not where is modern poetry going, but where has it gone.[1]

Although some memorable verse was written in the thirties, no major figures or important movements originated during the decade. As Warren French points out, several of the most promising poets of an earlier generation died by their own hand in the late twenties and early thirties.[2] Those who continued to live and write often found that their best work was either behind or ahead of them. (The one notable exception was Wallace Stevens, who labored in virtual obscurity during the decade.) Probably the two most representative American poets of the thirties, Archibald MacLeish and Kenneth Fearing, are today regarded as talented propagandists whose work seems curiously dated. Davidson was asking many of the same questions as the more fashionable leftist poets of the age, even as the answers he offered were fundamentally different.

The passion (some would say intransigence) of Davidson's Agrarian commitment raises a question about his poetry as poetry. One of the major doctrines of the New Critics was that poetry and propaganda don't mix. As Yeats observed, we make rhetoric out of our quarrels with others, poetry out of our quarrels with ourselves. What made the literature of the Southern Renascence different (and better) than that of the Old South was a dialectical and self-critical sensibility. In Cleanth Brooks's famous formulation, "a poem does not *state* ideas but rather *tests*

---

1. Morton Dauwen Zabel, "Two Years of Poetry: 1937–1939," 569.
2. See Warren French, *The Thirties: Fiction, Poetry, Drama,* 116.

ideas."[3] One has difficulty imagining the politically defiant Davidson agreeing with this notion. For that reason, his Agrarian poetry would not seem to lend itself to the close reading extolled by some of his closest friends and admirers. Such a view is an oversimplification, however. If some of Davidson's poems are too shrill for their own good, others incorporate the sort of internal resistance that makes for a vision earned.

I

"Aunt Maria and the Gourds" is one of several poems from *Lee in the Mountains* that transcend mere statement to achieve something akin to drama. The title character is an old southern woman who tries to maintain cherished customs in a land defiled by industrialism. (The regional references clearly mark the setting as Nashville and the surrounding area.) Although she despairs of cultivating a sense of regional piety in the rising generation of young people, she continues to plant her gourds every spring. The speaker in the poem is apparently neither as old as Aunt Maria nor as young as the friend he is addressing. Occupying this middle ground, he has the ideal vantage point from which to view the Old South and the New. At one point, the speaker says to his listener:

> You who walk in callous innocence,
> Pacing, as once I paced, the long street,
> Pause, look down, remember how this stone
> Slid and avoided when you set your foot.
> Hear the rattle of gourds over Babylon.[4]

As attractive and charming a figure as Aunt Maria might be, the real focus of the poem is on the younger inhabitants of the modern South (just as the real focus of Tate's ode is on the solipsistic modern man, not the heroic war dead). The danger of innocence (which has been a common theme in American literature at least since the time of Hawthorne) is presented here as an ignorance of the past. Fortunately, those who pace the long street of history can acquire some perspective. What this perspective reveals, however, is the instability of the ground under one's feet. Like ancient Babylon, the modern industrialized South is an opulent kingdom, but it is also a place of spiritual exile.

Davidson's celebration of the Old South continues in "The Last Charge." It is an eloquent poem and one that Davidson chose to keep in the volume of

3. Cleanth Brooks, *The Well Wrought Urn: Studies in the Structure of Poetry,* 229.
4. Donald Davidson, *Lee in the Mountains and Other Poems,* 9–10. Subsequent references will be cited parenthetically in the text.

selected verse he published nearly thirty years later. In many ways, it reminds one of Tate's ode. As in Tate's poem, the speaker is a modern southerner who stands in a Confederate cemetery, lamenting the lost valor of an earlier age. He even imagines the dead rising up for one last assault on federal troops. His final resolve is to remember the honored dead even as the elements continue to take a toll on their graves. What makes "The Last Charge" inferior to Tate's ode (and to some of Davidson's own more successful poems) is the lack of a fully developed double perspective. The speaker is simply a one-dimensional surrogate for the poet himself. All that this poem tells us about the modern South is that it ain't what it used to be. How it got to be that way is an issue that is never really examined.

"The Deserter: A Christmas Eclogue," which Davidson dropped from his selected poems, is much more effective at developing a dramatic situation. It is an historical poem in two important senses. First, and most obviously, its action is set in the past. Beyond that, however, Davidson is using the past (in this case a plausible but imagined incident) as a parable about the present. The two speakers in this poem are not shepherds in a pastoral setting but Lester and Jamie, two Confederate veterans suffering through Reconstruction. Of the two, Jamie appears to be in the worse straits. What little crop the June drought left him has already gone to pay for mortgage interest on his farm and for the funeral expenses of his late son-in-law. Much against his natural inclinations, he has come to Nashville because he has heard that the Tennessee state government has voted pensions to Confederate veterans.

Although Jamie served through all four years of the war and was wounded twice, he is denied his pension because he has been labeled a deserter. He had left his company briefly to visit his family, just two miles distant, so that he could warn them of the imminent approach of Yankees and bushwhackers. His family had already departed, and Jamie himself was captured by the Yankees before he could rejoin his unit. "In sixty-five," Jamie says, "men took my word, men knew / That Jamie Hines was captured near Pulaski / Trying to reach the army" (20). Unfortunately, the war ended too soon for him to set the record straight. In the meantime, the scalawag who controls the pensions has blacklisted Jamie because he had opposed the railroads back in 1880. Thus, Davidson makes Jamie a victim of two of the forces he hated most in modern society—bureaucracy and industrialism.

Like the speaker in "Aunt Maria and the Gourds," Lester is a man who lives between the two worlds of the old and the new. When Jamie complains of the dirt in Nashville, Lester replies: "But soot means money. / More smoke, more trade. That's what I've been taught to say" (16). (The self-deprecating tone suggests that he does not believe the platitudes he has learned to mouth.) Because of his status in the new social order, Lester would be in a position to help Jamie secure a bank loan. He describes himself as a spy behind enemy lines. In words that Davidson himself might have spoken, Lester announces:

Nashville was occupied by Federal troops
In eighteen sixty-two. *They hold it still!*
The only difference is, they do not wear
Blue uniforms. (21)

There is a tendency, especially among those who know Davidson's political views, to read Lester's statement as naked polemicism rather than as a dramatic utterance. Nevertheless, a close reading of the context might cause a careful observer to wonder whether Lester is really Davidson's spokesman. Certainly, his diagnosis of the ills afflicting modern man would square with Davidson's. We live in a world where those in power prefer "The written word to any word made flesh. / They cannot think until they think in print" (21). Lester's response to such a situation is to try to succeed in the new world while secretly acknowledging the moral superiority of the old. Lester's recommendation to Jamie, on this particular Christmas Eve, is to renew his Christian faith:

. . . This wretched world prefers
The formula to the form. But we shall give
Our worship to the undefeated form,
Forever green as in these holly boughs. (22)

Had the poem ended there, it could easily have been taken for a tribute to religious stoicism. Davidson, however, concludes with nine lines of narration, in which Jamie and Lester pass through a city of artificial wreaths, gilt festoons, and a sign that proclaims CHRIST SAVES in letters ten feet high. Clearly, Davidson is mocking commercial religiosity, not genuine faith. Still, this concluding narrative keeps us from endorsing Lester's facile piety as an adequate response to either Jamie's situation or the agony of the modern South. If there is an answer to these dilemmas, it probably comes from something closer to Tate's "knowledge carried to the heart." When Lester and Jamie pass through the vulgarity of Christmas Eve in postbellum Nashville, "Their eyes / Were bent on other fields, on charities / Unblazoned and unrecognized." But the final perspective is that of the modern world itself: "They walked, / Arm in arm, through crowds that knew them not, / And went, as old men will, their secret way" (22).

Davidson's "Two Georgia Pastorals" consist of one of his most admired poems—"Randall, My Son"—and the potentially embarrassing "Old Black Joe Comes Home." They should be read in tandem. The poem about Old Black Joe seems to owe a debt to Joel Chandler Harris's "Free Joe and the Rest of the World." Like Harris, Davidson writes about a black man who is victimized by emancipation. Unable to prosper in freedom, he returns to the only home he has ever known. All of Davidson's patronizing attitudes toward black people are present here. Nevertheless, the poem transcends race. One is reminded of the parable of the prodigal son and of Robert Frost's "Death of the Hired Man" as much as of Joel Chandler Harris. Like the prodigal son and Frost's hired man, Old Black Joe returns, after a long absence, to the home that has to take him in. Freedom has turned out to be lonelier than he thought it would be, but "home" has changed as well. The ravages of Reconstruction have driven the old master to the grave, and the farm itself is to be seized the next day. Joe is welcomed for the night and offered what little food is left in the kitchen, but the old life to which he had hoped to return is irrevocably gone for both races of southerners.

The title of the poem can't help reminding readers of Stephen Collins Foster's song "Old Black Joe Comes Home." The pathos of both works lies in their ability to convey the sadness of a lost home. (The Pittsburgh boy Foster did this in several of his most memorable songs, including "My Old Kentucky Home" and "Old Folks at Home.") In "Old Black Joe," the good and faithful slave casts a longing glance back to the cotton fields even as he is preparing to enter Heaven. Despite his religious faith, the memory of past happiness seems more real than the expectation of future glory. This is even more true for Davidson's Old Black Joe. Having discovered the hollowness of political millennialism (the "year of Jubilee"), Joe finds his old home as irrecoverable as the one in Foster's song.

The situation in the second Georgia pastoral, "Randall, My Son," is almost the opposite of that in "Old Black Joe." Here, we have not the return of the prodigal but his departure. The speaker is a southern mother who realizes that her home has gone to seed but tries to persuade her son to stay anyway. She bids him mount the stair and lie down in his old bed as the lamp burns low. "Within the changeless room where you were born / I wait the changing day when you must go." There is in her voice the sense of weariness one hears in the speaker of Ransom's "Antique Harvesters." This is particularly true of the third stanza, which concludes with these lines:

> Cold is the mistress that beckons you from me.
> I wish her sleek hunting may never come to be—
> For in our woods where deer and fox still run
> An old horn blows at daybreak, Randall, my son.

The hectoring tone of Ransom's poem is absent here. The mother is not angry as wasp music, and she even seems resigned to her son's departure. What she offers him if he stays, however, is more substantial than a phantom fox who exists as simply an archetype of chivalry. The hunting may not be as sleek as in distant lands, but the deer and fox and old horn remain. If Randall abandons his home region, he will have broken the bond of the generations. All that he will have to bequeath to his unbegotten son is "The lustre of a sword that sticks in sheath, / A house that crumbles and a fence that's rotten." The alternative is to remain and "Hear, what I hear, in a far chase new begun / An old horn's husky music" (39). Thomas Daniel Young and M. Thomas Inge believe that this new chase is the Agrarian movement itself.[5] If that is the case, Davidson must have despaired that the cause would be adopted by a younger generation. There is no indication that Randall reconsiders his decision to leave or that his mother's words have had any impact on him.

If "Randall, My Son" is a triumph of rhetoric, "From a Chimney Corner" relies for its effect almost entirely on dramatic situation. In the present tense of the poem, an old woman and her grandson sit by the fireside as she reminisces and he listens. Her recollection is of "a dank morning near Christmas, sixty-four" (40). A mere girl, she could see the remnants of Hood's army "drenched with December and sore defeat." As these men limp up the road, the women who live along the Lewisburg road wait helplessly for "the armies in blue / That soon will break through the distant cedars" (41). Neither the grandmother nor the third-person speaker of the poem tells us what to think or feel about this experience. Davidson trusts his dramatic powers enough to believe that we will get the point of the story on our own. Based on what we know of his life and family background, it is easy to imagine the grandmother as Rebecca Patton Wells and the child as Donald Davidson. Although this knowledge is not essential to appreciating the poem, it may account for the fact that Davidson did not feel the need to generate emotion through explicit statement. The feeling was already there in search of an objective correlative.

II

Unlike Tate, Lytle, and Warren, Davidson never wrote a biography of a major figure from the Civil War era. Nevertheless, important historical personages appear in his verse. This is true not only of "Lee in the Mountains" but also of such lesser poems as "The Last Rider" and "Twilight on Union Street." "The Last Rider" is specifically addressed to Andrew Lytle. (The beginning—"You, Andrew Lytle" may be an echo of Archibald MacLeish's "You, Andrew Marvell.") The speaker recalls Lytle telling him of a darky's reaction to "a bold / Image of Forrest mounted / By Mississippi side." In this image (presumably a statue) the general's horse seems spent, as if he had been riding all night as he often did in

---

5. Young and Inge, *Donald Davidson*, 96.

wartime. The speaker imagines that Forrest has come back "To the bluegrass that sired him / And the roads he fought on" (44). However, if he has come back from Mississippi side, it is to a place "where the living do not fight / And only the dead can ride" (45). Certainly, for Lytle and Davidson, Forrest was the yeoman general who epitomized the backwoods South at its best. His valor, or that of his ghost, is an indictment of less committed modern southerners. Although the poem does not explicitly endorse the rides of the Ku Klux Klan, which Forrest founded, "The Last Rider" is an unabashed statement of resistance. There is no suggestion, however, that the docile "darkey" of the first stanza has anything to fear from Forrest—living or dead.

In "Twilight on Union Street," Davidson reaches even further back in history, using Andrew Jackson as his touchstone. In the morning of his career, the "high-booted, quick-oathed" Jackson was a man of action, whether it be according to the laws of the court or of the gentleman's code. By noontime, his mere reputation was enough to strike fear into the hearts of men: "They knew where General Jackson left his dead." One detects no sense of irony or doubleness in the poet's admiration of Jackson. Instead, we are left with the feeling that modern man lacks the vitality and conviction that made Jackson such a forceful leader.

> And now the twilight. History grows dim.
> The traffic leads, we no more follow him;
> In bronze he rides, saluting James K. Polk,
> His horse's rump turned to us in the smoke. (52)

Images of industrialism pervade this final stanza. The twilight is made even more obscure by the smoke of factories. The modern southerner is more likely to follow the car ahead of him than the historical example of Old Hickory. And the Jackson legacy itself has been reduced to a statue that prominently features a horse's rear end. (Although there is no evidence of direct influence, one cannot help thinking of the contrast between the statue of Colonel Shaw and the underground parking garage in Robert Lowell's later poem "For the Union Dead.") The fact that Jackson is saluting the less impressive James K. Polk may suggest that the process of historical decline has been going on for some time.

The meretriciousness and vulgarity of what passes for high culture in the New South is the subject of Davidson's "On a Replica of the Parthenon." Obviously thinking of the plaster monstrosity that dominates Centennial Park in West Nashville, Davidson asks: "Why do they come? What do they seek / Who build but never read their Greek?" Because the Nashville Parthenon represents art and ancient history as a mere commodity, it is a perfect symbol of a rootless society. As in "Twilight on Union Street," automobile traffic figures prominently here.

Near this replica of classical civilization are "aimless motors that can make / Only incertainty more sure."

Centennial Park is also a place where the repressed sexuality of the Bible Belt comes uncomfortably close to the pagan sensuality of Ancient Greece.

> Shop-girls embrace a plaster thought,
> And eye Poseidon's loins ungirt,
> And never heed the brandished spear
> Or feel the bright-eyed maiden's rage
> Whose gaze the sparrows violate;
> But the sky drips its spectral dirt,
> And gods, like men, to soot revert. (50)

The soot that claims both gods and men is not the inviting burial ground of Bryant's "Thanatopsis" but the debris of an industrial civilization that has lost touch with both art and nature. The men who have built the modern Parthenon are bearing witness not to their great learning but to their great pretension. The poet sees it as the work of "men who slew their past / Raised up this bribe against their fate" (51).

One does not need to have an opinion about the relative merits of the Old South and the New to appreciate this poem. The replica of the Parthenon could have been erected in the Midwest by a George Babbitt or in New England by a Silas Lapham. Agrarianism is more tenable when it is offering a critique of modern life than when it is simply refighting the War Between the States. If Davidson occasionally succumbed to southern chauvinism, he was most interested in finding a *usable past*. The builders of the new Parthenon have not done even that. Because they are ignorant of the real past, they have had to create a manufactured one. But, as any student of classical civilization could have told them, it is not possible to step in the same river twice.

The degeneration of nature itself is the subject of Davidson's "The Horde." From a technical standpoint, it is one of Davidson's most interesting and uncharacteristic poems. The language is made to sound anachronistic by the use of compounds and inverted word order and the frequent omission of definite articles. (There is also more enjambment than one finds in a typical Davidson poem.) "The Horde" sounds like nothing so much as a fairly literal translation from Anglo-Saxon verse. The opening stanza of the poem illustrates these points.

> Father remembered the wild pigeons crowding
> Beech groves, mast-rich. The flutter in boughs, the cloud
> Darkening all, a hurricane circling and surging.

> Eye lost count, ear could not measure sound.
> Mind hurled measureless with them, feathered the sky.

The world in which wild pigeons lived gave promise of lasting forever. The second stanza of the poem is filled with images of harvest and fruition. "Field was fat. . . . The muscadine / Spilled on the clearing."

> . . . And everywhere birds' cries
> Flung forever, whirling with hurried leaves,
> Clans of the trampled skies that echoed back
> Thunder of buffalo hooves, the plunge of fish. (53)

In the third stanza, we are introduced to an aging man of the woods, who could have come straight from a novel by James Fenimore Cooper or William Gilmore Sims. (He still oozes of cider and reeks with fur.) In his childhood, the speaker remembered this man telling him "The pigeons came / Thus, when I was a boy, in autumn time, / And still come on, for wilderness is ripe." Even if this statement is true, the very fact that the backwoodsman feels compelled to make it suggests that it is far from self-evident. There is also a suggestion that the wilderness, although still ripe, is a bit farther removed than in the frontiersman's youth.

After a string of ellipses, the speaker begins the fourth stanza with the stark statement: "This is an autumn when they come no more." The landscape is now infertile, hollow, and rotten. "There is frost on the grandson's eyes, / And only rumor upon the skies . . ." [ellipses in original]. In place of the wild pigeons, starlings now come. They are "an immigrant horde" that seem merely nervous and finical. "[T]hey squawk / Against too few boughs, complain to have no better." The speaker regards these birds as a nuisance and throws a stone at them. In response, "They fly from me / To some other wilderness grandson's tree / And dream their protest is the pigeon's thunder" (54). In this last line, the poet attributes to the birds themselves some sense that a glory has passed from the earth. Like the speaker, they can only dream of an heroic past.

Davidson concludes part one of *Lee in the Mountains and Other Poems* with "Sanctuary," which is one of his most visionary poems. Conceived as a father's instructions to his son, "Sanctuary" imagines some future holocaust when industrial civilization will have made human life unendurable. Although the father knows that he will be gone by then, he urges his son (and his grandsons yet unborn) to take to the wilderness, where they will be more at home than the enemy. Drawing on some long-buried racial memory of the backwoods, the survivors will burn or hide what they cannot carry. They will level the remaining crops, being careful to leave the enemy nothing to take or eat. Taking only the bare essentials for their three-day wilderness ride, they will leave at once. "Do not wait until / You see *his* great dust rising in the valley. / Then it will be too late" (56). Like Lot's family leaving Sodom and Gomorrah, these refugees are warned not to turn, not even to look back.

This poem would seem to be part of a postapocalyptic tradition in American literature that stretches back at least as far as Hawthorne's "The New Adam and Eve." The year after *Lee in the Mountains and Other Poems* was published, Nathanael West would give us an image of Los Angeles in flames in *The Day of the Locust*. When the threat of nuclear warfare became a fact of our collective existence, the postholocaust narrative also became a staple of our popular culture. In *Lost in the Cosmos* (1982), Walker Percy imagines civilization beginning over again in Lost Cove, Tennessee. (This tale was itself greatly influenced by Walter M. Miller's science fiction novel *A Canticle for Leibowitz* [1959].) In his hit song "A Country Boy Can Survive" (1981), Hank Williams, Jr., celebrates the ability of rural people to start life over again after urban society has destroyed itself.

Because the title of his poem is "Sanctuary," not "Holocaust," Davidson's emphasis is less on the ruined world left behind than on the idyllic refuge that nature can provide. Returning to this refuge is not just an expedient in a time of difficulty but a preferred way of life. Within the long tradition of literary primitivism, there has always been a myth of the once and future utopia.[6] The arcadian retreat that Davidson depicts is nothing less than the authentic man's true home.

> There in tall timber you will be as free
> As were your fathers once when Tryon raged
> In Carolina hunting Regulators,
> Or Tarleton rode to hang the old-time Whigs.
> Some tell how in that valley young Sam Houston
> Lived long ago with his brother Oo-loo-te-ka,
> Reading Homer among the Cherokee. . . . (57)

This mountain retreat is a place from which the descendants of the tall men can witness the dust and flame of the enemy camp and plan a new attack. Such a strategy might well have appealed to the combative side of Davidson. But the alternative he presents in the final six lines of the poem is far more seductive:

> Or else, forgetting ruin, you may lie
> On sweet grass by a mountain stream, to watch
> The last wild eagle soar or the last raven

---

6. For a discussion of the "Theory of Decline and Future Restoration," see Arthur O. Lovejoy and George Boas, *A Documentary History of Primitivism and Related Ideas* (Baltimore: Johns Hopkins University Press, 1935), 1:3.

Cherish his brood within their rocky nest,
Or see, when mountain shadows first grow long,
The last enchanted white deer come to drink. (58)

III

The title poem of *Lee in the Mountains* represents Davidson's Agrarian muse at its best. The poem contains as much conviction and passion as anything he ever wrote, but it manages to embody these qualities in a dramatic situation. To be sure, writing about Robert E. Lee involved hazards as well as benefits. Lee has loomed so large in the southern imagination that it is difficult to write about him as less than a demigod. (Allen Tate abandoned a proposed biography of Lee because he could not find enough complexity and ambiguity in the man's character.) Davidson wisely concentrates on a period of Lee's life when he was no longer a public figure or a leader of the southern cause. During the five years that he served as president of Washington College in Lexington, Virginia (1865–1870), Lee was trying to educate young men in the postbellum South, while editing his father's memoirs in his spare time. These commitments to an earlier and later generation are less spectacular than Lee's exploits on the battlefield, but they may also be more relevant to the situation of a contemporary southerner such as Donald Davidson.

"Lee in the Mountains" was one of several poems that Davidson conceived while living in Marshallville, Georgia, during the 1932–1933 academic year. ("Old Black Joe" and "Randall, My Son" were also from this period.) He had the idea for the poem clearly in mind by the time he left Marshallville that summer. In late August he completed a draft of a poem that he called "General Lee Remembers." This draft of 61 lines differs substantially from the final version of 121 lines, which Davidson completed in January 1934 and read later that month at a United Daughters of the Confederacy luncheon in Nashville. Between August 1933 and January 1934, Davidson wrote five versions of the poem that he finally called "Lee in the Mountains."[7]

After completing the fourth version, Davidson sent a draft of his poem to Allen Tate and Caroline Gordon, who made important suggestions before "Lee in the Mountains" was published for the first time, in the May 1934 issue of the *American Review*. Despite recommending a few revisions, Tate expressed great admiration for the text Davidson sent him. "Your Lee poem is the finest you have ever written," he declares in a letter to Davidson dated January 19, 1934. "I

---

7. See Thomas Daniel Young and M. Thomas Inge, *Donald Davidson: An Essay and a Bibliography*, 5.

say this deliberately after much meditation and study of it. I thought your other recent poems, in the last couple of years, too argumentative and documentary. This new one is about Lee and about a great deal more than Lee. It is a very fine poem. If you lose what you've got here and relapse into documentation, I shall come over and cut your ears off" (*Literary Correspondence*, 290).

Most commentators agree with Lawrence E. Bowling that "Lee in the Mountains" can be divided into five movements and possesses the dramatic structure of a five-act play.[8] The action begins with Lee walking to his office one morning. His reverie is interrupted by the greetings of some boys already gathered on the cold grounds before the morning bell. Lee is struck by the contrast between the eagerness of these young men and his own world-weariness.

> The young have time to wait.
> But soldiers' faces under their tossing flags
> List no more by any road or field,
> And I am spent with old wars and new sorrow.
> Walking the rocky path, where steps decay
> And the paint cracks and grass eats on the stone.
> It is not General Lee, young men . . .
> It is Robert Lee in a dark civilian suit who walks,
> An outlaw fumbling for the latch, a voice
> Commanding in a dream where no flag flies. (3)

The images of decay and ruin suggest the plight of the South during Reconstruction. At the same time, there is something of a biblical cadence to the declaration "I am spent with old wars and new sorrow." The suggestion is that Lee is like an Old Testament prophet or patriarch reduced to hard times when God seems to have turned his back on his people. The man who was once a general is now considered an outlaw and a traitor (at least by the radical Reconstructionists). He is just "Robert Lee in a dark civilian suit, . . . a voice / Commanding in a dream where no flag flies." The question facing him at this juncture is what to do with the rest of his life. The bulk of the poem is devoted to justifying the choice that he has made.

The next two verse paragraphs take us into the remote past. Lee is recalling the sad fate of his father, the Revolutionary War hero Light-Horse Harry Lee, who faced bankruptcy and imprisonment for debt during the last years of his life. In addition to losing all financial security, Harry Lee was physically attacked by a drunken mob in Baltimore because of his opposition to the War of 1812. He left America in 1813 in an attempt to make a new start in the West Indies.

---

8. Lawrence E. Bowling, "An Analysis of Davidson's 'Lee in the Mountains.'"

After five years of exile, he returned home, making it only as far as Cumberland Island before his ill health required his being put ashore. Shortly thereafter, he died and was buried in a "lone grave." According to the poem, Robert vowed beside that grave to finish his father's memoirs. Whether this is literally true or not, he did visit the grave during the War Between the States and began editing the memoirs soon after the war was over.

There are several reasons why Robert may have felt obliged to finish his father's memoirs. As the child of Harry Lee's old age, Robert remembered his father only as "a broken man," either in prison or in exile. Finishing the memoirs was a way of acquainting himself with a father he never really knew. Also, the enterprise helped bring back memories of his mother, who used to tell her son much about the past, even as she fingered the pages of the uncompleted manuscript. As he finishes the task of defending his father's reputation, "Her voice comes back, a murmuring distillation / Of old Virginia times now faint and gone, / The hurt of all that was and cannot be." What is less clear is why Lee chooses not to tell his own more compelling and timely story: "He would have his say, but I shall not have mine. / What I do now is only a son's devoir / To a lost father. Let him only speak" (4).

One possible explanation for Lee's choice has to do with the nature of historical truth. In Robert Penn Warren's *All the King's Men,* Jack Burden, as a young Ph.D. student, tries to edit the Civil War diary of an ancestor named Cass Mastern. He soon discovers, however, that the truth of Cass's life eludes him. It is only after Jack has learned some of the same lessons that Cass derived from life that he is able to return to the project and make sense of it. By the same token, Robert E. Lee is able to make sense of his father's life largely because of what he himself experiences during the War Between the States. Just as his father's house was seized by creditors, Lee's own house in Arlington was taken by the U.S. government. Like his father, Lee has also gone from being a hero to a pariah. When he thinks of his father as "a broken man," it is with empathy, not just filial pity.

Lawrence Bowling argues that there are political as well as personal similarities between the circumstances of Harry Lee's life and those of his son. Robert E. Lee was not fighting primarily to preserve the institution of slavery, which he opposed, but to defend the autonomy of local government. He believed that the gravest threat to political liberty lay in a coercive central authority. The union that was saved by the federal victory in the War Between the States was not the same one that had existed prior to the war. Having lost much of their sovereignty, including the simple right to determine whether or not they wished to remain part of the union, the states were no longer partners in a federal enterprise but colonies of a remote and despotic national government. At least, this was the way it seemed to Robert E. Lee and many other white southerners in the depths of Reconstruction. (As an agrarian regionalist opposing cultural nationalism,

Davidson saw the contemporary southern situation is similar terms.) Light Horse Harry Lee and other American patriots had fought the American Revolution to assert the right of local self-government at the end of the eighteenth century. In a sense, then, both Robert and Harry Lee (and, by extension, Davidson himself) were fighting for a similar vision of corporate liberty.

If the reasons for Lee's commitment to his father's memoirs are apparent by this point in the poem, it is still unclear why he refuses to tell what he knows about his own wartime experiences. In the next twenty-seven lines of the poem, Lee contemplates the probable consequences of doing so. At one level, making a full report of the sufferings of the Confederacy would absolve Lee of the guilt he feels for trusting the seemingly honorable terms of surrender offered by the enemy. In line seventy, he asks, "And was I then betrayed? Did I betray?" Had he held out longer, taking to the mountains to wage guerrilla warfare, he might have secured better terms from a battle-weary foe. Certainly many of the young soldiers of the Confederacy would have followed his lead.

Unfortunately, one cannot reverse the course of history. If Lee were to tell all that he knows now, he would succeed only in inflaming controversy and delaying the painful process of reuniting a sundered country. Although it might appear courageous to do so, to plead the cause of the South at this time would be suicidal.

> If it were said, as still it might be said—
> If it were said, and a word should run like fire,
> Like living fire into the roots of grass,
> The sunken flag would kindle on wild hills,
> The brooding hearts would waken, and the dream
> Stir like a crippled phantom under the pines,
> And this torn earth would quicken into shouting
> Beneath the feet of ragged bands. (5–6)

It is more than a little ironic that Davidson, who has often been accused of wanting to refight the War Between the States, seems to be endorsing the passive and conciliatory stance of Lee.

It should be remembered, however, that this poem is not the assertion of a doctrine but the rendering of a dramatic situation. Lee feels no sense of satisfaction or complacency about the current condition of the South. Rather than having retreated to the mountains to fight, he is now trapped there, pursuing what must seem to be a thankless civilian calling. Here, his responsibility is not to relive his immediate past but to do what he can to prepare the young men of Washington College for a better future. The surrender he made at Appomattox was honorable, even if the federal government failed to keep its part of the bargain. The only alternative that is left to him is to preserve his personal integrity. His stance of restraint and submission actually reflects a higher courage because it goes against every natural impulse that he feels. Presumably his sense of anger and wounded virtue will now be poured into his work on his father's memoirs, while he leaves the polemical defense of the Confederacy to a later generation.

Had the poem ended here, Lee's stoic resignation to the inevitable might seem the better part of valor, but it would also be a sign of spiritual and physical defeat. Instead of succumbing to such an attitude, Davidson ends the poem on a note of affirmation. The final stanza (which Bowling equates with the fifth act of the drama) begins with three lines that connect the conclusion of the poem with everything that has been said up to that point: "It is not the bugle now, or the long roll beating. / The simple stroke of a chapel bell forbids / The hurtling dream, recalls the lonely mind." In place of the bugle and the hurtling dream, Lee possesses a religious faith that can survive military defeat. Like Henry Timrod, he seems to believe that blood shed for a lost cause is more sacred than any spilled for a gained one. In the final fifteen lines of the poem, Lee reminds the young men that the God of their fathers is just and merciful and that He "measures out the grace / Whereby alone we live." Lee believes that at some point in the future, God will:

> . . . bring this lost forsaken valor
> And the fierce faith undying
> And the love quenchless
> To flower among the hills to which we cleave,
> To fruit upon the mountains whither we flee,
> Never forsaking, never denying
> His children and His children's children forever
> Unto all generations of the faithful heart. (7)

At first glance, the stance that Lee is endorsing would seem to resemble the problematical piety of Lester in Davidson's "Christmas Eclogue." The tone is entirely different, however. Lee's faith is not undercut by images of a commercialized celebration of Christmas. In fact, the vision of Providence that Davidson gives us in "Lee in the Mountains" is not even specifically Christian. He seems to be describing a tribal deity not unlike the God of the Old Testament. (When this poem was originally published in the *American Review,* it ended with the word "Amen.") We know that the historical Lee believed that the sacrifices of the recent past would be redeemed in the future. As confident as the general might have been about that future in the late 1860s, Davidson and his readers must have seen the situation from a somewhat different perspective. Living in Lee's future, they had not yet celebrated the triumph of the South and the revenge of its Old Testament God. If anything, industrialism represented to them a second wave of reconstruction. The Agrarians saw themselves as keeping the old dream alive even in the face of likely defeat. As a teacher of the young who was also trying to pass on the lessons of history, Davidson must have found his own situation mirrored in that of the aging Lee. Even though he had been born too late to be a Confederate general, he could still plead the cause of the South. It was a vocation that Lee himself had vouchsafed to future generations of the faithful heart.

TAKING THEIR COUNTRY BACK

If Donald Davidson could have seen something of his own situation reflected in Robert E. Lee's role as a southern educator, his tenure in that position was far longer than Lee's, and the students he influenced far more distinguished. Certainly one of the most unusual of these was Randall Jarrell. Having matriculated at Vanderbilt from 1932 to 1937, Jarrell was one of the earliest inheritors of what Charlotte H. Beck calls the "Fugitive legacy."[1] Coming from a thoroughly unbookish middle-class family in Nashville, Jarrell seemed an unlikely candidate for the literary life. Although he did pose for the statue of Ganymede on the Parthenon frieze at the age of six, he received a public education rather than attending one of the fashionable Tennessee prep schools. Even after choosing study at Vanderbilt over a career in his uncle's candy business, Jarrell majored in psychology not literature. After a few classes in English, however, he developed into a gifted and haughty young poet, who reminded both John Crowe Ransom and Robert Penn Warren of the creative ferment that had thrived on Whitland Avenue a decade earlier. It seems only natural that he forged close ties with Allen Tate, a similarly brash and talented figure from that earlier period.

Jarrell's debt to Ransom, Tate, and Warren is well known. Because his relationship with Donald Davidson was less important, it is virtually unknown. Nevertheless, Jarrell came under Davidson's influence at an important time in his academic career. When Ransom left Vanderbilt for a position at Kenyon College in 1937, the task of directing Jarrell's master's thesis fell to Davidson. A year earlier, Jarrell had written a paper on lyric elements in the ballad for

1. Professor Beck has explored the Fugitive legacy in a book forthcoming from Louisiana State University Press.

Davidson's graduate course in the English lyric. Typical of Jarrell's critical writing, the essay reflects a wide range of reading, a pronounced point of view, and virtually no scholarly documentation. Although such an idiosyncratic paper would not have passed muster with more conventional pedagogues, such as Walter Clyde Curry, Davidson gave it an "A" without comment. The thesis, which required the approval of more than one professor, would not experience such easy sailing.

Apparently the first draft of this thesis was a breezy critical discussion of A. E. Housman's poetry, complete with references to Jarrell's own verse. Writing to Jarrell at Kenyon, where Ransom had secured him an instructorship, Davidson urged his student to make the text more scholarly and to delete the chapter on his own poetry. When Jarrell reluctantly complied with those suggestions, Davidson was able to garner the necessary faculty approval for "Implicit Generalizations in Housman." Given his commitment to poetry and the relative informality of his own criticism, one can only conclude that Davidson put young Jarrell on such a short leash not to cramp his style, but to prevent less tolerant members of the faculty from blocking the thesis altogether. Over a decade later, a graduate student named James Dickey presented the draft of his master's thesis on Herman Melville's poetry to Richmond Croom Beatty, who had been the second reader on Jarrell's thesis. When Beatty told Dickey that he could not get the project approved by the graduate faculty without footnotes, Dickey checked "Implicit Generalizations in Housman" out of the university library, counted the number of footnotes, and put one fewer in his own thesis.[2]

If Randall Jarrell seems an unlikely Davidson protégé, Jesse Stuart could have been sent over by central casting. A rough-hewn young man from the mountains of Kentucky, Stuart was descended from his own tribe of tall men. Davidson might very well have seen in Stuart an exaggerated version of some aspects of his own earlier self. If his autobiographical writings are any indication, Stuart suffered even greater poverty than Davidson while growing up. Receiving only a rural public school education and lacking the example of educated parents, Stuart might never have turned to literature had it not been for a profound dissatisfaction with the drabness of life in the mountains. He ran away with a passing carnival, tried army life for awhile, then left to work in a steel mill in Ashland, Kentucky. The trauma of seeing a young man disemboweled prompted him to leave the industrial world after he had saved enough money to pay his debts.

Already a compulsive reader, Stuart enrolled in the only school he could afford, Lincoln Memorial University in Harrogate, Tennessee. It was here that he first read the work of the Fugitives and Agrarians and dreamed of eventually being among them. Following graduation, however, he returned to teach school in his native Greenup, Kentucky. When he made the mistake of asking for a raise in pay,

2. Thomas Daniel Young in conversation.

he was promptly fired. With no place else to go, Jesse Stuart headed for graduate school at Vanderbilt with a trunk, an old Oliver typewriter, and $130 in cash. He later observed that he had more manuscripts than clothes in his trunk.

Because of his extreme poverty, Stuart worked as a campus janitor (one of the few white men in that position) and could afford only eleven meals a week. His memories of his time at Vanderbilt are filled with recollections of physical hunger, as he would sit in class trying to keep his stomach from growling and his mind focused on the subject at hand. If anything, Stuart was consumed by an even greater appetite for literature. His approach to school was so undisciplined that he would sometimes write poetry when he should have been writing term papers. Even when he did his assigned work, it tended to be unorthodox. When he handed Edwin Mims what he thought would be an "A" paper on Thomas Carlyle, Mims refused to accept it because it had nothing about Carlyle in it. Stuart later reread the paper to discover that he couldn't find Carlyle in it either—"only in three places I had imitated his prose."[3]

When Mims asked his students to write an autobiographical paper of no more than eighteen typed pages, Stuart spent the next eleven days unburdening himself of memories of his youth. When the paper came due, he realized that he had written 322 pages from margin to margin. To conceal its bulk, he slipped the paper between two pieces of cardboard and bound it down with two heavy rubber bands. When Mims felt the weight of the paper, he exploded: "There you go, Stuart, you hand me a paper like this when you are failing my class. And you know I read every word of a paper handed to me by one of my students." Three days later, Mims returned this monstrosity to its author. " 'It's the finest paper handed to me in my career as a teacher,' he said. 'So crudely written and so beautiful and it needs punctuation.' "[4] Six years later, with a final chapter added, this paper became Stuart's third published book, *Beyond Dark Hills*.

It is probably just as well for Stuart's literary development that the Fugitive group had disbanded several years before his arrival at Vanderbilt. Like Merrill Moore, Stuart would write sonnet after sonnet with little or no revision. He always found it easier to start a new poem than to try to perfect an old one. Had he attended the Saturday evening sessions on Whitland Avenue, one can imagine Allen Tate attacking his shoddy craftsmanship. (Although Tate initially thought that Stuart had promise as a writer, he gradually became disenchanted with the Kentuckian's persona; writing to Davidson on May 15, 1950, he says of Stuart: "His dramatization of himself as the Hill-billy, for New York consumption, has disgusted me for years, and I suppose I can't be fair to his work" [*Literary Correspondence*, 351].)

3. Jesse Stuart, *Beyond Dark Hills*, 256.
4. Ibid., xv.

During his time in Nashville, Stuart did seek out the original Fugitive, Sidney Hirsch, who offered encouragement and no criticism of the sheafs of poetry that Stuart would show him. Having slipped back into isolation and obscurity, Hirsch probably needed the attention of a young disciple as much as Stuart needed the support of an older patron. Stuart later recalled that "in addition to the bread of dreams he gave me along with the other youth of the land who'd come and stay a week or longer with him, he gave me big plates of potatoes, big slices of cheese, green onions, milk, bread. . . . Ah, those feasts there when I ate food until I was ashamed, and then he stacked more on my plate." As he was busy filling Stuart's stomach and reading his poetry, Hirsch would wax nostalgic: "Your teachers used to come here. Donald Davidson came to me when he was just a boy in Vanderbilt University. I have many of his youthful poems now. He was the handsomest youth I've ever seen."[5]

The affinity that developed between Davidson and Stuart was due in part to their shared love of Elizabethan ballads and lyrics. "I was always the first one to Donald Davidson's class and the last to leave," Stuart noted nearly forty years later. " 'You are a good student, Stuart,' he said to me. He marked me down an A. No one except the recipient of this grade will ever know what the A's he gave me at Vanderbilt meant." (His first semester, Stuart had made three C's.) Because of the kinship he felt with his teacher, Stuart showed Davidson the poems he had tried to write. Many were frankly imitative of Carl Sandburg, Rupert Brooke, and other popular poets of the time. But when he brought out the poems he had written about his home region, Davidson detected Stuart's authentic voice. He boldly suggested that Jesse send one of these poems, "Elegy for Mitch Stuart," to H. L. Mencken at the *American Mercury*. Even though Stuart had had his submissions regularly rejected by much smaller magazines, Davidson was shrewd enough to identify a poem that he thought Mencken might like. When Stuart pointed out that Mencken had recently been quoted as saying that there was no poetry being written in America that was fit to publish, Davidson simply smiled and said, "His bark is bigger than his bite."[6]

When Mencken accepted "Elegy for Mitch Stuart," Jesse's career as a published writer was well launched; however, his academic career was over. After his nearly completed master's thesis was destroyed in the Wesley Hall fire, Stuart decided to leave Vanderbilt in the spring of 1932. Almost four decades later, he recalled his departure. "When I got ready to leave, my possessions all in a small borrowed suitcase, I said my 'goodbys' to friends; then I went over to say a last goodby to Donald Davidson. This was the meeting—though I didn't know it then— that would change my whole life. 'Go back to your country,' he told me. 'Go

---

5. Ibid., 264.
6. Jesse Stuart, "America's Pindar Was My Guide," 18.

back there and write of your people. Don't you change and follow the moods of these times."[7]

Jesse Stuart took this advice to heart, and his former teacher continued to promote his work. Davidson sent some of Stuart's poetry to Louis Untermeyer, who praised it. Writing to his old debate opponent Stringfellow Barr at the *Virginia Quarterly Review* on June 3, 1933, Davidson notes that "my mountain friend, Jesse Stuart, writes me that he has submitted to you a MS of his sonnets. I hope very much that you'll give them serious consideration. If you are looking for an American Robert Burns, Stuart is the man—the first real poet (aside from ballad makers) ever to come out of the southern mountains."[8] That October, Barr published twelve of Stuart's sonnets in his magazine. That same month, the *American Mercury* published thirteen under the general title "Songs of a Mountain Plowman." In May 1934, a third group appeared in *Poetry*. The following October, E. P. Dutton published Stuart's *Man with a Bull-Tongue Plow*, a collection of 703 sonnets written in a year's time. This book so impressed the Irish poet A.E. that he declared it "the greatest poetic work to come out of America since *Leaves of Grass*."[9]

In several of the sonnets in *Man with a Bull-Tongue Plow*, Jesse Stuart imagines himself addressing his old teacher from beyond the grave. It is in these poems that we get the strongest sense of the shared Agrarian values that bound Davidson and Stuart together. A fairly typical example is sonnet number 617.

> I do belong to these men of the past.
> I am one of a sleeping generation.
> I have gone to weed roots and dust at last.
> I may not have been a builder of the nation.
> But I was just one of the many millions,
> Lover of earth and trees and blackberry blossoms,
> And a one-horse scrap of land, Don Davidson.
> But now the blackberry roots grow in my bosom.
> My fields wait for the plow and weeds are growing.
> They soon will be too tall to turn them under.
> Cow birds swarm to my fields for April sowing.
> Blacksnakes crawl out after the first loud thunder.
> Don Davidson, I speak: Go use your pen,
> And let peace come from tangled grass and wind.[10]

7. Stuart, "America's Pindar," 18.
8. See Ruel Foster, *Jesse Stuart*, 56.
9. Ibid., 55.
10. Jesse Stuart, *Man with a Bull-Tongue Plow*.

I

The connection between the Agrarians and the *American Review,* which had seemed so promising at the outset, soon began to sour because of the personal and political eccentricities of Seward Collins. In a letter to John Gould Fletcher, dated April 16, 1933, Davidson expresses enthusiasm about the prospects for the review, but he concedes that all of his fellow Agrarians entertain doubts about Collins. Davidson's primary reservation was that Collins, as a New Yorker, would not be able to get the magazine before the audience it ought to reach. By June 7, he was pleading with Collins to pay him for a recently published review, so that he could pay some pressing bills before leaving Marshallville later that month. Apparently, this plea went unheeded. Writing to Frank Owsley on July 29, Davidson asks, "What is the state of affairs with Seward Collins. If he has treated the rest of you as he has treated me, some united action ought to be taken, at least to enable us to keep our self-respect and to warn other writers of his ways. . . . [H]e has maintained complete silence toward me ever since our meeting last spring."[11] In a letter to Davidson, dated August 5, Owsley complains even more bitterly of Collins's failure to answer letters and to extend promised payment. He is also chagrined by Collins's arbitrary editorial practices and his failure to build up circulation of the magazine. Prospects for the future were not enhanced by the fact that Collins was in Europe recovering from a recent nervous collapse.

Like many unstable people, Seward Collins was attracted to extreme political commitments. The Agrarians, distributists, neoscholastics, and neohumanists were all social reactionaries who rejected at least some of the basic assumptions of liberal democracy. Although such skepticism was not unusual during the Great Depression, Collins went several steps further to embrace a kind of medieval authoritarianism that he frankly identified as Fascism. As his espousal of Fascism became more explicit and more strident, the Agrarians became increasingly uncomfortable with Collins. To begin with, even if they were elitists, the Agrarians were not monarchists. They instinctively distrusted strong charismatic leaders such as Mussolini and Huey Long (two men whom Collins greatly admired). Moreover, as unabashed regionalists, the Agrarians rejected the nationalist ideal on which Fascism was based. As Albert E. Stone, Jr., observes, "their goal for America was not the 'one folk' ideal of Mussolini; quite the opposite. Agrarians welcomed regional, social and racial differences as healthy manifestations of time, place and tradition."[12]

---

11. Except where otherwise indicated, this and other letters cited in this chapter are housed in the Fugitive Collection of the Heard Library.

12. Albert E. Stone, Jr., "Seward Collins and the *American Review:* An Experiment in Proto-Fascism, 1933–37," 13.

If the Agrarians were becoming personally and politically disenchanted with Collins, the real break with his leadership was initiated by the foremost American distributist, Herbert Agar. While serving as London correspondent for the *Louisville Courier-Journal* from 1929 to 1933, Agar had become enamored with distributism and had even served as an editor for the distributist *English Review* at the time that *I'll Take My Stand* was published. Upon his return to the United States in 1934, he became fast friends with Allen Tate, an ally of the Agrarians, and a contributor to the *American Review.* Agar was interested in direct political action and tried to persuade Collins to move the *American Review* from New York to Louisville and to share the editorship with himself and Tate. When those plans failed to materialize, Agar formed an Agrarian-distributist weekly called *Free America,* which began publication in 1935.

Even if Agar and the Agrarians had not been moving in a different direction from Collins, their association with the *American Review* would not have survived the winter of 1936. In February, a small pro-communist publication called *Fight against War and Fascism* published an interview in which Collins showed his true colors. He told his interviewer, Grace Lumpkin, that he wanted to destroy factories and return to a medieval guild system. He expressed his longing for a king, his disdain for negroes, and his contempt for Jews. He declared himself a Fascist and seemed to imply that all the contributors to the *American Review* were of the same persuasion. If Agar was already in the process of distancing himself from Collins, Allen Tate did so even more vociferously. In a letter to the *New Republic,* Tate dissociated himself and the Agrarians from the sentiments Collins had expressed. He declared himself so deeply opposed to Fascism "that I would choose communism if it were the alternative to it." He also rejected Collins's romantic medievalism. "I do not want to restore anything whatsoever," Tate writes. "It is our task to create something."[13]

If Collins's affinities for Fascism and monarchy were foreign to Agrarian sensibilities, his racial views were not. Four years earlier, Allen Tate had been involved in a racial controversy that would be used to tarnish his memory over half a century later. In January 1932 Thomas Mabry, a young English instructor at Vanderbilt, invited Tate and Davidson to a party he was giving at the end of the month. Among the other persons invited were the novelist James Weldon Johnson, who was a guest professor at Nashville's predominantly black Fisk University, and the poet Langston Hughes, who was also on the Fisk campus at the time. Not only did Tate refuse to attend the party, he responded to Mabry's suggestion that he bring a beautiful woman by saying that the most beautiful woman he knew was his colored cook, but that her sense of decorum would prevent her from coming. Although he would be glad to meet socially with

13. See Stone, "Seward Collins," 17.

Johnson and Hughes any place outside the South, he insisted on maintaining local racial customs while in Nashville. The liberal Mabry was appalled by Tate's attitude, while Johnson was greatly embittered by the whole incident.[14] In 1985, at a literary conference in Baton Rouge, Louisiana, the African American scholar Houston Baker brought up the story of the Mabry party as an occasion for publicly referring to Tate as a "son of a bitch."

Although the Tate-Mabry correspondence is cited in biographies of both James Weldon Johnson and Langston Hughes, Davidson's role in this whole affair remains undocumented. Given his general racial views, which are quite well documented, one cannot imagine his taking a more liberal stance than Tate on this matter. Nevertheless, his racial attitudes appear to have been less rigid early in life than they would later become. As we have seen in his essay on Kipling, Davidson was far from enamored of the racist policies imposed by the British on the people of India. He was obviously pleased when William Stanley Braithwaite published his poems "Drums and Brass," "John Darrow," and "Ecclesiasticus" in the *Anthology of Magazine Verse* for 1923. Also, Davidson included Thomas W. Telley and other black professors from Fisk University as contributors to his book page.

Although his views might well have hardened by 1932, one can imagine Davidson wanting to meet James Weldon Johnson a few years earlier. On September 4, 1927, Davidson wrote in the "Spyglass": "Among books just published I should put James Weldon Johnson's 'The Autobiography of an Ex-Coloured Man' (Knopf) on the list of the most important. It is fiction; that is its characters are not taken from specific individuals. But as an expression of the mind of the negro it is not fiction, but truth, in a gentle and rather compelling garb."[15]

In his review of Johnson's novel, published in the "Spyglass" a week later, on September 11, Davidson begins by mentioning the debate between Negro writers with a sociological emphasis—W. E. B. Dubois, Walter White, Jessie Fauset, and Countee Cullen—and those, such as Langston Hughes and Jean Toomer, who are more interested in art for art's sake. He then argues that *The Autobiography of an Ex-Coloured Man* represents a successful combination of the two types. In an extraordinarily astute and sensitive discussion, Davidson goes on to write the following:

> Probably James Weldon Johnson has revealed as much of the negro mind as could be revealed within small limits. The reader gets a sense of privilege, for he knows only too well that "It is a difficult thing for a white man to learn what a coloured man really thinks, because . . . his thoughts are

14. See Eugene Levy, *James Weldon Johnson: Black Leader, Black Voice,* 327–28.
15. Donald Davidson, "The Spyglass," September 4, 1927.

often influenced by considerations so delicate and subtle that it would be impossible for him to confess or explain them to one of the opposite race." And the mellow, ingratiating style in which the book is written, the easy discursiveness, the simplicity of approach, and the entire absence of any belligerency or ugliness of spirit, make the work astonishingly impressive, all the more because it treats a delicate and dubious question.[16]

If Davidson was not yet committed to white supremacy by the time he was writing for the *American Review,* Seward Collins's attempts to turn him into a raging anti-Semite were even less successful. Apparently Collins wrote to Davidson some time in the fall of 1934 to chide him for not launching a more explicit attack on Jewish activists in his essay "New York and the Hinterland." Davidson responded in a letter dated October 10, 1934. Although he concedes a high incidence of Jews in the enemy camp, Davidson believes that ethnicity is at best a peripheral issue. "The new Jewish influence seems only a part of the larger problem," he writes, "and a part which, under the circumstances, would only serve to muddle the issues if it were stressed. Besides, I can't really believe that [Ludwig] Lewisohn, much as I dislike his views, or [V. F.] Calverton, or any one of a number of prominent Jewish writers, does any more damage than a number of altogether Gentile writers, editors, critics, philosophers, educationalists, etc. who could easily be named."

Later in that same letter, Davidson consults his personal experience to argue against a blanket condemnation of the Jewish people. Perhaps remembering his friendships with Sidney and Goldie Hirsch and other members of the fugitive race, Davidson writes:

> The Jews themselves are not all of the same school. Like the "New Negroes," they are divided. In the South there has never been any real anti-Semitic feeling—at least until the Scottsboro case. We have in this city, for example, a number of old Jewish families who are all but assimilated. To all intents, they are as much Southern as Jewish. They have little in common with the new element among the N. Y. Jews. I know some of these people very well, and respect and like them. Their danger of course is that they may be drawn into the vigorously "Pro-Semitic" ranks, and will so lose all that they have gained in the way of native roots.[17]

By mid-1936, the Agrarians had effectively distanced themselves from Seward Collins and the *American Review.* That same year, Franklin Roosevelt won an

16. Donald Davidson, review of *The Autobiography of an Ex-Coloured Man,* by James Weldon Johnson.

17. For a fuller discussion of Davidson's view of the Scottsboro case, see chapter 15.

historic landslide victory over the Republican presidential candidate, Alf Landon, who carried only Maine and Vermont. The *Literary Digest,* which had confidently predicted a Landon victory, went out of business. (Because the *Digest* conducted its poll by telephone, it greatly underestimated Roosevelt's support among the dispossessed.) Throughout America and Europe, writers were choosing sides in the Spanish Civil War. In England, A. E. Housman and Rudyard Kipling died. Adolf Hitler's theory of the master race was dealt a severe blow when the black American athlete Jesse Owens dominated the Berlin Olympics. Another American, Eugene O'Neill, won the Nobel Prize for literature. The best-selling fiction and nonfiction books in the United States were Margaret Mitchell's *Gone With the Wind* and Van Wyck Brooks's *The Flowering of New England.* Also, in 1936, the long-awaited sequel to *I'll Take My Stand* was finally published.

II

After the break with Seward Collins, the Agrarians began desperately looking for a new forum. Despite the interest generated by *I'll Take My Stand,* no publisher in the mid-1930s wanted a purely Agrarian book. Consequently, Davidson's efforts to put an exclusively Agrarian symposium together had been abandoned by the summer of 1935. At that point, Allen Tate and Herbert Agar proposed a more broadly based book attacking monopoly ownership. With little difficulty, Tate secured a contract from Houghton Mifflin and began recruiting a wide range of economic decentralists to contribute to the project. This eventually included eight of the Twelve Southerners whose work had appeared in *I'll Take My Stand* (for various reasons, H. C. Nixon, Stark Young, John Gould Fletcher, and Henry Blue Kline did not take part), the younger neo-Agrarians Cleanth Brooks and George Marion O'Donnell, several major distributists (principally, Herbert Agar and Hillaire Belloc), and a host of lesser lights. The book was rushed into print in an effort to influence the 1936 presidential campaign. (Agar even claimed that Roosevelt had made it the basis of his speech accepting the Democratic nomination for president.[18]) The revolutionary character of the anthology was suggested by its title—*Who Owns America? A New Declaration of Independence.*

With twenty-one essays, *Who Owns America?* was a more diverse collection than *I'll Take My Stand.* Lacking the sustained sectional polemicism of the earlier volume, the new symposium was less controversial. And, perhaps for that very reason, it was also widely ignored. Despite Agar's confident predictions, the book did not become a blueprint for Roosevelt's second term or for any subsequent

18. See Edward S. Shapiro, "American Conservative Intellectuals, the 1930's, and the Crisis of Ideology," 373.

presidential administration. Although aspects of the philosophy espoused in the volume are still being debated, one would search the corridors of power in vain to find a neo-Agrarian or a neodistributist. Even if one were to be found, it would be difficult to know where to place him on the conventional political spectrum. (Patrick Buchanan is the closest approximation of such a figure in contemporary American politics.[19]) The latter-day Jeffersonians were clearly wrong in thinking their program the only alternative to the Hobson's choice between Communism and Fascism. (Both varieties of totalitarianism were defeated in America by an increasingly Hamiltonian consensus.) They were much closer to the mark in predicting the havoc that unchecked industrialism would wreak on traditional ways of life.

Over sixty years after the publication of *Who Owns America?* it is more clear than ever how far the Agrarian position deviates from the worship of laissez-faire economics that now passes for conservatism. Not only were the Agrarians distrustful of capitalism, they were willing to use the powers of the federal government to redistribute property and income in a more equitable manner. In his essay "Big Business and the Property State," Lyle Lanier stops short of advocating government ownership of the means of production, but he does urge increased government regulation of business and even amending the Constitution to achieve that goal. Such regulation was accomplished by the New Deal after a few timely deaths on the Supreme Court made changing the Constitution unnecessary. When the surviving Agrarians gathered in 1980 to celebrate the fiftieth anniversary of *I'll Take My Stand,* Lanier was praising Barry Commoner, the presidential candidate of the ultra–left wing Citizen's Party.

We tend to think that the most important distinction in economic philosophy is between those who favor collective ownership of the means of production and distribution and those who advocate private ownership. In "Notes on Liberty and Property," Allen Tate argues that a far more important distinction is the difference between concentrated and widely distributed property. Big business has tried to rally small property owners to its cause by maintaining the illusion that all property rights are essentially the same. For small property owners, however, the right to property involves both legal and effective ownership—the right to sell and the right to use what one owns. This is clearly not the case for the small stockholder in a large corporation. The piece of paper that gives him part ownership in that corporation may produce dividends in flush times, but it gives him no real voice

19. At first glance, Buchanan's support for the American industrial worker would seem to make him an unlikely poster boy for the Agrarians and distributists. Nevertheless, his distrust of corporate elites and the global economy has endeared him to southern conservatives. (He has served as senior editor and regular columnist for the neo-Confederate *Southern Partisan* magazine.) Moreover, his Catholic social conservatism is congenial with the thought of such distributists as Chesterton and Belloc.

in the way his property is used. For that reason, Tate agrees with Marx that corporate capitalism in the necessary and inevitable prelude to Communism.

"The collectivist State," writes Tate, "is the logical development of giant corporate ownership, and, if it comes, it will signalize the final triumph of Big Business. 'All the arts,' said Walter Pater, 'strive toward the condition of music.' Corporate structure strives toward the condition of Moscow." (As a practical matter, the Communists could much more easily take over an economy that was already centralized than one in which property was widely dispersed.) Viewed in this light, a Jeffersonian economy would not be the via media between Hamiltonianism and Communism or Communism and Fascism but the opposite extreme from all of these various faces of collectivism. Tate summarizes his position in the following maxims: "Ownership and control are property. Ownership without control is slavery because control without ownership is tyranny."[20]

If *I'll Take My Stand* was long on diagnosis and short on cures, the same could not be said of *Who Owns America?* Although the contributors to this volume do not propose a single program for dealing with the ills of society, several of them suggest very specific and sweeping economic reforms. In "What the South Wants," John Crowe Ransom argues that because of the greater economic vulnerability they face, farmers are entitled to special treatment by the government. This would include such benefits as better roads, cheaper electricity, and more educational advantages. Farm laborers would also be ensured greater job security and a better standard of living. (Farmers would help to alleviate their own plight by engaging in a combination of money farming and subsistence farming.) Although the New Deal did many of the things that Ransom recommended, it did not halt the greater centralization of farming in America. As a result, agricultural policy gradually evolved into a system of government benefits for the wealthy, as increasing numbers of small farmers were forced off the land.

As radical as such economic prescriptions must have seemed at the time, the Agrarians and distributists believed that they would ultimately serve a conservative purpose. This thesis is suggested by the title of Andrew Lytle's essay—"The Small Farm Secures the State." A nation of small landowners is by nature socially conservative, he argues. The small farm "is a form of property . . . that the average man can understand, can enjoy, and will defend. Patriotism to such a man has a concrete basis. He will fight for his farm in the face of foreign or domestic peril." To maintain such an environment, Lytle concludes, "should be the important end of polity, for only when families are fixed in their habits, sure of their property, hopeful for the security of their children, jealous of liberties which they cherish, can the State keep the middle course between impotence and tyranny."[21]

20. Allen Tate, "Notes on Liberty and Property," 83, 93.
21. Andrew Lytle, "The Small Farm Protects the State," 238, 250.

20. Allen Tate, "Notes on Liberty and Property," 83, 93.
21. Andrew Lytle, "The Small Farm Protects the State," 238, 250.

In his own contribution to the symposium, Donald Davidson deals only peripherally with economics. The title of his essay, "That This Nation May Endure: The Need for Political Regionalism," ironically alludes to Lincoln's obsession with preserving the political integrity of the union but offers a much different prescription for achieving that end. By this point in his career, Davidson had become convinced that America was neither "one nation indivisible" nor an association of sovereign states, but a congeries of regional cultures. It was therefore a mistake to look to either the federal government or the individual states for solutions to our political and economic problems. These solutions would come only if the nation became a confederation of regional commonwealths. Just such a radical constitutional reform had been proposed by William Yandell Elliott and Frank Owsley. Endorsing this notion, Davidson argues that, at the very least, regional governments should have the power to tax and regulate commerce within their borders and to nullify objectionable federal laws.

Although the issue of slavery had been settled by the War Between the States, regional differences had not been obliterated. The subjugation of the South by the federal army was a military act with political consequences, but it could not impose an alien culture on a conquered territory. At their worst, the unionists were authoritarians interested only in political control. The totalitarian sensibility, however, insists on controlling the minds and hearts of people, as well. In the 1930s, Nazism and Communism posed that threat in an unmistakable manner by joining the totalitarian sensibility with the brute power of the police state. But totalitarianism is perhaps even more insidious when it wears a benign and genial face. The Agrarians believed that industrialism, with its promise of the good life, did wear such a face. Davidson puts the matter as follows:

> [I]t is the nature of industrial enterprise, corporate monopoly, and high finance to devour, to exploit, to imperialize; and a region which specializes in these functions is by that fact driven to engage in imperial conquest of one sort or another; . . . [on the other hand,] it is the nature of small business, well-distributed property, and an agrarian regime to stay at home and be content with modest returns. The region that specializes in these things, or that balances them with its industry in fair proportions, is a good neighbor, not desiring conquest. Whatever restores small property, fosters agrarianism, and curtails exaggerated industrialism is on the side of regional autonomy. If we had a fair balance of this sort in America, it is possible that the Old Federalism, with very small changes, would suffice our modern purposes.[22]

22. Donald Davidson, "That This Nation May Endure: The Need for Political Regionalism," 133. Subsequent references will be cited parenthetically in the text.

Six decades later, one is struck by Davidson's celebration of cultural diversity. In the last decade of the twentieth century, that concept became a shibboleth of the cultural Left. In practical terms, diversity all too often came to mean a racial and ethnic spoils system enforced by the protocols of political correctness. The ideal of a national or "American" culture, which had once been championed by political liberals, now came to be seen as a conservative notion. It is interesting, though probably pointless, to wonder whether Davidson would have altered his vocabulary had he lived to see the cause of multiculturalism extolled by black nationalists, radical feminists, and militant homosexuals. Certainly one of the challenges facing a principled conservatism is finding a way to achieve harmony in an increasingly pluralistic society.

Properly understood, the values of diversity and tolerance are more natural to a conservative sensibility than to a schematic leftist mind-set. Among his "six canons of conservative thought," Russell Kirk identifies an "affection for the proliferating variety and mystery of traditional life as distinguished from the narrowing uniformity and equalitarianism and utilitarian aims of most radical systems."[23] Political decentralization is one way of maintaining and enhancing that proliferating variety. As Davidson himself notes, "Independence, signifying as it does the end of colonialism, is a sacred word in American history. Among other things, it means that the land and the region belong to the people who dwell there, and that they will be governed only by their own consent" ("That This Nation," 134).

III

Although Agrarianism would continue to flourish as a literary sensibility, it ceased to function as a political movement shortly after the publication of *Who Owns America?* Ironically the group began to fall apart at precisely the time that it had the best opportunity to disseminate its views. It was of little consequence that the connection with the *American Review* had been severed by the midthirties. The Agrarians themselves controlled two of the top literary magazines in the country by the end of the decade. The first of these was the *Southern Review,* which was founded in Baton Rouge, Louisiana, in 1935, by Cleanth Brooks and Robert Penn Warren.

At that time, the only American literary quarterly that could rival the *Southern Review* was the *Partisan Review,* a nonacademic left-wing magazine of cultural criticism published in New York City. Because of their different emphases, the

23. Russell Kirk, *The Conservative Mind: From Burke to Santayana,* 7.

Partisan Review and the *Southern Review* were able to coexist quite easily in the same literary universe. (Before it was suspended by LSU in 1942 in the interests of alleged wartime austerity, the *Southern Review* was regularly publishing several of the most distinguished *Partisan Review* intellectuals.[24]) Then, in 1939, the *Southern Review* began to receive stiff competition from a quarterly published in the tiny village of Gambier, Ohio. Its editor was John Crowe Ransom.

In the spring of 1937, Ransom had seemed ensconced at Vanderbilt for life, when Gordon Keith Chalmers, the newly appointed president of Kenyon College invited him to come to his school in Ohio to "teach philosophy and write poetry." Although Ransom never did teach philosophy at Kenyon and wrote very little poetry after arriving there, Chalmers had other chores in mind for him. A truly visionary leader, Chalmers had convinced himself that the way to bring distinction to his small and obscure campus was to publish a literary quarterly that would achieve international acclaim. Plans for the *Kenyon Review* began shortly after Ransom's arrival in Gambier in the fall of 1937, with the first issue of the magazine appearing two years later. Because of the prominence of the *Southern Review* and the *Kenyon Review*, it was widely believed that the Fugitive-Agrarian fraternity (or mafia, if you will) exercised an iron-fisted control over American literary criticism during the late thirties and early forties. This impression was strengthened by the fact that several members of the fraternity and their younger disciples began publishing in the pages of both magazines.

Although Donald Davidson was a frequent contributor to the *Southern Review*, he was greatly disappointed that that magazine was not more programmatically Agrarian. (The *Kenyon Review*, to which he had contributed only one short review, seems to have had no social and political philosophy at all.) This disappointment boiled over when he tried unsuccessfully to place the fiction of his student Mildred Haun in the Baton Rouge quarterly. As a result of Davidson's efforts, a graduate program in creative writing was started at Vanderbilt in the late 1930s. On January 22, 1939, he wrote to Red Warren identifying Mildred Haun as the first graduate fellow in the program. He added that he "would be much pleased if the *Southern Review* would present her to the world." Davidson believed that to encourage Haun would also enable him to persuade the Vanderbilt administration to provide heartier support for the writing program. When Brooks and Warren rejected Haun's stories, Davidson wrote a strong letter of protest to Brooks. He was

---

24. For an authoritative history of the original series of the *Southern Review*, see Thomas W. Cutrer, *Parnasus on the Mississippi: The Southern Review and the Baton Rouge Literary Community, 1935–1942* (Baton Rouge: Louisiana State University Press, 1984). For a discussion of the relationship of the *Partisan Review* intellectuals to the *Southern Review*, see Mark Royden Winchell, *Cleanth Brooks and the Rise of Modern Criticism* (Charlottesville: University Press of Virginia, 1996), 107–9.

particularly chagrined that his "sponsorship . . . of a young author has availed nothing in the quarter where I should have hoped it might count, at least, to the extent of securing a 'debut.' " He then demanded to know the editors' general policy in choosing stories and whether they were "interested in 'discovering' able young Southern writers."[25]

Although Mildred Haun's rustic storytelling art appealed to Davidson, it was not sophisticated enough for either the *Southern Review* or the *Kenyon Review.* (Ransom claimed to like her work but did not feel that dialect stories were right for his magazine.) Fortunately, Lambert Davis at the *Virginia Quarterly Review* proved to be more receptive. Perhaps more important, Bobbs-Merrill published a collection of Haun's stories, *The Hawk's Done Gone,* in 1940. After leaving Vanderbilt, Mildred Haun entered the creative writing program at the University of Iowa in the fall of 1939. Correspondence from that time indicates that Davidson was pushing her work among his contacts at Bread Loaf, while giving her fatherly pep talks through the mail. Apparently, Haun was a shy girl who felt progressively more uncomfortable the farther she got from the Tennessee mountains. She was miserable at Iowa and welcomed the opportunity to return to her home state for further graduate work at Vanderbilt and eventually for a position at the *Sewanee Review,* which was published at the University of the South, approximately thirty miles northwest of Chattanooga. It was in this capacity that she gained dubious notoriety for an incident that may never have happened.

Although the *Sewanee Review* had been founded by William Peterfield Trent in 1892, it had not even been one of the leading literary magazines in the South for the first fifty years of its existence. That situation would change in the mid-1940s. When the original series of the *Southern Review* was discontinued in 1942, Alexander Guerry, who was vice chancellor of the University of the South, resolved to transform the *Sewanee Review* into a first-class literary quarterly to take its place. After Guerry persuaded the magazine's eccentric editor, William S. Knickerbocker, to leave, he turned the *Sewanee Review* over to Andrew Lytle, who improved the quality of the journal in his position as managing editor. (The temporary titular editor was T. S. Long, chairman of the Sewanee English department.) In 1943, the magazine increased the space devoted to poetry and began publishing fiction in each issue. The quality and timeliness of the criticism also became noticeably better. When Allen Tate came on board as editor in 1944, he redesigned the format of the review, began paying contributors, introduced prize competitions, and quadrupled the circulation of the magazine. (Even though the *Southern Review* was gone, Ransom at *Kenyon* and Tate at

25. The correspondence between Davidson and the *Southern Review* is housed in the Beinecke Rare Book Room and Manuscript Library at Yale University.

Sewanee maintained the Fugitive-Agrarian dominance of the nation's top literary quarterlies.) During this time, Mildred Haun was Tate's editorial assistant.

Despite his historic service to the magazine, Tate remained at the helm of the *Sewanee Review* for less than two years. Although he cited his impending divorce from Caroline Gordon in 1945 as the reason for his departure, Tate had also scandalized the Sewanee community with his compulsive lecheries. His fate was probably sealed when Mildred Haun reported to Guerry that Tate had propositioned her. As with so many cases of alleged sexual harassment, there was no independent evidence of what happened. Because no one could convincingly argue that this was not the sort of thing that Tate would do, his defenders resorted to claiming that Mildred Haun was simply not his type of woman. According to Walter Sullivan, "she was homely of face and figure, which would not necessarily have been crucial, except that she was . . . seemingly devoid of the spark and wit and sophistication that most of Allen's mistresses possessed."[26] When Davidson called Tate to warn him that Mildred's brothers were looking for him, Allen turned to Peter Taylor and others, who happened to be with him at the time, and said, "we must arm ourselves."[27]

As Brooks, Warren, Ransom, and Tate were gaining power and prominence in the larger republic of letters, Davidson found that his own influence was waning even within Fugitive-Agrarian circles. He had had more luck persuading his ostensible adversaries H. L. Mencken and Lambert Davis to publish his students than he had had advancing their cause with his friends and allies. Moreover, Vanderbilt's failure to retain Warren (whose temporary instructorship expired in 1934) and its willingness to allow Ransom's departure for Kenyon must have reminded Davidson how little the efforts of the Fugitive-Agrarians meant in their own backyard.

26. Sullivan, *Allen Tate*, 87.
27. See Ann Waldron, *Close Connections: Caroline Gordon and the Southern Renaissance*, 240.

GOOD FENCES MAKE GOOD NEIGHBORS

The one place where Donald Davidson was always able to escape the sense of isolation he felt in Nashville was at Bread Loaf. From a practical standpoint, spending summers in Vermont allowed him and his family to flee the stifling heat of Tennessee. The rural setting and the community of scholars devoted to literature made Bread Loaf a synthesis of both the Agrarian and Fugitive ideals. Because classes were held in the morning, afternoons were free. The evenings were often filled by visiting lecturers on literature, musical programs, and plays performed by the students in drama. Bread Loaf was also a place where old friendships could be renewed. So many of Davidson's colleagues and students from Vanderbilt visited him over the years that Allen Tate was prompted to say: "If anyone were to ask where the Nashville Fugitives came from, no one could answer, but if anyone were to ask whither they have flown, the answer would be 'to Bread Loaf.'"[1] No matter how vigorously the southerners were opposed elsewhere, they were always treated with respect on the mountain.

During his early years at Bread Loaf, Davidson boarded with the legendary local farmer Homer Noble. Something of the nature of their relationship can be gleaned from a letter Noble wrote to "Mr. and Mrs. Davidson" in Marshallville on November 15, 1932. "We love our rock ribbed Vermont," Noble begins, "but would like to see other places, including Tenn. 'You all' seemed to have enjoyed our company, as well as our climate, and scenery. We think you put it on rather thick. So we disclaim any fine qualities of character from natural tendencies but acknowledge that we are simply passing on what we have received from higher up." Noble goes on to say: "'We all' enjoyed your company, although

1. Bain and Duffy, *Whose Woods These Are*, 24.

201

we belonged to different political camps, and I think it is a good thing for Ladies and Gentlemen from North and South to mingle, for it brings about a better understanding. The trouble comes from those who are not Ladies and gentlemen mingling too freely and airing their opinions without any regard for common decency."

After a report on kittens Mary Davidson had doted on and news about a boy of French descent who had been shipped to the Nobles from the state industrial school, Homer concludes by contemplating the relative leisure he imagines the Davidsons to be enjoying in the South: "My mind wanders down to Georgia and I think of Katie Lou starting your fire for you and getting your serial, toast, and coffee ready. It makes me think how quickly I would join the Ancient Order of the Sons of rest if I were thus favored. I am now covering the inner walls of our cabbin with wallboard for we are to have it filled with hunters when the Deer Season opens, and we will have all we can accomodate in our house. So the family may have to sleep under the clothes line with a ladder over us."[2]

Davidson revealed much about the appeal Bread Loaf held for him in an address he delivered to the graduating class of 1938. While he gives community and tradition their due, he sounds more like a primitivist than an Agrarian. In fact, certain passages read as if they could have been written by Henry David Thoreau. Davidson clearly relishes the fact that residents of Bread Loaf are forced to do without some of the conveniences of industrial civilization. Reflecting on the tenuousness of man's control over nature, he notes:

> We have made acquaintance with the invisible stinging gnat, the persistent fly, the imperious skunk. We may witness the progress of milk from cow to table. We know that the drinking water comes from a pool 20 minutes walk up the hill. We feel the brunt of storms as well as witness the glory of sunsets. The rain thunders just as the excellent lecturer begins. The power goes off just as we are about to commit to paper the sublimest sentence of our lives. And then by the flicker of a candle we return for an hour to the terms of man's most ancient conquest: the little flame that obeys us and not the hired power company.[3]

Another one of the attractions of Bread Loaf is the nonacademic nature of the community. "The vast files of *PMLA, Anglia, Englische Studien,* and *Modern Philology,* cannot be transported up Ripton Gorge," Davidson observes.

---

2. This letter is housed in the Fugitive Collection of the Heard Library. I have neither corrected Noble's misspellings nor littered the text with bracketed *sics* in an effort to prove that I can spell better than a Vermont farmer.

3. Donald Davidson, "At Bread Loaf," 3. Subsequent references will be cited parenthetically in the text.

"We make that defect a virtue." Because they are not distracted by scholarly apparatus, the inhabitants of Bread Loaf are forced to become reacquainted with the masterworks themselves. If criticism is an act of discrimination, an essential part of the exercise is knowing what one can afford to do without. "A little of the best historical scholarship we must have, and do have, but it is surprising how much of it can be dispensed with, when we are obliged to make a choice and say what few books we really want to take with us to our figurative desert island" (4).

Davidson concludes by depicting Bread Loaf as a pastoral environment, in which the mechanized pace of life in civilization gives way to the older and freer rhythms of nature.

> [W]ith us everything is direct, personal, easy, concrete. I see you ten times daily at Bread Loaf. In the city I might see you once a year if I could gather courage to leave my engagements, brave the traffic, find the street and number where you live, and, having laboriously parked and locked my automobile, ring your doorbell and enter your apartment, only to find you obviously flustered and distraught by the appearance of an unexpected caller. But here, I tap at your door, I call across the lawn. We need no network of communication and transportation to manage our work and play. . . . Our time-sense, or our experience of time, is different. By the clock, our day is still 24 hours; but a certain leisureliness comes into our use of time. Hours become elastic. The days of the week lose their identity, we forget how to date letters. The days are longer at Bread Loaf, but they are pleasantly longer. We have more time, yet it does not drag, and presently we are surprised to find the summer gone so soon. (5)

Peter J. Stanlis, who studied at the Bread Loaf School of English from 1939 to 1944, vividly remembers Davidson as both a classroom teacher and a presence on the mountain. Stanlis's first class with Davidson was in British poetry of the fin de siècle period—with the chief text being Davidson's own anthology *British Poetry of the Eighteen-Nineties* (1937). Stanlis recalls that even though most of the poets they studied were more Victorian than modern and more minor than major, Davidson made them come alive in terms of the interests and problems of the twentieth century. What most appealed to him about such diverse poets as Wilde, Henley, Stevenson, Kipling, Dowson, Symons, Lionel Johnson, and John Davidson was their strict adherence to the traditional forms of the English lyric. "Davidson held to the same view on poetic form as did Robert Frost—that it takes not less but more originality to say fresh things in traditional forms."[4] Stanlis recalls that one highlight of the summer was James Southall Wilson's reading of

---

4. Stanlis's observations, which are paraphrased and quoted in the next few pages, are contained in a five-page single-spaced narrative he sent to M. E. Bradford in February 1991.

Thompson's "The Hound of Heaven" for those unable to attend church services in Middlebury. Davidson was in the audience that Sunday morning.

As fellow southerners, Davidson and Wilson would often team up to defend their home region in discussions about the War Between the States, even to the point of violating the ten o'clock rule. On the subject of more recent politics, however, Davidson and Wilson were in different camps. This fact was vividly demonstrated one afternoon during a croquet game, which pitted Wilson and his wife against Stanlis and Walter Pritchard Eaton, a professor of drama at Yale, with Davidson as spectator. The Wilsons were dedicated, even ferocious, croquet players, who specialized in knocking their opponent's ball as far out of play as possible. It usually was a winning strategy. On this afternoon, however, Davidson shattered the liberal Wilson's concentration by continually badgering him over his favorable view of the New Deal. This caused Wilson to miss some easy shots, which enabled Stanlis to knock his ball about thirty yards out of play. When Stanlis and Eaton won the game, Mrs. Wilson proved a hard loser, turning on Davidson for so distracting her husband. This was the only time Stanlis ever "witnessed a loss of sweet composure by this Southern lady."

In the summer of 1942, Stanlis took a class called "American Ballads, Folk Songs, and Folk Tales" from Davidson. Because of the anonymous character of the ballads, the class was never diverted into biographical criticism. What they concentrated on in their papers were the "American adaptations and variations that made balladry ever in the making." This process of continual re-creation was confirmed when Davidson invited a couple of Vermont balladeers, Grandpa Dragon and Grandma Fish, to Bread Loaf. Mrs. Fish said that "during the cold dark winters, when the country folk were frozen into their houses, they would weave baskets and also weave new verses to their ballads." Davidson helped the class see that the techniques employed in ballads could teach valuable lessons in the practice of writing—"with simplicity itself paramount; with actions above thought; the concrete above the abstract; the objective above the subjective." There need be "no elaborate psychological motives in the characters, who plunged into action *in medias res,* just as in the epic." Ballads "required no aesthetic apologia to accept the fiction, and the dream visions and prophecies were not sung for an emotional exploitation, but for the added flavor of the profound pathos that so often ended in a calm acceptance of death, because the tragic vision was an assumed fact of living."

In discussing the element of irreverence in American ballads, Davidson seemed to be of two minds. Although he praised irreverence as a reflection of our democratic character and frontier heritage, he also believed that ballads in America had ceased to be epical or tragic but had become the stuff of popular song lyrics. "This was a sign that American culture was becoming more secularized, because there were no objects that could command reverence. Davidson lamented this development, which was accelerated by industrialism and science, and made genuine faith in tragedy less and less tenable."

In addition to the folk music provided by local artists, more sophisticated musical performances were also very much a part of community life at Bread Loaf. Sometimes these were put on by the students themselves. At other times, professional musicians would be brought in. One summer, when Harry Owen was dean, an opera troupe from Philadelphia spent two weeks on the mountain, putting on a series of light operas. Madame Schuman Heinke gave concerts during two summers. In fact, musical programs were almost as frequent as lectures about literature. Recovering the connection between music and poetry that modernism had done so much to efface, Bread Loaf was a very congenial environment for someone of Donald Davidson's aesthetic convictions.

In the summer of 1944, Stanlis made the acquaintance of another southerner at Bread Loaf. Eric Bell, who had built a successful practice as a psychiatrist since finishing medical school, had come to Vermont to court Mary Davidson. Bell and Stanlis spent many an evening that summer drinking beer and talking politics and literature at the Pine Room in Middlebury. Eric claimed that, as a "damnyankee" Peter put an unnecessary "R" in just about every word he spoke, an accusation that Peter firmly denied. Then, just to watch his friend's reaction, Peter would deliberately add an "R" to words that were almost pure vowels. Eric's home state became "Allerbammer"; "whereupon he would be driven to despair." Because the ten o'clock rule did not apply in the Pine Room, Peter Stanlis learned much that summer about the War Between the States, particularly about army atrocities committed by General Sherman and others.

Stanlis credits the southerners he knew at Bread Loaf, particularly Donald Davidson, with giving him a proper appreciation of the importance of the war in American life. He came to realize that the conflict involved more than just a disagreement over slavery. Also at issue were contrasting views of state sovereignty. These, in turn, were rooted in fundamental philosophical differences—with the South defending a concept of corporate liberty and the North crusading for an ideal of individual equality. But even beyond all these causes, there was a more deeply rooted difference between North and South that Davidson enabled him to see. Stanlis writes:

> The war was between an agrarian society aiming at independence against an industrial society which demanded interdependence through a centralized authority. The superiority in numbers and power was clearly with the North. The harmonious integration of life in community, combining the spiritual and the secular, with reverence for nature, which was the view of the South, was destroyed in favor of all the agents of modernity in science, industry, and abstract secular reason, which triumphed through the Northern victory.

These forces continued to function after the war was over and have shaped American society ever since.

I

Donald Davidson found two different versions of Agrarian heaven in Marshall-ville and Bread Loaf. That he could feel totally at home in two such different regions of the country increased his regard for the geographical and social diversity of American life and his distrust of any attempt to produce a homogenized national culture. Not surprisingly, his best known and most frequently anthologized essay, "Still Rebels, Still Yankees," is a product of his experience in Marshallville and Bread Loaf. In highly evocative prose, he creates representative figures from both regions, Cousin Roderick and Brother Jonathan, based loosely on John Donald Wade and Homer Noble. Although he rejects any notion of *economic* determinism, geography is another matter. In Davidson's opinion, "the people were a great deal like the land" (*Leviathan,* 137).

Objections can easily be raised to this essay as sociology. As Michael O'Brien observes: "The farm of Homer Noble in Middlebury, Vermont, and the plantation of John Wade in Marshallville are not synonyms for New England and the South."[5] But Davidson is functioning here more as poet than as social scientist. Whether typical or not, the very fact that Cousin Roderick and Brother Jonathan could exist at all lent a certain plausibility to the Agrarian dream. Davidson begins "Still Rebels, Still Yankees" by approvingly citing Laurence Stallings's preference for a "Balkanized America." At a meeting of southern writers some years earlier, Stallings had said: "What I like about Charleston is that it has resisted Abraham Lincoln's attempts to put the country into Arrow Collars. If the South had won the war, the country would have had lots more color" (*Leviathan,* 131).

Neither during the War Between the States nor at any subsequent time did the South wish to alter the culture and customs of the North. Davidson was willing to accept the proposition that if Americans came to know each other, they would come to love each other; however, he believed that that proposition "ceased to have any meaning if America was to be subjugated to the ideal of uniformity, or to the ideal universe that some one section might generate. . . . To one who did not accept Lincoln's quaint idea that the United States must become 'all one thing or all the other,' it seemed more than ever true that the unity of America must rest, first of all, on a decent respect for sectional differences" (133, 136).

As Davidson proceeds to describe New England and the South, his essay moves away from abstraction and generalization and begins to resemble the

5. O'Brien, "Donald Davidson," 198.

kind of mythic vision evoked by Andrew Lytle and John Donald Wade in their contributions to *I'll Take My Stand*. Here is how a New England sunset appears to southern eyes:

> As the sun passed below the distant Adirondacks, we looked at the Green Mountains around us, and at the trim Vermont fields where all the weeds were flowers and all the grass was hay. In the clear detail of the afterglow we saw the forests of spruce and balsam and maple, and spoke of how the very wilderness, in this New England State, had uprightness and order. The woods were as snug and precise as a Yankee kitchen—no ragged edges, no sprawling, nothing out of place. In the clearings the farm-houses were all painted; and the barns were painted, too. The streams were orthodox streams, almost model streams, with water always translucent and stones rounded and picturesquely placed among moss and ferns. They were often called "brooks"—a word that for Southerners existed only on the printed page. (132–33)

Born and bred in such an environment, Brother Jonathan is a model of order and efficiency. His barn is arranged in two stories to accommodate both his hay wagon and his animals. He has built his house to economize space and retain heat. "The pantry and cellar are stored with vegetables, fruits, and meats that [his wife] Priscilla has put up with her own hands" (145). Brother Jonathan retains enough of a Puritan sensibility to revere President Hoover and loathe the "liquorish Al Smith." (In a letter to the Davidsons, Homer Noble's wife had expressed her fear that the election of Franklin Roosevelt would mean the end of Prohibition.) "But in the South, he supposes, he would be as good a Democrat as the next one" (146). Although he is too much of a rationalist to understand how Catholics can believe in the doctrine of transubstantiation, he has no difficulty affirming the Apostle's Creed when attending Sunday morning worship at the local Methodist Church. When an eccentric local landowner (obviously Joseph Battell) bought up much of the surrounding woodland and farm land, Brother Jonathan adamantly refused to sell out. The only hint of apostasy is "a faded photograph of a more youthful Brother Jonathan with his fellow baggage-clerks, taken in the days when he went west and got a job in Chicago" (145).

Life is not nearly so predictable and fastidious below the Mason-Dixon line. "If New England encouraged man to believe in an ordered universe, Georgia—and a good deal of the South besides—compelled him to remember that there were snakes in Eden" (140). Cousin Roderick may be as set in his ways as Brother Jonathan, but his are different ways. He "is the opposite of Chaucer's Man of Law, who ever seemed busier than he was. Cousin Roderick is busier than he seems. His air of negligence, like his good humor, is a philosophical defense against the dangerous surprises that life may turn up" (150). Distrustful of a market economy, "he tells how, when he was a young fellow, just beginning to take charge, his father came out to the plantation one day and asked for a ham. Cousin Roderick explained that hogs were up to a good price; he had sold the entire lot, on the hoof, and had good money in the bank. 'Sir,' said the old man, 'let me never again catch you without hams in your smokehouse and corn in your crib. You've got to make this land take care of itself' " (151).

Social and political equality are jealously preserved in Yankeetown. Everyone has his (and even her) say in the town meeting. If anyone in Brother Jonathan's family disagrees with the way the state is being run, he might very well stand for election to the legislature. In Rebelville, however, society is run through informal arrangements, which rely on a hierarchy with commonly understood privileges and obligations. As Davidson views the situation, noblesse oblige is most evident in the racial caste system. Speaking of Cousin Roderick, he writes:

> On his several tracts of land, the gatherings of inheritance and purchase, are some one hundred and fifty Negroes whom he furnishes housing, food, and a little money; they do his labor—men, women, children together—they are his "hands." He is expected to call them by name, to get them out of jail, to doctor them, even sometimes to bury them when "lodge dues" may have lapsed. They are no longer his slaves; but though they do not now utter the word, they do not allow him to forget that he has the obligations of a master. (151)

II

The sectional thesis expounded in "Still Rebels, Still Yankees" dominated much of Davidson's social criticism throughout the 1930s. As we have seen, it was central to his contribution to *Who Owns America?* and to several of his essays in the *American Review*. In 1938, the University of North Carolina Press published a collection of Davidson's sectional writings in a volume entitled *The Attack on Leviathan: Regionalism and Nationalism in the United States.* The animating spirit of that book was Frederick Jackson Turner, whose historic lecture on the significance of the American frontier had been delivered in the year of Davidson's birth.

Although not as well known as his pronouncements about the frontier, Turner's theory of sectionalism seemed to give scholarly validity to much of what Davidson felt instinctively to be true. Early in *The Attack on Leviathan*, he summarizes Turner's thesis as follows: "the sections are not vestiges from an older time, archaic and negligible, but have been and still are functions of the national life. They are real entities, not sentimental fictions: they have a place in the making of events, along with the Federal government and the state governments, although their place and power are not yet fully recognized or understood" (*Leviathan,* 9).

Sectionalism has become so pronounced in the United States for a variety of reasons, not least of which is the sheer size of the country. "The distance between Charleston, South Carolina, and the west coast is comparable, Turner points out, to the distance between Constantinople and the west coast of Spain; and the distance from our northern to our southern border is comparable to the distance between the Baltic coast and the island of Sicily" (21). According to Davidson, the character of an authentic section of the United States is "determined by its permanent physiographic situation, and by its less permanent, but persistent, population features" (22). The notion of sectionalism ideally suited Davidson's neo-Confederate sympathies. It allowed him to think of the South as culturally a separate nation, even if its aspiration to actual nationhood had been suppressed by the "War of Northern Aggression."

Davidson's interest in regionalism put him in an improbable and uneasy alliance with a group of liberal sociologists operating out of Chapel Hill, North Carolina. The leader of this group, Howard W. Odum, was professor of sociology at the University of North Carolina and founding editor of the *Journal of Social Forces.* Although Davidson had praised Odum's magazine in his book page during the twenties, he had fallen out of sympathy with its New South progressivism by the time the Agrarian movement was launched. For his part, Odum maintained a civil personal relationship with Davidson, while seriously mistrusting the prescriptions of Agrarianism. The one common link uniting the two men and their respective movements was a belief that the South had to be understood as a distinctive region. In his essay "Social Science Discovers Regionalism," which is the third chapter of *The Attack on Leviathan,* Davidson uses two recent books by the Chapel Hill group—Odum's *Southern Regions* and Rupert Vance's *Human Geography of the South*—to bolster his own position.

In his analysis of the South, Vance finds the region deficient by every measure of economic and social well-being. The reason for this does not lie in a lack of natural resources or in the biological inferiority of the population. Even the ravages of war and Reconstruction are not adequate explanations. In a conclusion that might seem anathema to the Agrarians, Vance cites the agricultural economy of the South as the reason for its backwardness. The problem is that the South's dependence on agriculture makes it particularly vulnerable to exploitation by the dominant industrial economy. Davidson argues, as Vance does not, that this exploitation represents the imperialism of the Northeast against the South. The Agrarian solution to this dilemma would not be to abandon agriculture but to find a more effective means of defending agricultural interests.

The term *regionalism,* as it is used by Vance and Odum, is meant to have fewer polemical connotations than the older word *sectionalism.* Although the regionalist and sectionalist may both recognize the same geographical and cultural divisions within the country, the sectionalist focuses only on parochial loyalties, whereas the regionalist defines local interests within a national context. The major problem that Davidson sees with regionalism, thus defined, is that it requires blind faith in the wisdom and benevolence of national planners. The sectionalist instinctively knows what is best for his own little postage stamp of soil. The regionalist must always be deferring to the good of the larger society.

In his fourteenth chapter, "Howard Odum and the Sociological Proteus," Davidson takes an even closer look at *Southern Regions* and its author. Despite his poet's discomfort with sociology, Davidson realizes that one kind of social science or another will greatly influence the future of both the nation and the region. He is, therefore, willing to endorse the moderate school of Vance and Odum as less objectionable than the militant one of Arthur Raper. (Raper had earned Davidson's undying enmity by writing a scholarly article critical of the locale in which Marshallville is located.[6]) Also, Odum's research lent statistical validity to the South's sense of grievance. "You cannot accuse a page of statistics of being nostalgic," Davidson writes. "There is no Jahveh-worship in a chart of taxation figures. It is impossible to charge Mr. Odum with renewing the War Between the States when he points out that the per capita farm income for New York state in 1929 was $493, while in Tennessee it was $137. Yet no doubt the South-baiters will have a verbal shillalah ready. They will probably call Mr. Odum a Fascist!" (291).

As much as the research of Odum might have to offer the South, Davidson is skeptical that it can be easily translated into a mass political movement. (The political failure of Agrarianism surely would have convinced him of the distance between the intellectual community and the population at large.) "If Mr. Odum, knowing what he knows, were a Huey Long in temperament, the sound trucks would be on the road tomorrow, to translate the deficiency indices into the language of the 'ignorant man,'" writes Davidson. How can the social science regionalists "achieve a united effort without unleashing the sectional antagonisms that they disclaim"? Only by discovering "some 'moral equivalent' for sectional antagonism" (308). Davidson believes that that will occur only if economic insecurity continues to plague the South.

Although Davidson was initially a cautious supporter of the New Deal, he soon became convinced that Roosevelt's attempts to forge a national political coalition would leave the interests of the South ill-served. (Andrew Lytle's image of the hind tit comes to mind.) In "The Dilemma of the Southern Liberals" (chapter

---

6. *Preface to Peasantry: A Tale of Two Black Belt Counties* (Chapel Hill: University of North Carolina Press, 1936). Davidson's reaction to this book will be discussed more extensively in chapter 17.

13 of *The Attack on Leviathan*), Davidson argues that the liberal movement in the South gradually abandoned its agrarian Jeffersonian roots to become an alien ideology. When Davidson published the original version of this essay in the *American Mercury,* he still regarded liberalism as an honorable philosophy, even if those who professed it were taking positions with which he disagreed. In a letter to Edwin Mims, dated January 24, 1934, he writes: "I feel that the younger liberals—Gerald Johnson & Co.—are far more blameworthy than [Walter Hines] Page and the leaders of his day, for they have had an opportunity that Page did not have for making a fresh estimate of the social and political history of the South." He concludes the letter by saying: "May I then subscribe myself, a liberal of some sort, I know not what."[7]

One can claim that modern liberalism is perpetuating the theoretical legacy of Jefferson while abstracting that legacy from its specific historical and social context. When Jefferson praises liberty for the common man, Davidson argues, he has a particular kind of common man and a particular kind of society in mind— "some Tom Jones of Virginia or Tennessee, a responsible individual with the stuff of God in him. Jeffersonian liberalism proposed to give Tom Jones his fair chance along with the 'rich and well-born' on whom Hamilton wished to confer power" (267). Although it is proper to defend a kind of metaphysical equality of persons within such a society, it would be foolhardy to destroy the society itself in order to enforce an unnatural equality of condition. That is why John C. Calhoun would claim the Jeffersonian mantle while defending slavery and opposing the tyranny of majorities. "Under Calhoun's leadership the South therefore abandoned the extreme equalitarian features of early Jeffersonian doctrine" (269).

While Southerners such as Calhoun were advocating an organic (even Burkean) interpretation of Jefferson, "their Northern brethren insisted on a thoroughly romantic application of Jeffersonian equalitarianism, and added to it (as if to parallel the South's paradoxical defense of slavery) their own paradox of a glorified Federal union which they did not concede would be in the least oppressive to the liberties of white Southerners or specifically partial to the 'peculiar institutions' of the North" (269–70). As a result, Davidson sees the War Between the States as "a struggle between two kinds of liberalism" (270).

The political struggles during the late nineteenth and early twentieth centuries often pitted a Bourbon elite against a populist insurgency. If the Bourbons had originally been gentleman farmers in the Jefferson mold, they eventually sold out to the railroads and other industrial interests. If the populists were yeoman farmers, their radical political and economic agenda clashed with Jeffersonian notions of limited government. The intellectual liberals, with their wholesale rejection of the southern past, struck Davidson as the least Jeffersonian of all.

7. O'Brien, "Edwin Mims and Donald Davidson," 911, 912.

"[I]t can hardly be said that the Southern liberals have any ancestors in the South. Their intellectual pedigree, so far as it is American, must be traced out on the northern side of the Potomac. They will discover their family portraits among the New England humanitarians. Their contemporary friends and relations may be found among the Marxians and socialists of various faiths who inhabit the metropolitan East, and, to some extent, the 'progressive' Middle West" (267). The dilemma of contemporary southern liberals, as Davidson sees it, is the failure of their idealistic vision to produce the promised utopia. This failure has evoked a variety of curious responses on the part of the liberals themselves.

> Some of them are undoubtedly quite ready to join the swing of the American Leviathan toward "social democracy," and these naturally hail the Roosevelt administration as a life-saver. Others are greatly attracted to the Russian experiment and are prepared to follow the Little Bolsheviks of the *New Republic* wherever the cries of the downtrodden proletariat seem to call them. Both directions, since they involve drastic curtailment of individual freedom, are strange paths for men who call themselves liberals. (263)

Despite his criticism of the direction that modern liberalism has taken, Davidson tries to convey the impression that he is writing from within the tradition rather than outside it. Nowhere does he propose a systematic conservative position with which to replace liberalism. (When the word *conservative* is used at all, it is as an adjective rather than a noun.) What he finally seems to endorse is a recovery of the original Jeffersonian vision, or liberalism properly understood. Davidson urges southern liberals to break their ties with industrial capitalism, which he assumes is doomed anyway, and once again unite its intelligence with the sentiments of patriotic southerners. "The Southern liberals, in short, may escape their dilemma by becoming more Southern" (284).

III

In urging a decentralized, regional approach to art, Davidson might seem to be reevaluating the distaste for local color that he expressed in his Fugitive days. In chapter 4 of *The Attack on Leviathan* ("Regionalism in the Arts"), he tries to confront this apparent contradiction by distinguishing between a kind of fashionable pseudoregionalism (which is really a form of cosmopolitan slumming) and the genuine article. Ersatz regionalism "may be distinguished by the explicitness with which it caters to a metropolitan audience. Its practitioners may establish art colonies in New Mexico or in the highland regions of the South. Its literary ladies, who once wore berets and smocks and drank gin while they read objectivist verse by candlelight, may don khaki and puttees and go into the hills to dabble in 'folk culture' or into the desert to collect pottery and watch snakedances" (82).

The salient distinction Davidson posits here is between cosmopolitan and provincial art. As in "A Mirror for Artists," he sees industrialism and urban civilization, particularly that of Manhattan, as the cause of all that is wrong with American art. (When Davidson would travel from Nashville to Bread Loaf, he would go out of his way to avoid passing through New York City.) In a culture dominated by the cosmopolitan aesthetic, "the mountain boy could get a college education, but the system that built him a school also took out of his mouth the traditional ballad that was his ancient heritage, and instead of a ballad gave him a 'mammy song' devised in Tin Pan Alley by the urbanized descendant of a Russian Jew" (74).

If Davidson sees New York as the center of artistic decadence, it is really serving as the port of entry for unhealthy European influences. But now that the expatriates have returned to America and the hinterland itself is developing an indigenous culture, America is beginning to experience a genuine renaissance of regional art. Many of the little magazines have folded, and the big New York periodicals are fast losing influence to such provincial journals as the *Southwest Review, Midland,* the *Southern Review,* and the *Virginia Quarterly Review.* (Even a maverick New York publication such as the *American Review* is really a manifestation of regional culture.) Theodore Dreiser and Sinclair Lewis have been replaced on the best-seller's list by Hervey Allen and Margaret Mitchell. "Van Wyck Brooks' indictment of the frontier, in *The Ordeal of Mark Twain,* was answered and exploded in Bernard De Voto's *Mark Twain's America,* a book which bristled with documentation and belligerency" (79). Charles Beard has been replaced by Vernon Parrington, and groups such as the Agrarians are vigorously searching for a usable past. Even as America is becoming more centralized politically and economically, Davidson believes that its culture is becoming more diffuse.

Davidson's concept of regionalism in art seems to shift when we get to chapter 11 ("Regionalism and Nationalism in American Literature"). Up to this point, he has used "regionalism" as an indiscriminate term of praise for the provincial art that he esteems, without realizing that the metropolitan art he disesteems is also the product of a regional culture, even if it is not as insular and self-sufficient as the regional cultures of the hinterland. Curiously enough, the Marxist critic Granville Hicks has erred in the other direction, dismissing as "regionalist" those works that do not advance the Communist Party line. In diametrical contrast to Davidson, Hicks has made "regionalism" into an all-purpose term of denunciation.

As Davidson is forced to admit in chapter 11, just about all works of American literature are regional. To see that this is so, we need only look for works that can be classified as purely "national" or "American." The sole book Davidson can think of that "attempts to interpret the 'typical' American . . . is Henry James's novel *The American*." "But the instance is embarrassing and inconclusive," he maintains, "for it suggests that a novelist must forsake America and become an exile if he is going to purify the American type from all the clinging alloys of local circumstance" (230). We are no better off if we try to define a national work of literature by virtue of its generalized subject matter. Whitman is one of the few writers who thought it was even possible to compose a national American poem. Although he writes voluminously on this subject in his prose, he was never quite able to turn the trick in verse. "[I]n every passage where he wishes to be quite clearly national, slighting no special interest and neglecting no peculiarity, he resorts to the catalogue, and gives us a list of all species and subspecies of Americana" (231).

The problem lies in assuming that there is such a thing as a national American culture, which can be embodied in works of art. "The concept of a national literature is a modern phenomenon, produced by the rise of the European nations to selfconsciousness during the later stages of the Renaissance" (233). A national literature does not come into being simply because a people share a common government. There must also be a single language, a single race, and a single culture. In addition, a national literature requires "a definite intellectual leadership associated with the centralizing presence of a capital like Paris or London; and besides, a long period of growth under aristocratic and learned guidance, and a second period, no less important from the modern standpoint, of critical and retrospective exploration of the cultural tradition." When such conditions exist, it is not necessary for anyone to ask of a given work: "But is it really English?" (234). In the United States, however, we are constantly asking whether a work is really American. Consequently, Davidson argues that we do not have a single national literature but many regional literatures. As long as this situation does not degenerate into a self-conscious antiquarianism or local color for the sake of local color, it is a welcome sign of cultural health.

If the growing regional consciousness in American literature was being reflected in advanced criticism and scholarship, Davidson found it strangely lacking in the textbooks that were being used to teach undergraduate college students. As director of freshman English at Vanderbilt, Davidson was painfully aware of the bias infecting even the best composition texts. In "Regionalism and Education" (a paper originally delivered before the college section of the National Council of Teachers of English), he takes a regional perspective on the phenomenon we now call "political correctness." Part of the problem lies with the changing role of composition teachers. No longer are they expected simply to instruct their charges in the intricacies of invention, organization, and style. Now they must also inculcate "desirable cultural attitudes." All too often those attitudes are defined by "the professional contributors to New York magazines: the men and women who have outdone all previous metropolitan generations in their disregard for the country west and south of the Hudson River" (246).

In the midst of his various reflections on regionalism, one subject that was never far from Davidson's mind was the role of the southern poet in the modern world. He had occasion to ponder this question once again when Allen Tate was called upon to edit a special southern issue of *Poetry* magazine in 1932. (Coming a decade after the southern number of *Poetry* edited by Dubose Heyward and Hervey Allen, this coup represented the triumph of the Fugitives over the Charlestonians, or, as Tate described it, a capitulation on the part of "Aunt Harriet.") Davidson saw the situation of the southern poet in 1932 much as he had when he wrote "The Artist as Southerner" half a dozen years earlier. The southern poet was still being urged to choose between two unsatisfactory alternatives—a cosmopolitan denial of his regional identity or an artless exploitation of that identity. Poets who choose the first of these alternatives are likely to abandon the South for New York, Paris, or London. Those who succumb to the second tendency might "commit monstrosities such as state songs on the model of Katherine Lee Bates' 'America the Beautiful' " or willingly appear in anthologies such as Addison Hibbard's *The Lyric South*. In other words, "a poet cannot be 'Southern' without behaving like a fool; and if he tries not to be a fool, he will not be recognizably 'Southern' " (341).

Not surprisingly, Davidson argues for a third way, which will allow the southern poet to be both a modern artist and a rooted member of his community. Although he does not mention the Agrarian movement by name, he believes that the artist can come to imaginative terms with the tradition of his region only if he is willing to take a stand on the social and economic issues confronting that region. At the same time, poets may be able to resist the cosmopolitan temptation more easily than writers in other genres, simply because they have less opportunity to pander to cosmopolitan prejudices. "For the poets are unpopular, the poets are never promoted, they escape the commercial taint that hangs over novelists and playwrights. Let them, then, write what they will, depending on their own integrity for a guide, and if they live like the Miller of Dee, envying nobody and with nobody envying them, they need not fear that their integrity will be impugned or spoiled" (346).

IV

As a collection of previously published essays, *The Attack on Leviathan* tends to repeat itself in ways that can be irritating to one reading it from cover to cover. Also, the organization of the book seems to be a bit arbitrary. The two chapters discussing the Chapel Hill sociologists appear over a hundred pages apart and in different sections of the book. Similarly, the chapters dealing with regionalism in the arts are found under different section headings. Although he extols regional diversity, Davidson is concerned primarily with the American South. In tone, the essays range from fiery polemicism to sweet reasonableness. (Only "Still Rebels, Still Yankees" reaches heights of near poetic lyricism.) What holds the book together (beyond its repeated affirmation of the regional thesis) is the metaphor implied in its title. In 1651, Thomas Hobbes used the term *Leviathan,* which was originally the Hebrew name given to the sea monster of the Old Testament, to refer to the all-powerful civil state. Unlike those of the nationalistic right (Fascists and big government conservatives), Davidson distrusted the Leviathan most when it seemed most benign. (Like Hamlet's devil, this monster had the power to assume a pleasing shape.) That is why he was more interested in attacking it than in teaching it to eats grits or speak with a southern drawl.

It is easy to accuse Davidson of overemphasizing the importance of regionalism in American life and underemphasizing other factors that distinguish particular cultures within the United States. Because we have become a much more mobile, even transient, society since the 1930s, more diverse populations have come to inhabit the traditional geographic regions. It can be argued that factors such as race, religion, class, ethnic heritage, political philosophy, recreational preferences, and sexual orientation play as great a role in determining a person's sense of identity as the location of his legal residence. If that is true, however, it is certainly no argument for uniform national solutions to the problems of our society. For better or worse, we are organized politically along geographic lines, not according to these other distinguishing characteristics.

For all the changes this country has seen, there is an irreducible core of regionalism that does persist. In the preface to his book *The Nine Nations of North America* (1981), Joel Garreau writes that "if Washington, D.C., were to slide into the Potomac tomorrow under the weight of its many burdens and crises, . . . North America would not suddenly look around to discover a strange and alien world. It would see a collection of healthy, powerful constituent parts that we've known all our lives."[8] I suspect that Donald Davidson would have agreed.

8. Joel Garreau, *The Nine Nations of North America,* xvi.

THE LAST AGRARIAN

In 1989, Russell Kirk recalled browsing through the library at Michigan State College as an "earnest sophomore" over fifty years earlier. It was there that he happened upon *The Attack on Leviathan.* "It was written eloquently," Kirk notes, "and for me it made coherent the misgivings I had felt concerning the political notions popular in the 1930s. The book was so good that I assumed all intelligent Americans, or almost all, were reading it."[1] As Kirk would learn later, nothing could have been further from the truth. After selling 206 copies in the 1937–1938 fiscal year, 204 the next year, and 76 the year after that, *The Attack on Leviathan* sold a total of 100 copies over the next nine years. Finally, in 1948, the University of North Carolina Press pulped the remaining unbound copies of the book and allowed *The Attack on Leviathan* to go out of print.[2]

Even as Davidson's defense of his homeland and his more general argument for cultural regionalism was going largely unnoticed, an eccentric book that was filled with unflattering caricatures of the South was sweeping the nation. In 1941, when *The Attack on Leviathan* was selling a grand total of six copies, Alfred A. Knopf published *The Mind of the South,* a debunking venture in cultural anthropology by a North Carolina journalist named W. J. Cash. Even though *The Encyclopedia of Southern Culture* (published in 1989) cites this book almost as often as it does the writings of Faulkner and Jefferson, *The Mind of the South* is not a work of philosophy, sociology, or intellectual history. It is a rambling interior monologue

1. Russell Kirk, "*The Attack on Leviathan* and the South's Conservatism," 1.
2. For a brief discussion of the publishing history of *The Attack on Leviathan,* see Michael O'Brien, *The Idea of the American South,* 257–58. Peter Smith Publishers brought out a reprint of Davidson's book in 1962. Then, in 1991, Russell Kirk reprinted it again in the Library of Conservative Thought, a series he edited for Transaction Press.

by a sensitive young man who loathed his small-town upbringing. Nearly six decades after its original publication, Cash's book remains in print and continues to stir controversy among scholars and ordinary readers alike.

Although the phenomenal success and enduring influence of *The Mind of the South* could not have been predicted at the time, Cleanth Brooks immediately feared the damage the book might do. It is therefore significant that he turned to Donald Davidson to critique it for the *Southern Review.* "I had to give the book a very cursory reading myself," Brooks wrote to Davidson on March 19, 1941. "The book seems to me more important than the material in it—for it will certainly be taken as a 'proof'—ordered and logical—of a whole set of preconceptions widely held, North and South. And for this reason the book needs an answer."[3] That answer came from Davidson in the summer 1941 issue of the *Southern Review.*

Davidson begins by arguing that Cash is simplistic and reductive. Reiterating one of the main arguments of *The Attack on Leviathan,* Davidson maintains that there is not a single South with a single mind but several different regions with distinctive interests and values. From now on, it will not be necessary to try to understand these different regions. One need only master Cash's pet term the "savage ideal." This "ideal" is simply the tendency to suppress dissent and variety in order to forge a more uniform society. Like Mencken, Cash lays the blame for this tendency at the feet of fundamentalist religion, although he does recognize the role of Reconstruction in strengthening the southern hegemony. The result is that we have in the South a society that Cash can compare only to those of medieval feudalism in the past or to Fascist Italy, Nazi Germany, and Soviet Russia in our own day. As Davidson is quick to point out, Cash's characterization of the South as a totalitarian society fails to account for the fact that this region was then exceeding all other sections of the United States in its support for England in its war against Hitler.

In his attempt to construct a psychological profile of the South, Cash says both too little and too much. He ignores the historical context for the antebellum defense of slavery, particularly the fact that this defense was part of a debate with strident abolitionists. Also, by concentrating so on the aristocrat and the backwoodsman, Cash virtually ignores the yeoman farmer, whom Andrew Lytle and Frank Owsley thought to be the real backbone of the South. Although Cash's study is supposed to be the intellectual history of a region, he says next to nothing about southern contributions to political theory, preferring to see southern politics as "a kind of rhetorical picnic."[4]

3. This letter is among the Cleanth Brooks papers housed in the Beinecke Library at Yale University.

4. Donald Davidson, *Still Rebels, Still Yankees and Other Essays,* 204. Subsequent references will be cited parenthetically in the text.

If Cash ignores many of the virtues of the South, he also tends to overlook the fact that there are endemic vices above the Mason-Dixon Line, as well. Giving the Mind of the North its due scrutiny, Davidson waxes vituperative against John Brown, William Lloyd Garrison, Thad Stevens, Walter Winchell, Fiorella LaGuardia, Aaron Burr, opponents of the Fugitive Slave Law, Abraham Lincoln, John L. Lewis and the CIO, northern Marxists, Mother's Day, feminism, Ralph Waldo Emerson and the transcendentalists, abolitionists, Irish immigrants (especially the Fenians), Ulysses S. Grant and his associates, Mayor Jimmy Walker, Eleanor Roosevelt, Henry Wadsworth Longfellow, John Greenleaf Whittier, Eddie Guest, James Whitcomb Riley, Edna St. Vincent Millay, and "all the movie people" (206).

Davidson believes the best that can be said about *The Mind of the South* is that it can do no permanent harm. As objectionable as the book might be, no true southerner would believe it, and no detractor of the South would find anything in it that he didn't already think was true, anyway. But what should we do with the scalawag Cash himself? Davidson takes up this thorny issue in a mock oration, which concludes his essay. "And now, fellow-Southerners, Proto-Dorians, the moon is setting, and the Fiery Cross is burning low. You all know what we all came out here for tonight, and let's get through with it. You all have heard what Mr. Cash has had to say, and I have tried, the best I could, to make plain to you what it means. Now what do you say? Shall we use the gun or the rope? Or ride him on a rail? Or just turn him loose?" (211–12). (The decision was to turn him loose and head home to whatever the womenfolk had spread out for the knights of the savage ideal.) In a macabre turn of fate, word reached Baton Rouge, too late to alter the review, that Wilbur Joseph Cash had hanged himself in a hotel room in Mexico City—the victim of no regional pathology but of private demons that have never been fully understood.

I

Davidson's fervent support of sectionalism and his continued loyalty to the Agrarian movement coincided with a growing sense of intellectual and personal isolation. By the time he left Vanderbilt for Kenyon, John Crowe Ransom had concluded that Agrarianism was a lost cause and had made his peace with the New Deal. As editor of the *Kenyon Review,* he would soon be devoting his full energies to literary criticism. (Although it had happened in fact almost a decade earlier, Ransom formally announced his break with Agrarianism in "Art and the Human Economy," an essay published in the autumn 1945 issue of the *Kenyon Review.*) Despite continuing to think of himself as an Agrarian, Allen Tate had an easier time than Davidson accepting the movement's lack of political influence.

Throughout the 1930s, the breach between Davidson and the rest of the Agrarians widened. Periodic bouts of depression led to stretches of inactivity that had Davidson's friends complaining among themselves. Writing to Tate from England on January 3, 1932, Ransom worried that "Don's going to get, not less, but more incapable of action. His trouble is pretty deep. He can't be jollied out of his melancholy, and as for intimidation, Don is like a large Tennessee knob of limestone." (Less than three weeks earlier, Davidson had refused to join Tate in protesting a charge of "criminal syndicalism" that had been brought against a group of New York writers who had supported striking miners in Harlan, Kentucky.) In a letter to Tate dated March 29, 1939, Ransom expressed his reservations about *Lee in the Mountains and Other Poems*: "Don is a real problem to me. I haven't been able yet to write about his book of selected poems, and I simply couldn't touch them in a published review; nor do I dare send them out to any good reviewer. Don just stopped growing before the rest of us did. . . . Don's case is partly private but partly, I'm afraid, the effect of ideology."[5]

In a long letter to Tate, dated February 23, 1940, Davidson confesses to feeling despondent:

> Well, I am certainly isolated. No doubt of that. I do not grieve, however, over the kind of isolation that may occur from the disregard of Mr. [Morton Danwen] Zabel or of the Communist reviewers of New York. I do not respect them; they can all go to hell. But I am decidedly grieved by being isolated from my friends. I don't mean physical isolation, deplorable though that is. I mean that I suddenly find myself at a disagreeable intellectual distance, for reasons that I do not in the least understand. . . . It is this intellectual isolation, this lack of communion, which I feel the most. And it began before any of you left these parts. Why is a mystery I can't solve. What fault was I guilty of? Did I just fail to keep up with the pattern of your thinking, and, though once worthy, thus become unworthy? I felt more than once, that there was a cloud between me on the one side and you, J. C. R., Andrew, and perhaps more on the other side. (*Literary Correspondence*, 323, 324)

Tate's response to these complaints was a letter of chastisement, written on February 28, 1940. On the matter of isolation, Tate contends that Davidson had always refused to enter casually into intellectual conversations, preferring instead to withdraw into his own ego. "In short, your arrogance has separated you from your friends," he writes. (Tate was particularly piqued at Davidson's failure to attend some function associated with the recent publication of Andrew Lytle's *At the Moon's Inn*.) "[Y]ou have done your level best to frustrate one of the finest intelligences and one of the finest poetic talents in this country; but you were

---

5. See O'Brien, "Donald Davidson," 191, 193.

so good to start with that you have achieved something very remarkable in spite of yourself."[6]

No doubt, part of Davidson's depression was owing to the lack of appreciation he felt for his efforts on behalf of Agrarianism. As with the Fugitive movement, Davidson saw himself doing most of the heavy lifting, while others were receiving most of the credit. Writing to Davidson on December 4, 1942, Tate sees the matter much differently. Although *Who Owns America?* "was not the symposium any of us preferred," he writes, "I took the view that it was either that or nothing." The blame for this situation he lays squarely at Davidson's feet: *"All through that period you simply would not act."* In the next paragraph, he accuses Davidson of having "a gift for persecution and martyrdom." "You have always had a steady job and security, and of late a considerable royalty income," he continues.[7] "I have had temporary jobs and insecurity, and right now I face great difficulties. So far as I can see you have not made any material sacrifices for agrarianism, while others certainly have" (*Literary Correspondence,* 328).

In his response to Tate, dated January 2, 1943, Davidson bristles at the accusation that he had been idle during the period between *I'll Take My Stand* and *Who Owns America?* "You forget what a difficult position I was in during that time," he writes: "burned-out of Wesley Hall, broke and in debt, ill with overwork and serious dental troubles, and my family ill too; my wife, in those years, had to undergo a serious operation which incapacitated her for a long period: we had to manage alone, unaided, without cheer or support from any quarter." Later in the letter, he reminds Tate that, while others in the fraternity were pursuing various non-Agrarian interests after *Who Owns America?,* he had published seventeen articles, several reviews, and *The Attack on Leviathan* between 1936 and 1940. All of these works (and, one might add, most of *Lee in the Mountains*) "bear rather specifically upon agrarian matters, as I understand them" (*Literary Correspondence,* 330). Davidson also notes that he had made several public appearances on behalf of the cause and had included various Agrarian writers in the courses he taught.

Even as Davidson's relations with his oldest Fugitive-Agrarian friends began to sour, he renewed his ties with one of the most distant and eccentric of the brethren, John Gould Fletcher of Arkansas. Fletcher had embraced the Nashville poets at the tail end of the Fugitive movement, in large measure because of his break with Ezra Pound, Amy Lowell, and the literary modernism with which he had been so deeply involved during his years in England. As if to compensate for his expatriation, Fletcher became the most patriotic of southerners upon his

6. This letter is housed in the Fugitive Collection of the Heard Library.
7. Tate is referring to Davidson's royalty income from *American Composition and Rhetoric,* which will be discussed later in this chapter.

return to Arkansas. When he tried to force a showdown between the Agrarians and the *Virginia Quarterly Review,* however, he succeeded only in alienating Ransom and Tate and embarrassing Davidson. His vitriolic attacks on Lambert Davis at a literary conference in Baton Rouge in April 1935 were the prelude to a nervous breakdown that left him hospitalized soon afterward. There was never any chance of his being asked to contribute to *Who Owns America?* which was published the next year. Fletcher's estrangement from what was left of the Fugitive-Agrarian movement became complete when Robert Penn Warren repeatedly rejected the poetry that he submitted to the *Southern Review* and eventually failed even to give him reviewing assignments.

Throughout this period Fletcher saw Davidson as a kindred spirit. In a letter to Davidson, dated November 5, 1937, Fletcher argues that he, Davidson, Owsley, and Nixon "are rapidly becoming the leading spokesmen of the group who want to preserve the best features of the Old South without recourse to such outrageous and bad economic and moral conditions as prevail, for example, in eastern Arkansas." In a longer letter, written on December 17, Fletcher contends that "the [Agrarian] group always contained elements that would tend, inevitably, to divide into a left wing and a right wing." He identifies himself with the left wing, while seeing "Ransom and Allen . . . on the right-wing side."[8] Apparently Fletcher, like so many democratic nativists throughout the forties, thought that literary modernism was an elite and reactionary movement. In contrast, he saw himself (and, presumably, Davidson) as belonging to a more authentically populist literary tradition. Also, in taking his stand with the Southern Tenant Farmers Union, Fletcher was siding with the Radical Left, even if his reasons for doing so could be most accurately described as Tory benevolence.

If several of the other Fugitive-Agrarians were enjoying literary fame and at least a modicum of economic comfort during the late thirties, these proved to be hard times for Donald Davidson and John Gould Fletcher. Their correspondence in 1938 is filled with laments about the neglect of their recently published books—Davidson's *The Attack on Leviathan* and Fletcher's *Life Is My Song.* A similar fate seemed to await Fletcher's *Selected Poems,* which was ignored by the reading public and panned by the reviewers. Then, in what appeared to be a miraculous turn of fortune, that book was awarded the 1938 Pulitzer Prize for poetry. Rather than giving him a new lease on life, this proved to be an isolated bright moment in a disintegrating literary career. Although Fletcher published two volumes of poetry in the 1940s (*South Star* [1941] and *The Burning Mountain* [1946]), his best book during that decade was a history of Arkansas. (For some time, the primary breadwinner in the family had been Fletcher's wife, the novelist Charlie May Simon.) When Davidson and Fletcher resumed correspondence (after a

8. Fletcher, *Selected Letters,* 185, 187.

break of several years), Fletcher was doing nothing more original than compiling an anthology of southern poetry for Rinehart.

On June 14, 1949, Davidson wrote Fletcher a long and mostly unhappy letter. The Vanderbilt administration was continuing to treat the remaining Agrarians badly. Frank Owsley had gotten so fed up with the situation that he had left for a position at the University of Alabama, while Davidson himself had just completed a leave of absence that had been only marginally productive because of Vanderbilt's unwillingness to arrange Theresa's work schedule to fit his travel plans. But his greatest lament was over the breach between himself and the other Fugitives. Thanking Fletcher for a generous blurb he had provided for a reissue of *Lee in the Mountains,* he writes:

> So far as I know, not one of my old friends of *The Fugitive* group has ever found occasion to commend my poems in public as you have done, and they seem ever more and more distant in all sorts of ways. I am like one beleagured in a lonely cabin, wondering whether I can hold out, then I hear the crack of your rifle and take courage. . . . It is true that I began to write the kind of poetry I prefer to write after the Fugitives discontinued their regular sessions, and I would rather think that it falls outside the sphere of so-called Fugitive doctrine.[9]

Although the Fletchers occasionally stopped in Nashville on their way east to New York, the Davidsons found it more difficult to get as far west as Arkansas. Nevertheless, in late April 1950, they did visit John and Charlie May at their country home near Little Rock. "Beyond the distant gate at the end of the narrow, winding driveway," Davidson recalls, "we knew that modern traffic sped on the paved road; but the Fletchers' house was like a place in the wilderness, quiet and removed as a pioneer homestead." Davidson was fully satisfied that "Fletcher, who in his time had been one of the most restless of wanderers, had found this spot in his own country, where he might spend in happiness the many years one hoped God would still grant him" (*Still Rebels,* 31).

The truth, alas, was more ominous. Fletcher's biographer, Ben F. Johnson III, notes that, at one point during their stay, "Fletcher told Davidson that he had been worried about Charlie May's health since her recent sinus operation. Although startled, Charlie May did not interrupt to explain that the operation occurred thirty-five years earlier." Immediately after the Davidsons were gone, Fletcher could not remember the conversation that had just taken place. "In addition, the table of contents for the Southern anthology remained unfinished because he began all over with the first page each time he sat down at his desk."[10]

9. This letter is housed in Special Collections of the University of Arkansas Library.
10. Ben F. Johnson III, *Fierce Solitude: A Life of John Gould Fletcher,* 252.

224   THE MEMORY KEEPER (1936–1950)

On the morning of May 10, the body of John Gould Fletcher was found lying face down in a cattle pond. He had drowned in two and a half feet of water—with his coat, hat, billfold, and cigarettes laid out carefully along the edge of the bank.

II

After the incredible productivity of the 1920s, each of the major Fugitives experienced periods of poetic drought. Although he continued publishing selections of his verse, John Crowe Ransom wrote virtually no new poetry after the twenties. For Allen Tate, the barren period came during the latter half of the 1930s. Even the remarkably fecund Red Warren published no new verse between "The Ballad of Billie Potts" in 1944 and *Brother to Dragons* in 1952. The wells of poetic inspiration also dried up for a considerable time in Donald Davidson's career. Between *Lee in the Mountains* in 1938 and *The Long Street* in 1961, he published only three poems. "Hermitage," which is the first and best of these, celebrates the values of the southern past, while warning against American involvement in the Second World War.

Davidson first presented "Hermitage" at a national meeting of Phi Beta Kappa in Williamsburg, Virginia, on December 5, 1940. ("Hermitage" was that year's annual Phi Beta Kappa poem.) The main speaker at the meeting, Marjorie Nicholson, made a spirited interventionist speech, which received considerable applause. That the same audience responded favorably to Davidson's poem probably suggests that they did not understand its underlying political message. In fact, after the poem appeared in the winter 1943 issue of the *Virginia Quarterly Review,* Allen Tate confessed: "I could never tell what you were saying exactly, and it seemed necessary to find out, because, unlike much modern poetry, it seemed to depend on an 'argument' about the pioneer. I know your ideas on that subject, and conjecture your thesis, but I felt it wasn't distinct enough in the poem" (*Literary Correspondence,* 334–35).

In "Hermitage," Davidson argues that an essential part of the American experience is liberation from the political conflicts of Europe. This leads logically to the isolationist stance he took prior to Pearl Harbor and never fully renounced. Although his views on contemporary politics influenced "Hermitage," the poem itself is a celebration of one of the original tall men—"Andrew Davidson, a Pioneer of Southwest Virginia and of Bedford County, Tennessee" (*Poems,* 68). Like "Horde," which precedes it in Davidson's *Poems, 1922–1961,* "Hermitage" employs archaic language reminiscent of Anglo-Saxon verse. Again we encounter inverted word order, figurative circumlocutions (such as the kenning), and a kind of ceremonial diction that identifies this as primarily a "public" poem and only secondarily as a meditation on the poet's own family history. The speaker is a modern persona, who, unlike the man by the gate in Tate's "Ode to the Confederate Dead," seems in fundamental harmony with his heritage.

In the first section of the poem, "Descending Chestnut Ridge," the speaker begins by saying:

> Now let my habitude be where the vine
> Tumbles the sagging rails, and the late crow
> Alone can challenge, whom for countersign
> I open these uncrafty hands,
> Unweaponed now, to seek upon the hill
> Stones where no filial tribute can be lost,
> Above the bones not laid in stranger's lands,
> But their own earth commingles with their dust. . . . (68)

The former home of Andrew Davidson has become a hermitage to which his descendant can retreat to ponder the history of his people in this country. In the background are the far-off "sapless nations" of an older world, bereft of their innocence and locked in an "unending cycle" of warfare. Unencumbered by the ideological passions that breed wars (he is "unregenerate by false faith"), the speaker is able to descend into Chestnut Ridge and recover a sense of his familial past: "To mark the clearing and to know the hearth / Where one smoke stands against the frosty sky / And one axe rings above the frosty earth" (68–69).

In the second section of the poem, "The Immigrant," the focus is on the "far-off sire" himself. Although the speaker "cannot see him plain" and cannot "tell what fire" brought him to these shores, he can at least hear the growing rumor of the immigrant's tale, "As voice to voice into the folk-chain melts / And clamor of danger brings the lost kin close" (69). (In other words, our present sense of peril brings the family together to seek the counsel of the past.) Through imagination, the speaker is able to visualize his ancestor as a kind of generic pioneer: "First of the host of all who came like him, / Harried from croft and chapel, glen and strath." In the new world ("where the beech-mast falls"), the pioneer is able to forget " . . . once how red / The dew lay at Culloden." Here:

> . . . Old feuds fail,
> And nevermore the axe sings on the wall—
> Since age on age we fled,
> Since we together, Gael and Gaul,
> Palatine, Huguenot, came in company
> And washed the old bitter wars in the salt sea. (69)

The third and longest section of "Hermitage," "In Blue-Stocking Hollow," ponders the frontier movement that brought Andrew Davidson to Bedford

County. The speaker tells us that "Our home is far across the western wave / Back of whose steeps, forsaken and foregone, / Lost continents ebb we have no power to save" (69). As the Virginian moves farther into the New World, he is "unshackled" by the fecundity of the land and the abundance of wild geese "hurling southward with invincible wing." These riches help to compensate him for what he has lost by turning his back on Europe: "To seal the firm lips of our unregret / To charm the door against the former age / And bless the lintel of our hermitage" (70).

In this new land, settlers can still share memories of the European past, still tell about "how Ilion fell" and "recall / Platonic converse." But a newer history has intervened between us and that older past. The nature of this newer history is spelled out in the closing stanza of the poem, where the "greybeard" of the new world tells the "men and maids" who seek his benediction:

> . . . This I leave to you!
> The Indian dream came on me in these glades,
> And some strange bird-or-beast word named me new.
> Peace to all who keep the wilderness.
> Cursed be the child who lets the free-hold pass. (70)

At first, it might seem strange to find Donald Davidson, who is constantly extolling a reverence for the past and its obligations in his patriotic southern poems, sounding like a member of Emerson's party of hope. If we can so readily forget the blood of Culloden, one might ask, why not the blood of Gettysburg as well? The answer would seem to be that Davidson was both an American and southern exceptionalist. In the original republic, it was possible to enjoy the life and liberties of a freeholder. Although the dream of such an existence is rooted in the philosophical tradition of Europe, it became a reality only in Jefferson's agrarian America. That society of noble yeomen was largely destroyed by the War Between the States and its restoration further imperiled by interventionist modern wars. The Agrarian vision involves a commitment not to our oldest patrimony but to a particular incarnation of the good society, which existed all too briefly on these shores. Whether or not this version of the American experience can withstand the scrutiny of history, it is apparently what Donald Davidson believed. Without some sense of this informing mythos, we must share Allen Tate's inability to understand what Davidson was trying to say in "Hermitage."

III

While Davidson was writing little Agrarian polemicism and less poetry in the early 1940s, his energies were devoted increasingly to composition and rhetoric. For several years, he directed Vanderbilt's program in freshman English, and he taught writing at all levels for his entire career. His opinions concerning this discipline are most fully developed in "Grammar and Rhetoric: The Teacher's Problem," an essay he published in the *Quarterly Journal of Speech*. Here, Davidson argues that the teaching of writing is plagued by two different but equally inadequate notions of grammar. There is the prescriptive conception that one finds in the workbooks used in many composition classes and the more scientific variety that is based on observation of actual usage.

Although the second view may seem superficially liberating, it is the mirror opposite of the first. "It enlarges the area of grammatical correctness without ever saying what is to be done with the larger correctness thus obtained. If the handbooks teach a petty kind of schoolmarm English, the new school of grammarians offers nothing really different in kind. It is just a bigger and looser kind of schoolmarm English."[11] The way out of this impasse is to follow the lead of those teachers (many of them novelists and poets) who regard writing as an art. This takes us inevitably from the realm of grammar to that of rhetoric.

Davidson's essay shows us how rhetorical analysis can illuminate the effectiveness of individual passages by such disparate writers as Robert Frost, Agnes De-Mille, Thomas Babington Macaulay, W. H. Hudson, Aldo Leopold, and Jonathan Swift. These close readings are meant to demonstrate the pervasiveness of rhetoric. When used well, it is the primary vehicle of effective communication. When used poorly, it is an impediment to understanding. Consequently, Davidson writes:

> Except in mathematics, and perhaps in scientific formulas, there is no discourse which can be "true" and at the same time "non-rhetorical." Scientists (particularly the social scientists) may be under the delusion that so-called scientific writing avoids all rhetoric and deals only in facts, uncolored by rhetoric, but they are mistaken. They are merely writing very badly; that is, they are using false rhetoric without knowing it. The best scientific writers are always good rhetoricians. They know that without the aid of rhetoric to set forth truth, this truth will issue in a weak or distorted form that makes the expression of it less than truth, if not a positive deception. (436)

Although this essay appeared rather late in Davidson's career (December 1953), its philosophy was implicit in his immensely successful textbook *American Composition and Rhetoric*. First published in 1939, this book was revised or reissued five times over the next thirty years. (In the world of textbook publication, a peculiar version of the Peter Principle dictates that a successful book be

---

11. Donald Davidson, "Grammar and Rhetoric: The Teacher's Problem," 428. Subsequent references will be cited parenthetically in the text.

continually revised until it is no longer in demand.) Davidson's volume is really three books in one—a rhetoric text, a selection of readings that illustrate the various rhetorical points the text makes, and a concise handbook of grammar. Although *American Composition and Rhetoric* is not primarily concerned with the composition "process," it does move from simpler to more complex forms of writing. It begins with the easiest and most natural mode—the autobiographical essay—then proceeds to simple expository writing. The book then digresses from the modes altogether to discuss the rhetoric of paragraphs, sentences, and words. This is followed by sections on descriptive and narrative writing, more complex forms of exposition (including the research paper), and finally argumentation.

One would be hard-pressed to discern an ideological agenda in Davidson's selection of writing examples, even though he was more concerned than many textbook authors of his time to include work by persons from the South and West. (He would later claim, in a letter to Allen Tate, that the prominence he gave to Agrarian writers limited adoptions of the book, especially in the South.[12]) Perhaps the most distinctive feature of *American Composition and Rhetoric* is the sophisticated stylistic analysis that one finds in the sections on paragraphs, sentences, and words. If Davidson's text were in use today, it would probably be restricted to classes in advanced composition. At the end of the twentieth century, the typical freshman does not enter the university with a Branham and Hughes education.

By the time the fourth edition of *American Composition and Rhetoric* was published in 1960, the book was seen as conservative, even reactionary. Not surprisingly, Russell Kirk's magazine, the *University Bookman,* gave the book (and its companion volume, *Readings for Composition*) considerable review space and an unqualified endorsement. On the basis of over two decades of college teaching, Warren L. Fleischauer pronounced Davidson's text "the best book currently available on the market for freshman composition courses." Its principal virtue was its concern with "the real problems of composition as these are posed by a mature and sound rhetorician and are faced by every student who ever nibbled a pen at midnight." After describing the organization of *American Composition and Rhetoric,* Fleischauer concludes: "There is nothing new in any of this, but there is much that is sound. It is the kind of thing to which we pay lip-service, then somehow fumble in the application."[13]

In the course of surveying seventy-one recent composition texts for *College English* that same year, John C. Sherwood was more tentative in his praise:

12. Davidson made this contention in a letter to Tate dated January 2, 1943. See *Literary Correspondence,* 330.
13. Warren L. Fleishauer, "College Textbooks in Composition and Rhetoric," 16, 17, 18.

Davidson writes on grammar in happy innocence, as if structural linguistics had never been, nay, as if Perrin had never written: he sternly labels constructions RIGHT and WRONG and states, apparently without fear of contradiction, that "Grammar is the servant of logic"—a statement which happens to be reasonable in the context of Davidson's book but which might cause comment in the present climate of opinion. Though dated in the one sense, Davidson's book has a kind of freshness still, for its humanistic values do not become stale as the values of socialized composition do.[14]

IV

Although Davidson occasionally received invitations to leave Vanderbilt, he rejected most of them out of hand. (Those that involved administrative work he found particularly unappealing.) The one offer that almost lured him away came in a letter of May 26, 1935, from Dean C. H. Barnwell of the University of Alabama. The position would have involved a substantial increase in salary and promotion to full professor. Davidson was favorably impressed by a subsequent visit to the Alabama campus and came close to accepting the position. In the end, however, personal ties kept him at Vanderbilt. (Although he never specified the nature of those ties, Ransom was still at Vanderbilt in 1935, and the Agrarian movement was still very much alive.) Vanderbilt refused to offer Davidson immediate promotion or to match the Alabama salary offer. The university did increase his pay by $500; however, an across-the-board cut in pay that went into effect that year limited his net increase to $220. When Davidson was finally promoted to full professor in 1937, after seventeen years of distinguished service and publication, Chancellor Kirkland informed him of the decision in a letter addressed to "My dear Dr. Daniel."

Because Davidson was the only one of the Fugitive-Agrarians to remain at Vanderbilt for his entire career, he had greater impact than any of the other brethren on the life of that institution. In particular, he exerted a profound influence on several generations of students, a number of whom became successful professional writers. The surviving correspondence documents the lengths to which Davidson would go in providing his students with both personal and professional advice. Some, such as Robert Penn Warren and Randall Jarrell, were too self-assured to need much counsel, but others probably owe their careers to Davidson's guidance. Nearly all came away with vivid memories of an extraordinary teacher and an enigmatic man.

14. John C. Sherwood, "Grammar and Tears: Seventy-One Composition Texts," 427.

Elizabeth Spencer, who entered the graduate program at Vanderbilt in 1942, would later write:

> There was something about Donald Davidson that scared students to death. I used actually to shake when I had to go into his office, stand in his presence, and stumble through whatever I had to say. I have heard strong men relate how as students they felt exactly the same. Feature for feature, nothing suggested the effect of his presence. He was scarcely above medium height, neither fat nor thin. He dressed in a mild, gentlemanly way. But he had steely gray eyes that seemed to look straight to the inside of your thoughts, a kindly tone of voice (until something angered him), brown hair growing thin, the small beginnings of what looked like a smile. It suggested many things: a willingness to listen? to sympathize? to laugh? to reject? You couldn't know which, but felt its quality was mostly one of waiting. When seated, he appeared taller than he actually was, a figure so erect behind a desk he might have been on horseback. What he had was authority.[15]

One of Spencer's most vivid memories of Davidson as a teacher concerned an incident that occurred in his class on the modern novel. She had written a critical paper in which she tried to demonstrate a connection between Faulkner's contemptuous behavior toward his fellow Mississippians and the social criticism she discerned in one of his novels. Davidson read Spencer's paper aloud in class and then "launched into a voluble attack" on it. Not only had she missed Faulkner's true intention by failing to read the text closely enough, she had committed the cardinal critical error of assuming that a writer's behavior could explain what he chose to write about. "Down on my small head came the whole weight of the New Criticism," Spencer recalled over fifty years later. When she went up meekly after class to request the paper back, "that is, if there is anything left of it," Davidson simply smiled and said: "A very fine paper, Miss Spencer. I thank you for it." "What contradictions there were in that man's makeup," she observes. "Now it seems clear that he had seen my mind at work, even if going off on the wrong track, and thought me of enough value to want to haul me back and set me down to start over again, think things through onto firmer ground."[16]

Spencer remembers Davidson's strong likes and dislikes among the writers he taught. Of Sinclair Lewis he said: "How can he do a serious subject when he can't keep a straight face?" Although Steinbeck was on the reading list, Spencer recalls Davidson pushing away a paper on *The Grapes of Wrath* as if it smelled bad. "He valued Thomas Wolfe but with so many reservations that Wolfe had a rough ride." (Davidson would gleefully rip into Wolfe's florid rhetoric: "What

15. Elizabeth Spencer, *Landscapes of the Heart: A Memoir,* 174.
16. Ibid., 177.

does he mean that he's lost, he's . . . *lost* . . . ? Where exactly are the 'ramparts of his soul'?") Hardy was lionized for his rootedness in the British countryside, while Conrad was seen as a writer without flaw. In reading James's *The Bostonians*, Davidson found himself cheering for the Mississippian Basil Ransom, who stood up well among the stuffy New England do-gooders. "He showed them all up," Davidson "rejoiced to say."[17]

Summing up her experience as a student of Davidson's, Spencer writes:

> College courses may be of some cumulative benefit, but few are absolutely defining, continuing through life as a means of judgment—in this case as a way of perceiving literature. This was what Davidson's course meant to me. What he personally meant is easier to see now than then. At the time I felt myself a humble worshiper, resentful a little that anyone should assume such a large degree of authority. Now I can see how much his perceptions of me were of benefit. For *he* could see me as a well-brought-up but totally unsophisticated small-town girl of a farming family, and he could approve of that; and furthermore only he could positively rejoice in my being able to excel not in spite of but *because of* this upbringing.[18]

Ruel Foster, who studied at Vanderbilt a few years before Elizabeth Spencer, remembers Davidson as a quiet man, constantly smoking cigarettes. His chronic ailments, along with the Nashville smog, noticeably affected his breathing, especially in morning classes, from late October until early spring. "Students liked and feared Davidson," Foster recalled in 1992. "They felt the mystery of the man and they liked his genuineness. There was frequently an other-worldly quality about Davidson. He would drift down a campus path with his hat firmly seated on his head and his striking, all-seeing eyes focused dreamily on some distant and other-worldy view."[19]

Foster continues:

> Fifty years afterward, I remember his piercing, penetrating eyes. He moved slowly, as if he were ever weary in those days—I feel that he was weary—worn down physically and psychically. In those days he sat at his desk to lecture and referred from time to time to an open notebook before him. But as ideas and emotions swept over him, his eyes sparked with energy and power as if all the things he couldn't say seemed to come out of his eyes—how if he disappeared all would melt away, save his eyes—like the eyes of a Chesire cat or the eyes of Dr. Eckleburg in *The Great Gatsby*.

17. Ibid., 178.
18. Ibid., 179–80.
19. Letter from Ruel E. Foster to M. E. Bradford, dated March 25, 1992.

Like so many students before and since, Foster fondly remembers Davidson's class in the English lyric. Not only was Davidson a fine scholar and an inspired teacher, he "added grace notes to the class when he sang melodiously a particular lyric we were studying [with] a fine voice and unselfconscious delivery." Although he did not enjoy the broad popularity of Walter Clyde Curry, whose Shakespeare class packed the undergraduates in every semester, "Davidson had generation after generation of student devotees who treasured his profundity of thought and his intuitive leaps in explicating texts." Employing a Socratic method in class, he would describe a crux in critical theory, state two possible solutions, pause, then ask a student which solution he would choose and why. Foster and his fellow graduate student Harry M. Campbell found Davidson's discussions of Faulkner so stimulating that, a decade and a half later, they published the first critical book on the Mississippi novelist.

Another early Faulkner scholar to study under Davidson was George Marion O'Donnell. Born in Mississippi in 1914 on Silver Home plantation, O'Donnell grew up on Blue Ruin plantation—"both places near a small town named Midnight."[20] While still an adolescent, he began reading Faulkner's novels and served as spokesman for a group of high school students who met Faulkner in 1930. Less than a decade later, in the summer 1939 issue of the *Kenyon Review*, O'Donnell published "Faulkner's Mythology," the first critical essay to be devoted to the work of his fellow Mississippian. (By the early 1990s, Faulkner had been the subject of over 6,000 essays and reviews, more than 300 books, and about 500 dissertations.[21]) While an undergraduate at Vanderbilt, O'Donnell became a contributor to *Who Owns America?* A year earlier, he had published two poems in the inaugural issue of the *Southern Review*. The fourth issue of that magazine contained six of his poems along with a critical essay on his work by John Crowe Ransom. At the same time, O'Donnell was writing a novel entitled *No More My Lady*. By the time Davidson offered him a fellowship in creative writing in 1939, George O'Donnell seemed well on his way to a major career in the world of letters.

After leaving Vanderbilt in the spring of 1940, O'Donnell appeared to have a hard time finding suitable academic employment. A letter from Davidson to Edwin Mims, dated August 6, 1940, suggests that the reason may have been vague rumors concerning his personal life. Although a Puritanical reserve prevents Davidson from spelling out the nature of those rumors, he argues passionately that O'Donnell should be allowed to defend himself rather than have his career destroyed by innuendo. When he finally landed a promising job at Louisiana State

---

20. Lewis P. Simpson, "O'Donnell's Wall," 193.
21. Lance Lyday, "Faulkner Criticism: Will It Ever End?" *South Carolina Review* 25 (fall 1992), 183.

University in 1947 (the year after Cleanth Brooks left LSU for Yale), O'Donnell had developed a bohemian southern persona. Lewis P. Simpson recalls that "the wall above his desk in his Allen Hall office was decorated with three objects. In the center, suspended horizontally, was the sword of an officer, CSA; to the right of the sword hung a vintage photograph of his maternal grandfather in the uniform of a major in his Mississippi regiment; to the left of the sword hung a photograph of the death mask of Marcel Proust." Simpson also recalls "a dinner party given by O'Donnell, at which, having made adequate spiritual preparation around a bottle of Dixie Belle gin, the guests dined ceremoniously by the light of a treasured family silver candelabra on mustard greens and corn bread."[22]

Other recollections of O'Donnell at this time suggest trouble lurking beneath the young man's surface flamboyance. In a letter to Cleanth Brooks, dated November 8, 1947, Robert B. Heilman writes: "Now that he has his boyfriend with him GMO is drinking worse than ever. He misses 2 or 3 classes a week. So far, everybody is only sorry." Then, on December 5, Heilman writes that Tom Kirby, the department chairman, "had to tell George O'Donnell to sober up or get out. George cried and said he knew it was true. It is really a sad case: he is a fine teacher, is much liked by mediocre students as well as good ones, and has won the approval of his colleagues. He apparently kills a fifth of gin daily."[23] O'Donnell eventually left the South for New England, where he died a quite natural death in New Haven in 1962. "According to a newspaper report, he got out of a chair to walk across a room and fell dead. The same report said that he had been for some years engaged in a work he called 'No More, My Ladies.' "[24]

22. Simpson, "O'Donnell's Wall," 192, 193.
23. This letter is among the Cleanth Brooks papers in the Beinecke Library at Yale University.
24. Simpson, O'Donnell's Wall," 200.

15

A TALE OF TWO RIVERS

Although Donald Davidson never abandoned his belief in the Agrarian cause, the failure of *The Attack on Leviathan* to reach more than a few hundred readers seemed to have ended his career as an polemicist for the movement. Moreover, after the appearance of "Hermitage," he virtually stopped writing poetry for the better part of two decades. The forties, however, were not bad years for Davidson. After the personal and professional struggles that had made the thirties a veritable nightmare, he enjoyed the greatest financial security he had known since the suspension of his book page from the *Tennessean.* In 1940, he was even able to purchase his first house, at 410 Fairfax Avenue, just a few blocks from the Vanderbilt campus.

Davidson's next-door neighbor on Fairfax was Ernest F. Goodpasture, Vanderbilt's most renowned research scientist and dean of the medical school during World War II. Because Goodpasture was both an empiricist and a secularist, he and Davidson conducted many lively but friendly debates over the backyard fence. The Davidsons and Goodpastures had been friends years before they became neighbors. The Goodpastures' daughter Sarah and Mary Davidson were both students at the Peabody Demonstration School in the late 1920s. Once, when Mary had measles and Sarah was suffering from chicken pox, the two girls exchanged notes through their fathers. (They called it the "scratch news.") Later, when the Davidsons were burned out of their home in Wesley Hall, Mary stayed for a couple of weeks with the Goodpastures. By the time the girls were living next door to each other, they were both undergraduates at Vanderbilt and Tri Delt sorority sisters.

Nearly sixty years later, Sarah Goodpasture Little remembered the Davidson household as a refuge from the strict discipline that prevailed in her own home. Living in a suite of rooms on the upper floor at 410 Fairfax, Mary forbade her parents from trespassing on her territory. (Sarah marveled at her friend's insolence.) It was a haven where the two girls could share confidences, sneak cigarettes, and pretend to be more grown-up than they actually were.[1] Although they remained friends, Sarah and Mary saw less of each other after they married. Eric Bell, the young psychiatrist whom Peter Stanlis remembers courting Mary in Vermont, won her hand. (Like Mary and Sarah, Eric had been an undergraduate at Vanderbilt.) Even more conservative than his father-in-law, Eric refused on principle to subscribe to a newspaper. Davidson used to warn him that one day he would see a machine gun pointed at his house and not know why.[2]

Eric's medical partner, who was a convert to Catholicism, led Mary and Eric into the Roman Church. Although Theresa eventually followed suit, Davidson himself did not. Nonetheless, his church attendance in his later years consisted largely of accompanying his daughter and her family to mass. (Mary and Eric had four children—three girls and a boy.) Davidson once told his student Robert Drake: "I can't be a Protestant like the ones they're making these days, though I was raised a Methodist. If I ever do go back to the Church, I'll either have to be a Catholic or join the most primitive, fundamentalist sect I can find, if it's nothing but a bunch of snake-handlers out under a brush-arbor."[3]

Although Donald and Theresa Davidson remained devoted to each other for their entire married life, they seem to have had relatively few friends in common. Whether it was because of cultural differences or personal temperament, Theresa never mixed easily with her husband's literary companions. In a letter dated March 27, 1936, Allen Tate lays the blame on Davidson himself: "Caroline and I," he writes, "have always found Theresa extremely charming and interesting, and felt that she would make a great addition to our social life; but Don, you have put such a dense barrier between your friends and your private life that we cannot penetrate it" (*Literary Correspondence*, 298).

Remembering Theresa Davidson from the perspective of the late 1980s, Walter Sullivan writes: "When I first met her, she must have been in her forties, though she seemed older. Like Mr. Davidson . . . , she wore plain clothes, made little effort at self-beautification. She was very much under Mr. Davidson's domination. Sometimes, when she tried to express an opinion, he told her to be quiet and she obeyed, though she talked intelligently when she was allowed to."[4] Perhaps as a consequence of living in her husband's shadow, Theresa acquired Donald's

---

1. Interview with Sarah Little, June 2, 1999.
2. Interview with Walter Sullivan, June 2, 1999.
3. Robert Drake, "Donald Davidson and the Ancient Mariner," 22.
4. Walter Sullivan, *Allen Tate*, 111–12.

suspicions and prejudices without the leavening effects of his many personal and professional ties. Shortly after Davidson's death, Mel Bradford announced his intention to bring his mentor's work back into print and to write his biography. Rather than see this as a gesture of affection and respect, Theresa threatened to sue him.[5] Other than members of her family, no more than ten people attended her funeral mass at St. Henry's Church in Nashville.

The only one of Davidson's siblings to follow him into the literary life was his brother Bill. A generation younger than Donald, William Wallace Davidson had been an undergraduate roommate of Cleanth Brooks. Although he achieved no great professional distinction, he taught for many years at the University of Georgia and even edited the *Georgia Review* after John Donald Wade retired. Because his wife would never let him drink at home, Bill Davidson made up for it at professional conferences. One night at the convention of the South Atlantic Modern Language Association, Walter Sullivan noticed that Bill was heavily into his cups and offered to walk him back to his hotel. The next day, Walter told someone he had gotten Bill Davidson back to his room at midnight. "That's funny," the other man said. "I got him back at one o'clock." Then, a third individual said: "I got him back at two." Apparently, Bill had just walked in the front door of the hotel and out the back. Some time in the early sixties, someone took a group picture that included the Davidson brothers. Upon showing it to Walter Sullivan, Randall Stewart observed: "The caption should read, 'What's wrong with this picture?'" The notoriously abstemious Donald Davidson was holding a drink, while brother Bill was standing there empty-handed.[6]

I

Although several of the Fugitive-Agrarian brethren had concluded that Davidson's best work was behind him by the end of the 1930s, some of his most notable literary achievements would actually belong to the last two decades of his life. If some writers work best under conditions of extreme poverty, Davidson's muse seemed to thrive when he was not worried about keeping the wolf from the door. After *American Composition and Rhetoric,* his most successful book (and his most distinguished work of prose) was a two-volume history of the Tennessee River, which appeared in the late 1940s. Originally published by Rinehart as part of its Rivers of America series, *The Tennessee* is easily Davidson's longest book (the two volumes run to nearly seven hundred pages of text). Here, he was able to reach a larger audience than had read any of his previous works. He

5. Tom Landess in conversation.
6. Sullivan interview.

was also able to demonstrate his skills as a narrative writer and (in the second volume) launch his most effective assault on industrialization, "progress," and the leviathan government in Washington. Finally Davidson was able to continue the love affair with the Tennessee frontier that he had begun with *The Tall Men*. As Clyde N. Wilson has observed: "In American historical literature there is nothing quite like Donald Davidson's *The Tennessee*—the history of a region and a people through the eyes of an epic poet."[7]

The idea for a book on the Tennessee was first raised in correspondence between Davidson and John Farrar of Rinehart in the spring of 1940. In a letter to Farrar, dated March 21, 1940, Davidson writes: "For a long time I have wanted a good opportunity to do a book, or some books, on Tennessee, the river included; but you are the first publisher to come at me with something concrete."[8] On May 12, he sent Farrar a longer letter outlining his plans for the book. In some introductory remarks he notes: "I should be writing of the Tennessee river, of course, at the moment of its transition into becoming less a river and more a lake. When and if the dam system of the TVA is completed, the Tennessee will be, I suppose, the most thoroughly chained, harnessed, and transformed river in the world—certainly in the United States. I approach the river, then, at this moment in its transition, which has elements in it of both hope and tragedy." In a classic understatement, he assures Farrar that his treatment of recent history will not be "either a touristic rave or a brief for the New Deal."

In the next paragraph, Davidson frankly confesses the bias that will inform his work:

> My approach to the general story of the Tennessee will naturally be that of a native Tennessean who stands neither with Left nor Right as those terms are commonly understood in the United States. My interest in "agrarian" and "regional" principles puts me personally in a category which is not very thickly inhabited nowadays. That interest naturally will affect my conception of how to tell the story of the Tennessee. . . . I cannot help feeling and believing as I do; and I hope that my way of feeling and believing might help me see and present many things that another kind of narrator might miss, or present too drily. At any rate I won't be copying other books in the series—as you intimated, in previous letters, some of your authors have been doing, against your desire.

On May 28, Stanley Rinehart wrote to Davidson, offering him a contract for a single volume on the Tennessee River for which he would receive a $500 advance.

---

7. This comment appears as a blurb on the J. S. Sanders reprint of *The Tennessee*, vol. 1.
8. This and other letters cited in this chapter are housed in the Fugitive Collection of the Heard Library.

At that time, Davidson intended to use the advance to support himself and his family during the summer of 1941, while he finished the book in lieu of teaching at Bread Loaf. (The editors with whom he was to work most directly were John Farrar, Carl Carmer, and Stephen Vincent Benet, all of whom were enthusiastic about the project.) On November 13, Davidson reported to Farrar that he had been doing a good deal of reading and was ready to prepare a prospectus for the first part of the book. "I hope I can get the focus right," he declares; "I hope I can make the river really my subject, and keep the reader always on it, conscious of it and of its being, rather than just take a general ramble among the legends and historical data."

By September 15, 1941, Davidson had 150 pages of "trial manuscript." Already, he was experiencing difficulty keeping his material within reasonable bounds. Because the historical context of the Tennessee was not as well known as that of other rivers, he felt the need to supply that context. "I can't 'tell the story' of the Tennessee without getting into enough of the history to give the story its full richness and meaning," he writes. "But in attempting to do this I have to avoid being just a chronicler; and my feeling is that so far as I have not altogether avoided that—too much of my first attempt is just historical summary, and therefore, I fear, pretty dead stuff, at any rate not yet thoroughly animated." It was already apparent to him that the Indians would play a greater role than the white man in his discussion of the early river. "The Tennessee has been pretty much of a damned nuisance to the white folks throughout most of its history," he notes. "They couldn't handle it; they got so they didn't like to think about it; they turned their backs on it and tried to forget about it."

Davidson had developed a thesis that was taking him away from his initial prospectus for *The Tennessee*. "This is the way I see the book now," he writes. "The Tennessee is a 'wild river,' and its story is mainly the story of its resistance to civilization. . . . The Indians, being 'wild' like the river, got along with it very well; and so did the Indian traders, who, I try to make clear, were true frontiersmen but of a very different sort from those who followed them." Davidson believes that the history of the Tennessee River can be understood in terms of three violent attempts to bring "civilization" to the region. The first was the settling of the West, when the federal government removed recalcitrant Indians from their homeland and moved them onto reservations. The second was the War Between the States, in which the inhabitants of Tennessee were forced back into the union. The final onslaught occurred in our own time. "The TVA represents the third attempt at conquest," Davidson writes. "Or the third major attempt. Ironically, the removers get removed, or the weakest of them do. The descendants of those who chased out the Cherokee are now chased out from their river bottom farms by order of the Federal government. And there stands the TVA. The question is, did the Indians leave a curse behind them, and will the TVA magic avail to circumvent that curse?"

Davidson had hoped to have the book finished by early 1942; however, a letter to John Farrar, dated January 8 of that year, indicates that he had fallen far behind his tentative deadline. (The letter also mentions worries about mortgage payments, taxes, and the remote possibility that he might be called back into the army at age forty-eight.) When Stephen Vincent Benet died later that year, his editorial position was taken by the South Carolina poet and novelist Hervey Allen. For the remainder of the project, Davidson's correspondence about *The Tennessee* was primarily with Allen, who appears to have been a remarkably astute and sympathetic editor. Writing on October 26, 1943, Allen suggests that Davidson complete the research that he might do for "a full dress history of this region."

> Its from that that you can write the river book. If you were going to write a long narrative poem you might possibly do it in the form of an impressionistic pageant of the high spots in your history. Well why not do something of that kind for the River Series in prose? Simply make your book on THE TENNESSEE in the River Series a kind of concentrated prose epic or running comment on your "history of the Tennessee valley" already filed away in the library of your mind?

Davidson responded with a long and appreciative letter to Allen on November 6. In it, he expresses his general feeling that he and his editor agree on strategy but differ slightly on tactics. Davidson sees the book as primarily a blend of narrative and exposition rather than as an extended prose poem. "I tremble a little," he writes, "before the 'prose epic' idea, so far as it might apply to the texture of what I write, since I would fear I might fall into rhetorical mushiness where I want concrete realities; but I would hope that the completed book would have, taken all together, something of an epical character." Davidson finds himself chafing a bit at the limit of 100,000 words for the book. He even observes wistfully that "it might have been better to plan two volumes for the Tennessee." Approaching the matter warily, he writes: "Herewith I deposit this idea in your lap, for what it may be worth." His new target date for completion is February 1, 1944.

On March 5, 1944, Davidson wrote to Allen to explain why the new deadline had not been met. Apparently, at some time during the winter, even as Theresa was recovering from a serious illness, Davidson had contracted neuritis of the left optic nerve. Although he was experiencing no pain, the vision in his left eye was partially blurred. To deal with this problem, he had to go to the doctor at least three times a week to take shots that left him groggy for hours. (At one point, he took some tablets that gave him "a raging four-day headache.") Under the circumstances, he had been able to do little more than meet his classes and fulfill a few other duties on campus. Begging the indulgence of the firm now called Farrar and Rinehart, Davidson promises to do everything he can to move the project forward but is reluctant even to suggest a new deadline. "I can remember no days as hard as these since childhood," he writes.

Unfortunately, things would only get worse. Late in March, Davidson's *right* eye became clouded. The doctor immediately ordered Davidson to stop reading and writing. He was able to finish the spring term at Vanderbilt only because his classes were so small that he could have his students read their papers to him. (The war had drastically reduced enrollments.) Although his condition improved gradually during the summer, full recovery was vexingly slow in coming. In a letter dated August 8, Davidson tells Allen that he will know in September whether his doctor will allow him to "return to normal eye-pursuits." In the meantime, he will press on with Mary's secretarial aid, while Eric prepares to leave for duty with the navy.

In September, Davidson's physician allowed him to "return to moderate eye-work," and Vanderbilt granted him a leave of absence. On December 30, he informed Allen that he hoped to begin sending the manuscript to the typist in January. "Unless I meet with some new disaster," he writes, "I ought to have the manuscript ready for you to see in February, or at any rate not later than early March." In the next paragraph, he indicates that he is feeling vastly better than he had earlier in the year. Although the shadow effect is not completely gone from his vision, he can read and write without the discomfort he had experienced in the spring and fall. "The doctor charges me to exercise restraint," he writes; "I have to stop whenever I begin to get tired; and I have to go easy on tobacco (I make a package of cigarettes last four or five days!). But I am no longer so completely disabled as I was."

On March 31, 1945, Donald Davidson finally mailed the manuscript of *The Tennessee* to Farrar and Rinehart. At 150,000 words, it was 50 percent longer than the typical book in the Rivers of America series. Even at that, Davidson fretted over the considerable amount of material that he had had to cut, condense, or ignore altogether. Writing to Hervey Allen the next day, he begged his editor to read the book as a whole before recommending changes. Allen did precisely that over the next month and a half. Then, on May 23, 1945, he wrote to Davidson: "I am deeply impressed by your contribution to American history and the fine integrity and tone of the theme and subject matter contained in your firm, clear prose." Less than a month later, the project took an unanticipated turn that must have brought Davidson a sense of liberation. In an uncharacteristically brief letter to his author, written on June 30, Allen announces that "we will not ask you to cut down on the book, but we are thinking of doing THE TENNESSEE in two volumes."

The most immediate consequence of this decision was to delay publication of the book even further, as Davidson rearranged the material from his over-sized manuscript into the two-volume format, while adding much that he had reluctantly dropped from his initial text. However, with the shackles removed and his health restored, putting volume one of *The Tennessee* in shape proved to be a relatively easy and pleasurable undertaking. In a letter to Allen, dated October 7, 1945, Davidson expresses the "great good cheer" with which he is approaching the task:

> I might not have had the courage, five years ago, to work toward such an end. I certainly didn't contemplate it at the beginning of my labors and would have been scared if it had been suggested at that point. But as I got more and more involved in my struggle with the Tennessee River I began to wonder how I was going to get through the enterprise without bursting a lot of stitches. The stitches did burst, after all. And now I am very happy at the chance to get the bulging Tennessee into a more comfortable and compendious garment.

II

"Down the valley of the Tennessee two rivers flow—two rivers blended indistinguishably where for centuries there was only one" (*Tennessee*, I:5). With this striking opening sentence, Donald Davidson establishes the underlying theme of *The Tennessee*—that it will be a tale of how one river became two. Volume one is subtitled "The Old River: Frontier to Secession." "One of the chief peculiarities of the old Tennessee," he writes, "is that, of all the great rivers east of the Mississippi, it has been least friendly to civilization. . . . It mocked the schemes of improvers. It wore out the patience of legislators. Tawny and unsubdued, an Indian among rivers, the old Tennessee threw back man's improvements in his face and went its own way, which was not the way of the white man" (6). It is for this reason that the river has inspired very little folk tradition and almost no formal literature.

It has become a commonplace of southern literary criticism that the South did not produce a great literature until the culture of the Old South was threatened with extinction, or at least assimilation. (Walter Sullivan refers to this as the "gotterdammerung theory of Southern literature."[9]) By the same token, it can be argued that the Tennessee River did not lend itself to literary treatment until it had been obliterated by the Faustian hubris of the Tennessee Valley Authority. It was only then that the old river, no longer a living entity, became fully accessible to the mythmaking sensibility. In implying as much in the opening chapter of his first volume, Davidson sets the tone for the tale that is to follow. The concluding paragraph of that opening chapter reads as follows:

9. Walter Sullivan, "The Southern Renascence and the Joycean Aesthetic," 110.

> Now, at long last, the old wild river is submerged, is lost in its great progeny,
> the river of the TVA. Destiny, or whim, or some man's bold wish, or some
> Platonic dream, has decided that this untamed river creature should become,
> of all the rivers of the world, the one most deftly chained, the one most
> thoroughly subdued to man's designing will. The Tennessee is now a civil
> and obliging stream. One flick of a switch by the tenderest human finger,
> and the Tennessee is any man's obedient slave, though he be a thousand
> miles away. Tourists stare at it in immaculate safety from observation booths
> placed on points where long ago, it was as much as a man's life was worth to
> be seen. The Indians are gone, and the Indian river wears the manacles and
> dress of civilization. How all this came about is a long story and a strange
> one. It begins with legend. It ends with statistics. (17–18)

Because of the two-volume format proposed by Rinehart, Davidson is able to give an ample account of the river during frontier times. Such familiar historical figures as Andrew Jackson, John Sevier, James Robertson, and John Donelson play roles in the narrative. We read of the rise and fall of Fort Loudoun and of the lost state of Franklin. Both the flatboat and the steamboat try with limited success to navigate the river. Next to man's conflict with nature, the theme that is most prevalent in this story is of the white man's encounter with the Indian. This particular drama is diverse enough to encompass elements of both tragedy and farce. One of the most unusual examples of the latter is the story of the Scots baronet Sir Alexander Cuming.

Sir Alexander arrived in the settlement of Charles Town in the Carolina territory in 1730 because, he claimed, his wife had seen it in a dream. Convincing everyone that he was a man of great wealth, he quickly established his credit by taking out several short-term notes and paying them back promptly. Before long, anyone in town who had any money to spare was investing it with Cuming in the hope of making a sizable profit. He then blundered naively into a local Cherokee camp and committed every possible breach of etiquette. He went into the camp armed and insisted that all of its inhabitants swear an oath of submission to King George. His very boldness and self-assurance so took the Indians off guard that they did exactly that. It was only after he sailed out of Charles Town harbor for London, with seven Indian chiefs aboard, that Sir Alexander's many investors discovered he was a fraud. When they broke into his treasure house, they found only empty boxes, old iron, and rubbish. Cuming "had carried off fifteen hundred pounds sterling of good Carolina money, and few people were entitled to laugh at the victims because Sir Alexander had played no favorites—he had taken in everybody who had money to invest" (85).

Unfortunately, there was more tragedy than farce in the white man's treatment of the Indian. Davidson respects the Cherokee as a noble and honorable people who were betrayed and brutalized by white politicians hungry for land and power.

Speaking of the forced removal of the Cherokee to western lands, Davidson bluntly declares: "It is one of the scandals of American history" (256). Andrew Jackson, who was the principal architect of the removal, had relied on the Cherokee during the Creek wars (particularly in the battle at Horseshoe Bend) and had won their trust and admiration. Now, for purposes of expediency, he was turning his back on them. Chief Junaluska echoed the prevailing sentiment of the tribe when he said: "If I had known that Jackson would drive us from our homes, I would have killed him that day at the Horseshoe" (258).

At this time, the Cherokee were actually more civilized than some of the backward white men who lived on the frontier. Their chief, John Ross, was one-eighth Cherokee and seven-eighths Scot. Under his leadership, the tribe had developed a republican form of government. It also had its own alphabet of eighty-five characters and a fairly sophisticated written language. In their agricultural practices and mercantile enterprises, the Cherokee were clearly entering the mainstream of the American economy. (They would also prove their southern loyalties a couple of decades later in the War Between the States.) Davidson concludes that "there is queer irony in the historical fact that the federal government, which during the eighteen-thirties denied citizenship to the Cherokees, who deserved it and wanted it, would within a quarter of a century confer it as an unsolicited gift upon four million ignorant Negro slaves, who had not asked for citizenship and did not know what it was" (264).

Davidson amply documents the deplorable behavior of assorted white men toward the Indians. This includes not only the official conduct of political hacks such as Martin Van Buren and military thugs such as Winfield Scott, but also acts of petty brutality and grand larceny on the part of ordinary citizens. Fortunately, a few whites also displayed a measure of decency and heroism. On one occasion, the steamboat captain George Washington Harris, who would later gain fame as the author of *Sut Lovingood's Yarns,* was taking a contingent of Cherokees downriver on his boat *Indian Chief.* When General Scott tried to countermand his orders, the diminutive Harris looked the six-feet-four general in the eye and said: "I am captain of this boat; my orders are going to be obeyed, and if you, in any way, attempt to interfere, my next order will be to place you ashore." Davidson assures us that "no more of Harris's orders were countermanded" (272).

Davidson concludes his account of the Cherokee removal by telling us about the Nunnehi, a band of supernatural visitants who presumably afforded protection to a few of their Indian friends. The Nunnehi transported the people of one town "to a place underneath the waters of the Hiawasse, where they live on forever. It is a place where fisher's nets always hang, as if caught on rocks. But it is not rocks, it is the hands of the people of the lost Cherokee town that clutch the nets and remind the fishermen that they are still there in the deep underwater home of the immortals" (279).

III

Davidson's painstaking research and his gift for narrative made volume one of *The Tennessee* a critical and popular success. "One reads 'The Tennessee' with a nostalgic reluctance to reach the end," wrote Harry Harrison Kroll in the *New York Times Book Review*. Avery Craven was even more enthusiastic in reviewing the book for the *New York Herald Tribune*. He argues that Davidson "gives the Tennessee a personality" and calls chapter 19 ("How It Was in the Old Days") "something of a masterpiece." Writing in the *Journal of Southern History*, Stanley J. Folmsbee notes that "Mr. Davidson has attempted to re-write the history of the Tennessee River region from the viewpoint of the river. Instead of looking upon the river from the surrounding country, he has reversed that procedure and has looked out upon the country from the vantage point of the river."[10] Several reviewers praised the woodcut illustrations that Theresa Davidson had done for the volume. With his first venture into popular history, Davidson seemed to have found the recognition that had been denied his previous work.

The first seven chapters of volume two read like a seamless continuation of volume one. The account that Davidson gives us of the Tennessee River during the War Between the States is charming and uncontroversial. Thomas Daniel Young and M. Thomas Inge describe it as "impressive in both style and historical authority."[11] Then, in chapter 8, "Parson Brownlow and the Klan," the polemical Davidson reemerges. His depiction of the horrors of Reconstruction is what one might expect from a southern patriot. Almost before the smoke had cleared from battle, the Tennessee Unionists elected the vindictive and fanatical William G. Brownlow as governor. Brownlow had once said in a speech in New York that "the war must be pursued with a vim and a vengeance until the rebellion is put down, if it exterminates from God's green earth every man, woman, and child south of Mason and Dixon's line."[12] With such a tyrant at the head of government, the former Confederates in Tennessee felt an understandable need for a means of self-defense. The solution to this need was the Ku Klux Klan.

Like Thomas Dixon, Jr., Davidson portrays the Klan as a noble and chivalric order. (He sees it as a kind of social fraternity that grew into something more as the need arose.) But, unlike Dixon, Davidson takes pains not to make the black man into a villain or to portray him as the particular object of the Klan's wrath. The Klan, he argues, "was not directed at the Negro as Negro; it was

---

10. Avery Craven, review of *The Tennessee*, vol. 1; Stanley J. Folmsbee, review of *The Tennessee*, vol. 1, 111.

11. Young and Inge, *Donald Davidson*, 143.

12. Donald Davidson, *The Tennessee*, vol. 2, *The New River: Civil War to TVA*, 121. Subsequent references will be cited parenthetically in the text.

not an anti-Negro movement. It was aimed at the powers that corrupted and exploited the Negro—the Brownlow regime and its hangers-on. But it was above all a movement in protection and self-defense" (124). Davidson nevertheless acknowledges that Klansmen often went on the offensive as well. But even here, they seem more like a band of pranksters than brutal vigilantes. He recalls one trick that D. W. Griffith would immortalize in his film *The Birth of a Nation:* "the thirsty spirit [white-robed like a ghost] . . . asked for water and, after downing a whole bucketful, remarked, in ghastly tones: 'That's the first drink I've had since the Battle of Shiloh' " (129).

Davidson's defense of southern autonomy is even more pronounced in chapter 12, "Trials by Jury and Otherwise." The "otherwise" refers to the scorn the northern press heaped upon the South during the Scopes "Monkey" trial in the 1920s and during the Scottsboro case a decade later. Characteristically, Davidson's treatment of religion proves much more measured and objective than his discussion of race. As we have already seen, Davidson was never able to share Ransom's indignation over northern reaction to the Scopes trial. (In his account, he fails even to mention the name of H. L. Mencken.) He presents the whole case as the misguided attempt of a small town to call attention to itself. The Butler antievolution law had been passed as an amendment to a funding bill for public education in the state of Tennessee. John Washington Butler had actually read Darwin's *The Origin of Species* and *The Descent of Man* and had no objection to his own children doing so, but he did not believe that public money should be spent on the teaching of a doctrine to which many Tennesseans would object. Because Darwin was not being taught anyway, the law seemed like something of a dead letter, and the liberal governor Austin Peay signed the bill rather than hold up funding for the state's education system.

The issue would have died there had a group of townspeople from Dayton, Tennessee, not seen the situation as an opportunity to create publicity for their otherwise obscure community. Davidson describes the situation as follows:

> So one day at a Dayton drugstore, over the Coca-Colas and ice-cream sodas, it was agreed among a group of ardent booster spirits that they would contrive to bring a test case under the anti-evolution law. . . . The ardent spirits were out for fun. No doubt they also wanted, as it was later said, to "see whether the law would stick." But their case was essentially a publicity stunt. They hurried their plans because they had learned that a test case was being prepared at Chattanooga, and they wanted to get ahead of Chattanooga. (198)

Because John T. Scopes was no longer teaching in Tennessee by the time that his case had worked its way on appeal to the Tennessee Supreme Court, he never paid the $100 fine that had been assessed for his violation of the law. Unfortunately,

Davidson argues, the international scrutiny that the case had generated made it difficult for the state to fashion any kind of educational policy that might be relevant to the actual situation in Tennessee. "Now, being under pressure, about all Tennessee could do was to try to get up money to buy a kind of education trade-marked 'progressive.' If it did not like the brand, it could hold its nose, shut its eyes, and swallow" (204).

With the Scottsboro case, it was Alabama's turn to represent the benighted South to the rest of the nation. On the night of March 26, 1931, a group of about twenty black youths boarded a freight train at Stevenson, Alabama. A fight broke out with some white boys who were already on the train. After the white boys were beaten up and thrown off the train, one of them saw that word of the altercation was telegraphed ahead to the sheriff in the next town. After eleven of the young blacks escaped, the remaining nine were arrested and charged with raping two white girls who were also on the train. When they were tried in Scottsboro, Alabama, in April of 1931, eight of the defendants were found guilty and sentenced to death. (The ninth boy, age fourteen, got off with a mistrial.) Shortly thereafter, the trial was branded a "legal lynching" in the North, and the forces of the American Left, particularly the Communist Party, championed the cause of the "Scottsboro Boys."

Any objective assessment of the case would indicate that the defendants had not gotten a fair trial. Their court-appointed lawyer was a notorious drunk, who was well into his cups by nine A.M. on the first day of the trial. Medical examinations of the two "victims" did not indicate any evidence of rape, and three of the defendants suffered from afflictions that made them physically incapable of the act of which they were accused. Davidson adduces none of these facts in his account of the case. He seems less interested in the guilt or innocence of the "boys" than in the fact that Yankee meddlers are once again vilifying the South (see *Tennessee*, 2:208). His argument is valid as far as it goes (the attorney who represented the "boys" on appeal, Samuel S. Leibowitz of New York, branded the people of Alabama as "lantern jawed morons and lynchers, . . . boll weevil bigots, . . . creatures whose mouths are slits . . . whose eyes pop out at you like frogs, whose chins drip tobacco juice"); however, his case would have been far more convincing if he had admitted that a miscarriage of justice actually was taking place. Davidson could have cited unfair trials in other regions of the country (such as the "legal lynching" of Sacco and Vanzetti in Massachusetts) to prove that the South was not a uniquely repressive place. The closest Davidson comes to evenhandedness is in presenting the NAACP as a responsible and "conservative" organization in contrast to the opportunistic and revolutionary Communist Party.

After dispensing with the Scottsboro case, Davidson devotes the remainder of his book (except for a lyrical closing chapter) to the phenomenon that makes the

Tennessee unique among American rivers—the Tennessee Valley Authority. As Edward Shapiro points out, all of Davidson's book up to this point (and much of his previous writing) foreshadows the attitude that he will take toward the TVA.[13] According to Davidson's vision, the history of the South, at least since the War Between the States, had been characterized by the region's attempt to determine its own fate in the face of interference from the North. This thesis makes Reconstruction, the Scopes trial, and the Scottsboro case all part of an unfolding drama. Sounding a theme that had run all the way through *The Attack on Leviathan,* Davidson concludes his chapter on Scottsboro with the following observation:

> To the new legend of the social depravity of the region was soon added the newer legend that all their ills and their sins were due to economic bad habits. The New Deal emphasized the latter legend in its open pronouncements and offered its services as uplifter. . . . The Tennessee Valley Authority, riding on the wave of the economic uplift, promised through economics to wipe all sins away. Behind its mechanical provisions for taming the Tennessee River was the open hint that social goodness would be substituted for supposed social depravity through the distribution of government-controlled electric power. (211)

In opposing the Tennessee Valley Authority, Davidson was not only placing himself among a minority of southerners, he was also breaking ranks with most of his Agrarian colleagues. Those Agrarians who took a public position on the TVA generally supported the enterprise. Anyone who has read *Who Owns America?* can easily see why this would be the case. If the South was ever to gain economic independence, it would have to break the hold that northeastern capitalists had over southern commerce. As we have seen, the Agrarians and distributists were not averse to using government as the instrument for achieving that goal. Through its flood-control projects, the TVA would aid southern agriculture. By providing residents of the valley with cheap electricity, it would free southerners from the grip of northern utility companies. "An intelligent use of electricity, the Agrarians contended, could foster a widespread distribution of property and help rectify the economic imbalance between the South and West and the Northeast."[14]

13. Edward S. Shapiro, "Donald Davidson and the Tennessee Valley Authority: The Response of a Southern Conservative," 443.

14. Edward S. Shapiro, "The Southern Agrarians and the Tennessee Valley Authority," 799. According to Shapiro, John Gould Fletcher, Frank Lawrence Owsley, and Allen Tate are all on record as supporting the Tennessee Valley Authority. Not surprisingly, the liberal Herman Clarence Nixon strongly backed the TVA, along with virtually every other initiative of the New Deal, while Henry Blue Kline worked for both the TVA and the Atomic Energy Commission.

Although Davidson never shared the enthusiasm of his Agrarian brethren for the TVA, he was initially hopeful that this program would do more good than ill for the South. Also, by being a regional authority that ignored the static and artificial distinctions between national and state interests, the TVA seemed to embody the social philosophy that Davidson endorsed in *The Attack on Leviathan.* "In principle," Davidson wrote in 1934, the TVA "is statesmanlike and highly imaginative, and it naturally excites the interest and wins the support of most thinking Southerners."[15] Within two years, however, Davidson became convinced that the TVA had become a kind of colonial presence, which ignored the wishes of the valley's residents and treated their elected representatives with outright contempt. In his contribution to *Who Owns America?* Davidson describes the Authority as "an irresponsible projection of a planned, functional society into the midst of one of the most thoroughly democratic parts of the United States" (*Leviathan,* 119).

Davidson believed that one of the main problems with the TVA was its complete independence from normal political constraints. It was exempt from both civil service requirements and political influence. "Thus the TVA personnel was entirely removed from the controls, partly federal and direct, partly local and indirect, to which most government agencies were subject" (*Tennessee,* 2:221). This made the TVA a law unto itself, not so much a fourth branch as a third level of government. "In other days, if you were discontented with a power company, you could appeal to the government. If you were discontented with TVA, to whom did you appeal? TVA was the government. In the Tennessee Valley there was nothing above it" (333). Moreover, because of the sheer scope of its activity, the TVA was a virtually unstoppable juggernaut. "One cannot repeal a great dam once it has been built, much less a system of great dams controlling a watershed of more than forty thousand square miles" (224).

In order to accomplish its technological goals, the TVA had to make itself a disruptive force in the life of the valley. By building a string of high dams, the Authority was able to achieve the maximum degree of flood control and produce the most electric power possible, but at the price of inundating much of the valley and destroying an entire rural culture. In some of his most evocative prose, Davidson describes the havoc wrought by progress:

> Hearth fires would be extinguished that were as old as the Republic itself. Old landmarks would vanish; old graveyards would be obliterated; the ancient mounds of the Indians, which had resisted both the plow of the farmer and the pick of the curiosity seeker, would go under the water. There would be tears, and gnashing of teeth, and lawsuits. There might even be feud and

---

15. See Shapiro, "Donald Davidson," 438.

bloodshed. Yet these harms, inflicted upon a sizable and innocent minority, weighed less in the TVA scales than the benefits that would accrue, in terms of industrial and social engineering, to the nearby or the distant majority who sacrificed only tax money. (237–38)

Although Davidson makes what he must have regarded as an heroic effort to concede the achievements of the TVA, Stanley Folmsbee is certainly correct in saying that he sounds as if he is only "giving the devil his due." In describing the inner workings of the Authority, he is particularly acerbic in his depiction of David E. Lilienthal, the youngest and most single-minded of its three directors. (Robert Drake recalls that, when Davidson said the name "Lilienthal," he made it sound "like it was one of the vilest words in the English language.") In Davidson's portrayal, Lilienthal comes across as the sort of liberal ideologue whom David Halberstam would later dub "the best and the brightest." In 1944 Lilienthal proclaimed the gospel of TVA in an ingenuous tract entitled *Democracy on the March*. Two decades later, Russell Kirk tells us, the former TVA director was on television boasting of the vast development schemes he was engineering for the Shah of Iran. As Kirk observes, "the consequences of such developments would fetch the Shah down to his ruin." Lilienthal's notion that wealth was equivalent to freedom appealed to neither "the Tennessee farmers dispossessed of their ancestral land, nor to their Persian-gardener counterparts."[16]

The success of the TVA lay not just in the extent to which it transformed the landscape and economy of the Tennessee Valley but in the degree to which it captured the hearts and minds of the majority of people who lived in the valley. At one point, Davidson compares the effects of the TVA program with those of the enclosures in England from the time of Henry VIII on. Such views were regarded as heresy in 1948 and for the remainder of Davidson's life. But the march of democracy has encountered some detours on the way. As Bob Holladay noted in the spring of 1997, "Davidson died before TVA became seriously involved in its nuclear power boondoggles, but it is easy to assume that he might have seen a kind of rough justice in the spectre of the empty cooling towers at Hartsville, or the controversies over safety at Watts Barr and Browns Ferry, and the fact that its nuclear power experiments left TVA $27 billion in debt."[17] Published eighteen years after *I'll Take My Stand*, volume two of *The Tennessee* is a fitting benediction for the Agrarian movement.

16. Stanley J. Folmsbee, review of *The Tennessee*, vol. 2, 283; Robert Drake, "Donald Davidson and the Ancient Mariner," 21; Russell Kirk, preface to *The Tennessee*, 2:xii.
17. Bob Holladay, "The Reactionary," 71.

Davidson, 1919

Davidson with unidentified French girls, 1919

Chaplains T. G. Vickers and J. T. Jenner of the 324th Infantry at the graves of Maj. L. C. Ward and 1st Lt. H. M. Smith, Handimont, France, November 14, 1918

2d Lt. Donald Grady Davidson

324th Infantry the morning of November 11, 1918, near Manheuelles, France

Davidson, probably around the time of the *Fugitive* magazine

Davidson with the John Donald Wade family. Wade is at the lower right.

Davidson and Robert Frost on the Bread Loaf campus

Bread Loaf faculty, 1962 (l to r) front row: Carlos Baker, Elizabeth Drew, Donald Davidson, Maurice Kelley; back row: Kenneth Connelly, John Berryman, Daniel Lindley, William Meredith, Reginald Cook (director), Peter Stanlis, Eric Volkert. Courtesy Peter J. Stanlis

Davidson with Grandpa Dragon and his ballad singers. Kay Morrison is on the far left; Robert Frost is on the far right. Courtesy Peter J. Stanlis.

Davidson at the piano. Photo by Jerome Drown.

(l to r) Walter Sullivan, John Crowe Ransom, Donald Davidson, and Peter Taylor. Photo by Gerald Holly.

Fugitives' Reunion, Nashville, May 1956 (l to r) back row: Allen Tate, Cleanth Brooks, William Cobb, Rob Roy Purdy, Richmond Croom Beatty, Frank Lawrence Owsley, Randall Stewart, Brainard Cheney, R. D. Jacobs, Alec Stevenson; middle row: Willard Thorp, Andrew Lytle, Jesse Wills, Alfred Starr, Louis D. Rubin, Jr.; front row: Robert Penn Warren, Dorothy Bethurum, Merrill Moore, John Crowe Ransom, Sidney Hirsch, Donald Davidson, Louise Cowan, William Yandell Elliott. Courtesy Louis D. Rubin, Jr.

Donald and Theresa Davidson on the Vanderbilt campus. Photo by Jerome Drown.

(l to r) Jesse Wills, Ellen Wills, Donald Davidson, and Theresa Davidson at the fifty-seventh anniversary dinner of the Coffee House Club, December 8, 1966. Photo by Bob Ray.

PART FOUR

MR. DAVIDSON
(1950-1968)

16

A JOYFUL NOISE

Like so many poets of the bardic tradition, and unlike so many modernists, Donald Davidson celebrated the ancient ties between songs meant to be sung and verse meant to be read. As we have seen, music and literature were both an essential part of his upbringing. Even though he decided against applying to music school at Harvard, he wrote his operetta, "Pandora's Box," before any of his Fugitive verse. Students in Davidson's class in the English lyric at Bread Loaf, as well as those at Vanderbilt, remember him bringing musical instruments to class and singing some of the texts they were studying.[1] It is therefore not surprising that Davidson became enchanted with the Sacred Harp style of hymn singing that he encountered while spending a year in Marshallville, Georgia, after he and his family were left homeless by the Wesley Hall fire. His memories of that year are preserved in his essay "The Sacred Harp in the Land of Eden," published in the April 1934 issue of the *Virginia Quarterly Review.*

"In the plantation country of Middle Georgia is a land which ought to be, but is not, called Eden," Davidson begins. As idyllic as the town of "Eden" may be, the surrounding countryside has preserved an even older culture. In the churches of the town, "the choir sings competently because it is made up of educated musicians with well-behaved voices. The congregation listens obediently because that is what it is supposed to do. When the service is over, they all go home to dinner without knowing exactly what is missing from the procedure to which all the people once said Amen—actually said it, did not leave it to a choir to intone" (*Still Rebels,* 138). The people of the town have been corrupted by such

---

1. See Herschel Gower, "Charles Faulkner Bryan and the Music of 'Singin' Billy,' " xviii-xix.

radio singers as Walter Damrosch and Lily Pons and by the ersatz prosperity of the New South. But if one leaves the neo-Gothic churches of the town and seeks out the "plain rectangular 'church houses' that stand beside lonely graveyards, in groves of pine or oak" (138), he will find the old-time all-day singings where everyone joins in.

It is in these backwoods, a cappella songfests that the South maintains one of its closest cultural links to Elizabethan England. The books the singers use, *Sacred Harmony* (1835) and *The Sacred Harp* (1844), preserve "some of the noblest and most ancient strains of folk and art music in combination" (139). The most orthodox of the Sacred Harp singers will use no instruments at all, not even a tuning fork or a pitch pipe. (This places a considerable burden upon the song leader, who must be careful not to set the tune too high.) Davidson observes that the Cedar Valley folk embody the purest form of Sacred Harp or shape-note singing, while the "new way" folks at Salem use "seven-shape" notes and have a new book every year.

In loving detail, Davidson describes his Sunday at the Cedar Valley church. " 'The lesson will begin,' announced Brother Oakes, 'with Number Fifty-nine.' (For this ancient ritual still keeps the procedure of the eighteenth-century singing school; it speaks of 'lesson' and 'class.')" Although not everyone expected is present, Brother Oakes decides to go ahead with the singing: "Now everybody jine in as we sing these songs of Zion, and if you ain't got a book, open yore mouth and make a noise anyway."

> He peered at his book and hummed under his breath to set the pitch. To right, to center, to left he swept his hand, and the groups of voices in turn proclaimed the pitch, leaning over to let the others try it with him. And now he had the pitch. Then with the downward stroke of his hand they went through the tune together, singing the syllables, *fa, sol, la,* and calling to life the ancient shape notes that told singers how the tune went. Without a fumble they syllabled the tune; and the pines outside, and the plowed fields, and the throng of folk on the rough benches heard again the ritual of fa-sol-la, kept for them in hard times and good, by men and women who knew how to worship in song. (144)

If certain modernist poets have helped to create a breach between words and music, so too have "trained singers who, in their zeal for pure tonality, obscure consonants and merge syllables so as to make words indistinguishable." The Sacred Harp singers do not do this. They love the words as well as the music and intone them to emphasize the "separateness of one word from the next." This is because "they believed in the words and loved the old figures of speech. They were happy to think that they 'were marching through Immanuel's Land to fairer worlds on high,' or that 'somewhere their troubles would be over' " (148). In these singings, Davidson saw poetry functioning as a communal bond, just as he believed in theory it ought to.

As close as Davidson feels to the ritual he has witnessed, he also realizes, perhaps regretfully, that he is not part of the Cedar Valley community, that he is a visitor in Eden town itself. Tennessee is farther north, and Nashville is a center of urban culture. Even worse, his wife is from a foreign country called Ohio. Although the local folk invite the Davidsons to stay and share the fried chicken and sausage and pie and cake that the women have spent all day Saturday cooking, they know they must depart. "We left the Sacred Harp folk under their pines, where in a moment the preacher would ask the blessing of the Lord upon the bounty that His hand and His earth, despite man-made hard times, had given His people; and went on our way with the strings of the *Sacred Harp* still vibrant in our minds, and saw the cotton springing up, the peach trees in full green, the grain already nearly ripe for harvest in the land of Eden" (151).

I

In 1950, a student gave Donald Davidson a dulcimer that he had discovered in his grandfather's attic. Davidson's pleasure in receiving this gift soon turned to frustration when his efforts to tune the instrument proved futile. In desperation, he began looking around for someone who knew something about dulcimers. That someone turned out to be Charles Bryan, a music professor at the George Peabody College for Teachers, just across the street from Vanderbilt. Bryan had been collecting dulcimers for years with the intent of tracking down their European origins. With Bryan's help, Davidson finally got his dulcimer properly tuned, and it soon became a fixture in his ballad class, where he would use it to play the old folk songs he was teaching. He also developed a friendship with Bryan that would be one of the most rewarding of his career.

By 1950, Charles Faulkner Bryan was already a prominent American composer. Born in Faulkner Springs, near McMinnville, Tennessee, in 1911, Bryan entered the Nashville Conservatory of Music as a scholarship student in 1930. Over the next two decades, his compositions included *White Spiritual Symphony* (1938), the Civil War opera *Rebel Academy* (1939), and a folk cantata called *The Bell Witch* (1947). Based on a Tennessee legend, *The Bell Witch* premiered at Carnegie Hall on April 14, 1947, under the direction of Robert Shaw. Shortly after Bryan began teaching at Peabody, Davidson's isolation in Nashville came to a miraculous end. Both men were small-town boys from rural Tennessee who shared a passion for folk music and a commitment to bridging the gap between high culture and popular taste. They were joined in this effort by George Pullen Jackson, a folklorist who taught in the Vanderbilt German department. Although the friendship of

Davidson, Bryan, and Jackson was not comparable to the fellowship that had bound the Fugitives thirty years earlier, it provided the most creative stimulation that Davidson had known since then.

Although Davidson greatly respected George Pullen Jackson, there was always a formal reserve in their relationship. Jackson was nineteen years older than Davidson and had established himself as a senior professor at a time when Davidson was just beginning his academic career. (Even in his diaries, Davidson refers to his friend as "Dr. Jackson.") In a sense, both men came to music as amateurs—Davidson as a poet and critic and Jackson as a professor of German. Davidson used Jackson's *White Spirituals of the Southern Uplands* when he taught the ballad and fully subscribed to Jackson's notion that Negro spirituals derived from white spirituals rather than being original creations of the black race. The experience at the Cedar Valley church that he describes in "The Sacred Harp in the Land of Eden" helped confirm Davidson's agreement with Jackson's thesis. "Songs like 'My troubles will be over,' 'Oh, who will come and go with me,' and 'On Jordan's stormy banks I stand,' were remarkably like Negro spirituals," Davidson writes, "but they were demonstrably older than the recorded versions of the Negro spirituals that resemble them. . . . Doubtless the Negro had adapted them in his peculiar way, but he had first of all taken his songs from the source where he had got his Bible, his plow, his language" (*Still Rebels*, 149).

If Davidson found a kindred spirit in "Dr. Jackson," he discovered an even closer soul mate in Charlie Bryan. Young enough to be his son or nephew, Bryan seemed to recharge Davidson's creative energies. When they first met in 1950, Davidson's earlier musical studies had long since been confined to a distant past. He had even stopped writing verse, publishing only two poems since the appearance of *Lee in the Mountains* a dozen years earlier. Before long, Davidson and Bryan were calling each other regularly: Bryan would telephone and sing a tune, and Davidson would return the call a few days later with a lyric to match. Or Davidson might send Bryan a lyric written out in longhand and soon receive a tune to accompany it. The end product of this collaboration was a folk opera called *Singin' Billy*.

This opera is an historical fiction based on the life and career of William H. Walker (1809–1875), the famous singing schoolmaster from South Carolina, whose songbook *Southern Harmony* (1835) is the most complete and authoritative collection of shape-note hymns ever published. Davidson had seen old editions of *Southern Harmony* (it sold over 600,000 copies in Walker's lifetime) at the Sacred Harp songfests around Marshallville in the 1930s. He became so interested in the book and its author that he seriously considered writing a definitive biography of Walker. However, Charles Bryan, who discovered *Southern Harmony* during the spring and summer of 1950, convinced him that they would be better advised to collaborate on a folk opera concerning Walker's life and music.

The story of *Singin' Billy* depicts an imaginary, but altogether plausible, trip that Walker takes from his home in Spartanburg to the backwoods of Pickens County, South Carolina. The purpose of this trip (and similar ones taken by the historical Walker) is to establish singing schools in areas remote from formal culture and education. What soon emerges is one of the most familiar themes in American life, the conflict between civilized manners and frontier vitality. In Davidson's rendering, this conflict also develops into a battle between the sacred and the secular. Interestingly, this is not the first time in American literature that the religious singing master has ventured into the wilderness. In James Fenimore Cooper's *The Last of the Mohicans,* the psalm-singing David Gamut serves as foil to the archprimitivist Hawkeye, who, despite having no cross in his blood, is spiritually more "redskin" than "paleface." The differences between Cooper and Davidson are crucial. Where Gamut is a ridiculous figure, a Darwinian misfit, the resourceful Billy Walker can hold his own in a strange country. Moreover Kinch, who is Davidson's primary spokesman for frontier paganism, is a backwoods roughneck who resembles Hawkeye less than he does a dim-witted bully.

Even if Singin' Billy and the values he represents finally triumph, Davidson was too much a descendant of the tall men to turn this tale into a moralistic parable of good vanquishing evil. In his instructions to the cast of *Singin' Billy,* Davidson describes its theme as being the power of music, which symbolizes the harmony of life. This harmony "cannot be achieved if we have a conflict between secular and sacred which results in the overwhelming triumph of the secular and the relegation of the sacred to a negligible and entirely separate place—as too often happens in our modern age. Nor can this harmony be achieved, either, if the sacred element so far triumphs that the secular is ruled out as unimportant— frowned upon and disregarded as being merely gross and sinful. We cannot exist in the flesh as mere spirits."[2]

If there is a conflict between the sacred and the secular in *Singin' Billy,* it is less a Manichaean struggle than a comic quest to adjust a balance that essentially exists already. Davidson believed that "life in Pickens County, at the time that Singin' Billy entered it, was already in a condition of approximate harmony" ("Some Remarks" 2). "[D]espite the rough and boisterous conduct of the Boys and Girls of Pickens County," Davidson continues, "there was really not much cultural distance, in that society, between secular and sacred. They did not have to go far to be reconciled. Even Kinch, the most rebellious and defiant of the Boys, is nearer to the principle of harmony than he himself knows" (3).

The characters and situations in *Singin' Billy* are standard comedic fare. Miss Callie Wilkins, the kindhearted, plainspoken matriarch of Oconee Town, is

---

2. Donald Davidson, "Some Remarks on 'Singin' Billy,'" 2. Subsequent references will be cited parenthetically in the text.

courted by Hezekiah Golightly, a Revolutionary War veteran whom everyone calls "Uncle Kiah." (The play is set in 1835 when Uncle Kiah is "going-on 75, and still a boy."[3]) Margaret Williams, the lead soprano, is in love with Hank MacGregor, a young blacksmith who has lost interest in the things of this world ever since he got religion. Kinch Hardy, who is Singin' Billy's main antagonist, is paired with the "little spitfire" Gussie Epps, who seems alternately drawn and repelled by his Dionysian ways.

Uncle Kiah begins the confusion by stealing Billy Walker's letters of reference. Playing the role of an aging Puck, he mistakenly mixes some of Miss Callie's love potions into the town's water supply. When Margaret, Gussie, and (presumably) other young girls in the singing school subsequently seem taken with the handsome young stranger from Spartanburg, Kinch accuses him of being an imposter who is using religion as a kind of seduction scam. (The missing letters of reference prevent Billy from establishing his legitimacy.) Because Kinch has, in effect, challenged him to a duel, Walker reserves the right to choose the weapons. Not surprisingly, he insists on a singing contest. The climax occurs when "Wondrous Love," as sung by Billy and his cohorts, drowns out the strains of "John Barleycorn," as sung by Kinch and Gussie. (Although they have different words and express vastly different themes, both songs share a similar tune.) Kinch and Billy shake hands, Uncle Kiah produces the purloined letters, and Singin' Billy invites his new friends from Pickens County to his impending wedding in Spartanburg.

In addition to the individual characters, the community itself is an active presence in *Singin' Billy*. The practical jokes played on the newlyweds in the shivaree illustrate this point. According to Davidson, "they are an assertion, of an almost ritualized character, that the community—and not merely the two love-struck individuals concerned—has a powerful interest in any wedding that takes place within its bounds. This is a 'low-level' but perfectly genuine assertion of a principle upheld at a high level by the church in the ritual of the marriage ceremony" ("Some Remarks," 4).

The sense of social continuity is emphasized by the pairing of old and young characters. Uncle Kiah, who is a comic figure from the frontier tradition, seems to have walked out of a tall tale from the Old Southwest. Kinch, who is headed to the New Southwest, seems destined to become a more modern version of Uncle Kiah, if he survives the Indians and the Mexican War. Should he carry out his intention of going to Texas with Gussie, "he will undoubtedly raise a lot of chillun and cattle on a good range, like Kiah in the Carolinas before him" ("Some Remarks," 8).

On the distaff side, Miss Callie is what Margaret is likely to become, a force for

---

3. Donald Davidson, *Singin' Billy: A Folk Opera*, 2.

stability and order in society. If she represents petticoat government in Oconee Town, it is a benevolent form of despotism, based on superior wisdom and endorsed by the voluntary deference of the community. (The rough-hewn Uncle Kiah is trying to wed her, not flee from her domestic tyranny.) Although one is not accustomed to thinking of Donald Davidson as any kind of a feminist, he does seem to endorse matriarchy in *Singin' Billy*. In his remarks to the cast, Davidson claims that even Aristotle failed to give women sufficient credit. "I am personally convinced," he writes, "that the women of 1789 must have had a good deal to do with the making of the American Constitution; but no Ph.D. thesis will ever be written on that subject, because the private and urgent complaints of the wives and sweethearts of the 'Fathers of the Constitution' about masculine mismanagement of civil affairs were, of course, not of a 'documentary' nature" ("Remarks," 9).

One hesitates to evaluate the literary qualities of *Singin' Billy* simply on the basis of the text. An opera that is meant to be performed and *heard,* it premiered at the Vanderbilt University Theater on April 23, 1952, and ran through April 28. Although it was performed two or three other times in the mid-1950s, *Singin' Billy* is now a largely forgotten work. (In 1985, the book and score were published by the Foundation for American Education, but neither sold very well.) Persons who attended the early performances in Nashville were favorably impressed with the opera and regret the subsequent neglect it has suffered. One enthusiastic admirer of *Singin' Billy* was Robert Frost. In his diary entry for August 10, 1952, Davidson describes a night at Bread Loaf: "Quite a merry evening. Frost wanted no talk or explanation *about* 'S. Billy'—only the songs. He was especially pleased with 'Low Country.' We repeated it for him—he followed the words from script & joined in. . . . At 12 midnight we were still going strong—but had to go home on account of early rising."[4]

II

America was no more safe for democracy in 1952 than it had been when Davidson left Vanderbilt for France in 1916. Communism was spreading throughout Asia and Eastern Europe. The cold war had escalated into armed conflict in Korea, with two veterans of the First World War—Sgt. Harry Truman and Gen. Douglas MacArthur—publicly feuding over the best way to wage the new war. Because he was now president of the United States and commander in chief, Truman prevailed. Relieved of his command, MacArthur returned to a hero's welcome in

---

4. Davidson's personal diary is in the possession of the Davidson family. Subsequent references will be cited parenthetically in the text.

America. Truman's public approval rating dropped so low that he decided not to run for a third term after losing the New Hampshire primary to Sen. Estes Kefauver of Tennessee. Marianne Moore's *Collected Poems* won the Pulitzer Prize for poetry; the award for fiction went to Herman Wouk's *The Caine Mutiny.* Francois Mauriac won the Nobel Prize for literature in Stockholm, while George Santayana lay dying in a hospital in Rome. On New Year's Eve, Hank Williams passed away in the back seat of his Cadillac en route to a concert in Canton, Ohio. The previous spring, Donald Davidson had completed his thirty-second year as a member of the Vanderbilt English department.

Many of Davidson's happiest memories of the fifties revolve around music. One spring evening in 1951, he gave a party for some of his younger colleagues. "Walter Sullivan brought his guitar & sang excellently," Davidson recalls. "He has a fine voice, sings with energy and feeling. He sang 'Lamkin' & 'Three Ravens.' [Rob Roy] Purdy sang an Elizabethan song, 'A bird or two' and an interesting version of 'Hugh of Lincoln.' I sang to dulcimer & guitar. Theresa showed Vermont pictures. It was a fine crisp moonlight night. We had a very good time" (diary, March 20, 1951).

Unfortunately, such evenings seemed to have been few and far between. As he grew older, Davidson found that even Bread Loaf was no longer the idyllic refuge it had been in years past. Birthdays were among the most difficult times for him, as he would often receive greetings only from his insurance agent, Frank I. Cherry. On August 18, 1952, Davidson recorded the following "reflections" in his diary:

> A difficult and almost desperate summer, all hard work and frustration. The sole accomplishment—finishing MS for 3rd edition of A. C. & R. Some preparation for the Stark Young piece. No real work of my own, only errands, chores, bread-and-butter work, anxiety, disgust with political conventions & parties, disgust with Southern leadership, no companionship, any longer, with BL faculty, no letters (much) except from people who want me to do things for them (without reciprocal interest). Count 59 as one of the loneliest birthdays. But how could it be helped? Each in his cell, as T. S. Eliot wrote. The finest thing is to look at mountains, clouds, trees, robins, hummingbirds, blooming flowers.

For years, Davidson was haunted by what he called his "railroad dream." In it, he finds himself in the middle of a railroad station, which seems so very familiar yet strangely devoid of facilities. Sometimes he has difficulty locating the train he is supposed to ride. On one occasion, he sees Theresa on the train, but he has to step off into the station to get tickets or something, and the train pulls out of the station without him. As he races around in a hopeless panic, he wonders if, just this once, he can take an airplane and catch up with the train. There is "the feeling, too, that *everybody else* had the right information, knew what to do, where to go, but I didn't—their knowing looks, their almost patronizing air" (diary, August 23, 1953).

Nineteen fifty-three had started badly for Davidson with the death of his longtime friend George Pullen Jackson. On January 2, Davidson had called on the critically ill "Dr. Jackson" in what would be their last meeting. Davidson recalls that Jackson didn't seem in as bad a condition as he had been led to believe. "Cheerful and alert—gestured freely with left hand—offered me cigarettes—smoked himself—gave me the Christmas card he had drawn. . . . His face was fallen, on right side, he could not talk, was relatively helpless, still seemed quite himself—and we conversed with Dr. J. nodding, gesturing, making signs." But when he left, Jackson's son-in-law Fitzgerald Parker told Davidson that the situation was hopeless. Less than three weeks later, on Tuesday, January 21, George Pullen Jackson was dead. Davidson drove out Franklin Road in heavy rain to attend the funeral that Thursday. He recalls it being "a sort of vague 'memorial service' rather than a funeral. The organist played 'Wondrous Love,' 'Poor Wayfaring Stranger,' etc. That was the only really appropriate part of the 'service.' " The eulogy was "clumsy" and "inadequate," because the speaker "didn't know enough about Dr. J. and his work to make even a decent 'talk.' He even missed the name—substituted 'John' for George.' "

A far more fitting memorial for Jackson was held that November at the annual meeting of the Tennessee Folklore Society in Cookeville, Tennessee. Davidson and Theresa got up at 5:30 that morning and left Nashville at seven. It was a hazy morning with few autumn colors because of a recent drought. The Davidsons arrived on the campus of Tennessee Polytechnic Institute at about 10 A.M. There was a full audience in the library auditorium by the time that Donald got up to read a tribute to his late friend. "The first paragraph nearly choked me," he reports, "—I could hardly go on—the picture of Dr. Jackson & his struggles before my eyes—I couldn't look at audience. Somehow steadied my voice and read on. Complete silence when I sat down—people said later this meant audience was greatly moved" (diary, November 7, 1953).

Less than two years later, Davidson would suffer another devastating loss. As he and Theresa were finishing breakfast at Bread Loaf on the morning of July 8, 1955, a telegram arrived from Tennessee. At first, Davidson assumed that Charles Bryan was sending good news about a proposed telecast of *Singin' Billy* on NBC television. "But no—it was from Edith announcing Charles' death, the day before, of heart failure—and from this moment everything was unreal, and I was dazed." The Davidsons drove to Middlebury to send a telegram to Edith Bryan and to order flowers for the funeral. "The tears kept streaming, but it was something to do" (diary, July 8, 1955). The only entry in Davidson's diary for the following day reads: "Unable, from grief, to do anything but the commonplace

& necessary." Then, on Sunday, July 10, he writes: "With difficulty, I composed a letter to Edith Bryan." The letter reads as follows:

> I have long felt that the Lord has been good to me beyond my deserts in allowing me during these later years the privilege of knowing Charles and joining with him in the creation of an art work that to me, and I think to him, was a joy throughout, a high experience of a sort rarely possible in the world as the world commonly goes. For me personally, Charles brought about the realization of a dream that never could have come true except through the beauty and power of his music. The happiest discovery of my life was to find that, under his inspiration, I could devise something that would help him to call that wonderful music into being. I have had no other experience in any way comparable to this.[5]

III

After the commercial failure of *Singin' Billy* and the untimely death of Charles Bryan, Davidson made no further attempts to write for the theater. Nevertheless, his collaboration with Bryan had started him writing poetry again, after a long dry spell. As we shall see, the verse of Davidson's final period is more varied in style and colloquial in voice than the explicitly Agrarian poetry of *The Tall Men* and *Lee in the Mountains,* just as that Agrarian poetry itself differs markedly from the writings of "Robin Gallivant." The final period in Davidson's poetic development is on full display in *The Long Street,* published by Vanderbilt University Press in 1961. In one section of that book, Davidson speaks through Joe Clisby—a persona whom M. E. Bradford sees as belonging "to an earlier South—a South that existed before World War I—or perhaps to a timeless Agrarian stasis."[6]

In a letter to Jesse Stuart, dated June 2, 1960, Davidson writes: "Perhaps you can see me hiding behind 'Joe Clisby.' He has been a help to me this winter. You never met him. Neither did I, exactly, but I seem to know him all the same." Writing again to Stuart a month later, Davidson notes: "It is a great help to have Joe Clisby as my 'mouth' (Indian fashion). He can say some things I personally could never say in direct form."[7] Although five of the seven Joe Clisby poems were first published in 1960 or 1961, one of them, "Crabbed Youth and Merry Age," dates back to 1934, and another, "The Swinging Bridge," appeared in the *Fugitive* in 1923.

---

5. See Carolyn Livingston, *"Singin' Billy:* An Introduction," 25.
6. M. E. Bradford, "Donald Davidson and the Use of Persona: A Reading of the Joe Clisby Poems," 126.
7. Ibid., 125–26.

These two older poems seem to belong to the Joe Clisby group by adoption rather than by initial intent. The original version of "The Swinging Bridge" contains something of the mysterious and romantic tone one finds in the poems collected in *An Outland Piper*.[8] The version in *The Long Street* is more nostalgic and whimsical, even Frostian. (One detects the rhythms and sensibility of Frost in the revision Davidson has made to the first line of the poem: "Not arching up, as some good bridges do" becomes "Not arching up as good stone bridges do.") Davidson brings the revised "Swinging Bridge" into the Clisby milieu by adding the following line to the end of the third stanza: "And the voices calling *Ezell!* and *Joe!* till comes the long, long night" (*The Long Street*, 51).

"The Swinging Bridge" vaguely recalls Frost's "Birches" (published in *A Boy's Will* in 1915). Davidson pictures a boy (now apparently identified as Joe Clisby) standing on a swinging bridge contemplating the allure of danger and uncertainty it projects. Standing on its ancient rotted planks, he has " . . . gone, like folks who have followed old desire / Into some heaven and long, long fallen asleep where they wanted to." In the original version, the experience was rendered with more immediacy and solemnity. There we read that the boy has " . . . gone, like his wild yesterday's desire, / Into the stream as things that fall asleep where they wanted to." The mature Davidson has connected the boy's desire with a more universal human impulse by mentioning other folks, while giving it a more archetypal resonance through his reference to "some heaven."

The *Fugitive* version of "The Swinging Bridge" ends with the boy looking to the future: "He thinks of the hill, dark, unclimbed of crest / And must be going there to see the blue mountain of his dream." Coming back to this poem nearly four decades later, Davidson casts the ending very much in the past tense. After introducing Ezell and Joe waiting for the long, long night, he writes:

> But the bridge stirs under his feet, the wizard bridge.
> "Cross me," it says, "and taste my sweet unrest."
> Beyond the whispering leaves, beyond the stream
> One dark hawk mounts the clouds to the sky's crest—
> Long, long have I remembered that sky, those wings,
>   that climber's dream. (51)

Although the poem is not written in the first person—except for the coy reference to "a boy (I know him well) . . ."—there can be little doubt that the speaker is wistfully recollecting his own youth from the perspective of age and wisdom. Of course, in revising the poem, that is precisely what Donald Davidson has been doing.

8. Donald Davidson, "The Swinging Bridge."

The two poems that follow "The Swinging Bridge" in the Joe Clisby section of *The Long Street* may belong there in spirit; however, neither mentions a character named "Joe," much less "Joe Clisby." "Spring Voices" is a quatrain that uses one of the oldest themes in poetry—the *ubi sunt* motif. Poets working in this tradition express an appreciation for the beauty of the world, which is all the more poignant because of the transitoriness of that beauty. (The term itself derives from the first two words of the Latin phrase *ubi sunt qui ante nos fuerunt?* meaning "where are they who before us went?") Significantly, the spring voices heard in this poem are not those of illustrious predecessors but of nature itself, not tall men but gray doves. The poem reads:

> Lovely in spring again flows Harpeth River
> While bough to bough I hear the gray doves calling,
> But the voices that answered me by Harpeth River
> Are gone with the flowing stream and the blooms falling. (52)

April may not exactly be the cruelest month, but the flow of the Hereclitian river (and the falling blooms) reminds the poet that all beauty, indeed all life, is fleeting.

"Crabbed Youth and Merry Age" is a slight but effective exercise in irony. Unlike "Spring Voices," which appeared for the first time in *The Long Street*, this poem dates back to the mid-1930s. (It was first published in the spring 1934 issue of *Quill*.) The point of the poem is expressed by the reversal of expectations one finds in its title. Rather than juxtaposing an heroic age of the past with a diminished present, Davidson champions the old over the new by contrasting living members of two different generations. The young men of this poem speak in "tongues of disaster muted with sleep and scorn." They seem used up and old before their time: "Before the time of resting they are tired; / Before the time of losing they are forlorn." Although we do not know where or how the young men live, their natural element is darkness. Perhaps they are coming in from a night on the town; at the very least, they are intoxicated with cynicism.

In contrast to these desiccated youths, we see:

> . . . the old men, risen at morning light,
> Unlatching country gates before the sun,
> To catch a horse and call with Stentor's voice
> The lazy boy whose ploughing's not begun. (53)

The agrarian imagery in this second stanza suggests that a life lived close to the earth (and bathed in morning light) results in sustained vitality, if not perpetual youth. The reference to Stentor's voice gives the stanza a mythological resonance. Old men speaking with such a voice have the moral authority to chastise indolent plow boys. The placement of this poem suggests that Joe Clisby belongs to the generation of merry age.

The Joe Clisby series opens with the three poems in which Joe appears most prominently—"Joe Clisby's Song, "On Culleoka Road," and "Second Harvest." "Joe Clisby's Song" is an affirmative lyric, which suggests that past and future are bound together in a seamless web. The speaker (presumably Clisby himself) begins by remembering an old song that said "something of youth and desire / And summer passing away." (Apparently, this song is Sir Walter Raleigh's "As You Came from the Holy Land," which, according to M. E. Bradford, "is a conversation about love and change."[9]) In agreement with this old song, the speaker asserts that "love is a durable fire / And will stay." At the same time, he realizes that neither he nor the song is made for a time "that reads only lust in a kiss / And shreds the magic of rhyme" (47).

The speaker goes on to describe the "old Bethel burying-ground" as a place bathed in moonlight, where "true lovers as ever were found." Among these lovers are he and Nettie Long and "Burt Whitson with his Ruth." There is nothing ghoulishly inappropriate about their being here. The dead people in this cemetery are just as much a part of the organic community as the young lovers who are courting on this summer evening. Indeed, the two couples "walked and sang to the low / Ranks of the good dead people." As Clisby tells us, "the old folks that lie there / We know were singers all" (47). He invites those who would join the song the dead people sang, but are afraid to raise a sound, to "Come walk with Nettie Long / And me, by the burying-ground." The poem concludes on a festive note:

> Burt Whitson and his Ruth
> And many couples more
> Can tune the lips of youth
> As they did mine before
>   To sing the truth. (48)

This poem is a celebration of romantic love within the bonds of community. The love shared by the young couples in "Joe Clisby's Song" transcends lust, at least in part because it is not merely personal. It is an experience that is shared with the singers in the graveyard and one that stretches back to Raleigh's time and before. As Bradford notes, "Davidson's poem transforms the old material of love and death into a negation of mutability, a music in tribute to that love which outlasts ordinary mortal limitations."[10] In a sense, this poem answers the *ubi sunt*

9. Bradford credits Prof. Ward Allen of Auburn University with identifying the song. See Bradford, "Persona," 131.
10. Ibid.

question by saying that those who have gone before are still with us because of the power of shared experience. That shared experience is another name for love.

The second poem in the Joe Clisby sequence, "On Culleoka Road," depicts Joe himself among the ranks of the dead. Here, he claims "the shadow's privilege" to stand at a river east of Culleoka, just south of Columbia, Tennessee. In modern times, a girl with yellow hair drives a blue sports car across a bridge spanning the river. Joe makes it clear in the second stanza such a girl would be incapable of asking the *ubi sunt* question. She could not possibly believe that someone such as Joe Clisby once crossed that same river. Not only is he an invisible spirit, the surrounding environment has been permanently altered: "apples are gone from the hill," "wild thickets of plum are stricken and chopped away," "strange weather keeps all water from the mill." Looking now toward the past, he recalls that "before there was ever a bridge" on Culleoka Road, he met a wagoner there, "an old man with merry eyes and sunset on his hair." The story he hears from this old man, with his primitive means of transportation, provides a striking contrast to the image of the girl in the blue sports car:

> "My girl," he said, "was a phoenix, dawn rosy on her breast;
> Five nights I rode courting till the heavens overflowed
> And I swam my horse to win her, for what young man can rest
> Who comes to find his phoenix on Culleoka Road?"

Joe can respond to the old man's tale because he too is on his way to court "one whose eyes are blue as day / And hair bright as morning on a sycamore in spring." Like the wagoner's beloved, Joe's girl has promised "that she will be my phoenix through all my journeying." This knowledge is sufficient to sustain him throughout life and to remove any horror from the prospect of death:

> When I rode from my phoenix the whippoorwills were calling;
> Midnight a meadow the stars had overflowed;
> On my lips her kisses and summer dew falling
> Till we should be shadows on Culleoka Road. (49)

Insofar as our focus is confined to the wagoner and Joe Clisby, the message of this poem is the same as that of "Joe Clisby's Song"—love is a shared experience of the living and the dead, indeed the very rationale of life itself. The wagoner has proved the intensity of his love by riding five nights and fording flooded rivers to court his "phoenix." The term *phoenix,* with its suggestions of resurrection (including the sexual connotations employed with such wit by John Donne in "The Canonization"), reminds us that love is a recurring paradigm. There is a strong suggestion, however, that the knowledge shared by Joe and the wagoner is inaccessible to the blonde in the sports car. The distance that it took the wagoner five nights to traverse can now be traveled in a matter of hours with relatively little hazard. The wagoner probably could not have imagined how things would become, and the girl in the sports car obviously has no memory of how they were. Because of his unique position, Joe Clisby is able to see *both* the elegiac past and the hollow present.

In "Second Harvest," the poem that follows "On Culleoka Road" in *The Long Street,* Joe Clisby is alive but far removed from civilization and the love of women. He is in the masculine wilderness of American myth, a land occupied by hunters from Natty Bumppo to Ike McCaslin. In the first stanza, Joe confesses that he and his companions, "at midnight, crowding the autumn paths," cannot sleep for the sound of the hunter's horn. In the second stanza, there is only the slightest hint that the land has declined since the days of their youth. They hunt in an area where only the hunter's moon now "sickles the frosty lanes where green corn once was growing." In order to enact their part in the ritual (they "know what play comes on so soon"), the quail and wild turkey must seek cover "beyond the ravished field." The tone of diminishment is far more muted than in a hunting tale such as Faulkner's "Delta Autumn," but one can hear it between the lines.

The third stanza sounds other familiar themes:

> Once I could ride where a man ought to a hill where horses
> Neighed and my old companions called—that starry place
> Where always the Ploughman drives the Bear on her changeless courses
> And no man hangs his head to dream of a woman's face.

The reference to "that starry place / Where always the Ploughman drives the Bear on her changeless courses" adds the context of Greek myth to an otherwise indigenously American fable. Because of the American tradition of male bonding, the note of misogyny in the final line is almost obligatory. It is then repeated in the first line of the last stanza: "Then no soft arms could hold me from my wilderness yearning. . . ." Because he is able to resist the blandishments of any domestic Eve (with apparently little effort), Joe is able to reap the "harvest of life that gives me life" (50). Because the poem is titled "Second Harvest" and Joe identifies himself and his companions as "the too-long born," we infer that this is a poem of old age. Like the indomitable old men in "Crabbed Youth and Merry Age," the Joe Clisby of "Second Harvest" finds nature to be a source of renewal and rebirth, if not perpetual youth.

IV

As a resident of Nashville with a keen interest in folk music, Donald Davidson could hardly ignore the country music industry. Nashville is one town where the high culture and popular culture of the South exist almost literally side by side. It is no more than a fifteen-minute walk from the Vanderbilt and Peabody campuses on Twenty-first Avenue to the legendary recording studios on Sixteenth Avenue. A sometimes creative, sometimes hostile, tension has always existed between the ballads Davidson so loved and the music played on country music radio stations and the stage of the Grand Ole Opry. Knowing of his love for the folk tradition, some of Davidson's most perceptive and devoted students have assumed that he must have held commercial country music in contempt.[11] The truth, however, is more complex.

As his diaries clearly indicate, Davidson enjoyed the *Grand Ole Opry* and was knowledgeable about the artists who performed there. For example, on Saturday, February 28, 1948, Mildred Haun gave him and Theresa sixth-row floor tickets to the Opry. Between eight and eleven that night, they heard Roy Acuff and the Smoky Mountain Boys, Bill Monroe and the Blue Grass Boys, the Possum Hunters, and Minnie Pearl. Bradley Kincaid sang "Robin Redbreast" and "Gooseberry Pie," but the best single song, in Davidson's estimation, was Monroe's "Molly Darling." He thought that the best fiddling was done by Curly Fox in "Whoa Mule." "Performances on guitars & mandolins, also bull fiddles, were amazing," Davidson writes in his diary. "They are skillful artists—virtuosos. Acuff was good in 'Pale Horse'" (diary, February 28, 1948).

It is not clear when Davidson first decided to write a novel about country music. We know that he tried to place such a manuscript with the publishers of his two most successful books. He sent the text of *The Big Ballad Jamboree* to Scribner's on May 25, 1953. A month later, on June 25, the book was rejected. On September 23, it was sent off to Rinehart. Apparently it fared no better there, because on November 6, Jesse Stuart was suggesting that Davidson try his publisher, McGraw-Hill. The editors at McGraw-Hill liked the book well enough to suggest revisions and even seemed on the verge of publishing it when the firm summarily abolished its trade division. At that point, Davidson appears to have abandoned the project altogether. For years, an early, incomplete draft of *The Big Ballad Jamboree* existed in the Davidson papers at Vanderbilt. It was not until late 1994 that Davidson's granddaughter Molly Kirkpatrick discovered the final completed typescript of the novel in her mother's garage. In the spring of 1996, over forty years after the book was completed and nearly thirty years after its author's death, *The Big Ballad Jamboree* was finally published by the University Press of Mississippi.

The protagonist of Davidson's novel, which is set in 1949, is a hillbilly singer named Danny MacGregor, whose girlfriend, Cissie Timberlake, has left show

11. For example, Tom Landess assumed that this was the case in an interview I had with him on June 8, 1997.

business to collect traditional ballads as she pursues an M.A. in folklore at the local teachers' college. Although he is closer to Cissie in his professional interests, Davidson uses Danny as the sympathetic narrator of the novel. He may poke fun at some of the cornier and more sentimental aspects of commercial country music, but his harshest satirical jibes are reserved for academia. By far, the most ridiculous and loathsome character in the novel is Cissie's thesis advisor, J. Chauncey Hoodenpyl, a pompous fraud who tries to take credit for Cissie's research. Next to him, the novel's redneck villain, the bootlegger Buck Kennedy, maintains a kind of roguish charm.

The only other character lampooned nearly as much as Hoodenpyl is Carlos B. Reddy, a populist congressman obviously based on the Tennessee senator Estes Kefauver. "His motto was 'Always Be Ready,'" Danny tells us. "He said it was because his Mamma had named him Carlos B. on purpose, and told him it meant 'Carlos Be Reddy,' but folks from his home town said no, that wasn't right; his Mamma's maiden name was *Bee* and she was kin to the man that first named Stonewall Jackson 'Stonewall.' Anyway, Carlos B. Reddy was always ready—especially when it came to getting elected, and he sure was good at that."[12] Like Kefauver, whose liberalism Davidson despised, Carlos B. Reddy wears a "Hollywood coonskin cap" and displays a lecherous interest in pretty young women.

Despite his depiction of Carlos B. Reddy, who comes across as a congressman devoid of ideology, cheerfully buying support with pork-barrel money, Davidson makes very little political commentary in *The Big Ballad Jamboree*. One exception is his description of Pegram's Crossroads at the beginning of chapter 7. Here, Danny and Cissie are discussing a desolate area in rural Carolina. (Although the novel is set in the fictional town of Carolina City, there is an actual town of Pegram in Middle Tennessee.)

> There wasn't any blacksmith at Pegram's anymore. There were hardly any wagon tires to put on anymore, or plow points to sharpen, or horses and mules to shoe. There wasn't any little auto repair shop, either, or even a gasoline pump. There were not enough folks left in Beaver Valley to support anything but their own selves. They had had plenty of practice in doing that. They had to be tough to stay.
>
> "It's worse than I remembered," Cissie said gloomily. "Pegram's store was open when we were last here. The old man sold us Coca-Cola."
>
> "The wholesalers closed him out. He's gone to live with one of his daughters, I heard."

12. Donald Davidson, *The Big Ballad Jamboree*, 6. Subsequent references will be cited parenthetically in the text.

"Then we'll have to work fast to get the ballads before the rest move away. And before the old folks die. I don't like to think about it. It's sort of—ghostly."

"It's still worse at Big Cataloochee and Little Cataloochee, where the Smoky Mountains Park came in and moved them all out. Nothing left but tombstones. If it was TVA land, there wouldn't even be tombstones. TVA moves even the dead folks, they tell me. Then puts water over empty graves." (73)

On the whole, the tone of *The Big Ballad Jamboree* is light and, in places, very funny. When Danny complains to his friend and barber Ed Cooley about the burden of toting a tape recorder all around the backwoods so that Cissie can record ballads, Ed tells him that he is lucky his girl is not crazy about religion. When Ed was courting his future wife, he had "to go to church Sunday mornin', Sunday night, prayer meetin', Christian Endeavor, box suppers, memorize the Golden Text, go to Sunday School, read the Bible ever' night, think about my sins and try to be sanctified" (59). And then the traveling revival meeting came to town, and he had to attend services three times a day for two weeks. (Fortunately, his girlfriend "didn't go in for the rattlesnake style of religion" [59].) Finally, Ed said, "Elora, my soul is saved but if you want it to stay saved you better marry me before I backslide" (60). Now that they are married, Ed and Elora spend Sunday mornings reading the newspaper and listening to the radio.

Davidson's depictions of the country folks whom Cissie records is also tinged with humor. If poor rural white people have not always fared well in American literature, Davidson gives them their due without resorting to the maudlin apotheosis that one sometimes finds in the work of John Steinbeck. Like Huck Finn, Danny MacGregor can describe a scene deadpan, never ruining the effect with overt commentary. Here is the matriarch Aunt Lou Watkins summoning the children in her household: "Elmer! Roscoe! Mary Lou! States Rights! Joe-Bob!" (76). In this scene, Davidson moves effortlessly from broad comedy to a precise observation of manners: "Aunt Lou began to dip snuff, not in the nasty white trash way of pouring it from the can into the lower lip, but in the old genteel way of dipping with a little soft twig brush and rubbing it very carefully into her gums" (84–85).

Danny's resemblance to a modern-day Huck is most evident when he is giving his bemused account of life on the college campus. The academic administrator as character type is rendered brilliantly in the following passage: "I don't know why, but I had in my head that a Dean would be an old, long-faced man in a black coat, something like an old-timey preacher. But Dean Bronson wasn't that way at all. He was a peart young blackheaded, black-eyed feller, so agreeable that I almost felt like I'd got into an insurance office by mistake and might walk out with a $50,000 endowment policy and forget all about reading the fine print" (127). A few pages earlier, Danny had described Dr. Hoodenpyl as "a young-looking fat little man grinning at us, with a tray in his hands and enough grub on it to feed two people" (121).

In his attempt to make small talk with Danny, Hoodenpyl comes off as fatuous and inadvertently patronizing. "I have been vastly amused," he prattles on, "immensely amused, and, I might add not at all displeased, to see how the hillbilly music has routed the crooners and the other jazzicians of Tin Pan Alley and Hollywood. Yes-yes. Jazzicians. Not musicians—jazzicians. The hillbilly performers, whatever else they may be, are certainly musicians. Not quite the genuine folk music, of course, Mr. MacGregor. Not quite. But not so far from it as some people would argue" (122). Davidson's ear for academic pretension (right down to the verbal tic "yes-yes") is as good as it is for the vernacular speech of authentic agrarian people. Also, by portraying Hoodenpyl as such a buffoon and scoundrel, Davidson makes the academic study of folk music seem anything but an invariably noble calling. There is enough that is meretricious in both academia and show business that Davidson feels no need to construct a facile morality play around the conflict between these two realms.

Dr. Hoodenpyl's greatest scholarly accomplishment is what he calls his Frank Sinatra chart. This is an elaborate series of graphs showing an inverse relation between knowledge of traditional ballads and a "radio preference" for Frank Sinatra. As Hoodenpyl himself explains the chart: " 'I am PROUD of Laurel Gap, North Carolina, where, among 43 students of high school age, the incidence of knowledge of traditional ballads is very HIGH.' He was standing on tiptoe, reaching up. 'In fact, almost ONE—HUNDRED—PERCENT. See-see-see-see-see! And the incidence of radio preference for Frank Sinatra is—ha, ha!—very *low!* Isn't that glorious? GLORIOUS!' " (171). When Danny tells his disc jockey friend Wallace Exum that this all seems rather obvious, Wallace observes: "He has a Guggenheim Fellowship—or somethin'. He gets paid for making charts of what everybody already knows" (173). A few pages later, when it becomes apparent that Hoodenpyl is going to take credit for one of Cissie's discoveries, Danny labels the act as "jest plain stealin'." Cissie replies: "Up in Beaver Valley, we'd call it stealin'. But in graduate school it's scholarship" (179).

The glimpses we get of the country music industry are less extensive. Obviously, Davidson was not nearly as much at home on Sixteenth Avenue as he was on Twenty-first. (A diary entry for May 31, 1954, tells of a lunch he had with Jack Dewitt, the station manager for Nashville's legendary country music station WSM, but such encounters appear to have been infrequent.) Nevertheless, as Curtis W. Ellison and William Pratt point out in their afterword to *The Big Ballad Jamboree,* "eighteen of the novel's twenty-five chapters include performances, and at least three give detailed accounts of musical events."[13] The first of these is a performance before the Future Farmers of America in chapter 4, and the last is the ballad concert that Cissie organizes at the college. Although we do not actually see Danny on the road, we hear his complaints about "the one-night stands for ten or twelve nights running" and the experience of fighting "the trailer-trucks along the two-lane winding Georgia roads." "Working for Rufus?" he asks rhetorically. "Yes, I was—and for fertilizer firms, drugstores, overall factories, purgatives, cosmetics, dog-biscuit companies, till it wore me out." Then, with a telling anticommercial image, he notes: "I could hear the adding machines underneath my guitar frets" (102).

The Big Ballad Jamboree is an extremely well crafted first novel. In addition to its pervasive humor, the action is fast-paced (concluding with a car chase that might have come right out of *Smokey and the Bandit* or *The Dukes of Hazzard*), and the characterizations are deft if not particularly deep. A likable protagonist with genuine agrarian values, Danny Macgregor is trying to restore his family farm with the money he makes as an entertainer. He shares Cissie's love for traditional ballads, if not her commitment to studying them. In the novel's comic resolution, Cissie secures a more permanent teaching position at the college, while Danny is hired as her audio-visual assistant. They even have time to pursue their musical careers on weekends. If this happy ending may seem to trivialize the conflict between folk and mass culture that has run through the novel, that conflict was never presented as absolute. And what well-intentioned reader would wish a less promising future for a couple as attractive as Danny and Cissie?

It is unfortunate that *The Big Ballad Jamboree* never saw the light of day during Davidson's own lifetime. With proper promotion, it might have been a commercially successful novel. If nothing else, it would have enhanced Davidson's literary reputation by establishing him as a first-rate humorist (something that readers of his poetry and essays might not have suspected). Patti Henson's cover drawing for the Mississippi Press edition of the book reminds one of a comic strip out of the fifties. The point, whether intended or not, is that the image of rural life harbored by most Americans at the time Davidson wrote his novel was derived from Al Capp's *Lil' Abner*. In *The Big Ballad Jamboree,* we have a more realistic and more respectful picture of a similar milieu.

It is significant that Davidson chose to set his novel in 1949. The country music historian Bill C. Malone has characterized the years 1946 to 1953 as the "boom period" for country music. During the postwar years, what had once been known as hillbilly music was gaining wide popular acceptance and enjoying great crossover appeal.[14] By the midfifties, when Davidson was actually writing *The*

---

13. Curtis W. Ellison and William Pratt, afterword to *The Big Ballad Jamboree*, 291–92.
14. See Bill C. Malone, *Country Music U.S.A.,* 199–243.

Big Ballad Jamboree, the situation was radically different. The emergence of rock and roll in the midfifties (beginning with "Rock around the Clock" by Bill Haley and the Comets in 1954) represented a severe challenge to all traditional forms of music, including country. Many of the most successful early rock-and-roll performers (including Elvis Presley himself) were rural white southerners who were influenced by both country music and black rhythm and blues. Several of these performers (Presley, Jerry Lee Lewis, Johnny Cash, Roy Orbison, Charlie Rich, and Carl Perkins among them) recorded for Sam Phillips's Sun Records label in Memphis and were known as rockabillies. A Danny MacGregor of 1956 would have found the conflict between the traditional folk sound and a more commercial brand of music far more pronounced than in 1949.

It is easy to see why Donald Davidson did not write a more contemporaneous country music novel. Even if the songs performed on the *Grand Ole Opry* in the late forties and early fifties were different from what he taught in his ballad classes, they were still far more familiar than anything Elvis Presley would record just a few years later. If Davidson felt comfortable attending the *Opry* in Nashville's Ryman Auditorium or lunching with the station manager of WSM, it would have been a far different proposition to listen to Jerry Lee Lewis play boogie-woogie piano in a barroom where chicken wire protected the performers from flying bottles. Had Davidson set his novel in the heyday of rock, he would also have been forced to deal imaginatively with the increasing role of race in American life.

WHO SPEAKS FOR THE WHITE MAN?

On May 17, 1954, Donald Davidson recorded the following entry in his diary: "U.S. Supreme Court handed down 9–0 decision against segregation—9 justices against how many million white folks in South and elsewhere! A black day. More black days to come. All foreseen, not for that reason either welcome or tolerable." Prior to this historic decision, Davidson had included support of the racial caste system in the South as part of his more general defense of regional tradition. After the Court transformed integration into a constitutional imperative, he made the fight to preserve segregation into a consuming passion. In fact, this was almost literally the case. When one considers the sheer amount of paperwork generated by his political activities in the fifties, not to mention the undocumented labors the paper trail merely suggests, it is remarkable that Davidson was also able to teach a full load at Vanderbilt and Bread Loaf, write a novel as good as *The Big Ballad Jamboree,* and produce the best sustained body of poetry in his career. It is no wonder that his health, which had never been good, began to deteriorate at this time. What is perhaps even more regrettable, though perfectly understandable, is the toll that Davidson's outspoken racial views would take on his reputation as man and artist. Nearly three decades after his death, *Nashville Life* magazine ran an article about Davidson under the provocative heading "Donald Davidson: Author, Prophet, Racist."[1]

What were Davidson's views on race? Perhaps the most measured and sympathetic assessment is offered by his friend and colleague Walter Sullivan:

1. This provocative phrase appeared on the cover of the April–May 1997 issue of *Nashville Life*. That issue of the magazine contained Bob Holladay's article "The Reactionary."

It seemed to be Mr. Davidson's misfortune that his political adversaries were able to define their conflict with him almost totally in terms of race; but in fact he collaborated in the definition. He told me that when he first came to Vanderbilt, he was friendly with the black professors at Fisk University, met with them socially as well as professionally, but ceased his intercourse with them when the push for racial equality began. In his judgment, the civil rights movement was a vehicle for political upheaval. Even had he not believed this, he would have opposed the movement on its merits, and his stubborn devotion to a platform built on the hypothesis of white supremacy caused both him and his friends a good deal of pain.[2]

When one considers his courting of William Stanley Braithwaite and his enthusiastic response to the work of James Weldon Johnson, one is tempted to think of Davidson as a onetime racial moderate who became embittered by the passage of time and the continual assault on southern tradition. But the truth seems to be that he was capable of holding and expressing conflicting attitudes in the same period of his life. In a letter that he wrote to John Gould Fletcher on June 13, 1927, over three months *before* his review of *The Autobiography of an Ex-Coloured Man,* Davidson bemoans the fact that New York publishers will ignore the work of poets such as himself and Fletcher but "will publish the trivial verses of negroes like Langston Hughes because niggers are a metropolitan fashion."[3]

Two and a half years later, Davidson expressed some concern about contributing to a very pluralistic symposium on southern culture being proposed by Howard Mumford Jones. Writing to Jones on December 18, 1929, Davidson imagined himself "condemning Dubose Heyward for taking New York's point of view on the negro while in another section [of the book] Langston Weldon White indicated that the South had at last been saved by a marriage, consummated in New York, between black literature and white." He argues that "this would be all the more embarrassing if my compatriots on the other side of the fence were vowing . . . to lynch Langston Weldon White, and if I were quite ready to do that too."[4] It is difficult to believe that the same man who, two years earlier, was capable of identifying Langston Hughes, Walter White, and James Weldon Johnson with three distinct traditions in Negro literature was now lumping them all together in a crude composite figure.

Even in his public writing, Davidson could be sharply, though not categorically, critical of what he regarded as black radicalism. Reviewing W. E. B. Du Bois's novel *Dark Princess* in his book page on July 1, 1928, he writes:

2. Sullivan, *Allen Tate,* 26.
3. This letter is housed in the University of Arkansas Library at Fayetteville.
4. This letter is housed in the Fugitive Collection of the Heard Library.

In more ways than one it is a disturbing and tragic book. It is by turns impressive and preposterous, and it is hard to say which quality dominates the book. So far as it gives a serious and detailed picture of an ambitious negro consciousness of varying degrees of idealism, fanaticism, wisdom, and sloth, it is keen and powerful. In its picture, given from the radical negro point of view, of a white civilization whose every purpose is directed toward suppressing and crushing negro aspirations, it is pitifully frenzied, laboriously ridiculous, and some of its shaky concatenations of events are as far-fetched as an Oppenheim thriller or Elmer Gantry's amorous intrigues with the woman evangelist.

Davidson concludes by observing that *Dark Princess* "has elements that make it dangerous, and from my point of view, regrettable, and I have a hearty distaste for its extreme propagandistic turn. But even with all its frenzy, it demands to be read, whether to study the workings of a radical negro mind or to see the clear, sharp pictures of negro life that the other elements tend to obscure. In this case it is more important to understand than to denounce."[5]

Davidson's irate response to Robert Penn Warren's essay in *I'll Take My Stand* has become the stuff of legends. In "The Briar Patch," Warren had written a defense of racial equality and justice, while expressing support for the economic advancement of southern blacks. Like Booker T. Washington before him, Warren believed that these goals could be accomplished even within a segregated society. (As we shall see, Warren would abandon his acquiescence to segregation by the 1950s.) Because Warren wrote his essay while away at Oxford, it was difficult for Davidson or the other editors in Nashville to discuss it with him. (To make matters worse, it had been submitted very late against a tight publication schedule.) Writing to Tate on July 21, 1930, Davidson expressed shock and disbelief that the Red Warren he knew could have composed such an essay. "It hardly seems worthy of Red, or worthy of the subject," he complains. "And it certainly is not very closely related to the main theme of our book. It goes off at a tangent to discuss the negro problem in general (which, I take it, is not our main concern in the book), and it makes only two or three points that bear on our principles at all" (*Literary Correspondence*, 251).

Undoubtedly, Warren's racial views were considerably more liberal than Davidson's (or those of any of the other Agrarians, with the exception of H. C. Nixon). Politics, however, seems to have been only one issue here. Davidson was convinced that Warren's treatment of the Negro had little relevance to the conflict between industrialism and Agrarianism. Had Warren written a sympathetic essay about the virtues of the rural black peasantry, it would probably have passed muster with

5. Donald Davidson, review of *Dark Princess,* by W. E. B. Du Bois.

Davidson. (After all, Davidson was closer to Thomas Page than to Thomas Dixon in his view of black people.) On March 17, 1930, he had written enthusiastically to Warren: "It's up to you, Red, to prove that negroes are country folks—'bawn and bred in a briar-patch.'" Davidson was advocating not race baiting but an attitude of benign neglect toward the political status of the Negro. As long as the racial caste system was in place, he felt no particular animosity toward his dark-skinned neighbors.

Black people are largely absent from Davidson's creative work, so much so that "Tate accused him of writing about only half the South—the white part."[6] Particularly from the 1930s on, Davidson's writing would deal with blacks almost exclusively in political and social terms. (In *The Attack on Leviathan* and elsewhere he voices concern that an ever more powerful federal government would eventually try to dictate racial policy to the South.) Even the lyricism and generosity of "Still Rebels, Still Yankees" are undercut by insensitive references to blacks. At one point, Davidson says of New Englanders: "They had freed the Negroes, replying 'I can' to duty's 'Thou must'; but they were fortunately exempt from the results of emancipation, for no Negroes lived among them to acquaint them with the disorder of unashamed and happy dirt" (*Leviathan,* 138).[7]

If anything, Davidson's unpublished views were even more contemptuous of enlightened opinion. Remembering her former teacher nearly six decades later, Elizabeth Spencer writes:

> His scorn for those who questioned the segregation of the races in the South was evident even back in the forties, when I was a student. He regarded those blacks highly who were able, always as individuals, to "find a place for themselves" in terms of the prevailing white culture. He remarked once in class that a plantation owner he knew had said that when a black worker misbehaved he had to do something about it, so he gave him a whipping. "They're just children, after all." Davidson admired a Disney movie that came out about that time, *Song of the South.* It celebrated the Uncle Remus stories of Joel Chandler Harris. It glorified, said Davidson, "the old fashioned Negro."[8]

6. See Conkin, *Southern Agrarians,* 152.

7. A few pages later, Davidson writes, "The Georgian, when reproached for his intolerance, told himself that actually nobody outdid him in fond tolerance of the Negro. Lynchings, the work of hot-heads and roustabouts, were regrettable; but what did a few lynchings count in the balance against the continual forbearance and solicitude that the Georgian felt he exercised toward these amiable children of cannibals" (142).

8. Spencer, *Landscapes,* 184.

I

Davidson's first extended essay on the race question, "A Sociologist in Eden," appeared in the December 1936 issue of the *American Review*. He was responding to Arthur F. Raper's recently published book *Preface to Peasantry: A Tale of Two Black Belt Counties*. Because Macon County, Georgia, the location of his beloved Marshallville, was one of the counties in question, Davidson believed that he was defending what was virtually home turf. Nevertheless, his tone is surprisingly moderate and reasonable. Ostensibly, Davidson's main concern is with exposing the limitations of abstract sociology in dealing with the rich particularities of social life in any specific community. "[A]s one goes from humanism to sociology," he writes, "something happens that is like what happened to the unfortunate young man in Tennyson's 'Locksley Hall': 'The individual withers, and the world is more and more.' "[9] Not only are Cousin Roderick, Sister Caroline, and the other white inhabitants of Eden absent from Raper's book, but so too are the many "black individuals, surely also individuals," whom Davidson proceeds to mention by name and identify according to personal idiosyncracies.

Much of the effectiveness of Davidson's essay lies in the fact that he appears to be knowledgeable about the black people in Macon County and genuinely concerned with their welfare. One might disagree with Davidson's analysis, but it is hard to dismiss his position as a mere Negrophobic rant. In fact, had Davidson himself contributed an essay on race to some future Agrarian symposium, he might well have taken the blacks he knew around Marshallville as prime examples of "country folks bawn and bred in a briar patch." Lacking such intimate personal knowledge of the region, Raper tries to function as a disinterested scientist. Unfortunately, he harbors an ideological bias that makes true scientific objectivity impossible.

Davidson cites, for example, Raper's reference to "the paradoxical feelings of affection and devotion which have always existed between many members of both races." The sociologist tries to illustrate this point by recounting the fact that a black schoolteacher made her pupils stand when a white visitor (presumably Raper himself) entered her classroom. "Bewildered, the visitor asked the children to sit down—he had little expected such obsequiousness" (188). Davidson responds by noting that "the 'feelings of affection' and the manners here called 'obsequious' are commonplace in the plantation South, as Mr. Raper well knows." Rather than admitting this fact, Raper renders what Davidson considers an erroneous and tendentious interpretation of social reality. This is

9. Donald Davidson, "A Sociologist in Eden," 184. Subsequent references will be cited parenthetically in the text.

hardly correct scientific behavior. "A physicist does not say that the magnet *paradoxically* attracts the iron filings" (189).

Davidson blames the social plight of the southern Negro on economic conditions that are not of the South's making. He argues that Raper "cannot relate the shabbiness of tenant houses to the glorious upsurge of the Empire State Building or realize that the thirty or forty cents a day paid to the Negro wage hand may, in a sense, represent what is left when tribute has been paid to Detroit, Wall Street, and the American Federation of Labor" (197). Even the doctrine of white supremacy is the fault of the Yankees. That doctrine has persisted, Davidson concludes, as a necessary southern defense against the economic and political imperialism of the North.

Any attempt by the federal government to elevate southern blacks from tenants to landowners "would result in the ultimate eviction of white owners . . . either, directly, by a process of purchase and government subsidy, or indirectly, through a process of competition, like that by which the Japanese peasant infiltrated into California" (201). Davidson believes that any attempt by outsiders to upset the current system would simply exacerbate race relations. Perhaps the ultimate solution would be for the American people "to define a place for the American Negro as special as that which they have defined for the American Indian" (202–3). Pending such a reform, it is perhaps best to let local communities work out their own racial customs. "The Negro's acceptance (which so piques Mr. Raper) of the role the South has given him would seem to indicate that he prefers an inferior status, if it be real, to being a bone [of contention]" (203).

By the time Davidson published his next lengthy discussion of race, increasing numbers of black people were eager to throw off their inferior status, even if they had to become bones of contention to do so. (In a symposium entitled *What the Negro Wants,* the black writer Sterling A. Brown had compared Davidson and other white southern intellectuals—including timid liberals such as Mark Ethridge—with the native Fascist Gerald L. K. Smith.[10]) When "Preface to Decision" appeared in the summer 1945 issue of the *Sewanee Review,* America was in the final stages of a war in which racism had been depicted as an alien ideology. Hence, any domestic system that could conceivably be labeled as racist seemed particularly vulnerable. If Davidson had been able to defend segregation in 1936 from a position of strength, he no longer enjoyed that luxury nearly a decade later. This weakened position is perhaps reflected in his more embattled tone and the general unpersuasiveness of his arguments.

Davidson concedes that, when considered in the abstract, segregation is an illogical system. It is only when we place it in the context of history and custom

10. See Sterling A. Brown, "Count Us In," in *What the Negro Wants,* ed. Rayford W. Logan (Chapel Hill: University of North Carolina Press, 1944), 308–44.

that it begins to make sense. Because of the conditions under which black people originally lived in this country, it is impossible for the descendants of slaveowners ever to think of the descendants of slaves as social equals. Only a sociologist (which by now has become something of an all-purpose term of invective for Davidson) or a Marxist could believe that a law or a hundred laws could change the attitudes of the white South. That there might be a moral argument for such a change in attitudes is a possibility Davidson does not consider. Rather, he sees segregation as the natural, even beneficent, condition for the Negro's continued presence in the South.

The problem with arguing from history is that one leaves himself open to being refuted by contradictory historical evidence. For two decades after white southerners regained control of their society from the Reconstructionists, racial segregation was virtually unknown. Black people may have remained socially inferior to whites, but they were not publicly separated either by law or custom. Curiously enough, the institution known as Jim Crow enjoyed a life span almost exactly contemporaneous with Davidson's own. It came into being (for reasons that continue to be debated by historians of the South) in the 1890s, when Davidson was a young boy in Tennessee, and was finally eradicated by a series of three historic civil rights bills passed by Congress in the 1960s.[11] The last of these, the Open Housing Act of 1968, became law in the year of Davidson's death. By ignoring the actual history of segregation, Davidson is guilty of the very error he attributes to utopian sociologists.

Davidson is on much sounder ground when he discusses the history of the Thirteenth, Fourteenth, and Fifteenth Amendments to the U.S. Constitution. Neither he nor the majority of white southerners have any quarrel with the Thirteenth Amendment, which freed the slaves. (He even suggests that emancipation would have come earlier had northern abolitionists not turned it into a sectional political issue.) He reminds us that that amendment "was ratified by the first governments set up in the Southern states after Appomattox—the governments later rejected as illegitimate by the Radical Republican Congress" (405). The Fourteenth and Fifteenth Amendments, however, were ratified by puppet southern legislatures set up by the federal government during the military occupation known as Reconstruction. These amendments, which gave black people citizenship and the right to vote, were passed by fraud and force. Consequently, Davidson believes that the white South has the moral right to disregard them. (Although he does not call it that, what Davidson is advocating sounds suspiciously like massive civil disobedience.) He candidly admits that the

11. The best-known and most influential study of Jim Crow is C. Vann Woodward's *The Strange Career of Jim Crow* (New York: Oxford University Press, 1955). Martin Luther King once proclaimed this book the "Bible of the civil rights movement."

racial caste system is the means by which the South effectively nullifies the two hated amendments.

In contrast to these amendments, forced on the South at the point of a bayonet, "the various state laws which uphold and fortify the bi-racial system throughout the South . . . represent genuine conviction and receive overwhelming popular support." Davidson even suggests that this popular support includes large numbers of blacks. (One is surprised that he fails to quote such conservative southern blacks as Booker T. Washington and Joseph Winthrop Holley, who would seem to lend credence to his position.[12]) "The [segregation] laws, in effect, forbid the Negro to participate as an equal in white society as such," Davidson readily admits, "but they acknowledge his right to flourish, so far as he is capable of flourishing, in the more general, bi-racial society of which both white and black are members" (406).

In an attempt to show that he is not anti-Negro, Davidson concludes his essay with praise for the majority of blacks, who he believes have flourished under the paternalistic indulgence of the white South:

> Even as a slave, the Negro won personal esteem, often great esteem, from the white man who ruled him. Today, despite the embarrassing inheritance of hostility engendered by events of the past and the endless stream of reproach that continues to be poured upon the South, the Negro still wins personal regard. How does it happen? It happens because the people of the South have always been face to face with the Negro, as a person, and because in that situation his individual and personal character is known directly and appreciated concretely, according to his deserts. Because this is true, there are thousands of unknown Negroes today who are doing their race infinitely more good than the educated Negro leaders can ever hope to accomplish through argumentative books. (412)

II

Although the majority of white Tennesseans did not welcome the Supreme Court's decision in *Brown v. the Board of Education*, the extent of *organized* resistance was not nearly as great as in the states of the Deep South. Tennessee, traditionally a two-party state, had a growing black electorate and a history of political progressivism. In 1954, the state's three highest elected officials (Gov.

---

12. The president of Georgia Normal (now Albany State) College, Joseph Winthrop Holley was a political ally of the arch-segregationist Gov. Eugene Talmadge. Although he did not publish his autobiography, *You Can't Build a Chimney from the Top*, until 1948, he was a well-known public figure at the time Davidson was writing "Preface to Decision."

Frank Clement and U.S. Senators Estes Kefauver and Albert Gore, Sr.) were liberal Democrats with ambitions for national office. (Clement and Gore both coveted the vice presidency, while Kefauver was preparing to make his second run for the White House.) Still, the state constitution of Tennessee prohibited public assistance to integrated schools, and no locality was eager to be the first to cross the color line. However, with the integration of Nashville's parochial schools in the fall of 1954 and the impending integration of the federally controlled schools in Oak Ridge the following year, the racial barriers in Tennessee appeared to be weakening. In defiance of this trend, the Tennessee Federation for Constitutional Government was formed on June 30, 1955, with Donald Davidson as president and Jack Kershaw as vice president.

In 1955, Jack Kershaw was a forty-two-year-old sculptor, who had long been a fixture on the local cultural and political scene. After attending Montgomery Bell Academy in Nashville, he entered Vanderbilt on a football scholarship in 1932. (Although an injury relegated him to the bench, he later played semiprofessional ball in Nashville during the depression.) While at Vanderbilt, Kershaw studied with both John Crowe Ransom and Robert Penn Warren; however, his original loyalty to the Old South went back to his childhood, when he listened to the Civil War stories of his grandfather, who had fought with Nathan Bedford Forrest. Although he had enjoyed cordial relations with black artists while working as an arts administrator for the WPA in the thirties, Kershaw never wavered in his belief that federally mandated integration would violate the sovereignty of the states and severely damage the social fabric of the South. He and Davidson had worked together to get Strom Thurmond's Dixiecrat Party on the ballot in Tennessee in 1948. It was only natural that they join forces again to confront the political crisis facing the South.

Judging from his correspondence and entries in his diary, it would appear that Davidson formed a close friendship with Kershaw during the latter half of the 1950s. This was a time when he was estranged from most of his former colleagues in the Fugitive and Agrarian movements. His brief but intense collaboration with Charlie Bryan had ended with Bryan's sudden death in the summer of 1955. Davidson had greater need than ever for a soul mate, but it would have to be someone who shared his political commitments. "From those he considered his friends," writes Walter Sullivan, "he demanded absolute loyalty: you had to agree with him one hundred percent—less would not suffice—and you had to put your agreement into action."[13] Jack Kershaw was such a friend.

In his diary for January 9, 1955, Davidson writes: "Called on Jack Kershaw and his wife Mary Noel, at their new modernistic home on Caldwell Lane. Saw pictures at his studio (old Oriental Golf Club) & in house, talked art and

13. Sullivan, *Allen Tate*, 26–27.

politics, 4 to nearly 6. Very striking masterly portrait of his wife; mural in studio of Negro women of city in county workhouse gang. Pleased in general with JK's views." A little over a year later, on January 16, 1956, Davidson's diary records an incident that suggests something of Kershaw's fiery independence and hatred of bureaucracy:

> Jack's story of the agricultural bureaucrat who refused to give gov't loan after Jack had labored over the "forms." Jack called him "cabbage head" etc. but didn't curse him. Bureaucrat grabbed surveyor's pole & hit at Jack, who fended off with a chair (as if he were a lion), while shouting for the man to take off his glasses. Jack finally broke through, grabbed man, removed glasses gently, laid them on desk, then socked him one good hard blow that laid man on desk. Uncle Oscar Noel and the Noels gave Jack a hero's welcome but bureaucrat had Jack arrested for assault & battery. Uncle Oscar got Jack Norman to defend Jack Kershaw. Bureaucrat appeared in court with black eye. Only witness was a farmer who was in office when fight occurred (also seeking agricultural loan)—a witness for prosecution, but favorable to Jack—swore Jack hadn't cursed man, etc. Jury of farmers glad to see bureaucrat with black eye, joyously gave Jack acquittal. Jack Norman charged Jack *nothing*—his usual fee, in advance, for defending "criminals," $10,000.

Although the Tennessee Federation for Constitutional Government was generally recognized as "the most respected and influential [resistance] organization in the state," it was not nearly as effective as segregationist groups in some of the more militant states of the Deep South. In a report to the membership of the federation in the summer of 1957, Davidson could boast of chapters in no more than fourteen of Tennessee's ninety-five counties. Although he could claim some following throughout the state, most of the members and almost all of the chapters were concentrated in West Tennessee, "where the bulk of the state's relatively sparse Negro population (16 percent in 1950) was concentrated, and where white attitudes on race most nearly approximated those of the Deep South."[14] It is therefore surprising that the first two major battles the federation waged were in East Tennessee.

The desegregation of the small public school system in Oak Ridge, Tennessee, was an unusual but significant development. Because Oak Ridge was a virtual fiefdom of the Atomic Energy Commission, the federal government was able to take unilateral action there with minimal involvement of local officials. As one can easily imagine, Davidson was none too fond of the Atomic Energy Commission

14. Neil R. McMillen, "Organized Resistance to School Desegregation in Tennessee," 325, 325–26.

to begin with. Oak Ridge was a synthetic federal reservation created by a land grab reminiscent of the TVA. It brought to rural East Tennessee a cosmopolitan group of outsiders of both races. In his pamphlet "Tyranny at Oak Ridge," Davidson notes that Anderson County, where Oak Ridge is located, "has had practically no Negro population in the past. Its people have the Southern uplander's traditional dislike for intrusion and interference by strangers, no matter who they are or how much law they claim to have on their side."[15]

Ironically, Congress had recently ordered that the town of Oak Ridge be appraised and returned to private ownership. However, by the time the town's schools became part of the statewide system in Tennessee, they would already have been integrated. When local resistance leaders asked Davidson and the federation for help, their strategy was to write to the state commissioner of education, Quill Cope, pointing out that Oak Ridge would be in violation of the state constitution if it integrated its schools. Cope refused to take action on the grounds that schools in Tennessee are governed by local boards. Unfortunately for those opposed to desegregation, the local board in Oak Ridge had no more autonomy than a southern legislature during Reconstruction.

As one defiant Oak Ridger put it: "The Supreme Court decision . . . is anything but democracy. However life in Oak Ridge is governed by a pure dictatorship—first the Army Engineers, then the Atomic Energy Commission. . . . [R]ebellion did not develop because the majority [of residents of Oak Ridge] have become acclimated to Dictatorship." As an example of the arbitrariness of government officials, the disgruntled east Tennessean cites the rents charged by the commission on housing it maintained. Because Oak Ridge was built on a hillside, officials declared that those living at the foot of the hill would pay the lowest rent. As one moved up the hill, the rent increased. "Thus the residents in this zone were forced to pay extra—not for locations near churches, schools, or shopping centers, most of which are in the low rent zone, but for a view of the God-given mountains. Might as well have levied a tax on the air we breathe" (see "Tyranny," 14).

III

In December 1950, five black students in Anderson County sued in federal court for admittance to the all-white high school in Clinton, Tennessee.[16] Because the

15. Donald Davidson, "Tyranny at Oak Ridge," 6. Subsequent references will be cited parenthetically in the text.

16. For fuller accounts of the situation in Clinton, see McMillen, "Organized Resistance," 317–19; and Hugh Davis Graham, *Crisis in Print: Desegregation and the Press in Tennessee,* 91–113.

case dragged on for five years, the original plaintiffs all eventually graduated from segregated schools. As a legacy of that case, however, Clinton was under court order to admit twelve Negroes (there were more than eight hundred white students) to the school in the fall of 1956. The preceding summer, the Tennessee Federation for Constitutional Government had tried to generate statewide resistance to this order with speaking engagements by two of the U.S. Senate's most ardent defenders of segregation—Strom Thurmond of South Carolina and James Eastland of Mississippi. Tennessee's own politicians, however, did not regard race as an issue of high priority. (That same summer, Frank Clement gave the keynote speech at the Democratic National Convention, while Estes Kefauver walked off with the party's vice presidential nomination, beating— among others—John F. Kennedy and his own Tennessee colleague Albert Gore.) When the federation distributed a questionnaire to all the candidates in the Democratic primary, which was to be held on August 2, fewer than a third even bothered to respond. Of these, more than one-fifth were in disagreement with the federation's position.

Having failed on the political front, the federation sought relief in the courts. On August 22, two days after the first Negro students registered for classes at Clinton High School, the federation filed suit in the Anderson County Chancery Court to enjoin the school's principal from admitting them. When Chancellor Joe M. Carden dismissed the suit as meritless on August 27, the federation appealed to the Tennessee Supreme Court. But by now the process of desegregation had begun. That meant that the focus of resistance had moved from the political arena and the courts into the streets. The initiative was seized by local hoodlums and by a bizarre outside agitator named Frederick John Kasper.

A native of New Jersey, the twenty-six-year-old Kasper worked in a bookstore in the Georgetown section of Washington, D.C. He had studied poetry and racism at the feet of Ezra Pound and was now embarked on a one-man crusade to preserve segregation in the South. He turned up in Clinton on Saturday, August 25, and began going door to door in an effort to get parents to boycott and picket the school when it opened the following Monday. He was soon jailed for vagrancy but released for lack of evidence. On Tuesday, the twenty-eighth, he entered the high school in an unsuccessful attempt to persuade the principal, D. J. Brittain, Jr., to begin resegregation. He then began holding mass rallies on the courthouse square, until his violation of a temporary federal injunction against his activities landed him back behind bars. Local sentiment eventually became so agitated (with a little help from Kasper's anti-Semitic sidekick Asa "Ace" Carter) that Governor Clement dispatched 100 highway patrolmen and 633 battle-ready national guardsmen to Clinton by the end of the week.

The troops began arriving on Saturday, September 1. Prior to their arrival, Clinton had been engulfed by a tide of anarchy and violence. One chilling United

Press photograph shows a group of young thugs rocking the car of Negro tourists from Michigan, who were unfortunate enough to be passing through town after Ace Carter had given a particularly incendiary speech on Friday evening, August 31. Jack Kershaw entered this volatile scene to speak at an outdoor rally the following evening. In an editorial denouncing the federation, the *Nashville Tennessean* claimed that Kershaw had been hurriedly dispatched to Clinton to foment more violence. The *Tennessean* proceeded to ridicule Kershaw for being "so brazen as to preface his harangue in Clinton Saturday night with the absurd statement that he had intruded upon that community 'to help maintain peace.' "[17]

If one follows the logic of the *Tennessean,* anyone who publicly opposed desegregation was, by definition, inciting racist brutality. Certainly that would seem to have been the motivation of John Kasper and Asa Carter. However, the Tennessee Federation for Constitutional Government was not trying to capitalize on the unrest these men had helped exacerbate. It had been in the fight long before their road show rolled into town. When Jack Kershaw appeared in Clinton, he was simply fulfilling a speaking commitment he had made two weeks earlier.[18] Moreover, if his pleas for peace had been heeded, there would have been no need for tanks in the streets of Clinton the following day.

Even if the vigilante element in the segregationist movement was never much interested in the niceties of constitutional law, things might have been even worse had Kershaw not been present in Clinton that night. In his diary for September 2, 1956, Davidson in faraway Bread Loaf records what his federation cohort Vaughan Dubose told him about the rally:

> Vaughan reported Federation went ahead and arranged most successful public meeting at Clinton, Sat. night. Judge had given permission to use Court House, but finally reversed & denied permission; so they went to a nearby vacant lot & had good outdoor meeting, all peaceable. Having heard earlier that Clement was sending in State Police, etc., the folks had gone after their guns & were getting ready to fight troopers. Jack & friends persuaded them to leave guns at home; they did. . . . *After* meeting dispersed, state police belatedly arrived & went around throwing tear-gas bombs at scattered groups of innocent children. Clement just making a grandstand play for nat'l publicity.

When Clinton was placed under virtual military occupation, the criminals simply went underground, attacking hapless blacks and their white sympathizers. (The school itself was dynamited in the early-morning hours of October 5,

17. Graham, *Crisis in Print,* 103.
18. Interview with Jack Kershaw, July 10, 1997.

1958.[19]) If the actual perpetrators of violence frequently eluded capture, citizens attempting to exercise their First Amendment rights were fair game. On the evening of Sunday, September 2, State Adjutant General Joe W. Henry's troops fixed bayonets and dispersed a crowd that had gathered in the town square. The following day, Henry prohibited outdoor assemblies within Clinton, outdoor public speaking, parking, or assembling in the courthouse square after 6 P.M., and the use of public-address systems out of doors.[20] In December, Federal District Judge Robert L. Taylor (nephew and namesake of the legendary Bob Taylor) ordered the arrest of sixteen vocal segregationists for contempt of court. In February, the American Civil Liberties Union issued a statement from Knoxville, condemning the injunction the "Clinton Sixteen" were accused of violating. The ACLU was particularly disturbed by what it regarded as the injunction's unconstitutionally broad prohibition of picketing and other attempts to interfere with desegregation "by words or acts or otherwise."[21]

Represented by seventeen southern lawyers (including Theresa Sherrer Davidson and future Mississippi governor Ross Barnet) and aided by the federation's Freedom for Clinton Fund, fifteen defendants faced a trial by jury in July 1957. (One of the original sixteen had died in an insane asylum while awaiting trial.) These fifteen included fourteen blue-collar citizens of Clinton and the infamous Frederick John Kasper. The federation made it clear that its financial support was provided for all of the accused except Kasper. He was regarded as an erratic and truculent outsider who was doing the cause more harm than good. When it was discovered that he had frequently participated in interracial social gatherings while running a bookstore in Greenwich Village (before he came under the influence of Ezra Pound), many southern segregationists began to suspect Kasper of being a double agent. On July 23, he and six other defendants were found guilty, while four others were pronounced not guilty. (The remaining four had been previously acquitted.) Desegregation (at least at a token level) had triumphed in Clinton and would soon sweep the entire state of Tennessee.

Donald Davidson's political crusade had been spectacularly unsuccessful. (When the Tennessee Supreme Court heard the federation's appeal of the desegregation order in Clinton in October of 1957, it was actually able to declare segregation in Tennessee unconstitutional earlier than would otherwise have been the case.) Even as the Vanderbilt administration was embarrassed by his high public profile (just as it would have been embarrassed by public zealotry on the

19. When a reporter for the *Tennessean* informed him of the bombing, Davidson deplored the act. Pressed to say how such acts could be stopped, Davidson replied: "Stop integration" (see diary, October 5, 1958).

20. See Graham, *Crisis*, 100.

21. Ibid., 109.

other side of the issue), Davidson expressed a point of view undoubtedly shared by many of his silent colleagues. Tom Landess, who was a graduate student in English at Vanderbilt in the midfifties, tells of a conversation he had with the department's resident neo-Platonist just prior to the desegregation of the Nashville school system. "You know," said the neo-Platonist, "those children will grow up without racial prejudice." Landess wondered if perhaps the opposite might not be true, that forced integration would only worsen the existing prejudice. "We can always hope," replied the neo-Platonist. "But I don't think I'd be quite that optimistic."[22]

IV

In retrospect, it is clear that the Tennessee Federation for Constitutional Government (and its sister organizations in other states) was doomed from the very beginning. It was more than a little naive to argue for the constitutionality of segregation *after* the United States Supreme Court had determined otherwise. The various legal arguments advanced by the federation (many of which were devised by Theresa Davidson) never stood a chance of success, simply because lower courts are not empowered to reverse the Supreme Court, no matter what the merits of the case might be. The only way the federation could have prevailed would have been by persuading five justices of the Supreme Court to reverse the precedent they themselves had recently set. Before the unanimous decision in *Brown v. the Board,* all that the segregationists needed to do was to persuade five justices to uphold the long-established precedent permitting separate-but-equal educational facilities. Facing this less daunting task, John W. Davis, who was certainly one of the most capable and distinguished lawyers of the twentieth century, was not able to convince even a single justice that the control of local schools should stay with local communities.

Had the federation survived another three decades, it would have seen an activist judiciary use the Fourteenth Amendment to extend federal control into virtually every aspect of American life and effectively nullify the Tenth Amendment. Whether or not this represents a triumph for progress and enlightenment, it does signify a sea change in our political system. To see how far we have come, consider the following excerpt from a letter that Herman H. Ross—a former Tennessee politician—received from a public official: "In my opinion, there should be some over-all rules in the matter of the relationships of the various segments of our population, particularly where election to Federal office is involved. Local problems, however, whether they be on [race] or any other subject, should be dealt with by local government. We cannot hope or expect to

22. Interview with Tom Landess, June 8, 1997.

have a vigorous democracy in America unless this is our firm policy."[23] These views were conveyed to Ross on June 5, 1948, by the sitting governor of California—Earl Warren.

Whatever else it may have been, Davidson's crusade on behalf of segregation did not represent an extension of the Agrarian movement. Some of his staunchest allies in the fifties were southern industrialists, whom he would have considered "the Enemy" twenty years earlier. Moreover, none of the other twelve apostles of Agrarianism were involved in the struggle for segregation. John Gould Fletcher and Frank Owsley, both of whom had vigorously defended the South during the Scottsboro controversy of the thirties, were dead by the midfifties. (Owsley succumbed to a heart attack in 1956.) Andrew Lytle, who was sympathetic to the cause, was busy writing novels, while trying to decide whether he wanted to be a full-time farmer or a university professor of creative writing. John Ransom wrote to Red Warren in 1955 that "their sympathies should be strong and decisive for desegregation." John Donald Wade could only throw up his hands and proclaim to Davidson, in a letter dated December 24, 1955: "Now here we are, with the entire reputable world bent, and bent with Power-at-hand, to convince us that what we took to be the 'highest virtue' is in truth the worst of vices."[24] On race, as on so many other issues, Allen Tate spoke out of both sides of his mouth.

Although Herman Clarence Nixon had always been the most liberal of the Agrarians, he had never been particularly close to Davidson; so his views scarcely mattered. Of deep concern to Davidson, however, was Red Warren's increasing visibility as an advocate of civil rights. His writings in the fifties made "The Briar Patch," which had so infuriated Davidson, seem almost reactionary by comparison. On August 22, 1956, Davidson wrote in his diary: "Rec'd Red Warren's horrible little book on Segregation. Red 'interviewing' himself—an egotistical spectacle one wouldn't have expected of hardboiled Red. He joins the 'enemy', pretty much; debates with his 'conscience' in public; and makes money out of it! Red has now committed to the dream-world of academia & the publishers' editors, including Luce publications—sad affair."

Nearly six months later, Davidson was still fuming. In a letter to Cleanth Brooks, dated February 17, 1957, he writes:

> Red's little book on segregation has caused his stock to take a precipitous dive among his numerous southern cousins, old and young. They are amazed and shocked (1) that Red would be so ill-informed as he seems to be; (2) that he

23. The most persuasive and scholarly discussion of the transformation of the Fourteenth Amendment is Raoul Berger's *The Fourteenth Amendment and the Bill of Rights* (Norman: University of Oklahoma Press, 1989). Earl Warren's letter, which was contained in the files of the Tennessee Federation for Constitutional Government, is now in my possession.

24. See Conkin, *Southern Agrarians,* 158.

would be so careless about the company he keeps and allies himself with in this book; (3) above all, that he would accept money from Henry Luce et al. . . . Red and the publishers sent me no less than three copies of the book. But I haven't been able to bring myself to write a line to Red.[25]

When I asked Warren's daughter Rosanna about Davidson in 1993, she replied: "Donald Davidson was a racist whose name was never spoken in our home."[26]

The legacy of Davidson's racial view continues to besmirch his memory in the town where he lived and worked. On May 23, 1997, shortly after Bob Holladay of *Nashville Life* had taken Davidson to task for his retrograde political sentiments, Larry Daughtrey, a columnist for the *Tennessean,* recalled his own experiences as a student at Vanderbilt in the sixties. While praising Davidson's teaching and scholarship, Daughtrey flatly declared that his old professor "hated blacks" and that he had "become a sort of metaphor for the university itself: the intellectual richness diminished by a moral flaw embedded deep in its soul."[27]

Infuriated by these observations and the renewed assault on their grandfather's reputation, Davidson's granddaughters, Molly Kirkpatrick and Theresa Sullivan, sent a letter of protest to the newspaper. This letter, which was written on June 9, 1997, but never printed, stresses the bonds of respect and love that often united black and white people in the segregated South:

> After reading Mr. Daughtrey's article, an old worn piece of paper came to mind and was soon found. This draft of a telegram dated April 22, 1962, was written by our grandfather to Cora Woods. Cora worked for our grandparents and parents for a total of almost 50 years. She was not only our housekeeper but a cherished member of our family. Her husband Bennie had just passed away unexpectedly and our grandparents were out of town. There are many changes to the original draft. But the end result reads in part:
> "Mrs. Davidson and I were much distressed to learn of your great loss and wish you to know that we deeply share your grief and extend to you, dear Cora, our most affectionate sympathy. For your beloved husband we have always cherished admiration and warm regard.
> We know that a host of friends throughout this city and county who have known Bennie Woods as a noble, true hearted person and outstanding citizen will feel as we do that his passing is a loss to us all."[28]

25. This letter is contained in the Cleanth Brooks papers in the Beinecke Library at Yale University.
26. Interview with Rosanna Warren, June 16, 1993.
27. Larry Daughtrey, "Moral Flaw Diminishes VU's Glory."
28. I am in possession of a typescript of this letter.

Four decades after the demise of the Tennessee Federation for Constitutional Government, most of its leaders are long gone. Jack Kershaw, however, has remained active in both politics and art. During the turmoil of the fifties, he had gotten his law degree at night school and proceeded to help clients of both races deal with the challenges of a new social order. The most famous of these was James Earl Ray, whom Kershaw represented briefly in the late seventies. Like many Americans, including the members of Martin Luther King's immediate family, Kershaw believed that Ray was involved in a larger conspiracy, which the government covered up by offering him a plea bargain in exchange for his life. Jack once considered raising money by selling Ray T-shirts, and his wife, Mary, wrote a song called "They Slew the Dreamer." The spring that Bob Holladay and Larry Daughtrey sat behind their word processors damning Donald Davidson and the excesses of the Old South, eighty-four-year-old Jack Kershaw sat twenty-two feet in the air, sculpting a statue of Nathan Bedford Forrest, just off an interstate highway outside Nashville. It now stands in the middle of a southern memorial park, encircled by thirteen flags of the old Confederacy.

18

WHERE NO FLAG FLIES

In 1957, the Louisiana State University Press published Donald Davidson's second collection of essays. Although it was titled *Still Rebels, Still Yankees* and included three selections that had previously appeared in *The Attack on Leviathan*, the focus of this volume was primarily literary, not social and political. The difference, however, was merely one of degree. Davidson's aesthetic philosophy remained as firmly rooted as ever in a particular vision of society and of the artist's role in that society. In a letter to his publisher, he writes: "The general theme that binds the essays—no matter what their specific subjects—is the conflict between tradition and anti-tradition that characterizes modern society, with tradition viewed as the living continuum that makes society and civilization possible and anti-tradition as the disintegrative principle that destroys society and civilization in the name of science and progress."[1]

In terms of understanding Davidson's aesthetic creed, the most important essay in *Still Rebels, Still Yankees* is the first—"Poetry as Tradition." Here, Davidson is joining the long-running lament over poetry's diminishing influence in modern culture. (As Dana Gioia has pointed out, that lament dates back at least to 1934, when Edmund Wilson published the first version of his classic essay "Is Verse a Dying Technique?"[2]) Like John Crowe Ransom, Davidson believes that the poet started to be displaced from his central role in society when science became dominant in our culture. Poetry has been on the defensive ever since, even as poet-critics have tried to argue for the cultural importance of their art.

1. See Lewis P. Simpson, "Donald Davidson and the Southern Defense of Poetry," xv.
2. Dana Gioia, "Can Poetry Matter?"

These defenses seem to have grown more shrill and desperate as poetry itself has become more marginalized. In continuing to re-create poetry in newer and more recondite forms, the modernists have lost the old audience for poetry without creating a new one to take its place. According to Davidson: "That [old] audience, which as late even as fifty years ago [i.e., the turn of the century], was attending in large numbers the performance of Tennyson and Browning, or at least of the Fitzgerald who found his way in limp leather to many a parlor table, has abruptly dwindled to a faithful, well-schooled few. The show is financially on the rocks; the poet-author-actors would starve if not supported by Guggenheim fellowships and lectureships in creative writing" (*Still Rebels*, 6).

The modern poet is separated from the society in which he lives, not only by his style of writing, but also by his deliberate stance of alienation. Today, the champion of poetry is likely to be the enemy of society. It is clearly an anomaly when a poet such as Archibald MacLeish assumes a role of responsibility within the dominant political regime. Davidson reminds us that such a phenomenon was not so uncommon before the modern era.

> A hundred years ago John Stuart Mill took comfort from the poetry of William Wordsworth and openly confessed the fact that Wordsworth had made a new man of him. This result could hardly have been achieved by Wordsworth's verbal eloquence alone. There must have been—and indeed there was—some common metaphysical ground between Wordsworth the poet and Mill the political economist. Between the modern political economists and the modern poets there is no such common ground. Every serious poem by Messrs. Eliot, Yeats, Frost, Tate, and their most able contemporaries is in fact a reproach, direct or implied, against the modern political economists—that is to say, the social scientists in general. It is difficult to imagine a member of the Academy of Political and Social Science as turning to these poets for restoration of spirits. (9)

Davidson believes that the decline of poetry began when the art started to assume an exclusively literary character. Poetry that exists primarily for the printed page is fundamentally different from songs that belong to an oral tradition. As recently as the seventeenth century, Robert Herrick's "Advice to Virgins to Make Much of Time" was both a literary poem and the most popular song of its day. Not only have song lyrics and printed poems become two separate genres, the literary poems of our time can hardly be said to be verse in the same sense that the poems of Tennyson were. In abandoning traditional prosody, the high modernists made poetry unsingable. "It is unimaginable to readers of Eliot or Tate," writes Davidson, "that those poets would be caught composing lyrics that actually could be used in a Rogers and Hammerstein type of Broadway musical.

[That was before *Cats*.] The distance between the literary poet of today and the jukebox might have to be measured in astronomical light years, but it would be a fair measure of the cultural distance between the finest poetry of the twentieth century and the general audience" (20).

In the second essay in *Still Rebels, Still Yankees* (one dealing with William Butler Yeats), Davidson argues that the ideal relationship between the art and the popular lore of a culture would be one of easy reciprocity. "The popular lore ought to pass readily and naturally into the art." It should not be a specialized body of knowledge, accessible only to collectors and antiquarians, to "be appropriated, at long range, by a very literary poet." Conversely, "the art ought to pass readily into the popular lore, and not remain eternally aloof and difficult" (25–26). Only in a provincial society would there be much chance for such a symbiosis.

Yeats's career exemplifies both the advantages and the pitfalls an artist encounters working in a provincial culture. The early Yeats wrote ballads and folk songs and seemed to derive spiritual sustenance from his identity as an Irishman. As he became more heavily steeped in modernism, however, the folkish elements began to disappear from his poetry. Myths and popular lore, when they appeared at all, were refined into symbols, which were then interpreted according to the eccentric private mythology of Yeats's *A Vision*. Even when Yeats maintained contact with his own roots, his work became too rarefied to pass back into the popular consciousness. "Thus Yeats might appropriate the matter or even the manner of the street ballad singer of Dublin, but the Dublin ballad singer could not make any use of the art of Yeats" (28).

To Davidson's mind, the one undeniably great modern writer who never abandoned his folk roots was Thomas Hardy. In the fourth essay in *Still Rebels, Still Yankees*, "The Traditional Basis of Thomas Hardy's Fiction," Davidson notes that "Hardy wrote, or tried to write, more or less as a modern—modern, for him, being late nineteenth century. But he thought, or artistically conceived, like a man of another century—indeed, of a century that we should be hard put to name" (45). Hardy "wrote as a ballad maker would write if a ballad maker were to have to write novels; or as a bardic or epic poet would write if faced with the necessity of performing in the quasi-lyrical but nonsinging strains of the nineteenth century and later" (45–46). If other critics stress Hardy's affinities with post-Darwinian naturalism and with pessimistic philosophers such as Schopenhauer, Davidson sees him primarily as a traditionalist whose approach to art was deliberately anachronistic.

In an act of audacious literary appropriation, Davidson makes Hardy into an honorary southern writer. If forced to "place" Hardy, Davidson is tempted to see him "as an American whose ancestors failed to migrate at the proper time and who accordingly found himself stranded, a couple of centuries later, in the wrong literary climate. . . . The truth is that his general affiliation with the frontier humorists of the Old Southwest is a good deal more discernible than his affiliation with Victorian romantic-realists or with French Naturalists" (46). Davidson does not deny that Hardy's philosophy of life was bleak and mechanistic. He simply believes that that philosophy is aesthetically less important than Hardy's reactionary approach to literary form.

Davidson places his discussion of Hardy in an even broader context in his next essay, "Futurism and Archaism in Toynbee and Hardy." The terms *futurism* and *archaism* were coined by Arnold J. Toynbee to describe the desire of people to break free from a disagreeable present by losing themselves in memories of the past or dreams of the future. Futurists are guided by two firm convictions: that the best is yet to come and that you can't turn the clock back. As a traditionalist (or archaist), Davidson is frankly skeptical of the notion that the future will necessarily be better than what we have known in the past, especially if our vision of the future is an extrapolation from present experience. Moreover, he finds the taunt about not being able to turn back the clock largely irrelevant. "Neither can you turn the clock forward," he replies, "for Time is beyond human control." Davidson goes on to say:

> But the Futurist's use of the clock metaphor is in fact an unconscious revelation of his weakness. He wishes to imply that his design, and his only, is perfectly in step with some scientific master clock of cause and effect that determines the progress of human events. The implication has no basis in reality, since the Futurist actually means to break off all connection with the historical process of cause and effect and to substitute for it an imagined, ideal process of quasi-scientific development which is nothing more than a sociological vulgarization of Darwinism. (63)

Davidson believes that Toynbee's schematics reveal the limitations of the scientific (or pseudoscientific) mind-set—"it cannot express, as works of art do, either the rich totality or the vital essence of human experience" (66). It is for this reason that Sir Philip Sidney, in his *Defense of Poesy*, regarded poetry as superior to both history and philosophy in painting a true and *complete* picture of reality. Accordingly, if we wish to see how futurism and archaism actually operate in the lives of people we would be well advised to forget about Toynbee and read Thomas Hardy instead. In novel after novel (but particularly in *The Mayor of Casterbridge*) Hardy shows the disintegrating effects that futurism can have on an archaist region such as Wessex. Depicting the futurist critic as a sociologist who comes into Hardy country with a questionnaire, Davidson writes: "To the majestic tragedies of the Wessex people, assailed among their heaths, forests, and earthworks by external and internal foes, the Futurist questionnaire applies the ridiculous illumination of a pocket flashlight" (69).

I

If the conflict between tradition and its antithesis could be found in Hardy's Wessex, it was present even closer at hand in the American South immediately after the Second World War. The depression and the war may have delayed the sort of industrial expansion the Agrarians had feared in 1930, but by the late forties, all interference had been removed. In "Some Day, in Old Charleston," an essay originally published in the *Georgia Review* and reprinted in *Still Rebels, Still Yankees,* Davidson describes the heroic efforts of Charleston, South Carolina, to hold on to its ties with the past, even as the new town of North Charleston represents the imperialistic vulgarity of the present and the future.

On a visit to Charleston in April 1948, Davidson witnessed a military parade. Having been steeped in antiquity, he found it easy to imagine uniforms of red coats or kilts or blue-and-buff or Confederate gray rather than the drab khaki of our own time. But his mood was completely destroyed by the contingent that brought up the rear of the parade:

> It was a band of youngsters not in uniform but in civilian dress. At the head of the band a girl dressed up in the stage costume of a blue devil turned dizzying cartwheels on the pavement of King Street. Up went the little devil's heels and around she went cleverly on feet and hands. And behind her pranced a whole squad of drum majorettes. They drew their knees high to the beat of the drums. They tossed and swung their batons, twisted hips and bodies, nodded their heads under their grotesque shakos. They simpered brassily, their girlish features frozen in a Hollywood smile. With them, not far behind the comely blue devil, trudged a youth carrying a large sign with the legend: NORTH CHARLESTON HIGH SCHOOL. (217)

North Charleston was spawned by the vast development that had occurred in connection with the navy yards during the Second World War. Workers and their families came in from all over, many from outside the South, and formed a community in the direction of the Cooper River. Rather than disappearing after the war, North Charleston continued to grow as its inhabitants found various peacetime occupations. The noisy, irreverent boomtown was convinced that it represented the wave of the future and even threatened to drop the "North" from its name. It would "let Old Charleston slide into a subordinate role, let it be the decaying suburb of a new city" (220).

The character of Old Charleston demonstrated to Davidson that Agrarian principles could flourish even in a city, so long as that city maintained a sense of tradition. Davidson notes approvingly that "the map of Charleston in 1948 was not substantially different from the map of Charleston two centuries earlier" (221). (This still remains true half a century later.) Although Charlestonians had to look after their material concerns just as other folk did, they chose not to wreck their Georgian homes, tear down their enclosed yards, junk their handsome iron gates, and radically alter their eighteenth-century architecture. Such resistance to change could not be attributed to happenstance. According to Davidson, the secret of Charleston's stability lay in its insistence that economic pursuits were means to an end rather than ultimate ends in themselves.

It has long been assumed that the southern code of chivalry, courtesy, religion, and conservatism was the creation of aristocratic planters, who then imposed it upon their less affluent neighbors. Davidson argues that this facile assumption mistakes cause for effect. The aristocrats assumed a position of leadership in southern society because they embodied principles that were widely held by all classes and both races in the antebellum South. Davidson maintains that, even today, one cannot increase the Negro's devotion to work by raising his wages. His conception of the good life still consists of the same amount of hunting, dancing, singing, talking, eating, praying, and lovemaking. Rather than being a sign of shiftlessness, this sense of life's priorities is one of the supreme virtues of African American culture in the South. "The Negro, so far as he had not been corrupted into heresy by modern education, was the most traditional of Southerners, the mirror which faithfully and lovingly reflected the traits that Southerners once all but unanimously professed" (223).

At the end of his essay, Davidson returns to the image of the marching band from North Charleston. In a humorous—if somewhat overwrought—manner, he sees the drum majorette as the incarnation of everything that is wrong with modern society. Unlike the drum major, she is not really leading a march that symbolizes martial gallantry. Instead, she is "a follies girl, a bathing beauty, a strip-tease dancer" (225). (When there are several majorettes, they constitute a chorus line.) Davidson suspects that the majorette came into being about the time that high school and college athletics, particularly football, were transformed from amateur contests of valor into commercial entertainment. "Communities that accept such perversions of the beautiful and the gallant," Davidson writes, "are no longer communities in any true sense" (226). Over the centuries, the inhabitants of Charleston had fought the Indians, the British, and the Yankees. (During the War Between the States, they set a still-unbroken record for being under siege longer than any other civilian population in the history of human warfare.) Now they faced a new and more menacing foe—modernity in the form of a half-naked high school girl twirling a baton.

II

No matter what the cultural or political situation in the South might be, come June, Donald and Theresa Davidson would pack up their belongings and head north to Bread Loaf. They eventually purchased a summer house there and entertained friends and former students who might be passing through. Elizabeth Spencer remembers visiting the Davidsons there in the summer of 1950, while she was at work on her second novel, *This Crooked Way*. She recalls that one evening, Davidson entertained Theresa and her "with some ballads, the sort of music he loved, played on a curious old-fashioned instrument held flat on a table, something like a cithara or zither." One of the songs she remembers was " ' *The Golden Van-i-tee*,' its sad tale of an English ship of that name at war with 'the Spanish e-ne-mee,' dating back to Renaissance days."[3]

The blessed isolation of Bread Load could also pose occasional problems. On June 21, 1957, Davidson received a phone call from Tennessee informing him of the sudden death of his brother Tom. Because Theresa was unwell, he would need to arrange for her to stay with someone while he attended the funeral. Upon looking into the airplane schedule, he realized that he would have to fly from Burlington to New York to Louisville to Nashville. Then, when he tried to call the Burlington airport, he couldn't even get an answer. Finally, in exasperation, he called his daughter, Mary, to tell her that he would not try to come.

Sometimes getting to Bread Loaf could be nearly as difficult as getting out. Before the interstate highway system was complete, the trip would take several days by automobile, and frequently the Davidsons were not able to get away from Nashville until the late afternoon or early evening. The night of June 12, 1959, found them in Newmarket, Virginia, trying to make a reservation for the following evening at the Golden Arrow Motel in Selinsgrove, Pennsylvania. The woman who answered the phone said that she could not take a reservation because it would be Saturday night and the motel was likely to be full. Davidson asked if she meant to say that the motel was already full twenty-four hours in advance. The woman kept stalling until it finally came out that the motel was concerned about problems with "the colored." Davidson assured her that he was a white man who had stayed there before and that she could look it up.

Carrying on his political activities by long distance was also inconvenient. Throughout the summer of 1957, Davidson and Jack Kershaw were in frequent correspondence about the trial of the fifteen defendants in Clinton. On July 24, one day after the verdict came down, Davidson wired Kershaw with the suggestion that the foundation consider preventive legal action against John Kasper. Writing in his diary that day, Davidson observes that "association with Kasper seems to be the focal & critical point in the whole Clinton affair[,] which without him is on the whole innocuous. *With* him, it looks like a 'conspiracy' worked up by the other side." Davidson had good reason for his suspicions. Less than two weeks earlier, Robert Frost's daughter, Lesley Ballentine, had told him that she

---

3. Spencer, *Landscapes*, 247.

knew Kasper's bookstore in Washington to be the notorious meeting place of a Communist cell and was almost certain that Kasper had been planted in the segregationist movement as an agent provocateur (diary, July 13, 1957).

Although Bread Loaf was isolated geographically, it was the one place that continually put Davidson in touch with the larger republic of letters. As stimulating as that may have been, he was never in awe of the more cosmopolitan literary figures he encountered on the mountain. When R. P. Blackmur spoke on "The Role of the Intellectuals" on August 4, 1958, Davidson found the lecture to be sound in principle but weak in application and illustration. "A certain abstractness & remoteness from the general American experience," he notes in his diary. "Too much Princeton?"

Two years earlier, he had had a similar reaction to a lecture delivered by Richard Eberhart, comparing Ralph Waldo Emerson's "Brahma" and Wallace Stevens's "Giant." In his diary for July 9, 1956, Davidson writes:

> Both poems, surely must be second-rate or worse, and so Eberhart's lecture was rather too forced, spun out beyond all reason. A pleasant person, Eberhart, so definitely Minnesota German with an Ivy League education—pleasant despite that. You like the man—but again it appears that he, with Rich. Wilbur, Ciardi, and the others of whom he kept talking, . . . doesn't have *much* to talk or write about. A genteel emptiness—knows everybody, everything, but can't convince he's ever known reality. The East can no longer fertilize the Mid-West, being itself sterile. The after-speech session at the barn was the same. E talked of the foolish "radicals" of California—one Ginsberg and his poem "Howl," rebelling against the New Critics, T. S. Eliot et al.—then read his poems about seals and terns, horsechestnut trees, etc.

Amid all the serious discussion of literature, there were also farcical moments at Bread Loaf. In his diary for August 9, 1958, Davidson reports that, in giving that year's commencement address, Moses Hadas delivered an eloquent defense of the humanistic tradition, using no manuscript. Everyone noticed that he had had some papers in front of him, which he glanced at and laid down. They later learned that his speech was supposed to have been placed on the lectern in front of him, but what he actually found there was the text of Elizabeth Drew's speech from the previous year. So, Hadas proceeded to deliver a masterful extemporaneous talk. When the faculty arrived at the cocktail party immediately following his speech, they discovered that all the whiskey had been stolen. Davidson surmises that "some malignant student disappointed in grades did both these acts."

Two years earlier, Davidson had himself given the commencement speech (just as he had in 1938). As he stood there addressing the faculty and graduating class on August 11, 1956, he recalled when he had first come to Bread Loaf in 1931. That summer a fire had swept away the classrooms, the icehouse, and other

buildings. So, classes met in the sitting rooms of various cottages. He remembered
teaching his first Bread Loaf class in Treman Cottage, with the class seated in "an
odd collection of chairs that ranged from Victorian plush to prim, uncurving,
right-angled Puritan."[4] With his book on his lap and his notes on his book, he
attempted to expound on the poetry of Wordsworth. He had now been coming
back for twenty-five years.

At the outset of his speech, Davidson recalled that Robert Louis Stevenson had
said "that one's first tropical landfall touches a virginity of sense" (1). Davidson
had had something of that same experience when he first saw Bread Loaf. "The
mountain light, coursing from Middlebury Gap to the Adirondacks," he said,
"falls on the pages of our books with an illumination that is not given to many
to enjoy. We are among the few who can rightfully exult to say: 'If you would
understand this book, look at that mountain.' We have renounced the company
of those, so lamentably stockaded, who work under a colder light and know
only how to say: 'If you would understand a mountain, look at this book'" (5).
Davidson concluded his address with a reference to the local genius of the place:

> A procession of days, such as we know at Bread Loaf, is not to be measured
> in time. Count it in friends, members of the Graduating Class. Measure it
> in poetry. Weigh it in stories. Tune it in songs. It cannot pass away. Read it
> in the lines of the poem that you know not only by the book, but best of all
> from the lips and voice of the poet who made it. You might have taken many
> other roads, Members of the Graduating Class. But you took this one—up
> Ripton Gorge to Bread Loaf. You can say it with me tonight—
>
> > "Two roads diverged in a wood,
> >   and I—
> > I took the one less traveled by,
> > And that has made all the
> >   difference."
>
> And one difference is that for us who come to Bread Loaf and go away
> remembering Bread Loaf, it is always—always—summertime. (10)

Although Davidson had been a little hoarse, he managed to get through the
speech and immediately discovered how well the audience had taken it. He was
almost reduced to tears by the general reaction, which reminded him of "an
old fashioned Methodist handshaking and embracement." He was even hugged
by "stately Elizabeth Drew and some other ladies!!" He had tried to put in this
speech everything that he knew his audience felt, everything that he had come

---

4. Donald Davidson, "Bread Loaf School of English Commencement Address, 1956," 6.
Subsequent references will be cited parenthetically in the text.

to feel after twenty-five summers. Curiously enough, these were "the things that can be said *publicly* that one never dares to say in *private* conversation" (diary, August 11, 1956).

But even at Bread Loaf, there were moments of emotional isolation and near despondency, which could be assuaged only by the presence of family. After Mary and Eric and their children left from a visit in the summer of 1959, Davidson recorded his reaction in his diary: "And now, what a loneliness—Theresa and I desperate to counter it somehow. Morning, we drove up to our 'parking place' near the Harvey Brooks cottage and walked slowly up the old road toward Clark's Clearing. A brilliant sky, crisp air. Rested—and in late afternoon drove to Bristol by the 'slab-of-the-mountain' road—dinner at Bristol Inn—back by the lower road around 8 PM—missed the Robt Frost reading—too tired to venture into the crowd" (August 22, 1959).

III

Over half a century after her experience as a student at Vanderbilt, Elizabeth Spencer described her image of what the Fugitive movement must have been like:

> I like to think of them, despite differences of whatever nature, all remaining eternally in touch. One thinks of some Valhalla reserved for them, of meetings still going on—the lengthy discussions, the ideas advanced for talk to turn on, the new poems brought in fresh to read aloud, frequent laughter at genuine wit, the rise and fall of excited voices. A large fireplace burns companionable logs in the somewhat rundown, pleasantly shabby Southern parlor, windows reaching to the floor, dogs snuffling out on the front porch in the night. Their joyousness in one another, the pure zest of the intellect they shared—all this should never die.[5]

Although it was hardly the scene that Spencer imagines, ten surviving Fugitives and ten other guests were invited to the Vanderbilt campus for a series of meetings, both public and private, on May 3–5, 1956.[6] Over thirty years after the *Fugitive* had ceased publication, this was the first time that Vanderbilt University had

5. Spencer, *Landscapes,* 184–85.
6. The former Fugitives who participated in the 1956 reunion were Donald Davidson, William Yandell Elliott, Sidney Hirsch, Merrill Moore, John Crowe Ransom, Alfred Starr, Alec B. Stevenson, Allen Tate, Robert Penn Warren, and Jesse Wills. The non-Fugitive participants were Richmond Croom Beatty, Dorothy Bethurum, Cleanth Brooks, William Cobb, Louise Cowan, Robert Jacobs, Andrew Lytle, Frank Owsley, Louis D. Rubin, Jr., and Willard Thorp. For the fullest transcript of this occasion, see Rob Roy Purdy, *Fugitives' Reunion: Conversations at Vanderbilt, May 3–5, 1956* (Nashville: Vanderbilt University Press, 1959).

officially recognized the poets who had made the school famous in the larger literary world. Chancellor Kirkland was dead, and Edwin Mims had long ago retired. It took a new generation of administrators to realize the greatness that had once flourished unnoticed a few blocks off campus.

The driving force behind the Fugitive reunion was Randall Stewart, who had been appointed chairman of the English department the previous year. Although never a part of the Fugitive group, Stewart had been an undergraduate at Vanderbilt before the First World War, when the first meetings on Twentieth Avenue were taking place. A distinguished Hawthorne scholar, he returned to Vanderbilt with a doctorate from Yale and nearly twenty years as a professor at Brown. After suffering for thirty years under Mims and another thirteen under his successor, Walter Clyde Curry, the department saw Stewart's arrival as a breath of fresh air. With the aid of Louis D. Rubin, Jr., the young executive secretary of the newly formed American Studies Association, Stewart secured a grant of $4,000 from the Rockefeller Foundation to bring Vanderbilt's wayward poets home.

Like most reunions, this was a bittersweet affair. Davidson was keenly aware of the awkward position he was in. He and Ransom and Tate and Warren were the only Fugitives who had written verse of any real distinction. It was easy enough for the group to meet as relative equals back before any of them (except Ransom) had accomplished very much. Now it would be more difficult. Most of the former Fugitives were strangers who had very little in common. In terms of status, they ranged from Bill Elliott and Merrill Moore, who had achieved great prominence in their professions in the Northeast, to Sidney Hirsch, who had remained unemployed in Nashville for decades. The four major Fugitives had all embraced Agrarianism. Others in the group (particularly Elliot) were contemptuous of the movement.

The reunion opened on Thursday, May 3, at three o'clock in the afternoon, with a public meeting in Neely Chapel. The room was filled to hear a panel of Allen Tate, Andrew Lytle, and Red Warren speak of days past. Davidson was moved almost to tears to hear Allen and Red talk about the irony of their position as poets at Vanderbilt. "How can a Fugitive poet remember the Vanderbilt past," Davidson wondered, " . . . without in some way almost insulting Vanderbilt, at least the VU administration? I nearly burst to think of it—but had to sit quiet & compose a countenance, make up a face, somehow" (diary, May 3, 1956). At a posh dinner held at the Belle Meade Country Club the following evening, Chancellor Harvie Branscomb said to the group: "You were young, brilliant, and restless, and I take it the University added considerably to your spiritual unrest and discontent, and maybe that was its contribution to the Fugitive movement."[7]

Davidson addressed a public session on Thursday evening, making essentially

7. Louis D. Rubin, Jr., "The Gathering of the Fugitives: A Recollection," 664.

the same argument he would make the following year in "Poetry as Tradition." At least implicitly rejecting the "literary" poetry of high modernism, he declared that "a poetry that puts itself in a position not to be recited, not to be sung, hardly ever to be read aloud from the page where it stands, almost never to be memorized, is nearing the danger age of absurdity." At the first private session, which was held from 9:15 to 11:00 that night at Randall Stewart's house, Tate responded to Davidson's argument, saying that "we haven't got a choice between literary poetry, as you describe it, and this pure Pierian spring, folk literature. It's a choice between literary poetry or none at all: the canned poetry, manufactured for a super-bourgeois society."[8]

Bill Elliott took this dispute in an entirely unexpected direction when he brought up the fact that none of the Fugitives had written an epic. "On the face of it, this was a silly enough matter," Louis Rubin writes, "the epic having properly died a natural death several hundred years earlier. But what the argument was really about was the poetry of modernism, and the line of allegiance was between those who had become professional men of letters and those who hadn't." When those battle lines were drawn, Davidson instinctively took his rightful place with the professionals and ceased to condemn modernism "for failing to be what it couldn't be, and joined Tate, Ransom, Warren, and [Cleanth] Brooks in defending its literary integrity against the demand that it perform the function of a Platonic absolute."[9] It seemed that, after thirty years, the old divisions still separated the group.

One poignant moment, which showed how little some things had changed, occurred at the session on Friday afternoon. As Davidson describes it in his diary: "At lunch Bill & Merrill ran off & kidnapped Sid Hirsch[,] who had obviously been sulking in his tent, & brought him in. Sidney with a beard like a Rabbi, like a M[errill] Moore! So Sidney took the center at the afternoon session & we had a demonstration of his 'mysticism'—same old style, no advance—right back, in my instance . . . , to the old Demon Brother theme" (May 4, 1956). Although the members of the group now possessed a sophistication they had lacked when they first met Sidney Hirsch in 1914, they showed him the same old deference.

As the weekend wore on, Davidson (and, no doubt, others) began to lose patience with Bill Elliott. Of the group, he had come the furthest in worldly terms. In addition to being a professor at Harvard, he was a member of the National Security Council and Richard Nixon's chief foreign-policy advisor in the pre-Kissinger era. Despite having given up poetry, he dominated most of the sessions, dropping names and continually referring to the sixty-eight-year-old Ransom as "Johnny." (In his diary for May 4, Davidson complains of Elliott's

8. Ibid., 666.
9. Ibid., 664–65, 667.

tendency "always to talk too much" and of "Bill lording it over us.") Finally, things came to a head at the public reading on Friday night, May 4. A tremendous, overflow crowd had gathered. Basking in the occasion, Elliott went on too long in his opening remarks, gleefully reminding everyone that he was a real farmer and the Agrarians were not. At that point, Davidson got up and challenged Elliott to debate him in any courthouse square in Tennessee.

IV

Although he did not debate Bill Elliott, in the courthouse squares of Tennessee or anywhere else, Donald Davidson did make some memorable speeches in the latter half of the fifties. In March 1958, he traveled to Baton Rouge to deliver an address at Louisiana State University. The following month, he was off to Brunswick, Maine, to speak about the New South and the conservative tradition at Bowdoin College. The previous November, he had returned to his beloved central Georgia to inaugurate the Eugenia Dorothy Blount Lamar Memorial Lectureship at Mercer University. (This lecture series has now become an annual event, in which distinguished scholars speak on the state of southern culture.) Davidson presented a discerning and affectionate account of the Fugitive and Agrarian movements, which was published in 1958 by the University of Georgia Press under the title *Southern Writers in the Modern World*.

By far, Davidson's most pleasant trips were ones he and Theresa took around the South to visit people and places that were dear to them. December 12, 1956, found them back in Greenville, South Carolina. In his diary entry for that day, Davidson writes:

> Afternoon—Mrs. Buck drove us out to 104 Broadus Ave (Mrs. Allen's house), where Theresa and I were married and had a room, June-July, 1918. The "Allen girls" (now middle-aged) met us cordially—and it became a sentimental occasion as we swapped reminiscences. Theresa & I stood in the very room where we were married. House not changed—or the large well planted yard. . . . The street little changed, too—a fine old tree-bordered street—but now endangered by business.

Davidson was in South Carolina in December 1956 primarily to see Mary Chevillette Simms Oliphant, granddaughter of William Gilmore Simms, at her home in Bamberg. This visit was prompted by the growing affinity Davidson felt for Simms and the values he represented. On December 14, Davidson suggests how far that affinity was taking him. "Rainy—late breakfast," he writes in his diary. "Packed up to leave. Earnest talk with Mrs. O. in her study about the Simms biography & my plans. I told her my situation. She says only a man who understands & can defend the South ought to write the biography. Biography of Simms is in principle a defense of the South & what it has stood for thro' the centuries—Simms the most *representative* of all Southern writers: he is *the* South." Although his many literary and political activities finally prevented him from undertaking a biography of Simms, Davidson did contribute in various ways to the renaissance in Simms studies.[10] Moreover, his poem "Woodlands, 1956–1960" depicts Simms's old home near Bamberg as a symbol of bygone southern felicity.

Like so many of Davidson's other works, "Woodlands, 1956–1960" contrasts our spiritually deracinated modern era with an heroic past. To employ a term from T. S. Eliot, Davidson had found the perfect objective correlative for that heroic past in the image of Woodlands. The poem, which is divided into two parts, consists of a speaker's invocation of the spirit of Simms. What is significant is the extent to which that speaker (obviously Davidson himself) is able to achieve communion with the vanished social order. Unlike Eliot's *The Waste Land,* Tate's "Ode to the Confederate Dead," and several of Davidson's own earlier poems (particularly "The Tall Men"), "Woodlands" is not so much an indictment of the present or a lament for the past as a celebration of the past in the present.

In the first section of "Woodlands," titled "Evening," the speaker arrives "late, by a hundred years," at Simms's former home. He alludes to the fact that in the years immediately preceding his death, Simms had had to rebuild the house twice when it was destroyed by fire. He describes this plantation on the Edisto as it once was—with its mule wagons and mossy oaks. But he concedes that the world is different now:

> No candle leads us through the shadow,
> No agate lamp within a window-niche,
> But a groping hand can find somewhere a switch,
> And light can give its modern relief. (*Poems,* 20)

In perhaps the most forlorn passage in the poem, Davidson writes: "It is a century of no belief / And cannot read your stories, Gilmore Simms, / If history is fabulous no longer" (20). But, significantly, the speaker is not content simply to bemoan such a state of affairs. As the "Evening" section of the poem ends, he asserts:

> We cannot live by that death.
> How could we still draw breath
> If ever the fable were lost?
> Be with us, unseen host! (20)

10. Davidson's introduction to Simms's collected letters provides an extensive discussion of the novelist's life and works.

In the second section of his poem, which he calls "Morning," Davidson evokes both the spirit of Simms and his rich gallery of characters—Captain Porgy, Will Sinclair, Mellichampe, Blonay, Mad Archy Campbell, Supple Jack, Nell on her "tacky" Ballou, and Hellfire Dick—all of whom are referred to collectively as "children of Homer." As M. E. Bradford has noted, Woodlands was for Donald Davidson what Lady Gregory's Coole Park was for Yeats —"a place of retreat and a source of moral and artistic rejuvenation."[11] At Woodlands, Davidson can easily merge with the past as he imagines it to have been:

> Acorns upon the roof for Angelus
> While the squirrel's muted bark and the hawk's cry
> Make pure the heart and bless the exile's eye,
>
> Till, practicing our redemption, we may see
> Beneath the Church Oak, by the sunny gate,
> Your household worshipping . . . (21)

Simms, however, is not a model of quietistic withdrawal. He was actively involved in the social and political controversies of his day, and he wrote about men who violently resisted the enemies of their own time and place. Similarly, Davidson saw his retreat to Woodlands as only a temporary quietus from the battles he waged and never put totally out of mind. "Hearth and rooftree," Bradford points out, "are opposed by 'the cold voice of the world-city's dream,' used here in place of court or town life as these tropes function in the English prototypes of Davidson's creation. . . . Against the Tarletons of the twentieth century, 'the center cannot hold' because their squadrons, following 'unearthly logic,' exercise power for its own sake and, even worse than General Sherman's plantation burners, release the 'bomber's levin' (lightning) to 'dragoon heaven.' "[12]

Bidding farewell to the master of Woodlands, Davidson writes:

> Gilmore Simms, we have watched the dust-cloud rise
> And heard the hoofbeats of the Great Dragoon.
> Who would not know that flag of death he flies?
> Who would not say Tarleton has come again?
> But we have seen beyond the dark lagoon
> Shapes mounting, hand to bridle, as of old;
> How could we doubt that they were Marion's men?
> And surely we are, too, when your tale is told. (21–22)

11. M. E. Bradford, "Donald Davidson and the Great House Tradition: A Reading of 'Woodlands, 1956–1960.' " This essay provides a thorough and perceptive discussion of Davidson's knowledge and use of the great-house genre.

12. Ibid., 89.

Back when Davidson was composing "Lee in the Mountains," his political activity had consisted primarily of writing essays extolling the virtues of American regionalism and warning against the dangers of a leviathan state. When he was staying at Woodlands a quarter century later, his engagement with social issues was both more specific and more intense. If his poem about Woodlands posits modernity as the generic enemy of the way of life symbolized by Simms's plantation, it is probable that Davidson saw the intrusive federal government as an even more immediate analogue to Tarleton and his men. In this hour of peril, Davidson looked to the example of Simms, who was also a defender of state sovereignty and traditional racial customs. When he sees Marion's men riding to the rescue, as if from the very pages of Simms's fiction, Davidson is identifying himself imaginatively with the efforts of earlier American patriots to maintain the corporate liberty of their communities against a distant and tyrannical government. Whatever one might think of these sentiments, they are surely less important than the fact that, after two decades of relative silence, Donald Davidson was writing poetry again.

19

THE LAST FUGITIVE

With the publication of *The Long Street* in 1961, Donald Davidson took even his oldest friends by surprise. His first book of verse since *Lee in the Mountains* in 1938, it consisted mostly of poems written within the previous two years. At a time when Ransom had long since finished writing poetry and Tate's best work was behind him, Davidson had not only experienced a rebirth of inspiration but was writing better than ever. Tate observed that *The Long Street* "is all the more remarkable for its appearance so late in Donald Davidson's career."[1] Equally impressed, Ransom declared that, of all the Fugitives, Davidson had "maintained continuity and development most steadily in his art."[2] As improbable as it might have seemed only a few years earlier, Davidson now ranked only behind Robert Penn Warren as the most significant and productive Fugitive poet of the postwar era.

Although the most sizable and important parts of *The Long Street* consist of Davidson's most recent verse, he concludes the book with a section of twelve poems entitled "Fugitive Days." Four of these ("Apple and Mole," "Martha and Shadow," "Cross Section of a Landscape," and "Litany") had appeared in *Fugitives: An Anthology of Verse;* however, none of the twelve had been published in either of Davidson's two previous collections. (Eight of them would be preserved in his final, definitive volume—*Poems, 1922–1961.*) Among the most interesting of these are several that appear to belong to a period of transition between *An Outland Piper* and *The Tall Men,* when the poet was no longer Robin Gallivant but was not yet Donald Davidson.

1. Allen Tate, "The Gaze Past, the Glance Present: Forty Years after the *Fugitive*," 38.
2. John Crowe Ransom, "The Most Southern Poet," 202.

"Wild Game," which was originally published in the *Nation* on June 2, 1926, seems to anticipate themes later developed in the fiction of William Faulkner and the poetry of James Dickey. Here, some incarnate principle of wildness, sometimes assuming the likeness of a deer or the form of a wild wolf, visits civilization:

> To drink or touch or taste
> Our flat and homely waters;
> Obeying no charm or the chaste
> Prayers of our virgin daughters

The speaker is not certain whether this wild thing is real or only a thought. In either case, it is occasionally trapped but never caught.

> Yet is seen of certain men
> Alone, who walk with eyes
> Glazed to all else but it
> And are long afterwards called wise. (*Long Street,* 75)

The implication is that the wildness of nature can be fully appreciated only by a special, compulsive sensibility. (Later readers might be reminded of Faulkner's Ike McCaslin.) Davidson's ironic tone leaves us wondering whether these men are to be admired for their discernment or scorned for their obsession. Whichever it may be, any praise they receive will likely come late, perhaps after they're gone.

The nature depicted in "Stone and Roses" is much tamer and more domesticated. This poem (which was first published in the October 1923 issue of the *Fugitive*) concerns a figure who has both a day job and a nighttime hobby. During the mornings and afternoons, he is a master builder or engineer, "commanding stone to cornices and blocks."

> At his curt nod the ranks of saws cut straight
> Columns and urns are born of stolid rocks.
>
> But evenings, with a manner not of stone,
> Reckless of dew he kneels and bows his head
> Before his roses, fingering one by one
> The twilight buds just stemming from their bed. (81)

This poem demonstrates the distinction that Ransom makes between work forms and play forms. The protagonist (actually Davidson's father-in-law, Frederick Anthony Sherrer) exercises unquestioned authority and power when cutting and molding stone. When he is cultivating his roses, however, he must display delicacy and care. In this situation, which he enters by choice and from which he apparently derives great pleasure, he is the one who is subservient. The roses "are his high-born queens and emperors, / Requiring with their courtly pantomime / The tribute of his gestureless devoirs" (81).

In "Fiddler Dow" (from the *Fugitive* of April 1924), Davidson is in the world of fantasy familiar to readers of *An Outland Piper*. However, the setting and characters seem to come from rural folklore rather than the imaginary world of dryads and satyrs (more Thomas Hardy than Aubrey Beardsley). The poem opens and closes with four-line stanzas; in each the first and third lines rhyme and the second and fourth lines repeat each other. In between are forty stanzas, each consisting of a rhymed couplet. This simple and straightforward prosody tells of a mysterious fiddler who enters the town of Thorn one morning at six and begins to disrupt the normal activities of the day with his seductive tunes. "Who sent for him, nobody knows" (82), the first line reads.

When the farmers' wives hear him play, they leave the bacon in the pan. Their sons leave the pigs unfed, and the farmers themselves allow the cows to go unmilked. As people from various professions and social ranks join in the dancing, Davidson reminds us that the fiddle is the devil's instrument. (That point has been made frequently in popular culture, as recently as 1978 in the Charlie Daniels song "The Devil Went Down to Georgia.") The bacchanalian juxtapositions resemble a Satanic bash in one of Hawthorne's tales:

> Tattletale Tabitha, gossip and thief
> Danced with the Judge like a thin mad leaf.
>
> Hunchback Willie, forgetting his crutch,
> Caught sweet Madge Lorn in his spidery clutch. (84)

Like a pied piper for grownups, Fiddler Dow leads the people of Thorn down the cobblestones to the bridge out of town. Presumably, they would have continued following him had not "cool swung six" and the moon begun to rise. Awakened from their enchantment, the sober townsfolk begin to cast stones at the fiddler, until he disappears in the distance. Whether he actually existed or was simply a manifestation of the town's collective id is uncertain: "The fiddle quavered, the tune was lost; / Dow was gone like a late damp ghost" (85). No one even knows who paid him.

Because the fiddler does his work during the day, this poem is far more sinister than, say, Milton's "L'Allegro." The people of Thorn are not unwinding after a hard day's work but seeking a kind of frenetic release from the drudgery of their daily lives. In banishing the fiddler at the unwitching hour of six, they signal that his work is now done. They seek only a temporary respite, not permanent deliverance. One suspects that the casting of stones may be more a ritual of denial than a recovery of moral seriousness. (Why else raise the question of who paid the fiddler?) Because the second and fourth lines of both the first and last stanzas are identical ("With a fa-la-la-la-lady"), there may even be a suggestion of cyclical recurrence. The fiddler will always be available—to be summoned when he is needed and dispatched when he has overstayed his welcome.

If anything, "The Old Man of Thorn" (published originally in the *Fugitive* of February 1924) is an even stranger poem than "Fiddler Dow." A fairly traditional ballad (four-line stanzas using an *abcb* rhyme scheme), this poem begins on a deceptively realistic note. Eph Dickon (the old man of Davidson's mythical town of Thorn) appears to be nothing more than an agricultural vandal who "plants thistles in cornfields / As other men plant corn" (86). He even has a thistle farm on a hill outside of town. The man is clearly demented to derive such glee from gratuitous destruction of the harvest. There is no discernible profit motive here, only what Coleridge called "motiveless malignity."

As we get further into the poem, Eph Dickon seems to be something of an inverted pagan, worshipping sterility and drought where others would celebrate the fertility of nature. His black masses are attended by an owl and whippoorwill, who assist him in his mischief. As the imagery and atmosphere grow increasingly bizarre, the sense of realism gradually diminishes. Then, in stanza thirteen, it becomes unmistakably clear that Dickon is himself a supernatural figure:

> Straight from his loft he bounces
> Into his kitchen door;
> The hoarse owl and whippoorwill
> Were waiting there before. (87)

As this improbable trinity pass a jug around, Eph pronounces curses upon the wise farmers of Thorn, whose puny crop of corn cannot compare to what he plants: "Sing a song of a field of thistles / And a crop that's never failed yet."

Vile as Eph's sensibility may be, the light, frolicsome tone of the verse makes it hard to take the old man seriously as a villain. He seems the stuff of fairy tales—ripe for conversion, like Ebeneezer Scrooge, or for comic defeat, like Mr. Barnaby. In fact, neither happens. Instead, the final stanza is actually a celebration of Eph Dickon:

> With a hey-down-down-down-derry
> For the old old man of Thorn-O!
> Eph Dickon, the fool old man,
> The good old man of Thorn-O! (88)

The implication would seem to be that Eph Dickon is a communal myth, who serves a communal need. Rather than believe that their crop failures are due to the caprice of nature or the wrath of an omnipotent deity, the farmers of Thorn find it much more comforting to believe that they are the victims of an absurd warlock, who incarnates natural evil with few if any moral overtones. Psychologically, it is far easier to battle Eph Dickon than it is to take on nature or nature's god. If primitive peoples are capable of creating a god of the gaps to explain the otherwise unexplainable, a devil of the gaps is perhaps even more useful in a world that all too often seems to be the devil's playground.

The Long Street concludes with "Spoken at a Castle Gate," a poem that had originally appeared in the *Measure* in November 1924. Despite having been anthologized on several subsequent occasions by both Louis Untermeyer and William Stanley Braithwaite, "Spoken at a Castle Gate" appeared too late to make *An Outland Piper* and seemed out of place with Davidson's later verse.[3] Like so many of the poems from Davidson's earliest period, this one evokes both the allure and danger of some strange romantic realm.

If this poem is more effective than other similar ones, it is because the allure and danger are only suggested rather than explicitly realized in a world of dryads and nymphs. The speaker and his implied audience (an unidentified "you") stand at the gate of a castle that may or may not be real. The only way to ascertain its reality is to unbolt the gate and enter. When one does that, however, it is with the full knowledge that he will never return. On the other side of the gate, there are surely nightingales piping and queens walking in their gardens: "Young men in murmurous dreams have heard them talking, / Leaped up, like you, and entered . . . vanished . . . where?" (89; ellipses in original).

As real as these perceptions may be, the speaker cannot verify the objective existence of the castle:

> For all I know, the castle's just a dream,
> A shadow piled to mask a dangerous ledge,
> A fantasy blown from devils' lungs in steam,
> Made permanent here, just on a chasm's edge
>
> Where you will tremble in a swoon of falling
> And yet plunge upward through the unearthly mist
> To hear once more the voice that you heard calling
> And win at last those lips you would have kissed,
>
> Even as you touch the bolt that locks this gate,
> Smiling, with patience such as fits old men
> Who prophesy. . . . (89–90)

3. Braithwaite included this poem in his *Anthology of Magazine Verse for 1925* (Boston: B. J. Brimmer, 1925), 94–95. Also see William Stanley Braithwaite and Margaret Haley Carpenter, eds., *Anthology of Poems from the Seventeen Previously Published Braithwaite Anthologies* (New York: Schulte, 1959), 270–71. Louis Untermeyer reprinted "Spoken at a Castle Gate" in the third, fourth, fifth, and sixth editions of his *Modern American Poetry.*

The speaker and his listener—and, indeed, the rest of us as extended audience—face the age-old metaphysical dilemma of having no knowledge beyond the possibly fallible evidence of our senses. To turn back in caution might mean losing the opportunity for aesthetic and spiritual fulfillment. To plunge ahead in the recklessness of faith might mean the loss of quotidian comfort and even life itself. The solution that Davidson poses is the Idealist notion that our perceptions actually create the reality of external objects: "Ah yes, what you create / You'll surely find—but never come back again" (90). Those who take the extreme romantic step of entering the castle gate will find whatever they create—but lose everything else. This option held obvious appeal for the young Donald Davidson, but ultimately he rejected it. He turned away from the castle gate and became the opposite kind of poet—one who creates what he finds. To paraphrase his favorite Yankee poet, it was a choice that made all the difference.

I

The first four sections of *The Long Street* are "Northern Summers" (five poems set in Vermont), a selection of verse that deals loosely with historical themes under the title "What City . . . What Land . . . ?" the seven Joe Clisby lyrics, and the verse drama "The Case of Motorman 17: Commitment Proceedings." Of these, "What City . . . What Land . . . ?" is the longest. John Crowe Ransom speculates that its title may come from Homer's *Odyssey* book 7, where the lovely Nausicaa's mother, Queen Arete of the Phaecians, asks the wanderer, "Who are you? What men are you from?" If that is not the source, Ransom suggests, it might be found in the passage in the *Aeneid* where Virgil's hero, newly arrived in Carthage, is first identified by Dido and her countrymen.[4] In addition to some slight and enigmatic verse that Davidson dropped from *Poems, 1922–1961,* "What City . . . What Land . . ." includes "Woodlands, 1956–1960," the two poems Davidson published between *Lee in the Mountains* and *Singin' Billy* ("Hermitage" and "The Nervous Man"), a "patriotic" poem called "Soldier and Son" (which seems to belong to the period of *Lee in the Mountains*), the semisatirical "Old Sailor's Choice," a surrealistic dream vision called "At the Station," and tributes to his two oldest friends of Fugitive days—John Crowe Ransom and Allen Tate.

If the verse in the final section of *The Long Street* belongs to Davidson's Fugitive era, "The Nervous Man" reads as if it could have been one of the satiric sections of *The Tall Men.* Published in the spring 1950 issue of the *Virginia Quarterly Review,* this poem seemed to signal Davidson's return to the sort of ironic modernism

4. Ransom, "Most Southern Poet," 204.

exemplified by Tate and Eliot.[5] Had he not met Charles Bryan and become involved with *Singin' Billy,* that might well have been the direction that his career would have taken. Of course, we can never know. As it is, "The Nervous Man" represents an anomaly in Davidson's career. In an arch and elliptical style, Davidson proceeds to satirize the scientific and bureaucratic mentality.

It only stands to reason that Davidson would see the advent of nuclear weapons as a validation of his animus against industrialism. The notion that the machine would eventually destroy civilization and everyone in it now seemed entirely possible. One of the more memorable stanzas in the poem lampoons the amorality of the nuclear age. After observing that the Church had shown a greater deference toward Einstein than it ever had to Copernicus, Davidson writes:

> Therefore, his clock is logical, and thought
> Can be dispatched and scheduled like a train.
> Therefore the difference between *can* and *ought*
> Becomes absurd. If millions have been slain
> Or the world exploded, it is no one's fault. (38)

"At the Station" was probably based on Davidson's recurring dream of being disoriented at a train station. Perhaps in an attempt to objectify the experience, he makes himself one of three "wise men," who appear totally helpless. In turn, these men are incapable of producing the time, a ticket, or a key. Why Davidson would create three victims and dub them wise men is an intriguing question. Like the biblical wise men, the characters in this poem are persons of genuine learning, who seem lost in a strange land. Unlike their biblical counterparts, they are bereft of divine guidance or a divine mission. In fact, the situation (if not the imagery) is so surrealistic that one cannot tell where these individuals are going or what they are trying to do. Moreover, by rendering the point of view as first-person *plural,* Davidson makes it less easy for us to read the poem as the dream of a single individual. What we have purports to be straightforward narrative, while lacking straightforward narrative logic. Davidson's diary entry about this dream is both more moving and more comprehensible than the poem he produced from it.

Far more typical of Davidson's public sensibility are the voices we hear in "Soldier and Son." Appearing for the first time in *The Long Street,* "Soldier and Son" is concerned with the question of patrimony, which had dominated "Hermitage" two decades earlier, and which constitutes the subtext of many of

5. Tate was effusive in his praise of this poem. In a letter to Davidson, dated February 18, 1950, he writes: "You were the first person so far as I know who said that the damned scientists would split the atom; and now they've gone and done it" (*Literary Correspondence,* 349–50).

the poems in *Lee in the Mountains*. Framed as a dialogue, this poem depicts a son's attempt to find his own truest identity by understanding his father's experience. "Without recollection, how can I truly be / Your son, or a true father of sons?" the young man asks. "What is kindred blood, and no memory?"

At first trying to hold his son off, or perhaps test his resolve, the father suggests that the son read history: "Go read in those who have such words to sell; / You will be thought an educated man." But it is the truth, not a reputation for facile erudition, that the young man seeks:

> Skim milk they give and call it history.
> I have read its lies—have you not said they were lies?
> Belief I want that surpasses easy knowledge.
> When I believe you, I believe myself
> And am myself, beyond my present self. (23)

Only after this admission does the father open up and tell of an incident when four soldiers rode into an ambush. Two of the soldiers fell, and one rode back to warn the advancing column. Only one of the four remained to return fire: "Alone, he meets the attack, defends the fallen." Without having to say so, the father has made it clear that he is the heroic soldier of the tale. Faced with the choice between life and death, "he chose death, yet lived—to beget a son." Paradoxically, the soldier becomes a father not in begetting biological life, but in transmitting the memory of what he did when honor was at stake. Although he offers to show his son his scar, the son is no Doubting Thomas who demands simplistic physical evidence of things unseen. "Why should I need the scar for my belief?" the sons asks. "Now I know you truly are my father." The soldier replies: "Now I know you truly are my son" (24), and the two walk off in a spirit of love and understanding.

The two most personal poems in *The Long Street* are those written for Davidson's longtime Fugitive brethren John Crowe Ransom and Allen Tate. The first of these, "Meditation on Literary Fame," had originally been delivered under the title "An Epinician Ode in Honor of John Crowe Ransom" during a festival at Harvard that William Yandell Elliott had organized to honor the Fugitives on July 31 and August 1, 1958. The argument of this poem is that Ransom in Tennessee continued the tradition of Pindar, not by aping classical models, but by doing for his people and region what Pindar did for his. The fact that Ransom was now more than two decades removed from both Tennessee and the writing of poetry did not negate Davidson's broader philosophical point.

The Theban's lyre cannot be retrieved in our time by a scholiast rummaging in Byzantium's funeral gleam. The most that he can do is to pluck "the mute, the shattered frame." When Yeats tried to remythologize classical civilization, he ended up with only " . . . the abstract Bird / Of charred philosophy" at the cost of losing "Usheen, whom once he knew, and his dear land, / And all the Celtic host." Here, as in "Hermitage," Davidson suggests that one can recover the truest essence of old world culture only by turning one's back on the ruins of that world and beginning anew in a distant land. Addressing Ransom (though not by name), Davidson argues that there is a better alternative than either arid pedantry or deracinated aestheticism: "Fleeing that bitter choice, your reverend great-grandsire / Sailed, where the Muses led, to this western strand."

Although the people of Tennessee do not play the same games as did the ancient Greeks, they too need poets to commemorate their exploits. Moreover, those poets could not sing their songs "Unless some God or Goddess had stood there / Likeness of Mentor in a hunter's coat, / And tuned the winged words to us. . . ." The result is not just an indigenously American poetic tradition but one that is rooted in a specific New World locale:

> By Isis or the Thames you found none fabulous
> As those proud men at any county fair
> Who wore the Southern gray or Tennessee butternut
> As if great Pindar sat in the judge's chair.

Davidson concludes by sending a song of "new praise and old remembrance" to the subject of his poem. Although this is not evident from the text, the reference is self-reflexive, pointing to the ode itself and the occasion for which it was written. In a more explicit sense, however, Davidson is writing about the locale of the final four lines:

> *Where are no griefs, can be no joys!*
> *Happy the land where men hold dear*
> *Myth that is truest memory,*
> *Prophecy that is poetry.* (37)

The entire poem, particularly in these concluding lines, provides a decidedly antiromantic meditation on literary fame. (It is appropriate that the subject of the poem is the author of two famous essays, titled "A Poem Nearly Anonymous" and "Poets Without Laurels.") The truest fame of the literary artist does not lie in individual recognition, much less in martyred alienation. The griefs from which he reaps joys are collective, not personal. Myth is memory—not something read in a book or contrived from a private vision. (The poet himself is the memory keeper.) Only by possessing the past through memory can we hope to gain the future through prophecy. Poetry is the means by which past and future are reconciled in the tradition of a living community.

These same points are made in a more personal and less abstract manner in "Lines Written for Allen Tate on His Sixtieth Anniversary." Read strictly as autobiography, this poem gives no hint of any differences within the Fugitive and Agrarian fraternities. The first and third stanzas, in particular, evoke communal evenings at Benfolly, when one saw "Owsley's uplifted head" and "Ransom's gray eye" while hearing "the Kentucky voice of Warren." Amid these topical references is a fully articulated argument about the role of poetry in a healthy society—in this case the contemporary South.

"The sound of guns from beleagured Donelson / Up-river flowed again to Benfolly's hearth," the poem begins. Not some great Confederate victory but a disastrous defeat is remembered at these Agrarian gatherings. This is due not to masochism or self-pity but to Davidson's belief (held by Henry Timrod before him) that sacrifices are more hallowed when made on behalf of a lost cause. As

> . . . Lytle cried out: "Earth
> Is good, but better is land, and best
> A land still fought-for, even in retreat;
> For how else can Aeneas find his rest
> And the child hearken and dream at his grandsire's feet"

If "Hermitage" expresses a view of American exceptionalism, "Lines Written for Allen Tate" posits a specifically southern exceptionalism.

Tate's particular virtue is his realization that the modern South is not falling as ancient Troy fell or even as the South of the 1860s fell. The enemy today is a kind of metaphysical arrogance, as exemplified in the philosophies of Descartes and Comte. (Tate's "Ode to the Confederate Dead" was less about the perils of the Old South than about the modern plague of solipsism.) As he had in his poem about Ransom, Davidson again alludes to Yeats as an example of what can happen to a poet who forsakes his native roots for a kind of higher aestheticism. The cry of the kildee, which one can presumably hear at Benfolly:

> . . . is more than phlox or image
> For us deliberate exiles, whose dry rod
> Blossoms athwart the Long Street's servile rage
> And tells what pilgrimage greens the Tennessee sod.

Tate has enabled young people to hear the kildee's cry and " . . . unlearn / The bondage of their dead time's sophistry" (21). Then, in a key pair of lines that echo the title of the section in which this poem is found, Davidson writes of Tate's young readers: "They know, by Mississippi, Thames, or Seine, / What city we build, what land we dream to save." Having first established a specific southern reference, Davidson now argues for the universal relevance of Tate's verse and for the view of poetry and the poet that it implies.

In his final stanza, Davidson returns to the personal voice, imagining himself "with shortened breath" being among those who bear garlands to Tate in his mountain home.[6] (By now, Tate was living in Monteagle, not far from where he had edited the *Sewanee Review* fifteen years earlier.) If the reference to "shortened breath" is a self-deprecatory way of admitting the advancing age he shares with Tate, Davidson says confidently to his friend that the muses continue to be his marshals, "who in other years did not veil their sacred glance / Or from you look askance / And will not cast you off when you are gray" (22). There is perhaps an unspoken hope in these lines that those same muses will sustain all poets who are true to their vatic function—who endeavor to build a city and dream to save a land.

II

Two of the most ambitious and impressive poems in *The Long Street* are "Old Sailor's Choice" and "The Case of Motorman 17: Commitment Proceedings." Both are derived, to varying degrees, from classical Greek sources. In "Old Sailor's Choice," we see a modern Odysseus trying to make his way home from an extended voyage. Because this poem features a single speaking voice addressing an implied listener in a narrative situation (Odysseus before Acinoos, king of the Phaeacians), it is technically a dramatic monologue. However, it does not possess the ironic distance between author and speaker that we find in the monologues of Robert Browning. Even less does Davidson's poem resemble Tennyson's heroically optimistic "Ulysses." Rather it is a peculiarly Davidsonian parable of modern life. As in Homer's *Odyssey*, the wanderer must face certain hazards before he can return to his hearth and the bed of his faithful wife. The choice of hazards that Odysseus elects will determine whether he makes it back home at all.

At the beginning of "Old Sailor's Choice," a crowd gathers around an unnamed man who has plummeted to his death from the low window ledge of a tall building. They are not his friends but curious onlookers—among them Odysseus and his crew, who are passing through town. Circe arrives on the scene in time to argue in favor of cremation and against outdated funeral rituals. She is clearly the voice of modern fashion. But she is also an alluringly sympathetic voice. She feels Odysseus' pain in all that he has endured and will yet have to endure. Her advice is that he choose the easier of the two hazards he might face: "Skip

6. The reference to "shortened breath" may be a veiled allusion to the fact that both Tate and Davidson were heavy smokers.

Charybdis. The going there is rough / Even with modern equipment. I advise / Passage by way of Scylla" (33). Because he has "seen the monster Scylla," Odysseus wisely rejects Circe's counsel. As he describes it, Scylla embodies all the seductive blandishments of both the corporate and the welfare state:

> Within her cliffs of sheer synthetic rock
> She glides on steely pathways. Plastic walls
> Checkered in pseudo-marble cavern her lair.
> These throw you offguard. "How," you ask,
> Can anything go wrong where all is right—
> Rectangular, slide ruled, and functional?
> Mercy, pity, peace can be manufactured.
> Scylla can end your pain Now that the
> State decrees a tax increase . . .

The poem continues in this vein for several more lines until "the secretary with half-naked breasts / Extends the telephone on a crimson claw / And murmurs *Washington is calling!*" (35).

Knowing that he and his crew will never survive the concealed dangers of Scylla, Odysseus heads toward the merely physical hazards of Charybdis. Against this threat the heroic virtues can prevail, and no fate worse than death awaits them: "There the vortex spins like Poe's own maelstrom, / But a man's courage wears out the night." Unlike the typically American tale of manly adventure, this encounter with Charybdis is a rite of passage toward home and family rather than an escape from petticoat government. In returning to the simple pleasures of domestic life, Davidson's Odysseus is simultaneously defeating the wildness of nature and shunning a meretricious vision of civilization. The Agrarian ideal is embodied in neither a skyscraper nor the forest primeval but in a freehold where one can live in harmony with nature.

If "Old Sailor's Choice" resembles an updated version of Homer's *Odyssey*, "The Case of Motorman 17: Commitment Proceedings" is further removed from its classical source. Although Davidson's epigraph from lines 517–18 of Aeschylus's *Eumenides* reads "fear is a good thing, and it ought to sit as watchman over the soul" (57), the story he tells suggests how far we have parted from that wisdom in the modern world. This passage, M. E. Bradford reminds us, comes from the long speech of the Angry Ones, delivered after Orestes flees to Athens to appeal for relief from his long punishment for the murder of his mother, Clytemnestra.[7] In Davidson's tale, a streetcar motorman named *Orestes* Brown, who has come from the hills to the anonymous city, has been apprehended trying to put out

7. M. E. Bradford, "Aeschylus in Nashville: 'The Case of Motorman 17: Commitment Proceedings' and the Later Poetry of Donald Davidson," 55.

a fire at the home of his cousin, a thoroughly secularized Protestant clergyman. Because Davidson's Orestes is believed to have started the fire, he is on trial to determine his sanity and, hence, his criminal culpability. Ironically, it is Orestes himself, not the court, who preaches the redemptive value of fear.

Not only is Brown accused of arson, he has also upset the community by telling of a revenant in anachronistic dress who has boarded his streetcar and paid her fare with an ancient coin. The fact that the motorman is able to produce the coin makes it difficult to dismiss his story out of hand. Nevertheless, two psychiatrists (here referred to by the judicial term *alienists*), Brown's clergyman cousin, and the judge are all determined not to accept it at face value. Significantly, the only witness to testify in defense of Brown's vision is a poet who plays a role somewhat similar to that of Apollo in the *Eumenides.*

In Davidson's verse drama (and, by implication, in the modern world in which that drama occurs), the only people who believe in the supernatural are poets and madmen. Orestes Brown himself is the sort of backwoods prophet who could have come straight from the pages of Flannery O'Connor.[8] Although the court judges him insane, it is the court itself that faces the judgment of the poem. In 1962, Russell Kirk sent Davidson a copy of his essay "Empty Churches," which condemns modernism and infidelity in the Protestant churches of Europe and America. Davidson wrote back that "The Case of Motorman 17" was his own contribution to the discussion. This imagined story is a far more serious treatment of the conflict between religious faith and scientific hubris than was the circus in Dayton, Tennessee.

The first alienist begins his testimony by urging the court to exclude irrelevant considerations of right and wrong and ignore metaphysical distinctions. Nevertheless, his own position is fraught with metaphysical certitude. He is convinced that, whatever Brown may have done, "he was no more responsible / Than for the smallpox if he caught the smallpox." At the same time, he must concede the inability of science to explain how an uneducated man could see "strange phantoms / Like pictures in a child's mythology book, / Especially on a twentieth-century streetcar." A thorough psychiatric examination has shown that the motorman is "quite ignorant of classical myth" (59). Because science cannot account for the phenomenon that is Orestes Brown, the only solution the first alienist can offer is to lock him up. Initially, the second alienist appears to show slightly more respect for the motorman's experience. As a Jungian, he at least believes in the possibility of a collective unconscious. "[F]or the sake of science

8. Davidson reviewed O'Connor's *The Violent Bear It Away* in the *New York Times Book Review* on February 28, 1960. There he writes: "Flannery O'Connor's new novel, like her preceding works, is strong medicine, but now we know, as we did not know earlier, that the medicine is for the soul and is not just realistic Southern Calomel and epsom salts" (4).

and much more," he declares, "A certain skepticism might be used / Toward shallow unbelief no less than shallow belief" (60). If this man's agnosticism seems an improvement over the first witness's epistemological conceit, he can go only so far as to declare religion a beneficial "mental disturbance and concern" (61). Rather than consign Orestes to the loony bin, he would let him stand trial in criminal court.

If anything, Orestes' cousin, the Reverend Dr. Brown, is even less sympathetic than the second alienist to the literal truth claims of religious faith. He tells the judge that "the Church today / Is not adverse where science and the law / Prove their authority." He denies the relevance of sin, "original or new," and claims that "the curse of Adam is a symbolic term / To the enlightened student of religion" (62). Although primitive Christian charity might demand that Orestes be released to his cousin's custody, the Reverend Dr. Brown recommends instead "a program / Of therapeutic attention / In a modern hospital" (63).

When he takes the stand, Orestes claims to have become concerned about his cousin's spiritual welfare when he heard him preach a sermon of secularized theology ("He said there are no golden streets in Heaven, / No angels, golden stairs, or harps, or saints . . ." [66].) He then begins to see all kinds of occult signs that convince him that Hell's ministers are out to get "the Reverend." When he runs to his cousin's house and sees the place on fire, seemingly superhuman strength enables Orestes to uncap the old well and draw water with which to combat the flames. It is at this point that he is arrested and faced with commitment.

In the midst of all this scientific and pseudoscientific testimony, the motorman's only defender is a poet, who says of himself and Orestes: "Down the Long Street we two have walked as strangers— / Strangers yet friends." Among the things that they have seen is the "spectral Parthenon," with its grotesque carvings of "winged shapes, the eyes / That drip red blood, the twining snaky locks." He then utters a warning, which is totally ignored:

> For when the Divine Vision is lost
> And the New Jerusalem is built by a steel crane
> And Satan is no more King of Hell,
> These others return. You, too, will see them, in time,
> As the City withers into namelessness
> And no man has a face or place
> And your neighbor becomes your foe. (64)

When the judge prepares to sign the commitment papers at the end of the trial, he observes: "We have heard with interest the Poet's words, / But Poetry has no standing in this Court"—or, presumably, in modern society at large.

Nevertheless, Davidson gives the poet the concluding words in this verse drama. In the epilogue to the poem, he wonders if we have "come full circle at last," if there is "no light but desert sun / On the Road to Damascus? Only a comet's flare / Brightening the wintry sky above Bethlehem?" But he refuses finally to succumb to skepticism and despair. As irredeemably decadent as the modern world might seem, life is short and art is long. Even if Davidson saw this poem as an attack on secularism, his final image of salvation is not of Christ but of the ancient poet himself:

> But if Orpheus bleed
> His singing head
> Will drift on the stream
> To redeem men
> Till poetry
> And justice come again
> Unless the world be dead. (70)

III

The five poems that make up "Northern Summers" might well have been entitled "Davidson in the Mountains." They derive from Davidson's years at Bread Loaf, when he came to know and respect the agrarian ways of Brother Jonathan. The first poem in the section (and the volume) is "The Ninth Part of Speech," a verse letter to his friend Louis Zahner, which had originally been published in the autumn 1960 issue of the *Virginia Quarterly Review.* Zahner lived near the Davidsons at Breadloaf in a restored country schoolhouse. As an outpost of civilization located on the edge of the wilderness, this schoolhouse is a veritable embodiment of the American condition. From the very beginning of European life on this continent, the primitive vitality of the frontier and the cultural values of the settlement have existed in uneasy tension with each other. To borrow the terminology of Philip Rahv, Davidson's poem suggests that the truly educated person has much to learn from both the paleface and redskin ways of knowing.

At the outset, Davidson makes it clear that he is no disciple of Rousseau, celebrating the noble savage. Hardly an egalitarian, he has nothing but contempt for "glass-front life-adjustment schools / Where Dunce and Master sit on equal stools . . ." (3). But if nature unimproved is no adequate norm for either morality or culture, Davidson is still too much of an Agrarian to want to see the wilderness completely subjected to human domination. At one level, this poem is about the adjustments that nature and humanity must make to each other if they are to exist in productive harmony. As Bradford notes, "The Ninth Part of Speech" "links Davidson to the long stream of hard pastoral in American literature: a severe discipline, as in Frost or in Wordsworth's 'Michael,' but not suggestive of Theocritus, Bion, or the *Eclogues* of Virgil."[9]

The title of the poem at once stresses and undercuts the importance of traditional grammar. Education requires a knowledge of the eight parts of speech; however, the person who stops there is a mere pedant:

> Whoever takes a schoolhouse for his house
> Must move beyond a printed grammar's reach
> And try some parleying among birch boughs
> With beaver, deer, and the neat scurrying grouse
> Who use what is their own.
> And from them learn the ninth part of speech
> That never yet was parsed or paradigmed. (4)

The notion that nature has a language all its own is not original with Davidson. This belief has long been part of the romantic's creed—Emerson devotes an entire section of his essay "Nature" to the subject of language. Davidson, however, is not suggesting that we go native. His view has more in common with the notion of natural revelation than with Emersonian transcendentalism. As Lawrence Dessommes points out: "The forest creatures who use what is their own stand over against men who by implication can use what is others'. The creatures as creatures are less than men; yet they stand as models of character; for their character is by nature proper to their status. By analogy the teacher, anyone who 'takes a schoolhouse for his house,' must assume a character proper to his role."[10] Thus does Davidson maintain the hierarchy of being without necessarily glorifying man or denigrating nature.

In principle, the sort of education that Davidson advocates would be universally valid. However, he is enough of a realist to know that Zahner's schoolhouse and others like it are glorious anomalies in a world dominated by "Dewey and consolidation." They exist largely because the parsimonious Yankees of Vermont would hate to see these old buildings go to waste:

> Old schoolhouses it has for lease or purvey,
> Enough to adult-educate a few
> Unlaundered brains—but only just enough
> For those who like their walking rough
> Up trails that slip around technology
> To gulfs of fern and banks of memory. (4)

9. M. E. Bradford, "To Sing the Truth: The Poetry of Davidson's Later Years," 62.
10. Lawrence Dessommes, "The Epistomological Implications in 'The Ninth Part of Speech,'" 24.

One such individual is Zahner's "neighbor down the road," who sits with bench and blackboard, raising the songs of Moses under his maple trees. Although Davidson does not tell us this in the poem, the individual in question is Rabbi Victor Reichert, a scholar who was equally at home in nature and in the study.

The wild creatures who inhabit the landscape of this poem have a primitive wisdom to impart. They are predatory beasts, who live according to nonhuman instincts we imitate at our peril. Nevertheless, their existence teaches us something about our own contingency in the world. This fact is illustrated by two stories involving Homer Noble's wife. One afternoon, Mrs. Noble, who was herself a lady schoolteacher, discovered a wildcat outside her schoolhouse as she was preparing to leave for home. It "kept her after school / Much as she'd kept her little scholars in . . ." (5). Clearly, Davidson sees this as a revelatory experience for Mrs. Noble. Poking fun at the educational bureaucracy, he notes that her official visitor "was no semi-literate school inspector." Her only choice is to bolt the door, watch the wildcat and the snow, and wait to be rescued.

> Till dark fell he was Master, she the class;
> She figured unknowns through her pane of glass,
> Chill binomials, hour by hour:
> She plus the burning eyes, the frozen grass
> Times weather to the nth power—
> Then horses' hoofs, a voice, deliverance. (6)

Mrs. Noble's other experience with a wild creature came when she encountered a wolf near her home when she went out to fetch a log of wood. In this instance, as in the other, she subdues her fear by waiting the beast out. In both cases, her patience saves her from an animal who is physically more powerful than she. Although Davidson does not say so explicitly, Mrs. Noble's ability to alter her behavior in the face of external peril can be read as a kind of Darwinian parable. Even though the Agrarians sided with the anti-Darwinians in Dayton, their sensibility was one of adaptation. It is foolish to try to be nature's conqueror or its subject. What is required is the sort of communion that is based on comprehensive knowledge and empathy. Davidson makes that point in his concluding words to Zahner:

> Few now are left who know the ancient rule
> That tame abstract must wed the wild particular. . . .
> To know this secret, you were not the first,
> And will not be the last, we hope, to pledge
> Redemption if the worst should come to worst,
> And bring the schoolhouse back
> Somewhere close to a wildcat's track
> And the forest's finite edge. (7)

If "The Ninth Part of Speech" is a poem whose very tone bespeaks a deep metaphysical seriousness, "Gradual of the Northern Summer" reads almost like light verse. Its lilting rhythms suggest a carefree romp in a tame natural setting. One almost expects to hear Browning's Pippa remind us, as she passes, that "God's in his Heaven and all's right with the world." If "The Ninth Part of Speech" stops just short of a tragic vision of life, "Gradual of the Northern Summer" appears to be thoroughly comic. Nevertheless, for all its whimsy, Davidson's "Gradual" is a complex and serious poem that presents a coherent view of both life and art.

The controlling metaphor of the poem is based on the venerable notion that being in nature is itself a sacramental experience. Throughout the poem, Davidson makes analogies between various natural epiphanies and different parts of the Catholic mass. The gradual is a time of transition between the epistle and the gospel. As such, it is a moment of elevation from the human to the divine, usually accompanied by a song of praise. To say that the speaker of the poem finds the divine in nature is not to say that the poem is pantheistic or even conventionally romantic. He imagines the "vesper deer" telling their beads and the wolves genuflecting in the forest. Rather than being objects of veneration themselves, these creatures implicitly acknowledge a higher power.

Davidson means for us to see his poem as a kind of verse gradual, in the sense that it provides a bridge between the plenitude of nature and the divine mysteries to which nature points. Such a bridging can occur more easily when we are removed from an urban industrialized world. There is at least a hint of religious primitivism in the following lines:

> Whoso would turn to our abode
> Must take the narrow, rain-scraped road
> And learn by one-way steeps and grooves
> God loves best where he unimproves. (10)

Commenting on these lines, Bradford writes: "In such a timeless 'unimproved' state it is possible to step out of the realm of practical objectives so that even the food [Davidson's landlady] Mrs. Scott brings in is 'grace in a grocery sack' and the burning of morning fires the 'plainsong' of a 'primitive choir.' Even the sounding of horns along a distant highway becomes part of the scene's liturgical whole and 'hails like a distant Gloria.' "[11]

Like "The Case of Motorman 17," this poem concludes with a homage not to God, but to the artist. (Bradford is convinced that Davidson is referring to his wife, whose illustrations appear throughout *The Long Street*.) It is the province of

11. Bradford, "To Sing the Truth," 68–69.

the painter to preserve the beauties that the poet has tried to describe. Seeming to confess his own inadequacies (whether through ritualistic or genuine modesty), Davidson writes of "reflections we could never frame / Images we would leave to burn, / Lines for which we lack an urn . . ." (10–11). (Is this an allusion to Cleanth Brooks's equation of poetry with a well-wrought urn?) All of these, the painter "gathers into perspective." She is able to render the true beauty of this scene because she can see beneath its surface prettiness: "The shadows that our eyes refused / Are light she will not leave unused. / By dark as much as sun we live. . . ." Such a vision allows her to see in the world a sacramental unity to which most of the rest of us are blind. The shattering of that unity is the work of the Devil, and its restoration is at least a partial act of redemption:

> The foe that tears our parts piecemeal
> Means to enslave, not to reveal.
> To sever parts was our mistake;
> The brush restores them for God's sake. (11)

"A Touch of Snow" is fraught with a sense of impending apocalypse, but the tone and manner of the poem are so restrained that one might initially miss the urgency of its theme. As much as any poem in his corpus, "A Touch of Snow" demonstrates the ways in which Davidson belongs to and deviates from the mainstream of modernism. In a manner reminiscent of the fable of the ant and the grasshopper, the poem depicts a colloquy between the speaker (presumably Davidson himself) and a couple of housepainters about the meaning of some summer snow glimpsed on a nearby mountain peak.[12] Although the speaker sees the touch of snow as a sign that the season will shift as soon as the fog lifts, the painters complacently dismiss the prospect, as long as they are able to "keep summer here below."

If the house painters refuse to look at the snow, the speaker not only sees it but sees through it:

> From where that summer stays we still can watch
> For any higher warnings man should catch:
> Stars old or new that course the telltale night
> Tree-shapes that blaze too fair for mortal sight;
> Or mist flurries writing MENE there on our mountain height
> With just a touch of snow. (13)

---

12. I am particularly indebted to M. E. Bradford for his reading of "A Touch of Snow." See his "Meaning and Metaphor in Donald Davidson's 'A Touch of Snow,'" *Generations of the Faithful Heart: On the Literature of the South* (La Salle, Ill.: Sherwood Sugden, 1983), 175–82.

The fire on Belmont Street, which had been a sign of apocalypse in *The Tall Men,* has now been eerily transformed into a sign so subtle that most people would miss it altogether. Perhaps the silence, distance, and whiteness of the touch of snow make it even more ominous than a conflagration on a Nashville street—just as the whiteness of Melville's whale affrights more than does the redness of blood. Students of the Bible will recall that MENE was the first of the words that appeared in the handwriting on Belshazzar's wall on the night of his downfall. Only the prophet Daniel was capable of interpreting those words and their significance for ancient Babylon. The speaker in "A Touch of Snow," especially if we assume that he is a poet, assumes the role of a modern Daniel in a twentieth-century Babylon.

In writing an apocalyptic (or at least eschatological) poem, Davidson joins company with such eminent modernists as Yeats, Pound, Eliot, and Tate. However, his handling of his theme is thoroughly traditional. We have straightforward exposition, a regular metrical pattern, convincing descriptions of the natural landscape, unobtrusive classical and biblical allusions, and a controlling metaphor that is wholly implied rather than asserted. Davidson is comfortable enough with these conventions of order to employ them in describing impending disorder, rather than resorting to the newer conventions that actually simulate disorder. His choice of form suggests that Davidson agreed with Frost in seeing poetry as a "momentary stay against confusion."

Although it would probably be overstating the case to say that "A Barren Look," the poem that immediately precedes "A Touch of Snow," is postapocalyptic, clearly some natural catastrophe has already occurred before the speakers in this dramatic dialogue appear on the scene. The first speaker is a sort of interlocutor who prompts his companion to describe what he sees. To all appearances, what lies before them is a pastoral scene in rural Vermont. Bright water courses through an unreaped meadow, and "the deep-tufted slender grasses / Dowse their tips and sway where the eddying ripple passes." This is certainly no wasteland or toxic-waste dump; however, there is no sign of higher life forms. One might imagine that the speakers had miraculously returned to some remote geological past, except for the fact that one of them carries a map showing a road "fully paved through Middlebury Gap." It is precisely this sign of industrial progress that alarms his companion, who concludes the poem with a troubled speculation: "No fish in the stream, no light in the head, / And what if, next, the land be dead!" (12).

The "Northern Summers" section of *The Long Street* concludes with "Late Answer: A Civil War Seminar," a poem that depicts Davidson's dilemma as an unreconstructed southerner among Yankee academics at Bread Loaf. Although not explicitly specified, the setting of the poem is apparently the faculty club at Bread Loaf. Here the speaker's colleagues are identified not by name but by metonymy—Harvard, Vassar, Amherst, Yale, and Dartmouth. Although congenial enough, these professors cannot understand the speaker's preoccupation with a war now nearly a century in the past. Gently teasing him, "Harvard" declares: "When I said 'war' I meant of course the late / Unpleasantness. I must say you surprise / Me with these dank Faulknerian memories" (15). When the northern professors see that they cannot disabuse the speaker of his obsession, "Dartmouth" good-naturedly asks him to demonstrate the celebrated rebel yell.

Davidson (who is obviously the speaker of this poem) simply asks himself: "How could he learn what history books forbade? / And why should I instruct him?" (16). For Davidson, the War Between the States was the defining moment of American history, one that is not yet entirely past. If his northern companions shared his sense of tradition (i.e., the continuing presence of the past), they would respond with similar fervor, although to a different set of symbols and a somewhat different history:

> "You who debate by night cannot be mourning
> Faroff kinsmen dead or a roof burning;
> Yet a burning roof, kin dead long ago,
> If you could weep, would give you right to know
> The sound of valor where it dwells with sorrow. . . ." (16–17)

Davidson ends up defending not the Confederacy or the cause of secession or even the culture of the Old South, but the importance of historical memory itself. In fact, preceding Robert Lowell's famous Civil War meditation by only a few years, Davidson could have called the concluding stanzas of his poem "For the Union Dead." "We mourned with you then in brotherhood," Davidson recalls, "And I'll weep with you now for those whose names / Burn on your monuments like altar flames" (17). He then proceeds to call the roster of northern martyrs who fell for the cause in which they believed. It is the depths of his own commitment that enable him to do this, when the urbane Ivy Leaguers with whom he is sharing drinks would just as soon forget their own regional heritage:

> "We, too, have names that blaze on mouldering stone
> And I have seen men's tears fall where they slept
> And heard a shouting while I wept,
> A century off yet louder in my ear
> Than all that's so much magnified and near." (17)

What Davidson is referring to here is something akin to what Tate called "knowledge carried to the heart" in his "Ode to the Confederate Dead." Unfortunately, all that Tate's solipsistic speaker can do is "set up the grave / In the house." If that were all that Davidson was doing, he would fully merit the derision of his colleagues. The late answer he is giving in this impromptu Civil War seminar, however, has nothing to do with refighting old battles. "Tradition is the living faith of the dead," wrote Jaroslav Pelikan, "traditionalism is the dead faith of the living."[13] Davidson's journey from *The Tall Men,* with its willed recovery of the past, to poems such as "Lee in the Mountains" and "Late Answer" is a movement from traditionalism to tradition. It is not so much a position asserted as a vision earned.

13. Jaroslav Pelikan, *The Vindication of Tradition,* 65.

DOWN THIS LONG STREET

On the morning of June 29, 1960, Donald Davidson awakened from a strange dream. In it, he had just bought a house with a large backyard suitable for a garden. As he looked out over the yard, he saw a bulldozer at work, digging up and carrying away his earth. When he rushed out to put a stop to this, the man on the bulldozer smiled and asked how carefully Davidson had read the deed to his property. It contained a concession, the operator said, that allowed him to carry off the earth. Not remembering anything to that effect in the contract, Davidson resolved to go back in the house and have Theresa read the papers again. In the meantime, he ordered the trespasser off his property. The man simply smiled from atop the bulldozer. As he prepared to rush into the house, Davidson awoke. It was one of the most vivid dreams he had ever had (see diary, June 29, 1960).

In the late 1950s, Davidson began to experience a variety of physical problems, even as his periodic bouts of depression grew worse. While he rode the train from Nashville to Brunswick, Maine, in April 1958, the chronic pain in his back was exacerbated by a bad seat angle. Writing in his diary on April 15, 1958, he describes the Pennsylvania countryside as he could see it outside his window. "A fair, pleasant day," he writes, "but little sign of spring. Snow still on the shady side of mountains, along the ravines. Everywhere, as in industrial areas South or North, the same sights—factories, acres of parked autos, no people, little of the pleasant—marred structures, homes tawdry, humanity obscured. Everywhere bulldozers have been tearing out buildings & gashing the earth."

His description of his passage from New York's Pennsylvania Station to Grand Central Station reads like a journey to the Underworld. Arriving at a crowded Penn Station at 4:00, he carried his own baggage to the taxi, which drove through jammed streets at the height of the rush hour. Great trucks were being loaded with dresses as he passed through the garment district. Arriving at Grand Central Station, he carried his bags to the twenty-five-cent lockers at the head of the great stairs and nearly fainted from the pain in his back. Jostled by the surging crowd in the concourse, he found a little coffee shop, where he ate a sandwich, drank some coffee, and took a pain pill. Finally experiencing some relief, he discovered the tunnel to the Roosevelt Hotel, where he ate a full supper. Still having plenty of time to kill, he browsed at Ligget's among the largest array of paperbacks he had ever seen, finally selecting a Somerset Maugham novel to read while waiting for the 10:15 train. At 9:45, he started for the train, only to be told by the conductor at the entrance that his ticket had been made out the wrong way. With little time to spare, he rushed to the ticket window, where a surly ticket seller made out an elaborate form for him to sign. Hurrying back to the train with his three bags in tow, Davidson collapsed in his seat at 10:05, racked with pain and exhaustion (see diary April 15, 1958).

The next day, despite the unpleasantness of his trip, Davidson delivered a well-received lecture at Bowdoin College, alma mater of Nathaniel Hawthorne, Henry Wadsworth Longfellow, and the copperhead president Franklin Pierce. An eloquent and well-reasoned political talk, which dealt only peripherally with race, "The New South and the Conservative Tradition" was published in a much shortened version in the September 10, 1960, issue of William Buckley's *National Review.* Realizing that Jeffersonian liberalism was a thing of the past, Davidson had now allied himself wholeheartedly with the conservative wing of the Republican Party.

Davidson's health deteriorated further the year after the Bowdoin lecture. On February 21, 1959, he was taken to the Vanderbilt hospital after experiencing a mild heart attack. He spent thirty-two days in the hospital and a long period of convalescence at home. In April, his doctor took him off the anticoagulent he had been using for six weeks and recommended moderate activity. Nevertheless, Davidson could not do such things as drive a car or lift heavy objects. He was also forbidden from taking part in a literary symposium then going on at Vanderbilt. Although he could teach at Bread Loaf that summer and resume normal duties at Vanderbilt the following autumn, the doctor warned him to stay away from organizational (i.e., political) activities.

On September 17, 1959, Davidson attended the funeral of his old chairman Edwin Mims. Knowing that he would not be able to park anywhere near the West End Methodist Church across from the Vanderbilt campus, he took a taxi from his home on Fairfax Avenue. "During old fashioned Methodist funeral service," Davidson writes in his diary for that day, "I was at one point so deeply stirred by memories & grief that tears began to flow & I almost sobbed aloud. This was when the congregation sang a hymn. I thought of Dr. M. and of my own father's funeral." After much scripture and prayer, the minister finally talked of Dr. Mims himself and read an old hymn, "The Wayfaring Traveler," that Mims had suddenly remembered and repeated a few days before his death. After talking to various people outside the church, Davidson decided against going to the burial at Woodlawn Cemetery.

Summing up the year on a memoranda page in his diary, Davidson writes: "I say goodbye to 1959 with no regret, except for that ominous regret for *time* that goes so fast & more and more carries—and uses—his sickle." He characterizes 1959 as "the most unlucky year of my life" and proceeds to enumerate the various defeats and setbacks he had experienced in the previous twelve months. "But on the other side," he concludes, "I have written some poetry again—several poems during the year. None of these has been rejected, yet. I cannot 'balance' the year. I never tried to before. Suspect a critic would say 'put a minus for 1959.' But with me the poetry weighs heavily. It has weight in itself and, for me, is the seed of more. *Pace*, 1959."

In addition to writing poetry, seeing any of the old Fugitives always seemed to raise Davidson's spirits. The reunion of 1956 certainly helped to bring back happy memories. Also, the mere fact of growing older may have made him nostalgic. His tribute poems to both Ransom and Tate were written in the late fifties. On December 16, 1959, Davidson found himself at the Joint University Libraries on the Vanderbilt campus looking over some old letters from Allen Tate, which he had not read in many years. He was convinced more than ever how much was revealed in them. "[F]rom 1922 on," he notes, "—all the letters so shapely, definite, beautifully written—and far-seeing, if not prophetic in the high sense, as to the state and direction of our culture, in U.S. and the South, & of the arts" (diary, December 16, 1959). Toward the end of a letter to Tate, dated November 29, 1961, Davidson says of his Fugitive and Agrarian brethren: "Dear friends, you are the law and the prophets to me as of old" (*Literary Correspondence*, 382).

On December 25, 1961, Davidson noted in his diary that he and Theresa had spent a delightful Christmas with Mary and her family, exchanging gifts around the Christmas tree after one of Mary's finest dinners. Then, in the late afternoon, the Davidsons returned to the emptiness of 410 Fairfax Avenue. Of late, Donald had been plagued by peculiar dreams. In one, he is a kind of visiting teacher, who comes into the lecture room unprepared. The room is filled with students, all looking at him. Knowing he must say something, he starts to improvise and wakes up.

I

On January 29, 1963, Davidson learned that Robert Frost had died in Boston from heart failure and a blood clot in his lungs. "His like will not be again,"

Davidson writes in his diary. "One of the last of the 'Old Americans,' even though he was in so many respects 'modern.' What a vacancy we shall feel at B[read] L[oaf]—for a long time—maybe it won't be something we can 'get used to.'" Davidson had first read the poetry of Robert Frost "by candlelight in the rather cold, upstairs room of a peasant's house in the Cote d'Or" as he was waiting to be sent home from France in the winter of 1918–1919.[1] A decade later, he met Frost in the flesh when the New England poet, then in his midfifties, gave a reading to the Centennial Club of Nashville in the autumn of 1928.

Later that afternoon, Davidson attended a tea given in Frost's honor in the wealthy Belle Meade section of Nashville. He remembers the hostess perching herself on the floor in front of Frost so that no one else could come near or even speak to him across the barrier. Then, when the party finally broke up, the Davidsons were informed that they could have Frost for dinner and the balance of the evening. As they all three climbed into the family's second-hand blue Essex, Davidson asked Frost whether he would like to eat at the Hermitage Hotel uptown or in the Wesley Hall cafeteria. When Frost replied, without hesitation, "the cafeteria, I would like that," an intimacy was born that would last for the balance of Frost's life.

Although Davidson probably did not know it at the time, Frost had already rendered an important service to the Fugitive cause when he recommended that Henry Holt publish John Crowe Ransom's *Poems about God* in 1918. Frost greatly admired Ransom's verse and never missed an opportunity to praise it; however, his own approach to poetry more closely resembled Davidson's. In their most characteristic verse, both Frost and Davidson shunned the difficult and elliptical diction of modernism. They were both masters of a colloquial idiom and sought to address an audience of ordinary readers rather than a literary coterie. It is not known whether Frost had read *An Outland Piper* or *The Tall Men* when he first met Davidson, but he must certainly have been aware of the Fugitive movement. When Davidson took three volumes of Frost's poetry down from the bookshelf of his Wesley Hall apartment that evening in 1928, Frost readily inscribed all three. "'For D. D.,' he wrote in one, 'from his friend and admirer, Robert Frost'" ("Recollections," 2).

In 1944, Frost was again in Nashville to read. Then seventy, he was convalescing from pneumonia but in high spirits. A guest in the Davidson home on Fairfax Avenue, Frost agreed to visit with the neighbors and displayed a keen appetite, particularly for the hot biscuits Davidson's cook Cora Woods knew "so well to bake." On his second night in town, with the time of his reading drawing near, Frost reluctantly consented to rest and to take a light supper of a single raw

---

1. Donald Davidson, "Recollections of Robert Frost," 1. Subsequent references will be cited parenthetically in the text.

egg. ("From Cora, later on, we learned that Frost slipped back into the kitchen when we were not looking, and said: 'Cora, do you have any more of those little biscuits?' She did" [4].) The reading in Neely Auditorium on the Vanderbilt campus was a spectacular success. On their way in, Davidson and Frost had to make their way through an overflow crowd of people who had not been able to find either seats or standing room in the building. After the reading, the rush of autograph seekers, and the postlecture party, the Davidsons were dog tired. But for Frost, the recovering pneumonia patient, the evening had just begun. "Hours later, he asks what time it is. It is well past two in the morning. And what time does his train leave? Six-thirty A. M.! Triumphantly, Frost holds out his glass for more ginger-ale and says, 'Then it's not worth while to go to bed. Let's stay up all night'" (5).

The Davidson-Frost friendship flourished at Bread Loaf over the years. When Davidson first went to Vermont in the summer of 1931, Frost was already a fixture on the mountain. In the early years of the Writers' Conference, he usually came up from South Shaftesbury as a visitor rather than as an official participant. (Davidson remembers one summer when he was boarding with Homer Noble that Frost came over for a New England corn roast.) As the years passed, his close ties to Roberta Teale Schwartz and her husband, Gordon Chalmers, enabled Frost to fill Davidson in on what was going on at Kenyon College. (When Frost turned down the invitation to be editor of the *Kenyon Review,* he suggested that Chalmers offer the position to Ransom.) Piqued at the coolness Ransom began showing toward her verse, Roberta Schwartz persuaded her husband to bring the antimodernist poet Robert Hillyer to campus. For several years, Hillyer proved to be a thorn in Ransom's side and even created a minor scandal when he published a pair of articles in the *Saturday Review of Literature* that accused T. S. Eliot and the American New Critics of being sympathetic to Fascism.[2] One evening in July of 1949, Frost asked Davidson why Ransom had not continued writing verse. Davidson replied that "basically, it was because he gave up his principles when he went to Kenyon" (diary, July 20, 1949).

Earlier that month, the Scottish critic David Daiches had lectured at Bread Loaf. He argued that the New Criticism (particularly as practiced by Cleanth Brooks) was limited in its ability to deal with the kind of poetry that Frost wrote. "Frost was in audience on front row," Davidson notes in his diary entry for July 4, 1949. "But Daiches apparently did not know he was there as his remark 'If Mr. Frost were here,' indicated. Frost smiled & pointed to himself. He seemed much pleased with the general turn of Daiches' lecture." When Frost spoke to

2. Robert Hillyer, "Treason's Strange Fruit," *Saturday Review of Literature,* June 11, 1949, pp. 9–11, 28; and "Poetry's New Priesthood," *Saturday Review of Literature,* June 18, 1949, pp. 7–9, 38.

the School of English a week and a half later, he picked up where Daiches left off. "Said he had been inclined to wonder whether, if Shakespeare had been writing in the manner of a certain school of poets, he would have handled the witches' answer to Macbeth in different terms. To the question, 'what do ye here?' (not exact quotation) would they have answered, 'We are turning in a gyre'?"

Warming to his topic, Frost remembered asking T. S. Eliot what he thought of Robert Burns. " 'Not a poet at all,' said Eliot. 'In fact, no good poetry had been written north of the Tweed—except perhaps Dunbar—*Ti* mor mortis centurbat me.' (Frost quoted him with a malicious accent on the long *i* of *Timor,* an 'ai' sound.) But wasn't Eliot a Border name, said Frost. No, we belong to the Somerset Eliots, said T. S. E. But couldn't one say that Burns was a good writer of songs? asked Frost. 'One might grant that modest claim,' said Eliot. (Frost said this with mischievous emphasis & a slight imitation of British accent)" (diary, July 13, 1949).

When Frost would call on Davidson in the house he eventually purchased at Bread Loaf, the New England poet was often accompanied by his Scottish shepherd dog, Gillie. On one evening in the 1940s, just as Davidson had settled down with his dulcimer and Theresa with her reading, Frost appeared at the door, a shillelagh in hand and Gillie in tow. They talked of many things that night, including their mutual friend Hervey Allen. Despite a substantial income from a series of best-selling historical novels (*Anthony Adverse* was second only to *Gone With the Wind* in popularity during the 1930s), Hervey seemed always on the brink of financial disaster. Trying to maintain an estate in Miami, he would find enough money to water his grounds one year and to fertilize them the next, but never enough to do both in the same year. Hervey had a habit of taking trips with Frost and then leaving Frost to pick up the tab. "I would let Hervey push me along as much as a thousand dollars worth," Frost said. "No more than that, though. Would trust him that far." On one recent trip to Havana, the man who drove them to their hotel had greeted them with some lines from "Annabel Lee": "Many and many a year ago in a kingdom by the sea." "That's Poe," he said. "I learned it when I was a student in Kansas. You are a poet, I welcome you to Cuba."[3]

In many ways, Frost and Davidson were kindred spirits. Although a native Californian who made the landscape of rural New England a fixture in our collective imagination, Frost had strong southern sympathies, as well. His father was a copperhead who named his son "Robert Lee Frost" for the most sainted of Confederate generals. Although he always remained a nominal Democrat and read at the Kennedy inauguration, Frost called himself a "Godawful Disgruntled

3. This incident is recorded in a notebook Davidson kept, which is currently in the possession of the Davidson family.

344   MR. DAVIDSON (1950–1968)

Democrat." Grover Cleveland was the last Democratic president to win his wholehearted approval. As Peter J. Stanlis recalls, "It was a toss up for me whether Davidson or Frost despised the politics of the New Deal more than the other. I got a double dose and was amazed at how closely they agreed with what was wrong with the New Deal. Frost even referred to it as the 'New Diel,' Scottish dialect for new devil. Both Davidson and Frost especially disliked Mrs. Roosevelt and the so-called 'brain trust.' She was a murky sentimentalist who made mercy everything and justice nothing, while the brain trust was to them sheer arrogance in the federal government."[4] Frost once told Davidson that his definition of a liberal was "a man who fumbles with Gordian knots" (diary, August 5, 1961).

During the summer of 1957, when Donald and Theresa Davidson were both involved with the defense of the Clinton dissidents and a major federal-state clash over integration seemed to be looming in Little Rock, Arkansas, Davidson and Frost discussed the southern situation on several occasions. After giving a lecture on the merits of insubordination, Frost remarked to Davidson: "You've been 'insubordinate' down there!" Feigning ignorance, Davidson replied: "I can't imagine what you mean!" Then, Frost asked: "D'ye suppose they'll send troops into the South?" (diary, July 3, 1957).

Later that summer, Frost expressed himself much less enigmatically on the issue of segregation. As Davidson recalls in his diary entry for August 17:

> Frost in his own cabin—looking so much older now—but blue eyes clear as ever. Wanted to be posted about integration-segregation fight in South, etc. He admires strategy of Southern group in Congress. . . . His figure of speech on segregation & states rights—how hard it is to carry a tray of water to the refrigerator without the separating partitions in it. "I want something to separate me from the world," he said. "That's what boundaries are for. My clothes to separate me from the cold; my room—walls—from other people; my house, fence; the township lines; the state lines; the national boundaries." Says he is down on the record as a States Rights Democrat. When he first spoke to us on this (2 summers ago) he didn't think we had a chance against Supreme Court—that's the supreme power; no prevailing against them. But now we've made more headway than he had dreamed possible. Seems to admire it.

In all likelihood, Donald Davidson and Robert Frost were the only members of the Bread Loaf community to support Strom Thurmond for president in 1948.[5]

---

4. This is from his reminiscence of Davidson at Bread Loaf, which Stanlis sent to M. E. Bradford in February 1991.

5. Although Frost's support for Thurmond is one of the lesser-known facts of his life, he confided this information to his friend Margaret Louise Coit, author of *John C. Calhoun:*

Frost had a delightfully ironic way of using language in an accurate but entirely unexpected way. When lecturing at Bread Loaf on June 30, 1958, he began by declaring himself an "integrationist." After a pause, he added: "I've taught every subject in the curriculum." Although he did not use the standard political terminology, his ensuing talk about education was thoroughly antiradical and antimodern. At the end, he even expressed disgust for agnostics and praise for fundamentalists. At that point, he glanced mischievously toward Davidson and smiled (see diary, June 30, 1958).

As everyone who has read Lawrance Thompson's biography of him knows, Frost could be difficult and demanding, as well as charming. Davidson recalls a reading and talk Frost gave at Bread Loaf on July 3, 1961. Nita Cook, wife of Reginald "Doc" Cook, the longtime director of the Bread Loaf School, had said ominously to Davidson that afternoon: "This *might* be the last time." Frost, however, seemed in fine form (if anything, less decrepit than in recent years), and he soon had a diverse audience laughing at his sarcastic, bantering remarks. In a far less jovial mood was Frost's secretary and friend, Kay Morrison. In addition to having had a small cancerous growth removed from her cheek, she had just survived a hard day of driving Frost to Hanover, New Hampshire, and back. "He talked from 9:30 to 4:00—and I had to listen all that time while driving," Kay said. "He doesn't drive & doesn't know what hard work it is. At 4:00, when we reached home, I said: 'Now you can have a good rest before your reading.'" Frost replied: "But didn't you say you had some letters to read to me!" In exasperation, Kay told him: "I'm just too god-damned tired to do any more." Frost returned to his cabin without saying another word. Later he sent word that someone should bring two eggs up the walk for his supper (diary, July 3, 1961).

Nineteen sixty-one turned out not to be the "last time" for Frost at Bread Loaf. But the following year was. On August 4, 1962, Frost and Kay Morrison and her husband Ted enacted the annual ritual of the lawn party. Cocktails were served at the Homer Noble Farm, which Frost had purchased after Noble's death. Davidson records the scene that day in his diary:

> Robt. Frost, his white head standing out above the clump of guests, stands a little uphill from the old lilacs, near the opening of the lane to his "cabin," and is surrounded by a respectful knot who come to clasp his fist momentarily, then stand and listen, listen, listen. Less than usual does he seem to "see" whoever is in front of him. His glance is far away. Is he in a fog? Or in a cloud? The latter one guesses—as the journey to Moscow is in near prospect. Whispers say it has been planned by Kennedy, who will go with an attendant

---

American Portrait. This fact was related to me in conversation by Prof. Clyde Wilson of the University of South Carolina.

train of worthies. Of these Frost is the "Laureate." . . . Kay Morrison says to me, "Yes he is going—he is failing, and the days ahead are hard to face."

Kay's flower beds are bright and varicolored around the old farmhouse. Across the pole fence in the old meadow, Davidson notices the glossy horses, "so well groomed," and fireweed grown high where the new wall crosses the lane. The old windmill is now gone, the place cleaned up. The other field has been cleared for a large parking space. Rumor has it that Kennedy's secretary of the interior, Stewart Udall, wants to take over the Homer Noble Farm as a memorial to Frost when he passes on. Udall is a friend and admirer of Frost, who carried him in his arms through the snow outside the inauguration party (diary, August 4, 1962).

By the summer of 1963, all that was left of Frost at Bread Loaf were the memories of his friends. At a memorial service held on July 11, Davidson recalled one "mild August night," when he and Arthur Endicott, James and Julia Wilson, Ted and Kay Morrison, and maybe one or two others sat on the lawn east of Endicott's house, listening to Robert Frost. There was no moon, but the stars were bright, and Frost was propped on his elbow, naming the stars and "the great constellations in the eastern heaven" in the same voice that he used to speak his poetry. *"The bright star is Vega, in the Constellation Lyra. Can we see where yonder is Sirius? Tomorrow we must look for the evening star at the place where Frost tells us it will be"* ("Recollections," 4).

II

Davidson was not only the last remaining Fugitive-Agrarian at Vanderbilt; he eventually became the longest-serving professor in the English department. Walter Clyde Curry had taught in the department forty years at the time of his retirement in 1955. When Davidson left in 1964, he had put in forty-four years.[6] By the end of his long term of service, he had become an institution at the university. Recalling Davidson toward the end of his career, Roy Blount, Jr., writes: "[W]hen you saw him on campus in his later years, wearing a tweed cap and walking slowly, he looked not only hard, intensely honorable and distant, like Faulkner, but also indignant, as though he could tell, just by looking straight up the footpath, that the campus, at least, had gone to blazes. He looked like a man ready to give somebody a thrashing." Later, when they were conferring in his office about a paper of Blount's, Davidson opened a letter and reported that it was his announcement of reappointment for another year

6. Walter Sullivan has already surpassed this mark. As of the spring of 1999, he had taught at Vanderbilt for fifty years, longer than any other professor in the history of the university.

as a Vanderbilt professor. " 'Yes,' he said. 'I'm just going on from one year to the next.' "[7]

Although Davidson was a generous mentor to his students, he could be so lost in thought that he was literally unaware of what was going on around him. A student is said to have traveled up to Vermont to see him one summer. After spending the night in a pup tent, the young man showed up on Davidson's doorstep the next morning. When Davidson answered the door, he was holding a copy of Warren's *Selected Essays* and was so absorbed in his reading that his visitor might just as well have been a Fuller Brush salesman. "I can see that you're busy, Mr. Davidson," he said and beat a hasty retreat. A few weeks later, Davidson saw this same student across the Vanderbilt campus. "How are you doing, Harry," he shouted. "I haven't seen you in months."[8]

In an age when many professors see the classroom as a bully pulpit for preaching their own beliefs, it is noteworthy that such an ideologically committed partisan as Donald Davidson maintained a scrupulous objectivity in teaching books and writers he personally disliked. As Robert Buffington recalls:

> A startling example came one day in Mr. Davidson's British novel course. He had spent several meetings carefully analyzing *A Portrait of the Artist as a Young Man;* it was only after we were done and he was preparing on another day to take up a new novelist that he said, smiling, "Well, it's nice to be finished with that old obscene James Joyce." He once wrote me his opinion of Joyce as "the biggest fakir, leg-puller, and dirty-mouth of them all." But formally he gave Joyce his due. A graduate student once began a question of Mr. Davidson with the words, "Do you maintain . . . ?" "I don't maintain anything," Mr. Davidson said quietly.

Elsewhere in his discussion of Davidson, Buffington notes that "Mr. Davidson paid his students the most flattering attention possible for a man of letters to pay: a scrupulously close attention to the work they gave him. He might draw up several pages of criticism of a student manuscript."[9]

The rigor with which he taught his literature classes was more than matched by the high standards he maintained in his writing courses. Tom Landess recalls a poetry-writing class that he and his roommate, Edwin ("Buddy") Godsey, took from Davidson as undergraduates in the early fifties. Godsey had written a poem that was designed to appeal thematically to all of Davidson's Agrarian sympathies.

7. This is from Blount's syndicated column and was published shortly after Davidson's death. The copy that I saw was an undated clipping from the *Atlanta Journal* in the Fugitive Collection of the Heard Library.

8. Interview with George Core, June 1, 1999.

9. Robert Buffington, "Mr. Davidson in the Formal Garden," 128, 126.

Unfortunately, the poem, "A Holstein Mountain Lad after the Ball," was not very good aesthetically. Landess remembers two egregious lines in particular: "Walking by the creek / How his breath doth reek." Davidson had written in the margin: "And so does this line." In another place, he had simply written the word "bad" three times.

Fortunately for Godsey, the story doesn't end there. While Landess was away in the army, his former roommate worked on his craft with the encouragement and example of Davidson. By the time Landess returned to Vanderbilt for graduate study in 1956, Godsey was pursuing a Ph.D. at Yale and writing accomplished poems. After finishing all his work at Yale except for the dissertation, Godsey returned for a brief stint on the Vanderbilt faculty. Uncomfortable with the role of traditional scholar at a research university, he left Vanderbilt—first for Converse College in Spartanburg, South Carolina, and finally for the University of North Carolina at Charlotte. Buddy Godsey died in January 1966, trying vainly to save his son, who had fallen into a pond behind their house some six or seven miles outside Charlotte. The following year, his collection of thirty-three poems was published by the University of North Carolina Press under the title *Cabin Fever.* Edwin Godsey was probably the last serious poet to benefit from Donald Davidson's guidance. As such, he was one of the last inheritors of the Fugitive legacy.[10]

Although he never succeeded in publishing his own novel during his lifetime, Davidson influenced three generations of gifted fiction writers at Vanderbilt. At the very least, these include Robert Penn Warren in the twenties, Jesse Stuart and Mildred Haun in the thirties, Elizabeth Spencer and Walter Sullivan in the forties, and Madison Jones and Jesse Hill Ford in the fifties. Of these, Ford was the only one to renounce his ties to Agrarianism and turn his back on the Vanderbilt tradition. Throughout the fifties, however, Jesse Hill Ford remained an ardent segregationist and a tireless worker for the Tennessee Federation for Constitutional Government.

Even after achieving success in New York with fiction in the best magazines and a powerful television play called *The Conversion of Buster Drumwright* (which he wrote especially for Davidson), Jesse Ford continued to hold the unfashionable racial views of his region. (In a letter to Davidson, dated March 25, 1960, he tells of his heroic efforts to avoid integrated social gatherings and his horror at the rumors that Ava Gardner sleeps with Negroes.) A year after the Vanderbilt University Press published *The Conversion of Buster Drumwright* (with a foreword

---

10. Landess interview. For a fuller account of the life and poetry of Edwin Godsey, see Lloyd Davis, "Edwin Godsey and the Vanderbilt Tradition," in *The Vanderbilt Tradition: Essays in Honor of Thomas Daniel Young,* ed. Mark Royden Winchell (Baton Rouge: Louisiana State University Press, 1991), 232–45.

by Donald Davidson), Ford hit the best-seller list with his novel *The Liberation of Lord Byron Jones* (1965). This book exploited the widely held image of a racist white South perpetually traducing injured black virtue. Four years later, in 1969, Ford criticized Donald Davidson, Andrew Lytle, and other southern writers of their generation for fostering a strident "us and them" mentality toward the North.[11] (Apparently, the author of *The Liberation of Lord Byron Jones* had ceased to be one of "us" and had become one of "them.") The following year, Jesse Hill Ford shot and killed a black man who came too menacingly close to his driveway. Over the next quarter century, Ford's career and personal life hit the skids. Then, on June 1, 1996, he achieved his own liberation by committing suicide.

In addition to the novelists who studied under Davidson, one should also mention the short story writer Robert Drake. A native of West Tennessee, Drake did not begin writing fiction until after he left Vanderbilt and was teaching English at the University of Michigan. Nevertheless, he did contribute an essay called "Donald Davidson and the Ancient Mariner" to the growing genre of tributes to Davidson by former students. At the outset of this charming memoir, Drake recalls hearing about Davidson's intimidating reputation even before he enrolled at Vanderbilt. By the time he had reached his junior year, Drake had actually worked up enough courage to ask Davidson's permission to take his creative writing class. "Mr. Davidson, I'd like to take your writing course," he stammered out during registration at Vanderbilt's Old Gym. "I've been writing poems, but they aren't very good, I guess." In his characteristically fierce "but somehow kindly" way, Davidson replied: "Well, if there's anything to them, we'll find it out. I'll see if I can make them *bleed*." Remembering that semester a decade later, Drake writes: "I never went into his class without feeling that during that hour my soul was probably going to be required of me and that I was more than likely going to be weighed in the balance and found wanting."[12]

This same feeling of subordination apparently was felt by many and lasted for years, even after several of Davidson's former students had established substantial reputations for themselves in the literary and academic world. Although he was a generous patron, Davidson did not welcome the sort of easy collegiality that had existed between professors and students during the Fugitive days. (Walter Sullivan, who was thirty-one years younger than Davidson and his colleague for fifteen years, says that he can never remember anyone of his generation calling Davidson "Don."[13]) The one notable exception to this rule was Jesse Stuart. Born in 1907, Stuart was a generation older than many of Davidson's other proteges. The voluminous correspondence between the two men (119 surviving letters

11. James Seay, "The Making of Fables: Jesse Hill Ford," 200.
12. Drake, "Donald Davidson and the Ancient Mariner," 20.
13. Sullivan, *Allen Tate,* 24.

written over a period of thirty-six years) reveals the sort of deep and abiding friendship that Davidson often found difficult to sustain with his Fugitive and Agrarian brethren. With the possible exception of Charles Bryan, Jesse Stuart appears to have been Donald Davidson's closest literary soul mate.

Whatever shortcomings Stuart may have had as a stylist, the people of his hometown recognized him as their bard. Given his own views about the role of the poet in society, Davidson probably envied Stuart this local honor more than he would have the international reputation of other artists. In a letter to his former student on the occasion of "Jesse Stuart Day," (October 28, 1955), Davidson writes, "Never was a tribute more richly and truly deserved. . . . It is wonderful that you can have this expression of admiration and devotion from *your own folks,* and have it now. That hardly ever happens. It couldn't have happened to Tom Wolfe. It can't happen to Ransom, Tate, Warren, or me—I would think. And Mississippi is certainly not going to honor Wm. Faulkner in such a way."[14]

When Davidson finally persuaded Stuart to lecture at Bread Loaf in the summer of 1953, the enthusiastic response of the assembled literati seemed to confirm Davidson's own high opinion of his younger friend. In a letter dated August 10, 1953, Davidson tells Stuart that only Robert Frost had ever enjoyed such a favorable reception at Bread Loaf. Stuart's feat was all the more impressive when one considers how deeply entrenched Frost had become on the mountain. "I don't think that Frost ever moved this audience as you did," Davidson writes; "he is cautious and elusive in his own way; likes to speak in riddles; and only now and then, when he is feeling just right, does he deeply *touch* his hearers and open their hearts by opening his." The fact that Frost himself attended Jesse's lecture and the informal session held later in the barn was all the more remarkable when one considers how he habitually avoided such occasions. When Davidson describes his personal reaction to Stuart's performance, it as if a dam were bursting. One is reminded of those classic cinematic moments when Professor Kingsfield (or Mr. Chips) is suddenly humanized. The reserve that Davidson had so strenuously maintained, not only with former students but with old friends as well, is blown away by a torrent of emotion and reminiscence:

> As for me—well, Jesse, I was "carried away"—moved not only by the truth and force of what you were explicitly saying but by all it implied, all that it called up in the way of memories reaching far back beyond the time when I first knew you. There were voices speaking in your voice that I haven't heard since I was a boy, some of them very beloved to me. You weren't trying, outright, to speak for them, but you couldn't help doing so. Whenever a Southerner speaks in the manner native to him, as you do, he is always

---

14. See Foster, "Jesse Stuart and Donald Davidson: A Literary Friendship," 214–15.

speaking not only with his voice but with the voices of his foreparents. That is one of the big differences between being a Southerner and not being one. Very likely I was the only person in that room who could know, out of full experience, somewhat like yours, what was back of your utterance. I've walked barefooted to school, with my younger brother Tom. We had to fight the Martin boys (Jimmy and Ezell) nearly every day, going or coming. Life was pretty rough at Lynnville Academy (so-called) where father was principal, and I can tell some tales. I can see my dear father, just as dinner recess was over, saying "Pshaw, Pshaw!" (he never said anything stronger) and tying up a boy's wrist that had just been slashed, square across, in a fight, right on the school grounds. I had my own troubles later, in the four years when I taught in country schools in Tennessee. Perhaps you and I were the only persons in that room who ever whipped a pupil at school. And I remember being threatened—and scared to death—by the town butcher when I chased his son off the school grounds for misbehavior. Much more could I tell about "education."[15]

III

Walter Sullivan remembers Davidson in the late 1950s and early 1960s as being very different from the man he had been only a few years earlier. Sullivan writes:

> In the last years of his life, he was greatly mellowed. He stopped fighting losing battles, renewed old friendships, some of which had faltered in the fifties, and he became the unofficial custodian of the Fugitive-Agrarian past. He renewed the copyright on *I'll Take My Stand;* he wrote the introduction for the Peter Smith reprint of the *Fugitive.* . . . By 1960, he would sit with a glass of bourbon in his hand, a radical departure from his abstemiousness of the forties and fifties, and talk of his friends and the work they had written in a spirit and mood that were generous and relaxed.[16]

Davidson also seemed to have recovered the sense of humor that had all but vanished during the 1950s. Once when he and Walter Sullivan were driving by an urban renewal project near the Vanderbilt campus, Davidson wryly observed; "This reminds me of the Western Front in World War I." He was even capable of dropping his austere demeanor to the point of getting off some one-liners in class. Over the years, the cover sheet had gotten separated from an old term paper in the files of the ATO fraternity. When a student submitted this paper to

15. Ibid., 214.
16. Sullivan, *Allen Tate,* 27.

Davidson, he immediately recognized the work and returned it with the single comment: "I can do better now!"[17]

Although his views had not changed, Davidson's obsession with race lessened after his failing health and general ineffectiveness took him out of the active struggle to maintain segregation. The Tennessee Federation for Constitutional Government ceased to function in the sixties. Although Davidson was instrumental in forming a local chapter of the White Citizens' Council, he was not one of its leaders. From the sidelines, he and other conservative members of the Vanderbilt faculty voiced their displeasure with the fact that James Lawson, a black student in the Divinity School, was organizing sit-ins at segregated lunch counters in Nashville. They felt vindicated when he was eventually expelled from the university.

On May 9, 1963, Jack Kershaw's wife, Mary, phoned Davidson to inform him of the progress their side was making in a segregation case in Savannah, Georgia. Jack wondered if Davidson knew the whereabouts of Zora Neale Hurston, who he thought might be a witness for their side. A major figure in the Harlem Renaissance during the twenties and thirties, Hurston had opposed the Brown decision and other attempts at forced integration. Unfortunately, her whereabouts at that time was an unmarked grave in Florida. The following month, Davidson expressed a surprising appreciation for the views of another black leader. In his diary entry for June 10, 1963, he writes of the "appalling & grotesque" performance of a panel of Negro leaders who appeared on a television program called "The American Experience." James Foreman, the head of CORE, an editor of *Ebony* magazine, and a representative of the Southern Christian Leadership Conference all come in for censure because of their support of racial preferences as reparation for slavery and segregation. According to Davidson: "Only sensible things were said by 'Malcolm X' of the Black Muslims, who constantly feuded with the other three & deflated them with realistic questions. . . . He wants either a return to Africa or a separate 'Negro state' over here!"

As Davidson began to turn his attention away from politics and back toward literature, he was able to reestablish ties with friends whom he had previously regarded as traitors to the one true faith. In 1955, the English department had talked about bringing John Crowe Ransom back as a guest professor. At that time, Davidson feared that Ransom would take an openly anti-Agrarian position, which he would then be compelled to oppose. "If he comes down talking socialism, racial amalgamation, and so forth," Davidson asked Randall Stewart, "what do you think would happen?"[18] But by 1961, when Ransom finally did come back

---

17. Sullivan interview; Herschel Gower in conversation.
18. See Conkin, *Southern Agrarians,* 158.

to Vanderbilt for a year, these fears had largely dissipated. Not only had the two friends been reunited at the Fugitive celebration in 1956, Ransom and Davidson had resumed correspondence. They also enjoyed each other's company when Ransom participated in a literary symposium at Vanderbilt on April 20 and 21, 1960. Davidson remembers Ransom's reading and comments as being "the best, most moving I ever heard him give" (diary, April 21, 1960).

During Ransom's guest year at Vanderbilt, he and Davidson shared an office. They would also take long drives in the countryside around Nashville and eat dinner at Davidson's favorite restaurant—Miss Martha's in the Allen Hotel near campus.[19] On January 13, 1962, they had a kind of old-time Fugitive meeting at Alec and Elise Stevenson's home. In addition to Ransom and Davidson, Randall and Cleone Stewart and Jesse Wills were there. After a buffet dinner, topped off with Irish coffee, they went around the circle as of old and read from their recent work. Ransom had a revision of his old poem "Conrad in Twilight," while both Wills and Stevenson shared new verse with the group. Davidson read from *The Big Ballad Jamboree.* In April, this goodly company was joined by Allen Tate and John Wade, who were in town for the annual spring literary symposium. Davidson and Theresa practically wore themselves sick hosting a small Fugitive and Agrarian reunion at their house on Fairfax Avenue. Because Bennie Woods had died unexpectedly, they were without Cora's help for the occasion.

Even the unmarked locations of early Fugitive activities became shrines that literary pilgrims asked to see. When Virginia Rock, a Canadian scholar who had written her doctoral dissertation on *I'll Take My Stand,* came to Nashville on May 12–13, 1966, Davidson took her to the approximate place on Twentieth Avenue where the original Hirsch circle had met. (It was now the site of the Anchor Motel.) They then went to 1210 Adelicia Avenue, where Davidson and Theresa had lived in an upstairs apartment in 1920 and 1921. Alec Stevenson, Stanley Johnson, and probably Ransom had come there to read poems as the members of the group began returning from the war. (Elise Stevenson recalled that there had been some meetings at her house shortly after she and Alec were married—as the men read poetry, she sat on the stairs and listened.) Their final stop was the James Frank house at 3802 Whitland Avenue, where the Fugitives were officially named and conceived the idea of starting a magazine. On the evening of May 13, Harriet Owsley hosted a party at her house on Mockingbird Road. Davidson, Virginia Rock, and two couples from the Vanderbilt English department were in attendance. Andrew Lytle and an Episcopal priest (probably Father William Ralston of Sewanee) drove up from Monteagle. They "had a feast to talk over Harriet's tall mint-juleps" (diary, May 13, 1966).

As Davidson grew older, he inevitably began attending more funerals. On

19. See Young, *Gentleman,* 449.

October 9, 1961, a little less than two years after Edwin Mims was laid to rest, Richmond Croom Beatty lost his long battle with throat cancer. A distinguished scholar of American literature at Vanderbilt, Beatty edited the revived book page of the *Tennessean* after illness forced him from teaching. (His funeral mass was celebrated at Christ the King Church on Belmont Boulevard in Nashville, the location of Davidson's early poem "Fire on Belmont Street.") Exactly two years later, Davidson's old friend Dick Dodd called from Marshallville to inform him that John Wade had died at three-thirty that afternoon. Theresa had experienced "a chill and uncanny premonition—" at precisely that time (diary October 9, 1963). At one o'clock the next morning, the Davidsons arrived at Union Station to board the train for Georgia. The Pullman conductor led them with quiet solemnity from the ticket office down by elevator to the tracks.

They spent the weekend in Marshallville paying their respects to Wade's memory and consoling his family. Davidson recalls that Sunday, October 13, was "a fine morning—externally—at Marshallville." He and Theresa talked with Dick Dodd part of the morning and then made one last trip to the Wade house. "Dick drove us through John's 'World Garden'—the arboretum thriving and all in fair order. But the master was not there to point out or explain what we should see. I could not say a word. Dick told me afterwards he could hardly bear that journey: I felt the same" (diary, October 13, 1963). Exhausted, the Davidsons arrived back in Nashville not long after eleven o'clock that night.

As the sixties wore on, Davidson continued to experience insomnia and strange dreams. (In one of several dreams he describes in his diary on January 11, 1964, he is "looking up a wide shallow river, a northern river like the Susquehanna. Water rushing in waves and ripples toward me, like a rapids. A cold light over everything.") Also, his health seemed to worsen with each passing year. In Bread Loaf, on July 17, 1965, he woke up in the middle of the night with a smothering sensation in his chest and an abnormal rattling or bubbling sound that accompanied his breathing. The young doctor in Middlebury who examined him told Davidson that he had liquid in his lungs, gave him some white capsules to take, and scheduled a chest x-ray. In addition to taking the medicine, Davidson was to sleep with at least three pillows to elevate his head and chest. In five days' time, the capsules had done their job. Almost all the liquid had been drained from his lungs. His problem, the doctor told him, was old age. Hardened arteries were weakening his heart, which in turn couldn't carry off all the blood from his lungs.

Back at Bread Loaf in August of 1967, Davidson was in the hospital for an operation on his bladder. He spent much of the time leading up to his surgery reading the books of the Old Testament in the Gideon Bible in his room. He celebrated his seventy-fourth birthday in the hospital. Theresa and several of his Bread Loaf friends threw a surprise party for him, complete with presents and a huge birthday cake. After the nurse brought a knife and napkins, Davidson "solemnly but joyfully" cut the cake. "We each talk and eat & have a good time," he recalls, "—me concealing my disabilities" (diary, August 18, 1967).

Davidson had hoped very much to attend a southern literary festival that Louise Cowan was organizing at the University of Dallas for late April 1968. The meeting would focus on the Agrarians, with Ransom, Tate, Lytle, and Warren all on hand. Unfortunately, a recurrence of his heart problems prevented Davidson from attending. (In addition to the coronary he had suffered in 1959, he had experienced heart failure in the fall of 1965, just prior to a trip that he and Theresa took to Europe.) In a letter dated April 21, 1968, Davidson informs Jesse Stuart that, after two weeks in the hospital, he is ready to go home. "Probably I had some digitalis 'poisoning' from the difficulty of adjusting the dosage in my changed condition," he writes. "Had a terrific case of insomnia. Became generally weak, nervous, no good."[20] A pint of fluid had been drained from his right lung, which was partially blocked.

On the positive side, Red Warren had stopped by on his way to Dallas. Despite their differences over race in the fifties, the bonds of personal affection between the two friends remained strong. Warren later told Allen Tate that Davidson was frail and feverish.[21] It must have been clear to him that this would probably be their last meeting. Davidson's failing condition was also apparent to Robert Frost's biographer Lawrance Thompson, who had come to the hospital to pump Davidson for information about Frost. Thompson's intrusion on such an occasion and his exploitation of an obviously dying man enraged Warren. Thomas Daniel Young, who had taken Warren to the hospital, said that Red kept his calm while in Davidson's presence but blew up afterward over Thompson's insensitivity.[22] Ironically, there is not a single reference to Davidson in the three volumes of Thompson's biography.

Although Davidson sent a statement to Dallas, which was included in the record of the Agrarian sessions, his absence cast something of a pall over the festivities. If the men who gathered there were looking back on Agrarianism as an enthusiasm of their youth, Davidson alone had carried the faith into old age. The diary he kept for most of his life ends on April 25, 1968, with a final entry in Theresa's hand: "This morning I found the lifeless body of D. D. on the floor of the downstairs bathroom. Apparently he had been up much earlier and had been reading—since the light was on in his study and he had a book with him in the bathroom." Donald Davidson's long battle with modernity had come to an end.

20. See Foster, "Jesse Stuart," 221.
21. See Blotner, *Robert Penn Warren*, 374.
22. Thomas Daniel Young in conversation.

IV

Davidson died in what he surely would have regarded as the worst of times. Nineteen sixty-eight was one of the most turbulent years in American history. In January, the North Vietnamese launched the Tet Offensive. Although this resulted in a military victory for the United States, it was a public relations defeat. Americans now realized that the determination of the enemy was such that there really was no light at the end of the tunnel. In March, Eugene McCarthy's surprisingly strong showing in the New Hampshire primary forced Lyndon Johnson to pull out of the race for reelection. In April, Martin Luther King was gunned down on a motel balcony in Memphis. Come June, the lifeless body of Robert Kennedy lay on the floor of a hotel kitchen in Los Angeles. At the Democratic Convention in August, the war was brought home to the streets of Chicago in a series of brutal confrontations between political demonstrators and baton-wielding police. That fall, the Pulitzer Prize in fiction was awarded to William Styron's *The Confessions of Nat Turner,* a sympathetic account of a slave rebellion written by a white southerner. In November, Richard Nixon was elected president in a three-way race with Hubert Humphrey and George Wallace. On Christmas Eve, three American astronauts orbited the moon. Technology had conquered even the heavens.

Whatever Davidson might have thought about the world he didn't live to see, that world has thought little about him. He has been excluded from all three editions of William Rose Benét's *Reader's Encyclopedia,* a volume that includes everyone from Jeppe Aakjaer to Ulrich Zwingli. Although a few of his poems appear in collections of southern literature, classroom anthologies of American literature have passed him by. (An excerpt from "Still Rebels, Still Yankees" is included in *American Literature: The Makers and the Making,* which Cleanth Brooks and Robert Penn Warren edited with their Yale colleague R. W. B. Lewis; however, that book, which lists the date of Davidson's death a year earlier than it actually occurred, is now out of print.) If his early rejection of modernism caused his verse to fall out of fashion during his lifetime, the subsequent backlash against modernism benefited traditionalists such as Davidson less than it did beat, confessional, and free-verse romantic poets. In recent years, however, the rise of neoformalism has led to a rediscovery of premodernist and antimodernist poets, who stressed rhetorical accessibility and musical cadences in their verse. Even narrative poetry is coming back into favor. The climate may be right for a sympathetic reassessment of Davidson's verse.

Although George Garrett reviewed it favorably in the *New York Times Book Review* and declared it one of the best novels of 1996 in the *Yearbook of the Dictionary of Literary Biography, The Big Ballad Jamboree* has not enjoyed wide popular or critical acclaim. This may be due in part to its having been published by an academic press. If Davidson's novel ever makes it on to the screen, even the cable television screen, it might finally reach the mass audience for which it was intended. With the continuing vitality of regional theater in the South, there is even hope that *Singin' Billy* will be rescued from its undeserved obscurity.

To the extent that the study of southern literature is a recognized academic specialty, much of the credit goes to Donald Davidson and those who followed in his footsteps. The first important textbook in southern literature, Scott Foresman's *The Literature of the South* (1952) was edited by three of Davidson's former students—Richmond Croom Beatty, Thomas Daniel Young, and Floyd C. Watkins. Davidson's longtime friend Louis Rubin started both the Society for the Study of Southern Literature and the Fellowship of Southern Writers. If Davidson was the most provincial of the Fugitive-Agrarians, he saw that as a virtue rather than a shortcoming.

Given his literary achievement, it is unfortunate that so much of Davidson's reputation rests on his social and political writings. Walter Sullivan was certainly correct in noting that his words and deeds made it far too easy for Davidson's enemies to define their quarrel with him solely in terms of race. Ironically, the defeat of segregation has now made it possible to consider the merits of Davidson's views on regionalism without reducing them to an argument over race. Although the Confederate flag has been displayed by some racist groups in the South and elsewhere, it has also been flown by patriots in the breakaway states of Eastern Europe. If ever the Quebec separatists win their independence from Canada, they have vowed to unfurl the Star and Bars and play "Dixie." From the Northern League in Italy to the League of the South and the Tenth Amendment Movement in the United States, political devolution has become an international phenomenon.[23] To understand the philosophy and social dynamic behind this phenomenon, one could do worse than read the relevant essays of Donald Davidson.

The principles of regional autonomy and cultural diversity extolled by Davidson represent a threat to the conservative establishment as well as to the more obvious enemy on the Left. When Davidson's former student Mel Bradford was rumored to be President Ronald Reagan's first choice to direct the National Endowment for the Humanities, his nomination was sunk by a cabal of neoconservatives who supported Brooklyn native William J. Bennett for the job. The case against Bradford held that he was a neo-Confederate believer in state's rights, who had supported George Wallace and criticized Abraham Lincoln. Although

23. Clyde Wilson, one of the founding members of the League of the South, informed me of the Quebec connection in December 1997. For a discussion of devolution as a national and international political phenomenon, see Thomas Fleming, "America's Crackup," *National Review* (July 28, 1997): 48–49, 64.

his mentor's name was never mentioned in the debate, Bradford's nomination was sunk because he was too Davidsonian. Southern conservatives of the Davidson mold have had little to show for their loyal support of the Republican Party. Nevertheless, their voices continue to be heard in such paleoconservative journals as *Southern Partisan* and *Chronicles: A Magazine of American Culture.*

As Davidson's public reputation has fluctuated, he continues to be remembered fondly by his former students. According to Robert Buffington: "What makes the great teacher of literature is not, finally, his ideas, however sound; these his students, like anyone else, can obtain in their best version in his books. . . . It is his personal example of dedication to the subject, a subject conceived as an art and as a type of knowledge." For this reason, students who disagreed with Davidson often ended up revering him. Buffington remembers something once said to him by "a graduate student who had been working closely with Mr. Davidson but did not happen to share his Professor's politics: the politics did not matter, he had discovered; one could meet Mr. Davidson on strictly literary terms and be his friend."[24] Even when friendship had faded, gratitude and veneration often remained. Over forty years after her liberal novel *The Voice at the Back Door* had created a breach between herself and her former professor, Elizabeth Spencer could still remember her experience in Donald Davidson's class as "absolutely defining." If Henry Adams was right that a teacher touches eternity, Donald Davidson continues to live in the memories and achievements of his former students.

Twenty-five years after Davidson's death, one of those students remembered him in a poem. Lloyd Davis's "To Donald Davidson in Heaven (Southern Section)" reads in part:

> On my way to the bank, two Nigerian students
> drive by in a Swedish car, and I think
> of you and how things used to be.
> I remember your saying that morning
> in the spring of '54 after *Brown v. Board*
> the girl in Rand Hall asked you if you
> wanted your coffee "straight." And two
> other mornings as in dreams the past
> has faded into: your singing in the
> middle of your lecture on *The Return of the Native:*
> " 'A boon, a boon,' cried Earl Mar-shall,
> 'A boon, a boon,' cried he"; and that time
> in your office you handed me your mother's
> guitar, inlaid with mother-of-pearl,

24. Buffington, "Mr. Davidson," 128, 121.

"a woman's guitar," you said,
and I began "Bonny George Campbell"
in the wrong key with a hangover
from a Natchez Trace bar where Reidy
and Godsey and I had drunk and talked
till dawn. . . . [25]

During those insomnia-ridden nights when he would drift in and out of a troubled sleep, one hopes that Davidson had good dreams, too. One might have been of a fall evening on Whitland Avenue, when everyone was young and poetry was the only thing that mattered. Another might have been of a winter night around the fire at Benfolly, where one could see the gray eye of Ransom and hear the Kentucky voice of Warren, with the guns of beleaguered Donelson sounding in the distance. In another, it might be a spring day in the peach groves of central Georgia some time before the Fall of Man. But one suspects that the best dream of all would find Donald Davidson breaking the ten o'clock rule in a place where no flag flies and the summer never ends.

25. Lloyd Davis, "To Donald Davidson in Heaven: Southern Section," 111–12.

PRIMARY SOURCES

The bulk of Donald Davidson's papers are housed in the special collections section of the Jean and Alexander Heard Library at Vanderbilt University.

Books

American Composition and Rhetoric. New York: Scribner's, 1939. Rev. ed., 1943, 1947, 1953, 1959.

The Attack on Leviathan: Regionalism and Nationalism in the United States. Chapel Hill: University of North Carolina Press, 1938.

The Big Ballad Jamboree. Jackson: University Press of Mississippi, 1996.

Lee in the Mountains and Other Poems. Boston: Houghton Mifflin, 1938.

The Literary Correspondence of Donald Davidson and Allen Tate. Edited by John Tyree Fain and Thomas Daniel Young. Athens: University of Georgia Press, 1974.

The Long Street: Poems. Nashville: Vanderbilt University Press, 1961.

An Outland Piper. Boston: Houghton Mifflin, 1924.

Poems, 1922–1961. Minneapolis: University of Minnesota Press, 1966.

Singin' Billy: A Folk Opera. With Charles Faulkner Bryan. Glendale, S.C.: Foundation for American Education, 1985.

Southern Writers in the Modern World. Athens: University of Georgia Press, 1958.

The Spyglass: Views and Reviews, 1924–1930. Edited by John Tyree Fain. Nashville: Vanderbilt University Press, 1963.

Still Rebels, Still Yankees and Other Essays. 1957. Reprint, Baton Rouge: Louisiana State University Press, 1972.

The Tennessee. Vol. 1, *The Old River: Frontier to Secession.* 1946. Reprint, Nashville: J. S. Sanders, 1991.

The Tennessee. Vol. 2, *The New River: Civil War to TVA.* 1948. Reprint, Nashville: J. S. Sanders, 1992.

Essays, Reviews, Poems

"The Artist as Southerner." *Saturday Review of Literature* (May 15, 1927): 781–83.

"At Bread Loaf: 1938." Commencement address delivered to the graduating class of the Bread Loaf School of English, August 1938.

"Bread Loaf School of English Commencement Address." August 11, 1956.

"Certain Fallacies in Modern Poetry." *Fugitive* 3 (June 1924): 66–68.

"Donald Davidson's Notes toward an Autobiography: The Early Years." Edited by M. Thomas Inge. In *The Vanderbilt Tradition: Essays in Honor of Thomas Daniel Young,* edited by Mark Royden Winchell, 199–210. Baton Rouge: Louisiana State University Press, 1991.

[As Robin Gallivant]. "The Dragon Book." *Fugitive* 1 (April 1922): 13–14.

"First Fruits of Dayton: The Intellectual Evolution in Dixie." *Forum* 89 (June 1928): 896–907.

"Grammar and Rhetoric: The Teacher's Problem." *Quarterly Journal of Speech* 39 (December 1953): 425–36.

Introduction. *The Letters of William Gilmore Simms.* 5 vols. Edited by Mary C. Simms Oliphant et al., xxxxi-lvii. Columbia: University of South Carolina Press, 1952.

"Joseph Conrad's Directed Indirections." *Sewanee Review* 33 (April 1925): 163–77.

[Unsigned]. "Merely Prose." *Fugitive* 2 (June–July 1923): 66–67.

"A Mirror for Artists." In *I'll Take My Stand: The South and the Agrarian Tradition,* 28–60. New York: Harper, 1930.

"The New South and the Conservative Tradition." Lecture delivered at the Biennial Institute of Bowdoin College, Brunswick, Maine, April 16, 1958.

"On Teaching Democracy through Literature." Lecture delivered at the Zeal for American Democracy Day Conference. Nashville, Tenn.: February 1949.

"Preface to Decision." *Sewanee Review* 53 (summer 1945): 394–412.

"Recollections of Robert Frost." In *Robert Frost and Bread Loaf* (Limited Edition). Middlebury, Vt.: Middlebury College Press, 1964. No page numbers.

"The Recrudescence of Kipling." Paper read before the Calumet Club of Vanderbilt University in the early 1920s.

Review of *The Advancing South,* by Edwin Mims. *Nashville Tennessean,* May 23, 1926, p. 6.

Review of *The Autobiography of an Ex-Coloured Man,* by James Weldon Johnson. *Nashville Tennessean,* September 11, 1927, p. 6.

Review of *Dark Princess,* by W. E. B. Dubois. *Nashville Tennessean,* July 1, 1928, p. 6.

"A Sociologist in Eden." *American Review* 8 (December 1936): 177–204.

"Some Remarks on 'Singin' Billy.'" Talk delivered to the original cast of *Singin' Billy.*

"The Spyglass." *Nashville Tennessean,* September 4, 1927, p. 6.

"The Swinging Bridge." *Fugitive* 2 (June–July 1923): 84.

"That This Nation May Endure—The Need for Political Regionalism." In *Who Owns America? A New Declaration of Independence,* edited by Herbert Agar and Allen Tate, 113–34. Boston: Houghton Mifflin, 1936.

"The Trend in Literature: A Partisan View." In *Culture in the South,* edited by William T. Couch, 183–210. Chapel Hill: University of North Carolina Press, 1935.

"Tyranny at Oak Ridge." Nashville: Tennessee Federation for Constitutional Government, 1956.

SECONDARY SOURCES

Bain, David Howard, and Mary Smyth Duffy, eds. *Whose Woods These Are: A History of the Bread Loaf Writers' Conference, 1926–1932.* Hopewell, N.J.: Ecco Press, 1993.

Barr, Stringfellow. "Shall Slavery Come South?" *Virginia Quarterly Review* 6 (October 1930): 481–94.

Batts, W. O., ed. *Private Preparatory Schools for Boys in Tennessee.* Nashville: No publisher listed, 1957.

Blair, Everetta Love. *Jesse Stuart: His Life and Works.* Columbia: University of South Carolina Press, 1967.

Blotner, Joseph. *Robert Penn Warren: A Biography.* New York: Random House, 1997.

Bowling, Lawrence E. "An Analysis of Davidson's 'Lee in the Mountains.'" *Georgia Review* 6 (spring 1952): 69–88.

Bradford, M. E. "Aeschylus in Nashville: 'The Case of Motorman 17: Commitment Proceedings' and the Later Poetry of Donald Davidson." *Southern Literary Journal* 25 (fall 1962): 52–61.

———. "Donald Davidson and the Great House Tradition: A Reading of

'Woodlands, 1956–1960.'" In *The Vanderbilt Tradition,* edited by Mark Royden Winchell, 84–91.

―――. "Donald Davidson and the Uses of Persona: A Reading of the Joe Clisby Poems." *South Carolina Review* 26 (fall 1993): 125–34.

―――. "To Sing the Truth: The Poetry of Davidson's Later Years." Unpublished typescript in the possession of the author.

Brooks, Cleanth, *The Well Wrought Urn: Studies in the Stucture of Poetry.* New York: Reynall and Hitchcock, 1947.

Buffington, Robert. "Mr. Davidson in the Formal Garden." *Georgia Review* 24 (summer 1970): 121–31.

Conkin, Paul K. *Gone with the Ivy: A Biography of Vanderbilt University.* Knoxville: University of Tennessee Press, 1985.

―――. *The Southern Agrarians.* Knoxville: University of Tennessee Press, 1988.

Cook, Martha E. "Dryads and Flappers: Donald Davidson's Early Poetry." *Southern Literary Journal* 12 (fall 1979): 18–26.

Cowan, Louise. *The Fugitive Group: A Literary History.* Baton Rouge: Louisiana State University Press, 1959.

Cowley, Malcolm. *The Dream of the Golden Mountains: Remembering the 1930s.* New York: Viking, 1980.

Craven, Avery. Review of *The Tennessee,* vol. 1, by Donald Davidson. *New York Herald Tribune Weekly Book Review,* October 27, 1946, p. 4.

Daughtrey, Larry. "Moral Flaw Diminishes VU's Glory." *Nashville Tennessean,* May 23, 1997, p. B-1.

Davis, Lloyd. "To Donald Davidson in Heaven (Southern Section)." *South Carolina Review* 26 (fall 1993): 111–12.

Davis, Louise. "He Clings to Enduring Values." *Nashville Tennessean Magazine,* September 4, 1949, pp. 6–8.

Dessommes, Lawrence. "The Epistemological Implications in 'The Ninth Part of Speech.'" *Mississippi Quarterly* 27 (winter 1973–1974): 21–32.

Doyle, Don H. *Nashville in the New South: 1880–1930.* Knoxville: University of Tennessee Press, 1985.

Drake, Robert. "Donald Davidson and the Ancient Mariner." *Vanderbilt Alumnus* (January–February 1964): 19–22.

Dykeman, Wilma, *Tennessee: A Bicentennial History.* New York: Norton, 1975.

Ellison, Curtis W., and William Pratt. Afterword to *The Big Ballad Jamboree,* by Donald Davidson, 287–94.

Epstein, Joseph. *Plausible Prejudices: Essays on American Writing.* New York: Norton, 1985.

Fleishauer, Warren L. "College Textbooks in Composition and Rhetoric." *University Bookman* 1 (autumn 1960): 15–22.

Fletcher, John Gould. *The Autobiography of John Gould Fletcher.* 1937. Reprint, Fayetteville: University of Arkansas Press, 1988.

———. *Selected Letters of John Gould Fletcher.* Edited by Leighton Rudolph, Lucas Carpenter, and Ethel C. Simpson. Fayetteville: University of Arkansas Press, 1996.

———. *Selected Poems of John Gould Fletcher.* Selected and introduced by Lucas Carpenter and Leighton Rudolph. Fayetteville: University of Arkansas Press, 1988.

———. "Two Elements in Poetry." *Saturday Review of Literature* (August 27, 1927): 65–66.

Folmsbee, Stanley J. Review of *The Tennessee,* vol. 1, by Donald Davidson. *Journal of Southern History* 13 (February 1947): 110–12.

———. Review of *The Tennessee,* vol. 2, by Donald Davidson. *Journal of Southern History* 14 (May 1948): 281–84.

Foster, Ruel E. *Jesse Stuart.* New York: Twayne, 1968.

———. "Jesse Stuart and Donald Davidson: A Literary Friendship." In *The Vanderbilt Tradition,* edited by Mark Royden Winchell, 211–22.

French, Warren, ed., *The Thirties: Fiction, Poetry, and Drama.* Deland, Fla.: Everett Edwards, 1967.

Fugitive: A Journal of Poetry. "Foreword." 1 (April 1922): 2.

Fugitives: An Anthology of Verse. New York: Harcourt, Brace, 1928.

Garreau, Joel. *The Nine Nations of North America.* Boston: Houghton Mifflin, 1981.

Genovese, Eugene D. *The Southern Tradition: The Achievement and Limitations of an American Conservatism.* Cambridge: Harvard University Press, 1994.

Gioia, Dana. "Can Poetry Matter?" In *Can Poetry Matter? Essays on Poetry and American Culture,* 1–24. St. Paul: Graywolf Press, 1992.

Gower, Herschel. "Charles Faulkner Bryan and the Music of 'Singin' Billy.'" In *Singin' Billy,* by Donald Davidson, xvii–xxiv.

Graham, Hugh Davis. *Crisis in Print: Desegregation and the Press in Tennessee.* Nashville: Vanderbilt University Press, 1967.

Grantham, Dewey W. "Henry W. Grady and the New South." In *A History of Southern Literature,* edited by Louis D. Rubin, Jr., et al., 241–45. Baton Rouge: Louisiana State University Press, 1985.

Hazlitt, Henry. "So Did King Canute." *Nation,* January 14, 1931, pp. 48–49.

Hesseltine, W. B. "Look Away, Dixie." *Sewanee Review* 39 (winter 1931): 97–103.

Heyword, Dubose, and Hervey Allen. "Poetry South." *Poetry* 20 (April 1922): 35–48.

Hobson, Fred. *Mencken: A Life.* New York: Random House, 1994.

———. *Serpent in Eden: H. L. Mencken and the South.* Chapel Hill: University of North Carolina Press, 1974.

———. *Tell about the South: The Southern Rage to Explain.* Baton Rouge: Louisiana State University Press, 1983.

Holladay, Bob. "The Reactionary." *Nashville Life* (April–May 1997).

Johnson, Ben F. III. *Fierce Solitude: A Life of John Gould Fletcher.* Fayetteville: University of Arkansas Press, 1994.

Johnson, Gerald W. "No More Excuses: A Southerner to Southerners." *Harper's* (February 1931): 331–37.

———. "The South Faces Itself." *Virginia Quarterly Review* 7 (January 1931): 152–57.

Johnson, James Weldon. *The Autobiography of an Ex-Coloured Man.* New York: Knopf, 1927.

Johnston, David E. *A History of Middle New River Settlements and Contiguous Territories.* Huntington, W. Va.: Standard PTG and Publishing Company, 1906.

Jordan, Michael M. "*The Tall Men:* Davidson's Answer to Eliot." *South Carolina Review* 26 (fall 1993): 50–70.

Kirk, Russell. "*The Attack on Leviathan* and the South's Conservatism." *Heritage Foundation.* Lecture 206. July 11, 1989.

———. *The Conservative Mind: From Burke to Santayana.* Chicago: Regnery, 1953.

———. Preface to *The Tennessee,* vol. 2, by Donald Davidson, vii–xiv.

Knickerbocker, William S. "Back to the Hand." *Saturday Review of Literature* (December 20, 1936): 467–68.

Krock, Arthur. "Industrialism and the Agrarian Tradition in the South." *New York Times Book Review,* January 4, 1931, p. 3.

Kroll, Harry Harrison. "History-Laden River." *New York Times Book Review,* December 8, 1946, p. 26.

Lasseter, Rollin. Unpublished interview with Donald Davidson. Summer 1961.

Levy, Eugene. *James Weldon Johnson: Black Leader, Black Voice.* Chicago: University of Chicago Press, 1973.

Livingston, Carolyn. "*Singin' Billy:* An Introduction." *South Carolina Review* 22 (spring 1990): 21–26.

Lytle, Andrew. "The Small Farm Protects the State." In *Who Owns America? A New Declaration of Independence,* edited by Herbert Agar and Allen Tate, 237–50.

Mabry, Thomas D. "Look Away, Look Away." *Hound and Horn* 4 (spring 1931): 436–39.

Malone, Bill C. *Country Music, USA.* Rev. ed. Austin: University of Texas Press, 1985.

Marx, Karl, and Friedrich Engels. *The Communist Manifesto.* Translated by Samuel Moore. New York: Penguin, 1967.

McMillen, Neil R. "Organized Resistance to School Desegregation in Tennessee." *Tennessee Historical Quarterly* 30 (fall 1971): 315–28.

Mencken, H. L. "The Sahara of the Bozart." In *Prejudices: Second Series.* New York: Knopf, 1920.

———. "The South Astir." *Virginia Quarterly Review* 11 (January 1935): 47–60.

———. "Uprising in the Confederacy." *American Mercury* (March 1931): 379–81.

Mims, Edwin. *The Advancing South: Stories of Progress and Reaction.* Garden City, N.Y.: Doubleday, Page, 1926.

Monroe, Harriet. "The Old South." *Poetry: A Magazine of Verse* 22 (May 1923): 89–92.

O'Brien, Michael. "Donald Davidson and the Creed of Memory." In *The Idea of the American South, 1920–1941,* 185–209. Baltimore: Johns Hopkins University Press, 1979.

———. "The Middle Years: Edwin Mims." In *Rethinking the South: Essays in Intellectual History,* 131–56. Baltimore: Johns Hopkins University Press, 1988.

O'Brien, Michael, ed. "Edwin Mims and Donald Davidson: A Correspondence, 1923–1958." *Southern Review,* new series, 10 (autumn 1974): 904–22.

Owsley, Harriet Chappell. *Frank Lawrence Owsley: Historian of the Old South.* Nashville: Vanderbilt University Press, 1990.

Pelikan, Jaroslav. *The Vindication of Tradition.* New Haven: Yale University Press, 1984.

Price, Don. "Wesley Hall Is Burned." *Vanderbilt Alumnus* (February 1932): 101–3.

Ransom, John Crowe. "Antique Harvesters." In *The Fugitive Poets: Modern Southern Poetry in Perspective,* edited by William Pratt, 26–27. Nashville: J. S. Sanders, 1991.

———. "The Most Southern Poet." *Sewanee Review* 70 (spring 1962): 202–7.

———. *The World's Body.* New York: Scribner's, 1938.

Robertson, David. "Frog-Gigging in a Leaky Skiff." *South Carolina Review* 25 (fall 1992): 177–83.

Rock, Virginia. "The Making and Meaning of *I'll Take My Stand:* A Study in Utopian Conservatism." Diss. University of Minnesota, 1961.

Rubin, Louis D., Jr., "The Gathering of the Fugitives: A Recollection." *Southern Review,* new series, 30 (autumn 1994): 658–73.

———. "The Passion of Sidney Lanier." In *William Elliot Shoots a Bear: Essays on the Southern Literary Imagination,* 107–44. Baton Rouge: Louisiana State University Press, 1975.

————. *The Wary Fugitives: Four Poets and the South.* Baton Rouge: Louisiana State University Press, 1978.

Seay, James. "The Making of Fables: Jesse Hill Ford. In *Kite-Flying and Other Irrational Acts: Conversations with Twelve Southern Writers,* edited by John Carr, 199–215. Baton Rouge: Louisiana State University Press, 1972.

Shapiro, Edward S. "American Conservative Intellectuals, the 1930's, and the Crisis of Ideology." *Modern Age* 23 (fall 1979): 370–80.

————. "Donald Davidson and the Tennessee Valley Authority: The Response of a Southern Conservative." *Tennessee Historical Quarterly* 33 (winter 1974): 436–51.

————. "The Southern Agrarians and the Tennessee Valley Authority." *American Quarterly* 22 (winter 1970): 791–806.

Sherwood, John C. "Grammar with Tears: Seventy-one Composition Texts." *College English* 21 (April 1960): 426–38.

Simpson, Lewis P. "Donald Davidson and the Southern Defense of Poetry." Introduction to *Still Rebels, Still Yankees,* by Donald Davidson, v-xvii.

————. "O'Donnell's Wall." In *The Man of Letters in New England and the South: Essays on the Literary Vocation in America,* 192–200. Baton Rouge: Louisiana State University Press, 1973.

Singal, Daniel Joseph. *The War Within: From Victorian to Modernist Thought in the South, 1919–1945.* Chapel Hill: University of North Carolina Press, 1982.

Spears, Monroe K. *Dionysus and the City: Modernism in Twentieth-Century Poetry.* New York: Oxford University Press, 1970.

————. "The Function of Literary Quarterlies." In *American Ambitions: Selected Essays on Literary and Cultural Themes,* 109–26. Baltimore: Johns Hopkins University Press, 1987.

Spencer, Elizabeth. *Landscapes of the Heart: A Memoir.* New York: Random House, 1998.

Stanlis, Peter J. "Acceptable in Heaven's Sight: Robert Frost at Bread Loaf, 1939–1941." In *Frost Centennial Essays III,* edited by Jac Tharpe, 179–311. Jackson: University Press of Mississippi, 1978.

————. "Robert Frost: Politics in Theory and Practice." In *Frost Centennial Essays II,* edited by Jac Tharpe, 48–82. Jackson: University Press of Mississippi, 1976.

Stewart, John L. *The Burden of Time: The Fugitives and Agrarians.* Princeton: Princeton University Press, 1965.

Stone, Albert E., Jr. "Seward Collins and the *American Review:* An Experiment in Proto-Fascism, 1933–37." *American Quarterly* 12 (spring 1960): 4–19.

Stuart, Jesse. "America's Pindar Was My Guide." *Vanderbilt Alumnus* (March-April 1971): 17–19.

———. *Beyond Dark Hills.* New York: Dutton, 1938.

———. *Man with a Bull-Tongue Plow.* New York: Dutton, 1931.

Sullivan, Walter. *Allen Tate: A Recollection.* Baton Rouge: Louisiana State University Press, 1988.

———. "The Southern Renascence and the Joycean Aesthetic." In *Death by Melancholy: Essays on Modern Southern Fiction,* 97–113. Baton Rouge: Louisiana State University Press, 1972.

Tate, Allen. *"The Fugitive,* 1922–1925: A Personal Recollection Twenty Years After." In *Memoirs and Opinions, 1926–1974,* 24–34. Chicago: Swallow, 1975.

———. "The Gaze Past, the Glance Present: Forty Years after the *Fugitive.*" In *Memoirs and Opinions,* 35–38.

Waldron, Ann. *Close Connections: Caroline Gordon and the Southern Renaissance.* New York: Putnam, 1987.

The War of Rebellion: A Compilation of the Official Records of the Union and Confederate Armies. Series 1, vol. 23. Washington: Government Printing Office, 1889.

Wills, Brian Steel. *A Battle from the Start: The Life of Nathan Bedford Forrest.* New York: Harper, 1993.

Young, Thomas Daniel. *Gentleman in a Dustcoat: A Biography of John Crowe Ransom.* Baton Rouge: Louisiana State University Press, 1976.

———. *Waking Their Neighbors Up: The Nashville Agrarians Rediscovered.* Athens: University of Georgia Press, 1982.

Young, Thomas Daniel, and M. Thomas Inge. *Donald Davidson.* New York: Twayne, 1971.

———. *Donald Davidson: An Essay and a Bibliography.* Nashville: Vanderbilt University Press, 1965.

Zabel, Morton Dauwen. "Two Years of Poetry: 1937–1939." *Southern Review,* original series, 5 (winter 1940): 568–608.

ACKNOWLEDGMENTS

Grateful acknowledgment is made to the following for permission to quote from protected material: Lloyd Davis for a passage from his poem "To Donald Davidson in Heaven (Southern Section)"; Vincent Davis for portions of his correspondence with William Pratt; Helen Ransom Foreman for a passage from "Antique Harvesters," by John Crowe Ransom and portions of Ransom's correspondence with Donald Davidson; Ruel Foster for portions of his correspondence with M. E. Bradford; Robert B. Heilman for portions of his correspondence with Cleanth Brooks; the Jesse Stuart Foundation for sonnet number 617 of *Man with a Bull-Tongue Plow,* by Jesse Stuart; Molly Kirkpatrick and the Davidson family for passages from the poetry and diaries of Donald Davidson and portions of Davidson's correspondence with various individuals; Peter J. Stanlis for portions of his correspondence with M. E. Bradford; and Wallace W. Wells, Jr., for portions of the correspondence between Wallace Wells, Sr., and Elma Wells Davidson.